Form and Fancy

Form and Fancy

Factories and Factory Buildings by Wallis, Gilbert & Partners, 1916–1939

Joan S. Skinner

LIVERPOOL UNIVERSITY PRESS

First published 1997 by
LIVERPOOL UNIVERSITY PRESS
Senate House
Liverpool
L69 3BX

British Library Cataloguing-in-Publication Data
A British Library CIP record is available

0–85323–612–7 cased
0–85323–622–4 paper

Set in 10½ on 12½ Palatino by
Wilmaset Limited, Birkenhead, Wirral
Printed and bound in the United Kingdom by
Redwood Books, Trowbridge

To Sue

Thomas Wallis (1872–1953), architect

Contents

Albion Motor Car Co Ltd, Glasgow, Scotland – J. Tylor & Son Ltd, Southgate, London – Brolt Ltd, Birmingham – Williams & Williams Ltd, Chester – Tilling-Stevens Ltd, Maidstone, Kent – D. Napier & Son Ltd, Acton, London – War casualties – Jones & Shipman Ltd, Leicester – Rubery Owen Ltd, Darlaston, Staffs – Singer & Co Ltd, Coventry – Clayton & Co Ltd, Huddersfield – Cambrian Candle Co Ltd, Holyhead, Anglesey, Wales – General Electric Co Ltd, Witton, Birmingham: Machine shop extension, 1918–20; Switchgear works, 1919–21; General administration building, 1919–21 – Caribonum Ltd, Leyton, London – Commercial Cars Ltd, Luton, Beds – Hayes Cocoa Ltd, Hayes, Middlesex – A winning formula – Houghton-Butcher Ltd, Walthamstow, London – William Stannard & Co Ltd, Leek, Staffs – Babbage, Friendship & Hicks Ltd, Plymouth, Devon – S. G. Brown – Barker & Dobson Ltd, Everton, Liverpool – James Hunt Ltd, Fulham, London – Finishing, standardisation and individuality – Transitional designs – Solex Licensees Ltd, St Marylebone, London – Wrigley Products Ltd, Wembley, London – Young, Osmond & Young, Welwyn Garden City, Herts – Gramophone Company Ltd, Hayes, Middlesex: Cabinet department extensions; Record store; Administration building extension; New power house; Research laboratory; Shipping building

Aluminium Co Ltd, Banbury, Oxon – Briggs Motor Bodies Ltd, Dagenham, Essex – Kelsey Hayes Wheel Co Ltd, Dagenham, Essex – Greaseproof Paper Mills Ltd, Dartford, Kent – Beaton & Son Ltd, Willesden, London – Frederick Parker & Son Ltd, High Wycombe, Bucks – Vandervell Products Ltd, Park Vale, London – Assessment of other designs

List of illustrations

Frontispiece: Thomas Wallis (1872–1953), architect [artist unknown]

Permission has been granted for reproduction of the following illustrations: *The Architects' Journal* 4, 5, 9, *Building* 13, 15, Dunlop Limited 25, 26. Every effort has been made to trace the copyright holders of illustrations 10, 11, 23, 34 to request permission for reproduction, but without result. The remainder are by kind permission of the companies who donated them, of Christopher Wallis, or are the author's own.

Note: There are many more photographs and plans of these factories in the author's possession than could be illustrated here; they are available for inspection by students who wish to pursue an interest in any of the buildings involved.

Acknowledgements

First, my thanks to my family for their constancy, patience and support during a long period of research in many parts of the country. For assistance in that research, I am very grateful to Christopher Wallis ARIBA and Tony Ash, Associate Architect of Wallis, Gilbert & Partners; to William Todd Roxburgh FRICS and Lawrence Butterfield FRIBA, one-time members of the practice; to Douglas Burford FRIBA, partner at Elliott, Cox & Partners; and Marjorie Bennett, daughter of Thomas Wallis.

My gratitude is also owed to the many companies and their employees and ex-employees who have given of their time, knowledge, assistance and archive material but who are too numerous to mention individually but whose names are well-remembered.

For other source material I am indebted to many people in public offices, again too numerous to mention individually, but whose help and advice is of great credit to their calling, as follows:

Museums at Biggar, Luton, Plymouth, Brent, Gunnersbury, the Museum of British Road Transport, Coventry, and the National Museum of Photography, Film and Television, Bradford.
Libraries at Glasgow, Birmingham, St Marylebone, Swiss Cottage, Burnley, Manchester, Chiswick, Dartford, Liverpool, the Aluminium Federation Ltd, Birmingham, and the Royal Society of British Architects.
Record Offices at Bedford, Coventry, Liverpool and Leicester.
Local Planning and Development Departments at Oldbury, Chester, Waltham Forest, Merton, Brent, Camden, Dartford, Southwark, Hertford, Hounslow and Ealing.
Archive Departments at the University of Glasgow, the Tate Gallery, London, Kirklees, Huddersfield, Doncaster, Westminster, the Dunlop Archive Project, EMI Musical, John Laing plc, Glaxo plc, and the Ford Corporate History Office, Brentford.

Further material assistance has been received from the Department of History, University of Keele; the School of Architecture and Planning, University of Belfast; and the Public Record Office, Kew, to whom my thanks are due.

To Dr David Thistlewood of the School of Architecture, University of Liverpool, for always being there when I needed advice and encouragement, my heartfelt thanks, as also to the Northfield Employment Development Initiative, Leicester, without whom the typing of this manuscript would have been almost impossible.

I thank the Royal Society of British Architects for an initial grant toward costs of travel and photography.

Joan Skinner
Leicester, 1996

Note: The fate of the factories, the companies that commissioned them, and their later occupants, is up-to-date only to 1990.

Introduction

LONDON, 1916: Thomas Wallis (1872–1953), architect, closed the private practice he had operated under his own name since 1900 and left an established post in the Architects and Surveyors Division of His Majesty's Office of Works and Public Buildings where he had been employed since 1901, to found a new practice—Wallis, Gilbert & Partner. The primary objective of this move was to collaborate with an American company, Trussed Concrete Steel, in the design of factories to be constructed of reinforced concrete, using the form of reinforcement invented by the founders of Trussed Concrete Steel, the Kahn brothers of Detroit, USA.

Hitherto, and particularly in the south-eastern regions of Britain, the designing of factories was not popular amongst architects seeking preferment or with a profession seeking statutory recognition and status. And many manufacturers regarded the employment of an architect to be a wanton extravagance. In 1916, the Great War of 1914–18 was in progress. The quantity of armaments and munitions produced by private companies was already inadequate and the Government was building its own munition factories. Building materials were in short supply; in the private sector government licence to build was available only to manufacturers producing war requirements. In 1916, moreover, Thomas Wallis had a wife and three children to support and was himself over 40 years of age.

To abruptly hazard his career by entering so unpropitious a field could be perceived as a reckless gamble or an admission of defeat in the more prestigious ranges of architectural design. The subsequent achievements of Wallis and his partners do suggest, however, that the choice had been well considered.

Chapter 1 explores the biographical background of Thomas Wallis to reveal the qualities, traits and experience that show, despite the seemingly inauspicious circumstances of the time, how well-placed he was to take advantage of the opportunity offered by the American company. Much, of course, in the way of success, depended upon the competence of Trussed Concrete Steel and therefore the background and contribution of the company are reviewed. Chapter 1 also surveys the history and organisation of the partnership and the many factors that contributed to its substantial reputation and prosperity throughout the interwar years.

The interwar years represent, perhaps, the period in which occurred the greatest changes in the shortest time in the modern history of Britain. Most of the changes were the product of scientific and technological advances but had a profound effect upon the social and economic life of a country that was recovering from the traumatic legacy of the Great War. The 'Janus' effect of looking backwards and forwards at the same time affected attitudes and beliefs in all sections of society. Chapter 2 offers a brief perspective of architectural thought and activity in the period and of the attitudes and influences on factory design to which Wallis, Gilbert & Partners had necessarily to be alert.

Although in that period Wallis, Gilbert & Partners executed many commissions other than factories, industrial architecture represented over two-thirds of the partnership's *oeuvre* and an even greater proportion of its income. Designs for some one hundred factories and factory buildings have been discovered. These buildings are analysed and assessed in Chapter 3, which is divided into four sections. Evident in Wallis, Gilbert factory designs is a series of basic stylistic patterns that can be grouped chronologically into (a) those of the early years to 1926 in what is called the 'Daylight/Masonry' style and includes a 'transitional' period in which tiles formed part of the decoration; (b) those of the mid-term years 1927–35—the 'Fancy' factories; and (c) the later works to 1939 that embraced 'British Modern' and a more sculptural and geometrical form. Although these groupings are based upon architectural style, they provide a convenient framework for the purpose of analysis. A final section, (d), accommodates designs that do not fit comfortably into the above sub-divisions; these also include the overseas commissions and a number of buildings under the heading 'Sheds' that are largely basic, utilitarian structures, although not all are. Unexecuted designs have been included, but these are few indeed, their abandonment owing chiefly to economic considerations.

As the design of the factories relates very closely to their contemporary background, so too does their commissioning. Accordingly, a short history of each client company is included, where available, in order to round off what is, retrospectively, the buildings' historical context. The non-industrial work of the practice included a wide range of building types. The complete *oeuvre* for 1916–39 is listed at Appendix A, but cannot claim to be exhaustive.

Information in respect of some factories and factory buildings is meagre. Some factories have been demolished or destroyed and many others have been altered or added to. In other instances, the original plans are no longer obtainable, are different from as-executed, have been lost through enemy action or other disaster, or simply disposed of through lack of storage space. In some cases, published sources are of minimal content; the early works, for instance, were often written about in the context of articles dealing with building techniques or materials. However, the enthusiastic response of many companies, even when not the original owners of a factory, has helped to fill many gaps. One or two companies have preferred to offer no cooperation at all. And it is always possible that, even when so many Wallis, Gilbert factory buildings have been discovered, there are still others that have evaded a nationwide search.

Fundamentally, the approach of Wallis, Gilbert & Partners to the designing of factories was to contribute, so far as architectural design is able to do so, to a more efficient and successful pursuit of business by the companies that commissioned them. The effectiveness of Wallis, Gilbert's philosophy is summarised in Chapter 4—in respect of the architects' methods and objectives and, since style has so largely informed comment on their work, in relation to their choice of styles. Why those styles? Why change? Why Egyptian? Noted too is the interesting aspect that, although the initial venture into factory design and the early Daylight/Masonry buildings were American influenced and several clients were of American origin, Wallis, Gilbert designs were different from their counterparts in America.

Since the reputation of Wallis, Gilbert & Partners was largely based upon their factory designs, it is important too to look at how those designs were more generally received. By the architects' peers and architectural commentators the early buildings were approved for their 'architectural treatment' of reinforced concrete. The later, more Modern designs were often illustrated but rarely commented upon. At the time of their completion and thereafter, however, the appearance of the Fancy factories was harshly criticised. Retrospective criticism has tended to perpetuate contemporary judgements, although the unexpected demolition of the Firestone factory in 1980 sparked some re-evaluation. But charges of vulgarity, novelty-seeking and façade-building aimed at the Fancy factories have long diminished proper appreciation of their planning, their place in the wider range of Wallis, Gilbert works and, more generally, the architects' major contribution to factory design.

From the outset, however, the Fancy factories met with the approval of the clients who commissioned them, of later occupants and the people who have worked in them. The general public, too, seems always to have delighted in their colourful attractiveness. Therefore, in Chapter 4 these differences of opinion are put into perspective, their character and content examined and some of the errors and superficiality of judgement corrected.

For more than two centuries factories have played an influential role in the life of this country, but their design has rarely caught the imagination of architectural historians. Perhaps the odour of appalling conditions and exploitation of operatives that pervades their history, the thought that their design and construction belong more readily to engineering and technological fields, or that they relate more easily to social and economic history, have been the cause of such neglect. Nowadays, to some extent, that neglect is being rectified. It is hoped that this survey of the works of one of the most prolific designers of factories may stimulate greater interest in the architectural history of such buildings, particularly when so many of them are being demolished or allowed to become derelict.

Chapter One

Thomas Wallis and Wallis, Gilbert & Partners

Thomas Wallis—Biographical Background

Apart from the chronological material given below, biographical information about Thomas Wallis is somewhat sparse. From what is available, however, from his personal background and within its historical context, from an increasing familiarity with his work, from his published writings and from the contributions of people who knew him, it is possible to reach some understanding of the man himself.

Thomas Wallis was born on 27 May 1872 at 34 Chapel Road, West Norwood, South London, the home of his parents Thomas James Wallis, bricklayer, and Sarah Ann (née Hinslea, born in Sheffield). The house, on the corner of Chapel Road and Woodcote Place, included a grocery shop run by Mrs Wallis. The family employed one servant, usually a young girl, who lived in. At the time of Wallis' birth, Chapel Road was clearly a very respectable, reasonably prosperous area.

At the junction of Chapel Road with Knights Hill Road, the Lower Norwood Working Men's Institute, built in 1859, was later to become the Norwood Technical Institute, then South London College, and presently Lambeth College, North Centre. The records of the institution date only from 1895, so that it is not possible to say if Thomas Wallis attended that conveniently-near establishment. Indeed, nothing has been discovered of his early education, but it was probably in the late 1880s that Wallis joined the architectural practice of Sidney Robert James Smith at 14 York Chambers, Adelphi, London.

On 4 October 1899, at Christ Church, Streatham, South London, Thomas Wallis married his first cousin Edith Elizabeth, the daughter of James Wallis, master builder, and Sarah (née Norris) of 42 Streatham Place. The respective fathers of Thomas and Edith were brothers, Thomas James (born 13 January 1841) and James, one year younger (birth not registered?). They were the sons of Thomas Wallis, bricklayer (later building contractor who was involved in the construction of Dorchester House, London in 1858) and his wife Charlotte (née Copling) who, in the 1840s, resided at Park Road, Norwood. After their marriage, Thomas and Edith Wallis lived at 3 Holmewood Gardens, Streatham, where their elder son, Douglas Thomas, was born on 3 November 1900. Their second son, James Courtney, was born on 12 December 1905 when the family lived at 'Doric', 30a Streatham Place, at which address their daughter, Marjorie Edith, was also born, on 26 December 1914. A family tree is given at Figure 1.

Douglas became an architect; on completion of his training at the Architectural Association, he joined his father's practice and became a partner. James was a medical student at Guy's Hospital, London, but his career in medicine and his interest in social problems and the socially deprived suddenly and tragically ended when he died on 3 July 1932 whilst undergoing a surgical operation. Marjorie became a Court dressmaker, at one time conducting her business from rooms at 15 Elizabeth Street, London, when the architectural practice of Wallis, Gilbert & Partners was also housed at that address (part of the London Coastal Coaches station, now Victoria Coach Station, designed by Wallis, Gilbert & Partners in 1931).

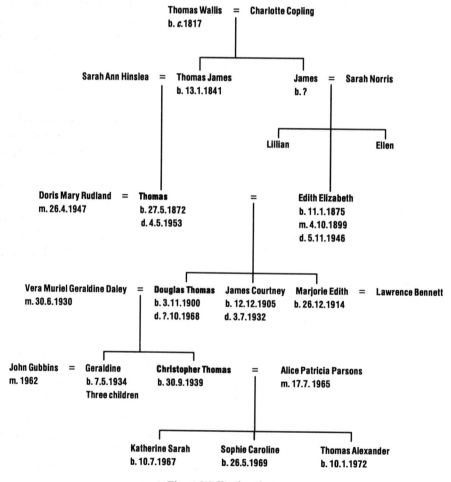

Fig. 1 Wallis family tree

The marriage of Thomas and Edith Wallis was threatened by Thomas' extra-marital activities. Shortly after the death of their son James in 1932, they lived apart for some months. A reconciliation in the following year was not successful and, in 1933, they separated irrevocably. Thomas then set up house with Doris Mary Rudland, his erstwhile secretary, some 28 years his junior and the daughter of Henry Thomas Rudland, jeweller of Chalfont St Giles, Bucks. They eventually married on 26 April 1947 after the death of Edith on 5 November 1946. At the time of the separation the family lived at 85 Woodbourne Avenue, Streatham; thereafter Thomas and Doris lived at Roehampton, West London, later moving to Chalfont St Giles, Bucks, to Ruislip, Middlesex, to Gerrard's Cross, Bucks, and finally to Worthing, Sussex.

Despite the disfavour that Thomas' personal life attracted and the problems arising from his persistently 'roving eye' (even into old age), he did maintain his earlier family in considerable comfort and take an interest in their welfare. In a letter to his grandson Christopher, of February 1948, he expressed his delight in classical architecture and promised later to extend the boy's interest in the subject. Like his father Douglas, Christopher became an architect, continuing to practise as Wallis, Gilbert & Partners, later as Wallis, Gilbert, Wolstenholme & Partners. The practice has more recently been subsumed into a larger company.

On 2 May 1953 Thomas and Doris Wallis moved house from Gerrard's Cross to Worthing. Thomas was then approaching his 81st birthday and barely survived the move. He died suddenly on 4 May 1953 at the new house, 37 West Parade, Worthing.

Thomas Wallis was a draughtsman and watercolourist of no mean talent. His leanings were as much in the direction of the art of his chosen profession as its basic structural aspects. Although always attended by a strong commercial understanding and ambition, his attitude to architectural design was always informed by an appreciation of the visual impact of buildings and the relation of buildings to their environment.

Architectural Training and Practice

Wallis received his architectural training in the late 1880s and throughout the 1890s in the office of Sidney R. J. Smith, then of 14 York Buildings, John Street, Adelphi, London. One of the best-known of Smith's commissions, and from which Wallis would have learned much, was the Tate Gallery in London. In March 1890 Henry Tate, a philanthropist whose wealth derived from the sugar refiners Tate & Lyle and who lived at Park Hill, Streatham Common, decided to present his collection of British art to the nation. Considerable controversy arose about where the collection ought to be housed.[1] None of the suggested places was acceptable to Tate, particularly as he regarded his gift as only the foundation of a national institution for exhibiting works by contemporary British artists. In 1892 he withdrew his offer and decided to build his own gallery.

Sidney Smith designed many of the free libraries gifted by Tate to the London boroughs,[2] and was appointed architect for the new gallery. Land was purchased at Millbank, overlooking the River Thames, where the Millbank Penitentiary once stood. In March 1892, Smith's view was that the only suitable style for the gallery was 'Classic; refined mouldings with Greek feeling and ornament sparingly introduced, the chief study being to get a good sky outline, proper front and carving and figures of the best character'.[3]

Despite Smith's contention that a picture gallery must, of necessity, be top-lighted and 'practically on one floor'[4] his first proposal was criticised for its lack of height.[5] Modifications attracted further criticism, including the comment that the added cupola was 'too high . . . its excessive frailty of material covering a building so dignified and solid . . . can hardly fail to appear incongruous and a little unfortunate'.[6] Compared with Smith's original design, the modifications were rather grandiose additions to a somewhat stocky building and a considerable departure from his initial concept. Compromise was reached, with a finally accepted design that included elements of both its predecessors. When members of the Architectural Association visited work-in-progress at the gallery in February 1896, they found that 'Although the plan has been varied but slightly from the original scheme, the elevations have been much remodelled. The principal alteration has been the lowering of the central dome'.[7]

The work was completed at a cost of £105 000 (some £15 000 over estimate) in 1897 and officially opened by the Prince of Wales on 21 July of that year.[8] The general contractors for the building were Higgs & Hill, the stone carving was executed by Mr C. Smith; fire resistance was aided by iron and steel concrete floors (by Dannett & Ingle) and brick-arched ceilings in the centre portion. Extensions, also designed by Sidney Smith, were added in May 1899 and opened in November of that year.

The building attracted public approval, albeit the interior was praised more than the exterior. When James Stirling designed the Clore Gallery extension in 1983, he insisted that his design would be a 'neutral, modest building that defers to the more assertive presence of the Tate', but commented upon the existing building

> . . . there is mannerism in the Classical conservatism of the Tate itself; . . . eccentricity in the proportions of the steps related to the Portico, and inconsistency in the way the busy areas of the façade—the corner pavilions and the Portico—are separated by neutral areas of wall.[9]

The perversities to which Stirling drew attention could well be the result of the building's compromise solution but could equally have arisen from more than one hand contributing to the design. Wallis was then still very young and not yet fully trained; at that stage of his career he would hardly have been entrusted, as anecdote has it, with the design of so important a building. But his hand is recognisable in the drawings and embellishments; there are similarities between the more grandiose additions to the design and the kind of work he later produced.

During his years with Sidney Smith, Wallis would have learned much about the designing of public buildings, in which circulation paths, appropriate and sufficient lighting, and fire resistance were important. Buildings designed by Smith were not always of outstanding architectural merit but they did, in the main, consciously relate to site and status—aspects of architectural design that became a forté of Wallis' later work. A particular feeling for monumentality appears, however, to be personal to Wallis himself, and his delight in decoration was to prove both a strength and a weakness. The latter trait, not yet fully disciplined, is for instance revealed in his first published design under his own name—a competition entry for the Herne Hill Library of 1904 which was premiated one of six but not executed.[10] The layout is well-planned and adheres to the brief but, as the elevations correspond to the layout, the various sections become almost discrete entities. The decorations, however, have no underlying explanation. Albeit in terracotta which lends itself to considerable freedom, the eclectic nature of the ornament—art nouveau, classical, Renaissance and Baroque, some bold, some delicate—results in not only a discordant hotch-potch but further emphasises the lack of coherence in the external appearance—an aspect of the Tate Gallery design to which Stirling drew attention.

On 13 December 1900 Wallis was elected a member of The Society of Architects. He was then practising on his own account at 15 York Buildings. At the end of 1900, however, he had a child as well as a wife to support. To ensure a regular income, he took employment as a temporary draughtsman[11] in the Architects and Surveyors Division of HM Office of Works and Public Buildings, on 1 April 1901.[12] At the time of Wallis' engagement by the Civil Service, examinations for an established post in the Architects and Surveyors Division were particularly onerous. Concern was expressed that too few good candidates were applying for or succeeding in passing the examination. In order to attract more trained architects, the nomenclature of the posts was changed on 30 December 1901 from surveyor to architect.[13] It was also recognised that many of the two hundred temporary draughtsmen and architectural assistants already in post had substantial cause to complain that they had 'no prospects, no settled position or status', although many of them were of a calibre to be retained. Some of the most able had been attracted to outside posts. Negotiations to arrive at suitable criteria in accordance with which appropriate temporary staff could be promoted to established positions took place over a number of years.[14] In 1913, of the 11 vacant posts for Architectural Assistant First Class, five were filled by temporary draughtsmen, promoted under the new conditions. Thomas Wallis was one of them. On 30 January 1913 he was promoted to that position, with effect from 1 January 1913, at a salary of £234 15s per annum, with half his temporary service counting toward his ultimate pension.[15]

No date is given in respect of Wallis' departure from the Civil Service or reason therefor, but a Minute of 4 December 1916 comments that 'There is a vacancy on the staff of Architectural Assistant First Class consequent upon the termination of Mr Wallis' employment'.[16] Whether Wallis chose to leave or whether he was asked to do so is not evident but, during his 16 years with the Office of Works, he had also been engaged in private practice. The only known work emanating from his office at 15 York Buildings is the competition entry for Herne Hill Library in 1904, although there could have been other commissions and possibly some overflow from his erstwhile mentor next door. Wallis was, after all, a very good draughtsman and, even if he was still having difficulty in settling elevations, he was particularly good at layouts.

From 1905 to 1913 Wallis collaborated, or was in some sort of partnership, with James Albert Bowden. They opened an office as Wallis & Bowden in *c.* 1908 at 33 Old Queen Street, London and, in 1910, at Queen Anne Chambers, Tothill Street, London. There is, however, at least one instance where plans show their names separately as 'joint architects'.[17] The only published works of Wallis & Bowden are competition entries. In 1906 their design for Southwark Public Library was premiated second, as was their entry for a boys' school at Maidenhead, Berks, in 1908. Also in 1908 The Bunker, Hythe and Rochdale Swimming Baths in Lancashire were premiated first and the designs executed. Designs were also entered for Barnsley Swimming Baths in Yorkshire (1911) and Middlesbrough Public Library on Teesside (1908) but not executed.

Three rather more ambitious competition projects, for the extension of Stoke-on-Trent Town Hall, Staffs, (1909, premiated first out of 27 entries), St Marylebone Town Hall, London, (1911, premiated second out of 180 entries) and the Port of London Authority Head Office (1912, one of six premiated designs out of 170 entries), enhanced both the income and reputation of the architects. The fees for their executed design of the Stoke-on-Trent Town Hall extension were £1696, which included a salary of £3 10s per week for the 'specially-appointed' Clerk of Works, Mr J. Billingham of Gillingham, Kent.[18] Even when reduced by that figure and divided with Bowden, such income in those years was not inconsiderable, particularly when additional to Wallis' steady salary from the Civil Service. How did he manage to oversee the building of the executed designs and, at the same time, work six days a week in London? Perhaps Bowden attended to all the site visits.

Wallis & Bowden designs were often chosen in preference to those entered by better-known architects, such as Lanchester & Rickards, F. Troup, Curtis Green and F. Atkinson. Their drawings were often praised for their clarity and excellence (surviving pencil drawings show Wallis often to be the author). Planning and layout requirements for the three last-mentioned competitions called for a high degree of understanding of the operative use of buildings in the placing of rooms and circulation patterns. Wallis & Bowden received considerably less criticism of their resolution of the problems than most other entries. Overall, their joint efforts reflect an increasing confidence, an awareness of style appropriate to the period and the expression of civic dignity, as well as an ability to understand and meticulously observe the brief. Given the general flamboyance of Edwardian architecture, none of the proposed designs is outrageously Baroque. Visual impact relies most strongly upon a powerful use of Doric-influenced neo-classicism articulated by projections, recession and set-back, so that delineation of the buildings is an emphatic part of their expression. Conversely, on such 'masculine' and often monumental designs, the decorative elements are sometimes overly feminine and frequently 'bitty'.

By 1913 the partnership with Bowden appears to have come to an end. Wallis' private practice remained at Queen Anne Chambers, Tothill Street, while Bowden moved to 6 Duke Street, Adelphi. From 1915 or 1916, Bowden was employed at the Ministry of Munitions Supply Department at Whitehall Place. His obituary of 14 October 1949 states that 'during the war he built many munition factories'.[19] For the first few months of the First World War, armaments were produced by the private sector but, because of the inadequacy and costliness of the arrangement, the Ministry of Munitions was formed on 9 June 1915 to 'stimulate and control government war supplies'. Royal Ordnance factories were expanded and multiplied under its management. The Office of Works, where Wallis served, was also involved: Frank Baines, then Assistant Architect and Surveyor First Class, was promoted to Principal Assistant of the Architects and Surveyors Division to design and oversee the building of munition factories.

More architects were recruited to cope with this unprecedented task. Choice of sites for the factories involved selecting large tracts of land that were sufficiently isolated to ensure safety from aerial bombardment and for internal security, where wind and flooding were not excessive, but whose geological foundations were often unknown. Access by rail, canal and road needed to be away from main routes but connectable to them. Power supplies for lighting, heating and motive power had to be reasonably available, but sewerage, water supply and special filtering devices had to be separate from public mains. At the chosen site, an adequate labour force would have to be housed and fed or transported thereto and from.

For the buildings themselves, very little steel could be drawn off from armament manufacture. Timber was in short supply—weathering kilns were designed so that new timber could be used to support very large uninterrupted spans. North-light roofs were essential to prevent risk of sunlight affecting many operations. No materials could be used that might cause fire and, in many instances because of the nature of the materials being processed, no heating could be installed. Convenient routeing of processes had to be planned amongst buildings that had to be dispersed for safety reasons. The appropriate placing of special decontamination and search areas, of cleansing rooms, sanitary facilties and locker rooms was also required. Adequate light and ventilation had to be balanced against contamination and fire risk. Structure and layout planning had to minimise the effect of possible explosion. In pursuit of maximum productivity, however, human life appears to have been a secondary consideration. For instance, in many cases, walls would be externally packed with earth revetments, but roofs would be flimsy so as to ensure an outlet for explosive blast should it occur, and for easy replacement.

As a member of the architectural staff of the Office of Works, Wallis was engaged on such projects (including that at Georgetown, near Paisley, Scotland, which became the Royal Ordnance Factory, Bishoptown) and thus learned at first hand about planning for mass production and the containment of hazards. This experience also contributed to his later insistence on improving working conditions for employees.

In 1916 Wallis moved his private practice to Caxton House on the opposite side of Tothill Street, to rooms on the seventh floor in close proximity to the offices of the American company, Trussed Concrete Steel Limited (Truscon). At that address Wallis founded the architectural practice of Wallis, Gilbert & Partner and entered into a collaborative arrangement with Truscon as designers of industrial buildings in which the company's own form of concrete reinforcement was to be used. In respect of the name 'Gilbert' in the partnership title, anecdotal evidence states that (a) Gilbert was a name plucked from the air and inserted with 'Partner' (in the singular) to provide a nicely-rounded title for the practice that could remain intact irrespective of whoever else might be recruited; (b) it was the first name of a member of the Kahn family, founders of Truscon, but who has never been identified; and (c) Gilbert was a member of the Canadian office of Truscon who proposed to emigrate to Britain but never actually did so.

Whether any real person was the original 'Partner' is not known. If it was Moritz Kahn of Truscon that may have been the reason for Wallis leaving the Civil Service, on the grounds of unprofessional behaviour arising from involvement with a member of a company that had been contracted to work for the Office of Works.[20] In any case, in 1916 Thomas Wallis as Wallis, Gilbert & Partner had collaborated with Truscon in the design and building of a factory for J. Tylor & Son Limited, that is, before Wallis left the Office of Works. When Frank Cox, architect, believed to have been lately of Verulam Buildings, Gray's Inn, London, was recruited to the practice in 1917, the firm's title became Wallis, Gilbert & Partners (in the plural).

Moritz Kahn was a member of the Kahn family who emigrated from Europe to the United States of America in 1880. Of the four sons of the family, Albert the eldest became a successful architect and achieved a worldwide reputation as a designer of industrial buildings; Julius and Moritz were engineers and

Louis found a career in real estate. Between them they developed the Kahn system of concrete reinforcement, first patented in America (filed 11 December 1902, bearing date 18 August 1903). Reinforcement consisted of the 'Kahn bar' which had members projecting obliquely so as to form the diagonal members of a part of a truss. The designers emphasised that a properly constructed concrete beam was, in reality, a trussed beam, so that stirrups could only transfer stress to the main tensional member when the two were rigidly connected together, the horizontal reinforcement taking not only the stress caused from adhesion of the concrete to it but also the summation of the horizontal components of the strain in each of the diagonals. Since the concrete surrounding the bars would not prevent loose stirrups from slipping, the shear members were attached rigidly to the horizontal reinforcement. A bar with two projecting wings or stirrups was used, the stirrups being bent up at about 45 degrees, so as to cross the planes of rupture at nearly right angles. At the centre span, where the horizontal tension is greatest, the web was left intact on the bar and served as additional reinforcement. The stirrups were part of the original metal of the bars, being merely sheared and bent. The bar was sent to the building site complete, ready to be incorporated into the concrete as a single unit. Floor slabs were reinforced at top and bottom with horizontal bars, while bars used vertically could reach diagonally across a column and be tied in. Other Kahn methods included a system of helical hooping and 'Hy-Rib', a sheet metal reinforcement.[21]

To exploit the system in America, the aptly named Trussed Concrete Steel was formed with its Head Office in Detroit, Michigan, and works at Youngstown, Ohio.[22] Shortly after Moritz Kahn's arrival in England seeking a market for the Kahn system, his expertise in a court case caught the attention and interest of the principals of building contractors Holland & Hannen, and led to the formation on 12 March 1907 of an English branch of the company at Caxton House, Tothill Street, London. Something over 50 per cent of the company's capital was issued to the American parent for the plant and goodwill, the balance being taken up by members of the Holland and Hannen families and their friends.[23] The patent bars were first manufactured in Britain by the Earl of Dudley's steel works at Brierley Hill, Staffordshire (later known as the Round Oak Steel Works) but the arrangement became unsatisfactory, as also did that with Joseph Sankey of Wellington for the manufacture of Hy-Rib reinforcement. In consequence, in 1912, the company founded its own manufacturing plant at Mellors Road, Trafford Park Estate, Manchester.[24]

The object of the Truscon Company was to design in reinforced concrete, supplying its own form of reinforcement. A list was compiled of contractors who were willing to tender in the Kahn system and of architects who were prepared to design for its inclusion. Few contractors were, however, experienced in the new building material and, not infrequently in the early years, Truscon would itself tender for a commission, appoint an architect, and negotiate with a suitable contractor.[25] Despite powerful competition from structural steel as a building medium, Truscon gained in reputation, owing largely to the technological and engineering competence of a staff drawn from most countries in continental Europe, and so gained many contracts. Most reinforced concrete buildings in the years prior to the First World War were clad in stone or brick, so an aesthetic in concrete itself was slow to develop. Truscon was mostly concerned with more mundane projects, which became typical of its work for the next 50 years, such as coal bunkers, swimming baths, quays, bridges, viaducts, aqueducts, breweries and factories, which emphatically justified the professed stability of the system.

Moritz Kahn was aware of the application by his brothers in America of the Kahn reinforcement system to a particular model of factory design. Based upon a regular grid of column, beam and slab, in which the concrete was fully exposed and external wall spaces were glass-filled, it was known as the 'Kahn Daylight System' of factory design. The earliest examples of like construction in Britain by Truscon were a factory for the Arrol-Johnson Motor Company at Dumfries, Scotland, in 1913 and an extension for the Albion Motor Car Company in Glasgow, Scotland, 1913–15 (see Chapter 3 below).[26]

As companies applying for government licence to build a factory or extension to an existing plant during the First World War were required to plan for as little use of steel and timber as possible, reinforced concrete was an obvious choice, since it used much less steel than steel-framing and concrete was not in short supply. It was also less vulnerable to fire and to vibration. When Truscon was looking for architects to design in its medium the field was not a wide one. Knowledge and experience of reinforced concrete construction was comparatively rare in Britain, as was the willingness (as yet) of the architectural profession to actively engage in such a pursuit or to become involved with a commercial company.

So what had Thomas Wallis to gain from collaboration with Truscon and what had he to offer to such a venture? During the First World War most engineering companies were required to turn over to armament production; new factories for that purpose certainly provided an immediate market for exploitation. After the war, however, many of those companies would expect to return to their peacetime product; they would need to retrieve a backlog of work necessarily abandoned in wartime but might also wish to produce some or any of the range of new products promised prior to the war by advances in science, technology and invention. The post-war years bid fair to be highly competitive if Britain was to recover her economic status. In 1916 the United States of America had not yet entered the war and was free to exploit and develop its industrial advantage. In competition, new British factories would need to be modern, efficient and flexibly planned, and designed in a style that reflected the stature and competitive edge of the owner company. Wallis appears to have recognised that, in the absence of professional competition, the designing of factories offered a niche to be filled, expanded and improved upon—a 'market opportunity' in which the earliest and most astute bird could catch the fattest worm.

Wallis was an ambitious man whose ambitions had by 1916 not been fulfilled and whose circumstances then offered little likelihood of their being so. To engage in factory design he needed access to a relevant clientele and a worthy product to offer. Truscon would provide both requirements. Reinforced concrete construction met many of the structural and planning needs of both wartime and later factories; it also offered flexibility in planning and a modern appearance. Moreover, Truscon could contribute in-house engineering skills and experience and, as a commercial company, was (unlike the architectural profession) free to advertise, to canvass for business and to recommend suitable architects to prospective clients.

For his own part, Wallis' youthful exposure to the construction industry in being born to a family engaged for at least two generations in the building trade and, in some small measure, to the commercial pressures of buying and selling in his mother's general store provided an early foundation. Truscon marketed its 'Daylight' system design as 'The Model Factory' in which the welfare of the labour force was as important as efficient production, indeed an essential contribution to that end. From his knowledge of the hardships of building labour and later those of munition workers, Wallis would appreciate that aspect of Truscon design.

In designing for efficient production lines, meeting the unique constraints and demands of munition factories' briefs provided a learning process of considerable value. Wallis' architectural training, his subsequent private practice and his post with the Office of Works were largely concerned with the designing of public buildings. In such roles he gained experience of planning circulation paths, appropriate means and levels of ventilation, lighting, heating and public safety, and in designing elevations that attracted public approval and recognition of status. Whilst Wallis may have appreciated, aesthetically, the essential massiveness of the Kahn Daylight factory, the austere nakedness of the unadorned concrete frame must surely have offended his artistic soul. From his understanding of the stylistic sensibilities of the British market he would know that some form of decorative enhancement of the basic structure would better attract British clients. That may, indeed, have been an important reason why Truscon was seeking British architects with whom to collaborate.

By the end of 1916 Wallis had already designed three factories in association with Truscon. Only one of them was built but Truscon used them as advertising material. In 1917 Technical Journals Ltd of 27–28 Tothill Street, London, published *The Design and Construction of Industrial Buildings* by Moritz Kahn. The majority of examples and illustrations of buildings in the Daylight system were American but, in his preface, Kahn singularly acknowledged his indebtedness to 'Mr T. Wallis of the firm Wallis, Gilbert & Partner,

Architects' for his assistance in compiling the book and for the inclusion of 'noteworthy English examples' of factories designed by the partnership. From 1914 onwards, Truscon published a bi-monthly magazine *Kahn-crete Engineering*, in which articles by architects and engineers explained the principles and nature (and also the virtues) of building in reinforced concrete—preferably in the Kahn system. These publications were a useful medium for disseminating information to prospective clients.

The Wallis, Gilbert Partnership

The marketing efforts of Truscon and favourable comments in professional publications ensured a good start for the partners, Thomas Wallis and Frank Cox. By 1918, with an influx of commissions and a concomitant increase in staff, larger premises were sought. The architectural part of the practice moved to 22 Cranley Gardens, London. Truscon took up residence at the same address in the same year. Wallis, Gilbert Surveyors were accommodated at nearby Claremont Street but this was a purely temporary measure while rooms at 29 Roland Gardens were being remodelled. The whole practice moved to Roland Gardens in 1919.

Truscon in Britain became wholly British owned in 1919; Moritz Kahn returned to America a few years later. Although the architects continued to use the Kahn system of reinforcement the close ties were loosened; Wallis, Gilbert & Partners were attracting work on their own account. Their main sources of commissions were word-of-mouth recommendation or cross-connections with principals of companies making similar products or inter-trading. Frank Cox was most frequently concerned with furthering the interests of the practice, particularly at the American Club in Piccadilly, London[27] and the Ritz Hotel where 'most of the business was done'.[28] Many clients became Wallis' personal friends. The partnership designed their houses and Wallis often joined them at shooting parties and other social gatherings. Family connections and social pursuits have ever oiled the wheels of commerce; aided by personal charm and a gregarious nature, Wallis was always willing to join the manufacturing fraternity in its pleasure and leisure activities. These were the satisfactions of entrepreneurial motivation that go beyond money-making. But at the same time, they offered means of attracting new business and, as importantly, more intimate occasion to learn the needs, problems and business methods of manufacturers—and to influence them.

Wallis understood very well that successful manufacturing was not simply a matter of efficient production—the goods had to be *sold*. The architectural practice itself was, in structure, execution and philosophy, closely modelled on production lines; here was Wallis mixing socially with manufacturers, 'selling' what the practice had to offer and speaking the same language as his potential clients. At the same time, he was keen to persuade clients that a well-treated workforce was more likely to be loyal and highly productive.

Stanley Thomas George Elliott (1899–1979), quantity surveyor, joined the practice in the late 1920s and became a partner, somewhat belatedly, in 1934. At much the same time, F. C. Button ARIBA was also elected to partnership in charge of the drawing office. When the building for London Coastal Coaches (Victoria Coach Station) was completed in 1932, the partnership transferred to that buildng as the first occupants of the rented offices that formed part of it, at 15 Elizabeth Street. Sub-offices were established in Brussels and Paris. It was in 1932 that the partnership went just a little too far in its marketing methods in publishing *Industrial Architecture*,[29] ostensibly from its Brussels office and printed in Geneva. The book's continental origins did not, however, protect the partners from the wrath of the British establishment. The Royal Institute of British Architects (RIBA) was concerned that, as the book contained illustrations of only Wallis, Gilbert works, the publication was tantamount to advertising. To some extent it was, since a copy was often sent to prospective clients to show the kind and range of work undertaken by the partnership. The book was banned by the RIBA and all copies ordered to be destroyed. A few are, however, still extant.

Through the interwar years the practice continued to grow, reaching an average of 75 members and staff. One of the major changes Thomas Wallis would have found in entering upon this venture was that, whilst prior to founding the partnership he had been designing to a pre-established brief, as Wallis, Gilbert & Partners, and particularly after ceasing to rely on Truscon, the practice would be involved in the important preamble of actually settling the brief. That called for recruitment of different kinds of expertise and for considerable cooperation within the practice and with commissioning clients. And not only with the principals of client companies. Consultation with works managers and technicians was considered essential when designing the most appropriate layout of a factory.

Increasingly, manufacturing companies recognised the necessity of devolving their activities into separate but intercommunicating departments, such as production, sales, research and development, and administration, and of organising production on direct-flow lines. All of which had considerable effect upon the designing and planning of their factories. Wallis, Gilbert had already appreciated the efficiency of the system, differentiating their own activities in a similar manner and setting an example to prospective clients. For instance, when Joseph Nathan & Company (Glaxo) was seeking to appoint an architect for its proposed new factory in 1934, it was able to include in its feasibility report to its board a description of the Wallis, Gilbert organisation:

> Item 6: The Partnership of Wallis, Gilbert & Partners consists of five members:

THOMAS WALLIS, FRIBA who concerns himself largely with the design of the buildings, particularly as to elevation and general development and presentation on site

FRANK COX, LRIBA the 'contact man', who up to the state of passing of the final plans coordinates all the activities of the firm with a view to securing a suitable solution of all problems as they arise. He also deals with details of contracts and exercises general supervision throughout the job

DOUGLAS WALLIS, ARIBA who, we are informed, deals with non-industrial work

S. T. G. ELLIOTT, PRSI who is concerned largely with quantities and prices

F. C. BUTTON, ARIBA who is in charge of the execution of all plans and drawings.[30]

The practice was divided departmentally as 'Architects' (with sections Design and Business respectively under Thomas Wallis and Frank Cox) and 'Surveyors' (sections Finance and Drawing respectively under Stanley Elliott and Frank Button). Each partner or head of department was responsible for the effective operation of his own section and for its cooperation with other sections. Every project was worked upon as a combined operation of teamwork, enhanced by cross-suggestion and exchanges of ideas. Stanley Elliott, chartered surveyor, was in charge of all financial and contractual matters in relation to construction work, but collaborated closely with Frank Cox, architect and business manager, in settling briefing requirements with clients, and in overseeing the execution of the brief. Elliott and Cox provided Wallis with all preliminary information for designing purposes, to which Wallis' personal acquaintance with the kind of client, his type of business, and the location of the commission would be applied. Wallis' designs would be passed to Button's section for drawings to be made. After practice meetings to resolve all features into an offer to the client, Cox would meet the client to arrive at a final design decision (Fig 2).

Specialist firms, such as engineers, were employed or consulted appropriately to the requirements of each commission. For major projects, a full-time Clerk of Works was employed on site; the best of such clerks were retained on the payroll to ensure their availability for future projects. Qualified junior architects and surveyors on the staff of the practice accompanied senior members to negotiating conferences and joined in deliberations as part of their general training, enabling them, on their own, to assume responsibility for minor projects.

Elliott and Cox devised a form of progress chart that could be applied to each project, on which the rate of progress of construction, the stemming of materials and the disposition of labour were plotted. It was therefore possible

Fig. 2 Wallis, Gilbert & Partners: group photograph of the practice, *c.* 1930s

not only to give an up-to-date account of progress at any one time but also to ensure adherence to schedule and to adapt progress to unforeseen circumstances. The practice also introduced the taking of photographs on site during construction, at fortnightly intervals from four or five set points, which could show levels of progress to the client and act as evidence for the resolution of any later dispute or complaint.

The major contractor for a project was generally chosen in consultation with, but finally decided by, the client, usually on the basis of tender; subcontractors were chosen by the architects but those chosen were made aware that 'if they let us down once, that was the end of them'.[31] High standards of materials and workmanship were extremely important; as Thomas Wallis stressed in his talk to the RIBA in 1933, although quality might be initially expensive, it would prove to be the most economic option in the long run.[32]

The main aim of the partnership was to deliver up the proposed building to the client complete on forecast date—or dates in respect of separate sections of the buildings, so that the client's production machinery could be installed and brought into operation while other parts of the project were still in process of completion. The partnership devised a form of contract that contained several measures to ensure the contractor's adherence to schedule. For instance, the inclusion of an 'acceleration' clause, whereby additional labour, overtime and shift working and/or better plant and materials could be brought in, was considered of greater value than the imposition of penalties or awards of bonuses in respect of completion dates.[33] Indeed, in the practice itself both members and employees worked to conditions similar to those contained in the acceleration clause when circumstances warranted. For example, the production of drawings, specifications, bills of quantities, and so on, within four days in order to compete for the Wrigley commission, was inclusive of four nights' work for the staff involved.

The way the practice worked, its methodology and its organisation, were major contributors to its success. The client's *interests* were always para-mount, in the giving of professional advice, in the nature and production of the design and its execution. But not necessarily the client's *wishes*; on occasion, persuasion might be exercised to demonstrate that the client company's wishes were not always in its best interest.[34] It was thus in the best interest of the partnership to manifest in its own operations the kind of efficiency, planning and production that the client company expected from its use of a building designed by them.

Client companies were not always newly founded since they had to be of some substance to finance a new building. But the industrial and commercial buildings designed by Wallis, Gilbert & Partners were often for the pro-duction of newly-developed products or services in a fiercely competitive market, and often in new kinds of locations. The designs were expected not only to incorporate the most up-to-date technology, planning ideals and convenience of operation, but to enhance and project the image of the client company as it saw itself and wished to be seen. It was essential therefore that, as well as their expertise, the character and personality of members of Wallis, Gilbert staff were compatible with fulfilling the needs of clients and dealing with contractors.

Frank Cox was a man as generous in spirit as in physical stature, very clear-minded and approachable but unrelenting against slackness or poor work-manship. The business was his whole life and, with no hobbies or outside interests, he was sadly at a loss after retirement in 1949 and died shortly afterwards, aged 68.

Sidney Elliott was an exceptionally clever man, 16 years Cox's junior, and also a worker, a driver, a taskmaster, complementary to Cox in keeping matters moving forward. Relations with business associates were excellent—and not always of a business nature. Elliott married Elsie Elgood, daughter of the principal of E. C. Elgood Ltd, flooring specialists, who were sometimes sub-contractors on Wallis, Gilbert sites; Cox's daughter married Gordon Buckle, engineer, who left E. Wingfield-Bowles & Partners (consulting engineers on some Wallis, Gilbert contracts) to set up on his own as G. H. Buckle & Partners.

Thomas Wallis was the senior partner. To members of his profession he was a popular, if unconventional, figure affectionately known as 'Tommy'.

He was good company, an asset to social gatherings and popular with his clients, many of whom were his personal friends. His talent was in composition, in the integrating of all briefing requirements, the constraints of site, the influence of location. Insight into the nature of his clients, wherein his extra-mural association with them was of advantage, informed the creation of an appropriate aesthetic. Ambitious for the reputation of the partnership, he regarded his designs as permanent contributions to what, in the future, might be considered the period style 'George V'.[35]

Thus the character of the partners was analogous to their professional role and relations with clients, client management personnel, contractors and others, with whom their particular role brought them into most intimate contact. Douglas Wallis, the elder son of Thomas, qualified at the Architectural Association and joined the partnership in 1927, but had little involvement in designing until the 1930s. As a student, he was influenced by his father's designs but, after visiting America, South Africa and Europe in the late 1920s, he came to favour the ideas of the Modern Movement and American-style factory building.[36] He opposed his father's belief in buildings being absorbed into their public environment as 'old friends';[37] in Douglas's view, once a building had served its initial purpose, it should be demolished and replaced by something more up to date.[38] Even so, his personal interests were in the world of art—with the Royal Academy and with artistic, impressionist sketching, but there is evidence of his involvement in the design of one or two factories and of certain original architectural features being taken up in the design of others.

The partnership cannot be said to have always worked in total harmony, but it certainly worked efficiently and gained a reputation of considerable substance. During the Second World War, the practice was engaged upon a number of exacting contracts of national importance. Site visits and supervision in wartime were frequently achieved with great difficulty. For example, for the torpedo base at Antrim, Northern Ireland, there was reliance upon the good offices of the Royal Air Force Transport Command in order to visit the site. Douglas Wallis was absent from the practice throughout the war; as a member of the Territorial Army he was fully occupied on a gunsite on the perimeter of London. Thomas Wallis was then an elderly man and, although still involved in designing, relied heavily upon Cox and Elliott to keep the practice going.

When Douglas returned to the partnership in 1945, Thomas Wallis announced that he intended to retire and that Douglas would assume his (Thomas') share in the partnership. Frank Button did not return after the war but Elliott and Cox, having so strenuously maintained the practice through the very difficult war years, were seriously put out by the absence of any consultation on or discussion of the suddenly imminent change. In their considered opinion, Douglas had 'never pulled his weight' in the pre-war days and had something of the reputation of a 'playboy'. Shares in the partnership were in descending amount from Thomas, then Cox, then Elliott, with Douglas very much the junior partner. The assumption by Douglas of his father's holding would have made him senior partner and thus very much in charge.

Elliott declared his intention to leave and to form a separate practice with Cox.[39] Circular letters to all members of staff gave each the option to remain with Wallis, Gilbert & Partners or to join the new partnership of Elliott & Cox. Client companies were also advised of the severance and asked to state which practice they would wish to be responsible for their current and future business. Agreement had been reached between the parties that whichever of them received the most staff and client options should retain the offices, still at Victoria Coach Station but now extended and re-addressed as 172 Buckingham Palace Road. The severance was operative from 1 January 1946, on which day Thomas Wallis retired. Wallis, Gilbert & Partners moved to 5 Cromwell Road, London SW7. Both practices continued to prosper but were never so large or so well-known as the Wallis, Gilbert & Partners of the interwar years.

Thomas Wallis had been elected a Fellow of the Society of Architects on 15 July 1920 (and thus, later, became a Fellow of the RIBA); his son Douglas was elected FRIBA on 9 October 1939. For many years Thomas Wallis served on the Science Standing, the Registration and the Salaried Members Committees of the RIBA. His contribution to improvement of working conditions in factories and his role as an 'important pioneer in the revolution in the general conception of factory buildings' were recognised in the obituary published by the RIBA in the Institute's *Journal*.[40] Frank Yerbury's comments there recall that Wallis was one of the 'characters' of the profession and was always popular in company. Yerbury also remarked that Wallis' views on building were 'quite his own' and that his 'approach to architecture was most unconventional'—an assertion supported by Wallis' own apologia and explanation of his work in factory design when he addressed the Institute in 1933.[41]

After his retirement, Wallis was free to indulge his artistic leanings in sketching old buildings and rural scenes (which were sometimes used to decorate the partnership's Christmas cards). His daughter, Marjorie Bennett, has a collection of watercolours painted by her father which are quite delightful. Wallis' preference for landscaping factories whenever possible, with lawns, flower beds and trees, was seen as both a humanising influence in an industrial environment and as a commercially viable contribution to image-making; it demonstrates, too, as do his pictures, a good eye for 'scene'. Perhaps he was always a frustrated artist but considered training as an architect made better economic sense. He came from common origins, with a building background. He flouted convention in his private and professional life, combined artistic talent with an understanding of industry and industrialists and, despite his pleasure in the 'good life', was committed to the view that there was no good reason why factories and other commercial buildings should not be pleasant places to work in and to look at. He was, too, both the founder and the destroyer of the Wallis, Gilbert & Partners practice that flourished so remarkably in the interwar years.

Chapter Two

Interwar architecture and factories

Thomas Wallis' attitude to architecture was 'unconventional' but during the interwar years there were, nevertheless, matters of moment affecting the architectural profession to which he had to give due cognisance.

The Architectural Background

After the First World War commissions did not increase as appreciably as the profession might have expected.[1] There was a shortage of building materials and skilled labour, which increased the cost of building. There was the influx of a new generation of architects seeking work, but much of the immense demand for domestic accommodation was met by local authorities, many of whom used in-house architects, and by speculative builders some of whom used none at all. Large contractors more often employed private practice architects to produce original designs but, even then, most residential estates consisted of large numbers of houses built to basic plans but with differently decorated elevations.

These circumstances did, however, give pause to the profession for reflection on the philosophical aspects of architectural design. A burgeoning belief that architects had a major role to play in the future improvement of society was, to some degree, an extension of the Victorian view that environment was character-forming, albeit there was a strongly felt desire to be free of Victorian historical eclecticism and the excessive decoration of that era.

The reaction against Victorian styles widened into debate upon exactly what style of architecture was appropriate to and representative of the twentieth century. The interwar period of architectural design is rather complex; it is here only briefly sketched but, at least, points to those aspects that most impinge on the designing of factories by Wallis, Gilbert & Partners. Within the debate, however, the emphasis on style was less superficial than at first apparent. Gloag pointed out that

> Architecture is an unescapable [sic] record of the ideas of any age and of the stresses and strains put upon any social structure. . . . The stage is set for a new renaissance.[2]

To be taken into account were the effects of new building materials and techniques, the use of electricity and other mechanical services, new health and building regulations, the influence of the expansion of transport, the increase in leisure activities and the broadening range of products and services becoming available to a wider range of the general public. Although these considerations would have their greatest impact upon planning, the major argument still revolved around style; most generally, battle was joined between Traditionalists and Modernists.

The former felt that the new era was more suitably represented in Britain by an updating of traditional forms, preferably of classical or Georgian origin, but neither imitative nor revivalist. It was a view that strongly supported the continuity of traditional British values and was essentially nationalistic: '. . . what might be endurable in a suburb of Paris or Berlin is quite intolerable in the Chilterns and the English countryside';[3] '. . . public buildings should show national character and be recognisable as belonging to that nation'.[4]

Commentators and critics who preferred the Georgian style admired its order and consistency. In Georgian times, they argued, there was only one source of style and one mould of fashion. The uniformity of the style handed down by the well-informed aristocratic patron ensured a rightness of taste throughout society.[5] Seemingly, the neo-Georgians saw themselves as fulfilling the same role. The Modernists, too, advanced an argument for uniformity, in that Modern-style architecture was adaptable to any building type and was therefore socially unifying, was also more up to date, and was more representative of the new age, which they described as 'technological' in character.

The Modern Movement was largely European in origin. Its aim was to achieve a more universally valid architecture that had its roots in the past but, in the 'rationality' of its form, was more appropriate to modern times. The Modern aesthetic was culled from the essence of classical Greek architecture, from Mediterranean vernacular, Cubist art, the absolutes of Platonic forms and the precision engineering of modern motor cars, ocean-going liners, aeroplanes and grain silos. It was manifested in unadorned white concrete, with an interplay of geometric forms and planes, made possible by frame construction. The modern 'machine aesthetic' promised a way of life that was clean, harmonious, uncluttered and efficient, since all purposive require-ments would be mathematically calculated like an engineering blueprint. At its best, however, the style had a poetry and lyricism that belied a mechanistic formulation. In Britain there were instances where, when the style was used for airport buildings, public houses, zoos and garages, it was regarded as pleasantly surprising, even exciting in its modernity. But, closer to home, the idiom was considered austere, soulless and alien to indigenous ideals. Moreover, it was not suitable for the British climate. In Britain, the romantic vision of Modern Movement architecture as the manifestation of universal absolutes, the saving grace of humanity, proved to be somewhat unequal to the task.

Less polemically than outright Traditionalist or Modernist, some British architects took a more median line. They had ideas of their own but were also influenced by styles from Sweden, Holland and the skyscrapers of America. Instances of combining new materials and methods with cleanly-defined and more humanistic styling were the headquarters of the Royal Institute of British Architects (Gray Wornum, 1932–34); Senate House, London University, and the London Passenger Transport building, St James, London (Charles Holden, 1936 and 1928–29 respectively); and Broadcasting House, London (Val Myers and Watson Hart, 1931). The many new municipal offices and town halls built during the period observed traditional civic dignity and beaux-arts planning but with a simpler, more stripped aesthetic than hitherto; and there were examples of brick-built massing of geometric forms taken from Dudok.

No consensus of opinion was reached regarding an aesthetic appropriate to the twentieth century, but there was general agreement that buildings should express their structure and function.[6]

Expression of function or purpose in a building was held to be essential in order to avoid pretentiousness and unnecessary decoration. Precisely how a building expressed its function was difficult to determine; even in respect of those with precedent, it was realised that '. . . at the moment there is no generally accepted idea of what a shop or office-block should look like in order to "look like what it is" '.[7] Gloag pointed out that if the purpose of a building should be boldly revealed by its form, that represented the dominance of individual design over every other consideration; and a building described as functional, because its form revealed structure and materials, represented the dominance of method over design.[8]

Expression of structure was, however, more important to the debate on the 'correct form' for concrete and steel. Oscar Faber's stricture that the 'best architecture must have form and structure conceived as essentially inter-dependent'[9] highlighted the necessity in concrete and steel construction for architects and engineers to work in close cooperation and to 'examine together the possibilities of suggestions as to treatment'.[10] Use of the new structural materials of reinforced concrete and steel frame had, in Britain, been hampered by the absence of technical knowledge and research, exacerbated by an almost total lack of interest by engineers.[11] Consequently, there had been no appropriate amendment of building regulations to allow full exploitation of the materials. For a number of years, almost all work in reinforced concrete was executed under the aegis of foreign companies, such as L. G. Mouchel & Partners (with the French Hennebique system) and Trussed Concrete Steel (with the American Kahn system). Prior to the First World War, buildings of frame construction, such as the Ritz Hotel, London (1904); the Royal Liver Building, Liverpool (1908–09); the General Post Office,

London (1914), were clad in stone or brick and adhered to masonry-based Edwardian styles of imperialistic neo-Renaissance or Baroque, so that the new materials had little impact on visual innovation. Early works in reinforced concrete were chiefly for industrial purposes.

Attitudes to Factory Design

An acceptable aesthetic for steel- and reinforced concrete-framed buildings was therefore of particular relevance to factory design. Restoration of the country's manufacturing base after the First World War was of considerable economic importance. The 'new' industries, mainly producing consumer goods and seeking to exploit a new, mass market, were more likely to engage the services of an architect. Factories for new industries offered the inducement that they, their products, methods of production and, in many cases, their location, were free of historical encumbrances. With the dearth of more prestigious work, architects were free to take the opportunity offered by factory design. Although this was as much a matter of expediency as of committed interest, by 1932 J. Dixon-Spain confidently expressed the view that

> Buildings for manufacture and transport may be said to be special to this age, and they will be the ultimate evidence on which the architectural intelligence of our time will be judged[12]

particularly, he said, since the First World War had 'ushered in an age of highly organised manufacture'.[13]

In the design and construction of National (munition) factories, it had been essential to design in accordance with the very hazardous nature of the enterprise and to organise speedy and efficient production. In those buildings architects met, possibly for the first time, the complex practicalities of factory planning that had to be resolved prior to drawing-board activities and that called for close collaboration with engineers. When reviewing his work for the Ministry of Munitions, Sir Frank Baines stated that he had 'dealt rather fully with the process of operations . . . because this is the real key to the problem of planning'. He appreciated that such work 'abundantly foreshadowed that the closest association and cooperation between these professions [architects and engineers] will be necessary in the future', but was nevertheless of the opinion that the architect was infinitely better qualified to 'carry out this work than an engineer'.[14]

It was not, however, quite so simple to dispense with the engineer. To meet the demands of industry in housing highly-mechanised, flow-line production for which the new constructional methods and materials were most suitable, architects had, of necessity, to work closely with engineers. Throughout the interwar years, books and articles were published giving information and guidance to architects on the planning of factories. Advice was offered on the practical considerations of rationalised production, services, locations and facilities for personnel. The point was made that good working conditions could lead to higher production; and, despite Sir Frank Baines' belief, the necessity was often stressed for cooperation with engineers and works managers, since no two industries' requirements were identical.[15] It is understandable that, when architects were entering a hitherto neglected field, constant reiteration of the fundamental aspects of that field was useful. But familiarity with the subject seems not to have entered the general body of knowledge.

In 1951, in his published talk entitled 'Industrial Buildings', Francis Wylie asserted that 'Factory building is no longer the Cinderella of the drawing office: it has become Industrial Architecture'.[16] Nevertheless, his talk was little more than a repetition of the basic facts of factory design that had been offered since 1917. As recently as 1982, Francis Duffy (architect) and Jolyon Drury (industrial consultant) found need to advise architects that, in order to 'invent better industrial buildings' they should

> . . . understand what goes on inside factories; which is far more varied than you might think. Different industries vary in size, in patterns of growth, in dirt, noise and messiness, in loadings, and in many ways which relate directly to building design.[17]

Dixon-Spain's forecast in 1932 of the criterion by which architectural intelligence would be judged seems not to have been fulfilled if, half a century on, architects were still being urged to 'understand what goes on inside factories'.

The educative and critical literature maintained an emphasis on factories purely as production units, which ignored the basic fact of commercial production—that selling is as important as making when the primary objective is financial profit. Manufacturers of the 1920s and 1930s were operating in a fiercely competitive market that sought to attract an increasing domestic demand. Many factories were located near, and were visible to, potential customers. The importance of aligning self-advertising and brand names with a company 'image' arose from new marketing methods that bypassed the old system of factors, merchants and wholesalers. Many manufacturers established their own depots and agents, at which selling points the company name or trade mark gave direct association with the point of origin. Sales departments were an important feature in the planning of the factory to which potential customers were invited. The kind of image projected by the buildings was therefore of some importance. In 1982, Duffy and Drury openly recognised that fact and stated

> Third, and most positively, the image that buildings project to suppliers, customers and bankers now becomes critical. A major task

of architecture is to express what the company wants to say about itself and to impress others.[18]

Was this not an aspect that had been critical to factory design throughout the long period of industrialisation? In the interwar debate on 'what a factory should look like', that aspect was often imperfectly understood and strenuously resisted. Professional appraisal was, all too frequently, imbued with the longstanding stigma of the vulgarity attached to trade.

A. Trystan Edwards felt that, if the ugly features of industry had to be tolerated in a city, they should be screened from view by means of a high wall or a thick bank of trees; if that were not possible, such building should show 'becoming deference to the aesthetic ideal'.[19] Dixon-Spain also thought the 'exterior of a factory should be unobtrusive'.[20] His own designs had a distinctly municipal air. L. Bucknell looked for a 'building which grows from the necessity and form of the machine'. He was convinced that once the architect knew all the facts of the process of manufacture, he would produce a building 'satisfying the requirements of economy, convenience and beauty . . . untramelled by prejudice and preconceptions and expressive of a great industrial age'.[21] Mr Bucknell belonged to the 'machine aesthetic' school and believed it should be applied where it most appropriately belonged. But again, all those attitudes tend to classify factories as purely mechanised production units, partly perhaps because production was the priority in munition factories from which some architects took their pattern, and partly because of the constantly expressed view that this was '*the* machine age'.

Influences on Factory Design

A further influence was the introduction of American-style mass production. At the close of the First World War, America was infinitely more prosperous than any other country involved in hostilities and was seeking outlets for expansion to mop up excess profits. To avoid the British imposition of import tariffs, to take advantage of the devaluation of the pound sterling, and to be able to break into European and British Empire markets, a number of American companies decided to build factories in Britain. American patent holders were often willing to license manufacture of patented goods in Britain by British companies; this too had an influence on production methods. Some British manufacturers felt it wise to visit the United States to research American methods before commissioning new buildings for themselves in Britain. During the interwar years in Britain there was also a gradual concentration of firms by merger or takeover to facilitate standardised, large-scale production. Volume production called for large, uninterrupted spans of floor space, organised into some or any of flow-line, conveyor belt, overhead track, gantries, or progressive single station methods.

Advances in the production of pre-fabricated, standardised building components reduced construction time and dependence on weather conditions, but imposed constraints upon both planning and the design of elevations. When constructing in frame, it was necessary to have plant and power on site so that this too entered into the logistics of planning schedules. The timing of deliveries of materials, the ducting of services in a monolithic structure while also allowing access for maintenance, the mechanics of lighting, heating and ventilation and more sophisticated sanitary arrangements (all usually put out to sub-contract), all called for precise organisation and stemming of operations by the architects in charge.

The application of electricity to manufacturing processes, though not yet used to its full potential, offered greater flexibility of process planning. As a much cleaner fuel, electricity also gave an aura of bright, cleaner, healthier factories that could be reflected in the overall visual appearance of the buildings.

That aspect was of considerable importance in the choice of location of many new factories. Although close proximity to London was important in economic terms, some distancing therefrom was often necessary to avoid the rigorous constraints upon concrete construction imposed by London Building Regulations, now no longer as flexible as in wartime.[22] The price of electricity, which varied from region to region, and the availability of labour were also decisive. A suburban, sometimes semi-rural, site invited landscaping of the buildings and called for elevations that gained from their setting, particularly when co-extensive with a new arterial road and clearly visible to the public. The opening up of hitherto undeveloped areas for large-scale building could, however, put considerable strain upon existing mains services; wells, water towers, tanks, disposal units and similar features were often required and had to be included in the overall designing process.

Concrete in its raw state did not lend itself too well to achieving the clean, bright image without some kind of enhancement. Appropriate treatment of concrete surfaces posed both technical and aesthetic problems,[23] but also extended the range of colours and textures that could be incorporated into a design.

The increasing use of road transport and the availability of sites beside major trunk roads attracted factories to those locations—albeit the additional congestion was somewhat self-defeating in regard to access. Nevertheless, in planning the layout of the site and buildings, access, routeing for delivery and despatch and for parking facilities had to be incorporated. Regulations in respect of covered, raised docking bays contributed to the improved appearance of factories when the use of cantilevering presented a more modern and elegant effect than did the traditional 'railway platform' type of shelter.

A combination of statutory regulations[24] and an appreciation that good working conditions and amenities were necessary adjuncts to higher productivity made for considerable emendation of traditional factory design.

Without disturbing the equilibrium of the production pattern, a variety of requirements had to be fitted into the overall plan. Adequate sanitary arrangements (that were heated, well-lit and externally ventilated), cloak-room facilities and rest rooms, could all be grouped to coordinate plumbing and to serve most personnel, or as single units at strategic points which saved on workers' time but required separate drainage. Always, facilities for men and women had to be geographically segregated but, in the siting of facilities, much depended upon how much time might be lost in getting to and from such places or upon the needs of those in specific areas of work. First-aid arrangements had to be accessible but free from contamination by factory processes. Canteens could be incorporated into the main structure or erected as separate buildings. Whilst one kitchen could serve the needs of all personnel, eating rooms were invariably separated in a hierarchical fashion and often also by gender; it was intended that access paths should not cross each other.

Although the provisions of earlier Factory Acts had often been ignored, healthier working conditions were important in the new factories and more easily achieved when electricity provided the main motive power. Work-places needed to have adequate lighting, heating and ventilation, air space, controlled temperature and humidity, and dispersal of smells and noxious substances. Sometimes, however, the environmental requirements of the product and/or product material took precedence over employees, but something extra had to be done for the thus disadvantaged employees to re-establish their well-being. Environmental provisions were also structural considerations; as particular services, they had to be included alongside the main machine power supply, but in a manner that prevented obstruction of any one by another whilst all of the services remained accessible for maintenance purposes. Precautions against fire hazard and the simplification of cleaning and painting for environmental cleanliness influenced the choice of structural materials; the need for rapid evacuation of a building in the event of fire affected planning arrangements.

An extension of the philosophy of the happy workforce was not only emblematic of an enlightened employer, but had a further role in reinforcing company loyalty. The provision of sports and other leisure facilities, in-house magazines and inter-factory contests, and the encouragement of family participation promoted a sense of community but also conspired toward arousing a competitive spirit that could be advantageous when translated into workplace activity. There were, however, no suggestions for changes in the conventional hierarchical system. Arrangements for effective and efficient supervision, in both production and administration areas, were expected to be included in planning schemes irrespective of whether other amenities and facilities were. Not all companies were prepared to finance all the improving facilities or, at least, not initially. Cost was persistently an overriding consideration. But, in view of the potential advantages, the architect was well advised to plan for the future implementation of such facilities and amenities.

The architect's forward thinking was even more important to the client in regard to future expansion. Although the primary commission would be based on little more than present capacity requirements, the possible/probable need for extra floor space demanded structures that were easily extendable, siting that left suitable free ground, or foundations sufficiently strong to support extra storey(s), as well as early planning for services and drainage in excess of original needs. At the same time, the original building should not look unfinished or as if requiring any future extensions to fulfil its conceptual promise. Extensions themselves were nevertheless expected to conform to and enhance the original design.

The variety of 'scientific management' systems introduced into manufacturing industry, although often embryonic in performance, affected planning arrangements. The move from having (family)owner's office and counting house integrated into production areas to the separation of administrative functions into departmental suites led to partial or complete separation of administration areas from those for production. This differentiation gave the architect some freedom of aesthetic expression and allowed companies more easily to establish individual and recognisable images. Even so, little attention seems to have been paid to an analysis of office operations or layout and planning other than the provision of easily-deployed partitioning within an open floor space. A certain extravagance of materials and design was permitted for the size and interior decoration of boardrooms, offices for senior management, entrance halls and any areas where a company had direct contact with customers. Waiting rooms were expected to be comfortable to reflect the status and prosperity of the company and, where appropriate, planning needed to include exhibition space in which to display the company's products.

Some companies made early endeavours to include accommodation for technical research and development, product testing and the training of personnel. Architects needed to collaborate closely with such expert advice as was available. Other companies, where the string-and-sealing-wax approach of traditional British innovation was still ingrained, came late to recognising the importance of purpose-built premises for such activities; but they were then able to take advantage of architects' longer experience.

Given that factories were hardly new upon the British landscape but that interest by many architects in their design *was* new, the coincidence of that interest with the arrival of new industry, new materials and products, new production methods and new constructional materials and techniques, gave credibility to Dixon-Spain's prophecy. That the prophecy was not fulfilled appears to rest with the intractability of traditional attitudes to industry. Wallis, Gilbert & Partners were, fortunately, less inhibited in their attitude to industry.

Gloag, in the debate about an architecture for the twentieth century, pleaded for a

> coherence of architectural taste and a new majesty of form, . . . strength and beauty [since] civilisation does not end with the provision and consumption of commodities.[25]

True enough! Consumerism may have contributed little to high culture but the provision of consumer goods was a valuable part of national recovery. It provided work in times of massive unemployment, fed the aspirations and well-being of the lower strata of society and put money in the pockets of the already well-off who, whilst preferring more 'civilised' pursuits, were not averse to investing in firms producing consumer goods. It was rather odd, too, that architects and commentators who readily accepted the modern machine as typifying the age regarded commercialism as an abhorrent phenomenon best excluded from modern culture. What, one wonders, did they think the machines were for? Even more odd, perhaps, is that the most vilified architectural styles—particularly those such as Wallis, Gilbert's Fancy factories—are now regarded as the most representative of the interwar years in catching the essence and character of the period.

Chapter Three

Analysis and assessment

Introduction

Although after the First World War there was the prospect of more commissions, there were also arguments and regulations, a variety of paradoxes and a degree of opprobrium awaiting Thomas Wallis. But, by that time, he and his new practice had already gained some valuable experience in their chosen field.

When Wallis began his career in factory design, the war was in its second year, with no certainty of its outcome. Although he had to design in accordance with government restrictions as to product and building materials, there was state financial assistance for war factory building; concrete construction was welcomed and the existing regulations in its regard were treated with some laxity; Wallis was free to create his own style. Most of the factories designed by Wallis, Gilbert & Partners during the war and until 1926 were the product of collaboration with Trussed Concrete Steel (Truscon). They show the most pronounced American influence—the 'model factory'[1] of the Kahn Daylight pattern of reinforced concrete frame infilled with large areas of small-paned glazing in narrow metal bars.

The increased penetration of natural light and cross-ventilation afforded by so much glass, often on all sides, and the wider spans permitted by frame construction, made a considerable contribution to efficiency in working arrangements and production planning. At the same time, the design provided an improved environment for the workforce. It was best suited to multi-storey buildings with under-one-roof operations and descending production flow—an arrangement of particular advantage where land was at a premium. But it was equally appropriate for storage and despatch purposes, was adaptable to single-storey operation, especially where future expansion must needs be upwards, and was remarkably flexible in respect of layout, alteration and addition.[2]

What typifies this group of early designs is that, despite their concrete frame, they affect a heavy, over-substantial bearing more appropriate to traditional masonry design. That these buildings were often over-stressed and over-solid looking was owed partly to the primal state of technical knowledge[3] and partly, after 1918, to building regulations not yet adapted to new building practices.[4] But aesthetically, too, there was the compulsion to conform to contemporary notions that large-scale buildings be impressively solid and stable. When designers in concrete were still seeking an expression peculiar to that medium, accentuation of its weight and density could be seen to counterbalance the apparent flimsiness of the glass-filled voids.

These early factories were most often commissioned by 'new' industries and/or for expansion for wartime production of goods that had a potential post-war demand. It was thus important that the buildings appeared modern and forward looking without completely losing touch with the past. Much less ornate than their Edwardian forebears, these factories were accorded professional approval; what decoration they carried was regarded as appropriate relief from the austerity of 'continental' versions. All these buildings were, in fact, variations on a basic theme. In keeping with that format, the decoration consisted of a small repertoire of concrete motifs that could be differently permutated to suit the client and the location of the building. The source of the basic design and layout was American; the styling and frontages of this early group were Wallis' own, derived from his neo-classical training.

From the mid-1920s, a new style emerged and new forms of layout. Steel was more readily available; a move away from cramped urban sites to larger areas of virgin land allowed a different approach to production layout. The discovery of the tomb of Tutankhamun in Egypt and the exhibition of some of its contents at the British Museum in 1923 gave impetus to the popularity of Egyptian styles and motifs; they became even more fashionable after the Arts Decoratifs Exhibition in Paris in 1925. Wallis included Egyptian styling in his designs as early as 1918 (including the interior of the practice offices), but this new popularity gave much freer rein to exercise his partiality. Most of the factories built between 1927 and 1935 were of modernised neo-classical style, but Egyptianising became more pronounced. Wallis' handling of the idiom showed, however, a more profound understanding of its cultural sources and implications than appears to have been the case in the wider commercial and industrial field. The imaginative use of coloured faience and a leaning toward popular taste in the design of frontal elevations attracted professional criticism.

The factories of this mid-term period are often referred to as 'Art Deco', in reference to some of the detailing, but the appellation ignores their basic concept and amounts to empty comment. There is no such *architectural* style. Other labels include *moderne*, modernistic, jazz-modern and, not infrequently, Fancy in denigration of their seeming novelty. 'Fancy' is, in fact, the most useful catch-all term with which to describe this group since its implications were intrinsic to Wallis' approach to factory design. The style too was Wallis' own; its association with American razzmatazz or Amerindian design, or the many other supposed sources, has no foundation.

The dominant feature of the later works to 1939 was an increasingly 'modern' (or Modern) approach, in which expression of materials and methods of construction formed the stylistic essence of a design. Geometric arrangements and accentuation of horizontals and verticals appear in brick and concrete; strong curves and semi-circles in the structure were reflected in sculptured decorative elements. Colour was not entirely abandoned but used to a lesser degree. In common with other areas of design and, indeed, with the social ethos generally, there was a greater feeling for tailored sophistication and, at times, something of the anonymity preached by the Modern Movement. But when not sufficiently well-handled it led to diminution, sometimes a loss, of the heroic character of the earlier designs.

The overlapping of the periods of these styles shows, to a large extent, a response to changing conditions and attitudes. Of equal consequence was the wish to relate a design to the wishes of a client and the location of the site. For some briefs, inevitably in such a wide field of clientele, an adaptation of the currently popular design was inappropriate. The final grouping contains a small, motley collection of designs that stand outside the basic themes outlined above. The overseas commissions and those for continental European companies for which Wallis, Gilbert acted in either a consultative or on-site capacity are of particular interest. The section, later in this chapter under the heading Sheds, refers to buildings designed for specific production processes at already-established works. The term is not meant to imply solely a series of minimally utilitarian adjuncts; although some are, many have architectural and technological features that confirm the expertise of Wallis, Gilbert & Partners as factory designers and demonstrate the correctness of their insistence on collaboration with works manager and engineers.

(a) The Early Years 1916–26—Daylight/Masonry Factories

Between 1912 and 1915, the British-based section of Trussed Concrete Steel was engaged in the construction of at least three major projects in Scotland: a three-storey E-shaped factory on a new site at Dumfries for the Arrol-Johnson Motor Works (1912–13);[5] a four-storey administration and drawing-office block for G. & J. Weir Ltd, engineers of Cathcart, Glasgow (1912–13);[6] and a four-storey block for the Albion Motor Car Company of Scotstoun, Glasgow (1913–15).[7]

The drawings for the Weir building bear the names of the company's in-house designers. In 1912, however, members of both the Albion and Arrol-Johnson companies visited America[8] to observe planning and production methods in motor manufacturing plants, particularly in Detroit, the home base of Truscon. In these instances, therefore, American influence on the design of factories for those Scottish companies was sought at source, rather than copied from factories built by American companies setting up in Britain.

The building at Albion was a modification of the 'unit-principle' described by Moritz Kahn in his book of 1917,[9] an alternation of multi- and single-storey units, which was then considered most appropriate for integrated, volume production. There is no direct evidence that Thomas Wallis was involved in the design of the Albion block; the original plans have been destroyed and those deposited with the local authority, and their records, appear to have been lost.[10] The clients assumed that 'Mr Kahn will probably employ an architect and pay him the fee himself'.[11] Wallis, Gilbert & Partners were, however, commissioned to design buildings for the Albion company in 1918, 1920 and 1927. The 1913–15 block, nevertheless, represents the prototype from which Wallis, Gilbert buildings of this period were developed. As such, it warrants examination, since that also gives some insight into the processes and programme by which such buildings came into being.

The Albion Motor Car Company Limited

This company, of 1272 South Street, Scotstoun, Glasgow, was founded in December 1899 to manufacture private motor cars. An increasing specialisation in commercial vehicles led to total conversion to that product and car production ceased in November 1914. The four-storey block was built in 1913–15 to centralise storage and redistribution as the company expanded into an integrated system of production of a comprehensive range of commercial vehicle chassis. Bodies were fitted to chassis in accordance with the customer's orders.[12]

In the conduct of their business affairs, the principals of the Albion Company had visited the United States a number of times prior to the First World War and had, in consequence, some knowledge of American factories and methods of production.[13] When planning the expansion of their own factory in 1912, it was decided that the Director, Dr Tom Blackwood Murray, and the Works Manager, Mr Keachie, should visit America on 1 June 1912, specifically to

> make a tour of inspection of the most up-to-date motor factories, machine tool shops, etc. so that the company may lay down extensions on the most approved lines.[14]

A multi-storey building was felt to be most appropriate because of the difficulties of feuing arrangements in Scotland and, thus, they paid 'special attention to Ferro-Concrete Buildings and the general arrangement of the various departments'. Much valuable information was obtained from the visit and it was decided to

> carry out further extensions to the Works largely on American lines, but with such modifications as appeared desirable and necessary to suit local conditions.[15]

Tenders for the concrete work were received from five contractors. On 9 May 1913 correspondence between Albion directors advised that

> Mr Kahn was up yesterday and we fixed upon the contract for the new Ferro-Concrete block going to Messrs S. Stevenson of Polmadie, for the sum of £8775. Of course, to this must be added the cost of the steel bars which will approximately come to £1824. Work will be started in the early part of next week.[16]

At the time of researching the building, the Albion works were situated on the north side of South Street, less than one hundred yards from the north bank of the River Clyde. Much of the land in that area is below sea level, with minor outcroppings of rock. Precise details of the foundations of the concrete building are not available but may well be those shown as 'existing foundations' in plans of 1927 for an adjoining extension. That is, stanchions resting on individual reinforced concrete platforms, with extra reinforcement rising seven feet from base to two or three feet above ground level around the lower end of each stanchion. Whatever their exact nature, the building sat comfortably on them for more than 70 years.

On completion, the building was designed as a hollow rectangle of four storeys rising to 60 feet in height, with the inner courtyard glazed over at single-storey level. The building had a north/south orientation. Its main entrance was on the south side, at the rear of but later connected to an office block built in 1912; access from the road was through a large service entrance to the east of the offices. Ideally, the whole of the ground floor was to have had no internal walls, but the units were built separately—the east unit, cross ends and lift/stair wells in 1913, and glazed throughout. The west unit was completed in 1915 and left open at interior ground level, the single-storey sheds in the well being glazed over when construction reached the first floor of the main block. Gantries for travelling cranes ran longitudinally down each side of the centre well and centrally below the furrow of the roof.

Each side unit measured 200 feet by 60 feet, with end connections each of 50 feet by 16, giving an overall ground coverage of 200 feet by 170 feet. Each floor was an open span of nine by three bays, 20 feet square, plus bays of 20 by 14 feet on the end walls. The internal hexagonal columns decreased in section in ascending order from 20 inches at ground level to 10 inches at the top floor. The top floors were each top-lit by a glazed, pitched roof over the centre aisle. The original windows, which have never been replaced, were metal-framed, twelve by five paned, with three centrally-pivoted opening lights, and have never leaked. Spandrels were of brick with concrete sills. Two windows on each side of the short connecting ends had only eight by five panes, but the variation in size was barely noticeable and did not detract the eye from the overall symmetry of the grille pattern. The variation reflected no interior function; it was simply a matter of fitting standard-sized windows into the dimensions of the building. Services were attached to cross beams and/or outer-wall piers and the building was steam-heated by wall-mounted pipes and radiators.

For many years, the building was used for storage of incoming materials and for finished goods, with light machine operations and a tool room on the fourth floor. As such, the 'Daylight' design was of great advantage but, when put to different usage, glare and solar heat-gain on the upper floors necessitated the fitting of blinds. The later installation and use of heavy machinery on the upper floors caused excessive vibration, with spalling of concrete on the walls surrounding the well, some cracking of brickwork and damage to the mechanism of a service lift. Only the ground floor was occupied when the building was visited and the problem, because of over-capacity, of reducing the building to single-storey or of total demolition when so closely surrounded by and attached to other buildings, had not then been solved. It is understood that the building has since been demolished.

The appearance of the building betrays its American influence in being dictated solely by its utilitarian purpose. Totally undecorated, the simplicity and abstraction of its form and 'fitness for purpose' convey no suggestion of art, artistry or beauty. Its visual impact in 1913 must have been considerable; a concrete and glass monster rising hugely from a sea of brick and slate, alien to both the ornamented office block and the familiar north-light sheds. More recently it was virtually lost sight of behind a replacement office block but it could have been more appropriately tamed shortly after its erection had the commission to Wallis, Gilbert & Partners in 1918 for four-storey wings to the office block been carried out.

The proposed wings, although of the same basic structure and monumentality as the concrete block, offered a more realistic compromise with contemporary aesthetic taste. The broken skyline, decorative motifs and a more complex articulation transmute a starkly modern structure into a classical façade. A relation would then have been established between the wings and the earlier concrete block in the similarity of their skeletal framework and between the wings and the existing office block in echoing the more accustomed grandeur of Glasgow's municipal architecture and massive tenement blocks.

The office block could well have been dwarfed by such large extensions but the hierarchical status of the 'management centre' was actually enhanced by the flanking towers, the projecting piers of the adjoining sections and the recession of the outer parts of the wings. In drawing the eye to the central offices, the threatening bulk of the 1913–15 concrete block would be stilled to a backdrop.

As architecture, the proposed wings were neither avant garde nor remarkably outstanding, or seeking a place in history, but the essence of the design lay in the architect's ability satisfactorily to integrate so many, often conflicting, demands into a building that obeyed the rules of proportion and unified composition. In reconciling appropriate references to industry, home and civic affairs, industry was given a proper place in the scheme of things. The design also reconciled traditional and modern approaches to architecture; it was neither as ornamental as Victorian or Edwardian buildings nor so aggressively austere and anonymous as the Modern inclination. Most of all, it was *suitable*—to its purpose and role, to its place and time, and to its clients, who were progressively commercial but still paternalistically-minded.

The wings were never built, possibly as a result of the economic situation at the time—the Government withdrew financial assistance to factory building once the war was won. As likely a reason, too, since the Albion Company manufactured commercial vehicles, was that as the war ended, some 60 000 ex-army vehicles were released for civilian purchase by the War Office Disposal Department.

In 1920, Wallis, Gilbert designs were executed at Albion for a boiler house and chimney to the west of the concrete block and, in 1927 as the economic situation improved, a machine shop extension of single-storeyed, trussed-roof sheds that matched fairly closely the style of the existing north-light sheds to the east.

The grid patterned, multi-storeyed, reinforced concrete frame-with-glass-infill design of the 1913–15 Truscon building at Albion can be recognised as the basic structure of most Wallis, Gilbert & Partners' factories of the early period. A series of 20 feet square bays gave flexibility to interior organisation of a variety of production methods. The regular pattern of stanchions and beams offered simple means of ducting, channelling or attaching power lines and other services. The format permitted freedom in the disposition of exterior openings, bays for lifts and stairs, and the installing of mezzanine floors for supervision, small processes, lavatories, and so on. The large, standardised windows provided a greater degree of cross-lighting and ventilation reaching over a wider area; the small glass panes, although more expensive to install, were more easily replaced and less hazardous to personnel in the event of breakage. Maintenance and painting of a vast array of glazing bars was a formidable task but the grille-effect did reduce glare to some extent, particularly if appropriate panes were of ribbed or ridged glass. Reinforced concrete columns, beams and floors gave better protection from fire and vibration, were cheaper and speedier in construction than brick or stone, and required less steel when that commodity was in short supply.

The plain frame building was very adaptable to the practicalities of manufacturing production, but its style was too stark and anonymous to commend itself as a total image of manufacturing industry. Though modern and progressive, its undifferentiated bulk was too reminiscent of dark Satanic mills and, for the population at large, too great a break with the customary decoration of large buildings. It is doubtful if the American origin of the format was generally recognised. When the Modern Movement concrete idiom imposed itself upon the British consciousness, it was regarded as 'continental' and, as such, heartily disliked by most British people. To become acceptable in Britain, the form needed to be anglicised and human-ised; for industry, it needed also to be customised to the inclination of the individual client.

The external shape of the plain frame building and the disposition of openings were dictated by the floor plans of internal layout and offered little scope for compositional enhancement. Generally, therefore, it could only be 'dressed'. The priority of layout planning and its effects on the elevations were always maintained by Wallis, Gilbert & Partners but, in all but a few cases, the most publicly visible part of the skeleton was always suitably dressed.

The importance of the Albion reinforced concrete block to a study of Wallis, Gilbert works, is evident in that

(i) even if Wallis was not personally involved in its design, he would have known of the building at the time the partnership was formed through assisting Moritz Kahn in the writing of *The Design and Construction of Industrial Buildings*, in which the Albion build-ing was cited and illustrated as an example. The first factory designed by Wallis, Gilbert & Partners, in 1916, repeated the hollow rectangle format of Albion.

(ii) For Wallis, the building was a seminal form of the frame/unit/daylight system; its construction in two parts demonstrated the potential of the system for comparative simplicity of extension, permutation of arrangement of parts, and its adaptability to production of operating requirements for many kinds of industry.

(iii) It establishes the American origins of the system and its con-struction in Britain at a date earlier than appears in much of the literature.[17]

(iv) The ease and speed of planning, designing, producing drawings for and constructing a building from a handful of units that could be juggled to meet a variety of requirements would present itself as a desirable and highly marketable commodity, in which indus-trialists might appreciate the analogy with their own large-scale production methods. For the architect, a set of aesthetic treat-ments that could also be permutated as appropriate to client and other determinants offered similar advantages.

By the time Wallis designed the proposed office block wings for Albion, he had, as Wallis, Gilbert & Partners, already designed five other factories, of which three were built. These designs were for firms which extended their premises under government licence and restrictions to meet wartime orders but whose products were also expected to find an expanding market in the post-war years. The design of such buildings had, therefore, to be appropri-ate to both contingencies. The plain, daylight frame and unit system was suitable on both counts in purely practical terms. Unadorned, however, the vocabulary was too limited for an urban setting, too bleakly insensitive in suburban or rural areas to which industries were beginning to migrate, and too bereft of recognisable symbolism to express how the client company saw itself in terms of either stability or modernity.

In the post-war years, manufacturers of new products (and speculative builders of cheaper housing) came to realise that the economies of standardis-ation could be reconciled with freedom of choice by the volume-production of a basic unit that could be individualised to identify the maker or to suit the customer's preference. That was a notion which Wallis, Gilbert appreciated from their beginnings. Thomas Wallis thus conceived a close range of compositional features and integrated decorative elements that reflected the basic frame but enhanced its countenance. That is, a burgeoning 'concrete aesthetic' that could be adapted to individual determinants or client's wishes.

As shown in the following analysis of three built factories, by the end of the First World War the Wallis, Gilbert format was well established, in a style that was as recognisable as any manufacturer's label.

J. Tylor & Son Limited

The first built design by Wallis, Gilbert & Partners in collaboration with Truscon appears to be that for J. Tylor & Son Limited at Oakleigh Road South, New Southgate, London, in 1916. The client company was established in 1768 as a manufacturer of tea urns. The business passed from fathers to sons and diversified into sanitary and hydraulic engineering and iron and brass founding, at Newgate Street and at Belle Isle, King's Cross, London.[18] At the turn of the century, the manufacture of petrol engines was added to the normal business. With an increase in orders for the War Department as from 1914, the petrol engine section required larger premises and, in 1916, a new factory was built especially for that purpose at New Southgate.

The site, of some 27 acres, was, in 1916, largely open fields bounded on the south-west by the Great Northern Railway and on the south-east by Brunswick Avenue and the Great Northern Cemetery. A private rail siding gave access to a small chapel on the site, where coffins trans-shipped from London rested, pending interment. The land slopes away from the southern corner, where access was established from Oakleigh Road and the railway bridge. The entrance is at a blind corner and therefore difficult for vehicular traffic; a roadway was built from that corner through the centre of the site, but access was not so problematical in the early years, as heavy goods were received and despatched via the railway sidings. When the railway was built in 1850, difficulties had been encountered with the layer of shale and gravel beneath the London clay subsoil and with natural springs that had to be culverted. The geological conditions continued to present problems of slippage and water seepage on the site. Of the proposed buildings only the machine shop, entrance lodge and meter house/transformer were built. The entrance lodge has since been replaced and the meter house was rebuilt when the original building suffered movement damage.

The machine shop was built on the site previously occupied by the chapel to take advantage of, and further extend, the railway siding. That building, now demolished, measured 440 feet by 180 feet overall, with ceilings at 14 feet 6 inches, and took the shape of a hollow rectangle. Floors, beams and columns, resting on individual platforms, were of reinforced concrete by Truscon, and disposed on a regular pattern of 20 feet square bays. Steel-framed windows, as infill, were of standard size, with twelve by five panes and three centrally-hung opening lights. The similarity to Albion is very clear. In contrast to the Albion building, however, this building was also to be used for administrative as well as production purposes. The main entrance, at the centre of the south wall, opened to hall, waiting room, telephone exchange and stairs; flanking secondary entrances gave access to offices and other administrative services, and there were shuttered openings at the corners to works and garage. Materials entered at the south end of the west wall and were despatched as goods from the north end. Stores and tool room were to be housed in the centre well. The design was thus intended, in the production areas, to facilitate a sequential line of processing.

It is not possible to say how production was actually organised by Tylors. The elevation plans show the first and second floors to be proposed extensions. Two of the storeys were built in 1916, with particularly massive longitudinal beams supporting the roof, in expectation of an additional third storey.

The company experienced considerable financial difficulties after the First World War and, although the main business continued at Belle Isle, production of 'Tylor' engines was transferred to a new company at Hendon and the site and buildings at New Southgate were purchased for £11 712 0s 9d in 1922 by the International Western Electric Company of Chicago, USA, for the manufacture of telephone equipment. In 1925 the company was purchased by International Telegraph and Telephone (ITT) of America and the name of the British subsidiary was changed to Standard Telephones and Cables Limited (STC). The site has been considerably extended and developed over the years.[19]

When purchased in 1922, the machine shop building was described as a 'modern, ferro-concrete structure, facing three sides of a rectangle, enclosing a pleasant open-paved courtyard'. STC roofed in the centre courtyard with saw-toothed north lights and closed the open end to two storeys in 1923–24. A third storey was added in 1933.

On 1 March 1980 the building suffered a partial collapse, when pillars in a corner of the ground floor were being repaired after suffering damage from the effects of chemicals and excessive heat from the ovens, in what was then the heat treatment department. Too much concrete had been removed by the repair contractors; two pillars sheared. The floors up to roof level in that corner descended some two or three inches. Core samples, taken from the lower floors, showed that the aggregate mix of the concrete had been of inadequate quality, but the reinforcing rods of the pillars were in excellent condition and did not buckle. ACRO props and steel scaffolding supported the section temporarily and the building remained in use until 1985. Further additional steel stanchions permitted sequential evacuation over time without interruption of manufacturing processes. The structure of the rest of the building was essentially sound, despite frequent overloading of floors, but the decision was taken to demolish the whole.[20]

The identity of the original contractor is not known. These early buildings were frequently over-stressed—a measure which, in this instance, probably prevented complete collapse of the building after more than 60 years of constant and varied use. The layout of the building, known by STC as Number 3, was considered by the company to be very efficient. When buildings 4 and 8 were erected, identical principles of design were followed. The uniformity of the design permitted easy re-arrangement of plant, and the 20 feet square bays were found to be admirably suited to different kinds of usage.[21]

The appearance of building Number 3 as it stood from 1933 until 1985 was something of a hybrid. The basic form was the Kahn Daylight unit system but Wallis added ornament, emphasising certain structural elements to articulate and balance the composition. The main entrance received its importance from its block-like appearance in the centre and its name-bearing pediment at roof level. A 'palace-front' effect was achieved through enhancement of the secondary doorways by projecting piers rising through three storeys flanked by substantial corner 'towers'. The towers delineated and powerfully enclosed the large, simple structure and, on the front elevation, broke the roofline to allow the eye to travel back to the centre and its main doorway. The proposed design of 1916 gave the impression of a classical masonry building in which the form work decoration could have been stone dressing of a brick building. The decorative details—'nail-heads', with or without supports, stepped, square pediments and tower terminals—became virtually the hallmark of Wallis, Gilbert & Partners' factories for at least a decade, and appeared first on the Tylor building. Highlighting of doorways by projecting piers on the west elevation contributed to a pleasing view of the factory seen by passengers on the railway.

As modified and extended in 1933 the building expressed more emphatically its simple, basic form. The doorways were accentuated only at their own level but the central entrance was made more assertive by additional mullions, at first and second floor levels, that rose into the short 'clock tower'. A plain cavetto cornice neatly terminated the whole structure. The Egyptian connotations of the cornice and the presence of the nail-head decoration on the clock tower suggest, in the absence of other evidence, that the extension of the third storey was also designed by Wallis, Gilbert. At some 17 years' distance from the original design, the 1933 extension completely altered the character of the building from modernised Edwardian to decorated Modern.

The proposed wings designed for the Albion Company in Glasgow demonstrated the adaptability of Wallis' concrete aesthetic to location; the Tylor building, in its progression from original design to final appearance, showed the adaptability of the format over time. The plan of the Tylor building repeats the hollow rectangle of the Albion concrete block but shows to a greater extent how the frame/unit system could be constructed part by part and the kind of freedom the structure afforded to the disposition of openings in the elevation to accord with internal planning.

Two designs of 1916 that were not executed were for Brolt Limited of Birmingham and Williams & Williams Limited of Chester.

Brolt Limited

In 1911 H. B. Brookes (a member of the family better known for the making of bicycle saddles) owned a small engineering business in Birmingham and was approached by C. A. Vandervell & Co Ltd of Acton to manufacture a dynamo patented by Vandervell's partner, A. H. Midgley. Brookes thereupon 'poached' from Vandervell one of his best engineers, W. Holt, and a company was set up in December 1911 by Brookes and Holt. Brolt Limited was a contraction of their two names and was founded to manufacture electric vehicle-ignition and lighting sets. Premises were leased at Princip Street, Birmingham. Most of the firm's business depended upon orders from commercial vehicle manufacturers, principally Albion, Beardmore and Jowett, and a few motor car companies.

In common with even the larger vehicle-oriented electrical engineering firms, by the early 1920s Brolt was facing financial difficulties. A new company was formed in 1920 and, within a year, the company moved to Oldbury (then in Staffordshire). The directors had made several requests to Joseph Lucas & Company to buy them out which, with some reluctance, Lucas did in 1924 for £50 000 but this was primarily a strategic measure to protect its own interests from predatory competition.[22]

The only evidence of the commission being given to Wallis, Gilbert & Partners is a sketch published in Moritz Kahn's book of industrial buildings in 1917,[23] from which it is fair to assume that the building was designed prior to 1917 and was to be of reinforced concrete under the aegis of Truscon. Where it was intended to be built is not clear, since the Princip Street premises occupied by Brolt are still standing and, without demolition of nearby property, there was no spare ground in the vicinity. There is no record of deposited plans, rate books show little variation in Brolt's charges over the relevant years, and the Princip Street premises during Brolt's occupation were rated under 'Offices, warehouses, shops and houses', not as 'Works' or

'Industrial buildings'. The Oldbury works have been demolished but a move to that area and a reorganisation of the company would not have been anticipated at the time the design was commissioned. There is no record of deposited plans relating to such a building in the Oldbury collection.[24]

The company's prospects may have appeared sufficiently favourable in 1916—probably through wartime orders—to consider a move from a small workshop to volume production, but the firm seems never to have been substantial enough, even with government support, to finance the building of a three-storey factory measuring 340 feet by 60 feet (given that the standard 20 feet square bays were intended).

The sketch suggests a double-storey at ground level for production purposes, with an attic storey of less height, possibly for offices and/or canteen use. The heavy cornice below the attic may have disguised a travelling crane gantry, but the firm was engaged in light engineering which would not require that type of plant. The design is again based on the reinforced concrete frame, infilled with metal-framed, small-paned windows of the Daylight system and is enhanced by the 'Masonry' effect. Advantage has been taken of the corner site, to make the short ends of the building more massive and to decorate the longitudinal elevations by projecting piers, one-bay in. The lower cornice is emphasised by additional formwork, of nail-heads, tassels and shaped panels, with the same arrangement repeated around the main entrance. Flanking the entrance, the corner towers are capped by stepped, enlarged versions of the nail-head.

Williams & Williams Limited

This company was a competitive offshoot of the family concern of Williams & Gamon Limited, established in 1859 as manufacturers of stained glass, architectural ironwork and metal-framed windows. Two sons of the founder registered themselves as Williams & Williams Limited and purchased, in 1915, a Georgian mansion in Liverpool Road, Chester, only a very short distance from their parent's firm. In that same year, the company was commandeered by the War Department for the large-scale production of metal ammunition boxes of the company's own innovatory design. For that purpose, single-storey sheds were built at the rear of the stone house. The plant became known as Reliance Works and, considerably extended, became part of the Heywood-Williams Group plc, whose products are chiefly in the aluminium field.[25]

For the Williams' buildings too the only surviving evidence is a sketch in Moritz Kahn's book of 1917. Plans deposited on behalf of the company in 1916 are not by Wallis, Gilbert & Partners and are for north-light sheds, to be built at the rear of the Georgian house, and these were executed under govern-ment licence. The inevitable conclusion must be that Wallis, Gilbert's proposal failed before the licensing authorities in competition with the built alternative.

The sketch shows another variation on the theme of the concrete frame structure with glass infill. Fronting directly on to the roadway, the building appears to be a double-storeyed block, some seven bays by four or five wide, with a single-storeyed, single-bayed aisle of the same width on the south side of the main building. The entrance at the north corner has bollards in place and large double doors common to a vehicular, service entrance and may well have been intended for access to a yard. The array and quantity of glazing bars are no indication of bay size; sketches of other buildings have not been equivalent to 'as built' in that respect, and the windows on the front elevation are, in any case, smaller, so that no overall measurement of the building can be gained from that evidence.

In the absence of floor plans, the interior layout is open to conjecture, but the apparent size does not suggest that the building was formed around a hollow central well. The works entrances on each side of the main frontage are treated identically, with stepped architraves and piers to roof height. The piers are repeated at one bay to the rear to form corner 'towers', with decorated capitals and stepped roofs to match the centre block and the boxed bay of the aisle. The piers, plinths and centre frieze are furrowed horizontally to imitate stone blocks—presumably to suggest a relationship between the concrete building and the Georgian house.

Assuming that the sketch represents a reasonably close likeness to what was intended if executed, the composition has a feeling of completeness that, despite its relatively small size, does not readily lend itself to extension. It is a compact, earth-hugging little building, designed to meet production require-ments and to pay due regard to its environment. The decision of the licensing authorities against the Wallis, Gilbert design may have been founded (as at Brolt) on the doubtful viability of the applicant company in repaying or leasing back the state-financed property. Williams & Williams Limited had had little time in which to establish itself, was in very close proximity to a competitor and the wartime product had a minimal post-war market. In the economic circmstances and given the provincial location, it would undoubt-edly appear that the state's expenditure would be more easily recouped by the sale or leasing of a cheaply-built, north-light shed than a substantial, comparatively expensive, reinforced concrete factory.

The Brolt and Williams designs have much in common besides their non-execution; they represent another aspect of the shapes available in the frame/unit/daylight system—single-, two- or three-storey, long, rectangular blocks, narrow fronted to the street, resembling one arm of the Albion shape. Together with the Tylor design, they represent too the exposition period of the Wallis concrete aesthetic that was developed into its prime exemplars with two built designs of 1917 and 1918.

(Coeval with the above designs were two large production units for the British Westinghouse Electric and Manufacturing Company at Manchester, which are examined under the heading 'Sheds', in section (d)).

Tilling-Stevens Limited

This company, at Victoria Works, St Peters Road, Maidstone, Kent, was formed in June 1906 to take over the business of Stevens & Barker at Maidstone and to manufacture 'Tilling-Stevens' commercial vehicles powered by petrol-electric transmission engines. When Thomas Tilling Limited, London's oldest omnibus operator (established 1847), converted from horse-drawn to motor omnibuses, petrol-electric transmission was favoured over geared engines as easier to drive, smoother in running and less subject to general wear or breakdown; as importantly, the erstwhile horse drivers were more easily trained to its use. At the 1906 Commercial Vehicle Show, Richard Tilling, grandson of the founder, met W. A. Stevens, who had converted his own motor car to petrol-electric and the decision was made to jointly manufacture their own vehicles. New premises were added to Stevens' works in 1912. Stevens left the company in 1917, when a considerable enlargement of the works was undertaken to accommodate production for war requirements.[26]

The site occupied by the company's works at Maidstone was admirably served by the transport amenities of the time. At the rear boundary was the River Medway, with a wharf alongside the deep water channel and a private siding from the South Eastern Railway that connected to the main London and south-east coast line. Roadways completed the perimeter at west and north. But the shape of the land available for development in 1917 presented considerable difficulties for the siting of a rectilinear building. Vehicular access was gained from the front of the new building through two large doorways at the corners, on the right to the building itself, on the left to the interior of the site, where a roadway circled around to the wharf at the rear. Footway access was served by small doorways on the outer sides of the vehicular entrances.

The original intention of the design was for a five-storey hollow-rectangle with a glazed single-storey centre well (Fig. 3) to be built progressively as at Albion and Tylors. The Truscon construction plan[27] (Fig. 4) shows the part that was actually erected; the vacant space for the proposed 'further extension' was, however, filled by a double-storeyed, pitched-roof shed. As the attic storey over the frontal block is centralised to complete the composition of the elevation, the decision not to fulfil the whole proposal was presumably made at an early stage.

The whole of the Wallis, Gilbert building was constructed of reinforced concrete, in collaboration with Truscon and employed the Kahn trussed bar system, again on a grid of 20 feet square bays. The core of the building

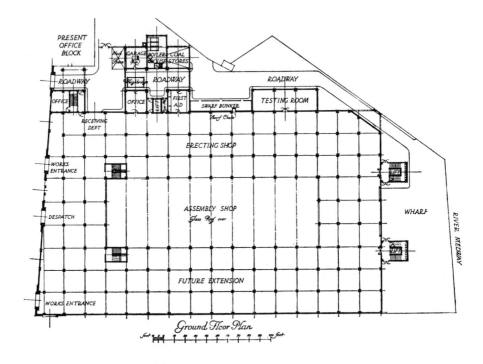

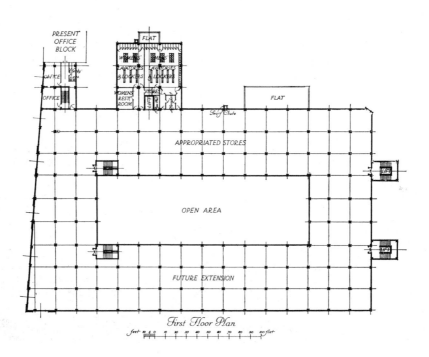

Fig. 3 Tilling-Stevens Ltd, St Peter's Road, Maidstone: plans—ground and first floors, 1917

Fig. 4 Tilling-Stevens Ltd, St Peter's Road, Maidstone: as-built, 1917

measures some 60 feet wide by 310 feet in depth and 60 feet by 60 feet perpendicular thereto at the rear, to which the proposed L-shaped extension would have been attached. The frontal areas gained some extra footage obliquely in a southerly direction as the façade was aligned with the roadway. The flat roof accommodated services and lift motors.

Company offices already existed. In the new building, other than a works office at the north-west entrance, all services and amenities were contained in the three-by-three bays abutting the main building on the northern side. At ground level were a garage, boiler house and coalstore separated from the office, first-aid centre and stair/lift well immediately adjoining the main building by a roadway with weighbridge. Locker and dressing rooms, rest rooms, sick bay and lavatories were also contained within the upper floors of the annexe. The unit system of construction was thus not only of advantage in exploiting the irregular space of the site but, in placing all services, etc. in annexed bays, the remainder of the 190 000 square feet of floor space could be dedicated to production processes.

That the building was government licensed and financed and production requisitioned, together with Wallis' experience of munition factories, would undoubtedly have influenced the planning of the Tilling-Stevens building. But the arrangements for integrated production under one roof reveal a modern attitude. Processes were arranged in a downward flow, facilitated by large electric lifts. The top floors contained, respectively, hardening processes and sandblasting (where ventilation for dispersal of airborne substances was of prime importance), and the tool and machine shops, where special tools, jigs and fixtures were fashioned; these latter were conveniently placed alongside the company's drawing office. Chassis parts were manufactured on the third floor; petrol tanks, bonnets and trays on the second floor; part of the first floor accommodated a self-contained electrical department manufacturing all the relevant equipment for petrol-electric motors. The remainder of the first floor was taken up by the production of engines, axles, and so on, for transmission to the ground floor where erection and assembly were carried out. Testing and inspection facilities were sited strategically to the relevant departments, a bay for engine testing being externally abutted to the ground floor to prevent excess vibration of the main structure.[28]

The building was centrally-heated throughout by low-pressure hot water, all pipes running in a duct in the reinforced concrete below the surface of the floors, and connecting to a rising-main channelled next to the main lift.[29] Power was transmitted by a series of overhead motors shafted to working stations, for which brackets were inserted during construction.

How a building appeared to the street was as important a part of its function as its internal operations: it is doubtful if the Albion board of directors would have chosen to place their concrete block directly on to the road, particularly as they intended within a very few years to build something more appropriate to the area in front of it. In the application of his chosen aesthetic for the Tilling-Stevens building, Wallis would have had to be aware of other determinants, such as the close proximity of the 1912 office building, frontage to a rather narrow roadway, the integrity of the elevation in both part-built and fully-extended forms, and that the new building was intended almost wholly for production purposes.

Only five years separate the new building from the standing offices but the disparities in concept, materials, construction and scale appear, at first sight, to be irreconcilable (Fig. 5). There is, however, a relation between the older building and the main part of the new in the regularity of window placement and in the stone string course of the one with the banding concrete and brick spandrels of the other that permit, however fortuitously, the juxtaposition without too stark a contrast.

What, in contemporary parlance, would have been referred to as the 'architectural treatment' of the 1917 building pertained, as in other factories of this group, only to the façade and one bay in depth, so that it was on the roadside elevation that any deliberate compatibility with the 1912 building was to be attempted. The 'complete' version of the building could have quite overwhelmed the older one, but the 'as-built' version being of lesser size (and differing only slightly from the original plans), has features that do counter-balance. A major problem would be the difference in height. Both buildings were flush with the roadway, so articulation and rhythm were achieved by narrow horizontals, recessed windows and strong, slightly-projecting verti-cals—Gibbsian in the 1912 building and stepped, low relief in that of 1917 and continuing through the cornice.

The strong central feature of the 1912 doorway was not repeated in the later building. The fairly plain vehicular openings, with bollard protection, and the small doors for footway access, preserved the utilitarian aspect of the production unit, in contrast to the important entrance of the offices. In comparison with the Baroque 1912 doorway, decoration of the later building was of a more restrained classical pedigree. It was contained within, and echoed, the overall geometry of the structure and, as part of the concrete framework, maintained the integrity of the constructional material. Further-more, the decoration was integral to the composition of the elevation, in visually reducing the height of the block in relation to its neighbour.

The heaviest and most projecting cornice is over the fourth storey; it has recessed vertical ribbing and nail-head corner stops—echoing the framing detail of the other building—and its terminal effect is increased by the 'capitals' which, as plain discs, are eye-catching as the only departure from angularity. Further downward movement is suggested by the pendant form of the supporting little 'piers'-cum-triglyphs. The pyramidal effect of the attic storey and the centralised half-storey pediment above it, with their heavy copings, and the relation established between top and bottom by the nail-heads with tassels on the half-storey and at the ground level doorway, also reduce the vertical emphasis.

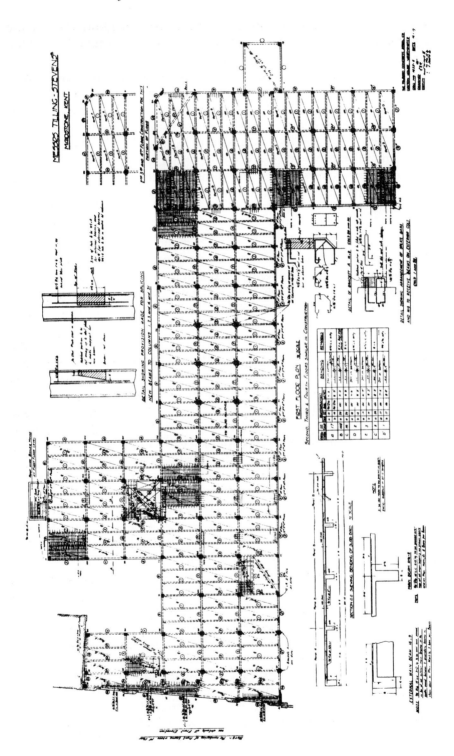

Fig. 5 Tilling-Stevens Ltd, Maidstone: constructional details, 1917

There is insufficient space in the foreground for a head-on view of the buildings from the road. But, from the main road on high ground behind the sheds, only the upper three storeys of the new building are visible. The concentration of decoration at that level not only helps to lower the vertical effect but also serves the viewer's perception of the Tilling-Stevens' works at a distance. The general air of classicism, the design of the decorative motifs and the prominence given to corner towers, even when they express no separate internal function, were wholly characteristic of Wallis' early masonry-style building. E. G. W. Souster considered the factory to be a worthy example of the modern manner, for

> all the main lines rise naturally from construction, and by concentra-
> tion on the supporting piers of the structure an astylar architectural
> character has been given to the whole construction.[30]

Other published comments on the building paid favourable attention to construction and planning and regarded its appearance as a 'satisfactory and thoroughly expressive architectural treatment for reinforced concrete'; Wallis, Gilbert designs were adjudged the 'best that have ever come to our notice'.[31]

At the conclusion of the First World War, the Tilling-Stevens company was restructured; by the end of the decade improved gear boxes were replacing petrol-electric transmission. A proposed amalgamation with Clayton's Karrier Motors Limited of Huddersfield, Yorks, was rejected in 1932. Richard Clayton left Karrier when the firm was purchased by Rootes Securities in 1934 and became managing director of Tilling-Stevens. He revitalised the company by the introduction and development of diesel-powered vehicles and took over the Vulcan Motor Company of Southport, Lancs. War Department orders kept the company in full production during the Second World War but, shortly thereafter, the predatory Rootes Group realised the necessity of the highly reputable Tilling diesel to its future expansion. Tilling-Stevens became part of Rootes in 1951 but, by 1966, the American company Chrysler had acquired a controlling interest and the group was again restructured as Chrysler (UK) Ltd.[32]

The Maidstone factory was closed in 1975. For nearly 60 years it had been in continuous use for the production of motor vehicles and engines; it had seen a number of reorganisations of processing, had accommodated the updating of technology and machinery, and still remained in good condition, other than some minor spalling at the edge of the uppermost front cornice. Its most recent occupation has been through its conversion to flatted industrial units.

D. Napier & Son Limited

The next-built Wallis, Gilbert design was in 1918 for D. Napier & Son Limited of Acton Vale, London, an engineering firm with a very long history, which had diversified into motor engine and vehicle manufacture at the turn of the century. In 1917 extra floor space was required for the building of aero-engines to government contract which could revert to motor car production when necessary.

David Napier, founder of the firm and a member of the famous Scottish engineering family, left Glasgow to set up business in London in 1808, to become a manufacturer over time of printing, munition and weighing machinery. From the time his son, James Murdoch Napier, was responsible for the business in the 1860s it gradually declined. Impatient of the lack of status accorded to manufacturers and manufacturing, James saw little reason to devote his life to the genre and the firm was virtually moribund when his son, Montague Stanley Napier, purchased the business after his father's death in 1895. In 1898 Montague designed a motor car; the manufacture of engines and chassis (with bodies supplied to the customer's choice by an outside firm) became the major concern for a number of years. A partnership with Stanley Francis Edge (erstwhile London manager for the Dunlop Tyre Company and fellow ardent cyclist with Napier) brought increasing success, owed largely to the advanced engineering of Napier and the commercial acumen and aggressive salesmanship of Edge. The firm preferred to make large, costly, custom-built vehicles for the luxury market, with only limited concession to popular choice, and had no desire to enter into large-scale, assembly-line production.

The company was incorporated as D. Napier & Son Limited in 1906. Although manufacturing and marketing were separately controlled, the mismatch of personalities brought the partnership to an end in 1909. Need for expansion had arisen, however, in 1902 and led to the purchase of three and a half acres of land at Acton, of which two and three-quarter acres were built upon by 1904. During the First World War, the Acton works became a 'controlled establishment'; the Napier car was virtually swept from the market as 2000 vans, lorries and ambulances were produced for the War Office. A government order for aero-engines and frames, initially taken as a 'stop-gap', brought complete conversion to those products. New workshops, designed by Wallis, Gilbert & Partners, were built in 1918, bringing an increase in floor space since 1914 to 100 000 square feet.[33]

No original plans or photographs relating to the Napier works at Acton have been discovered. More recently, the present owners of the buildings, Brixton Estates Limited, have carried out extensive modernisation of the premises. The shape and size of the original Wallis, Gilbert building are still evident, but that is all. The following analysis is therefore dependent upon secondary sources.

Sketches of the building that appeared in Kahn's *The Design and Construction of Industrial Buildings* and in *The Architects' and Builders' Journal* of 16 January 1918 differ only slightly from published photographs of the built version in *The Architects' Journal* of 24 March 1920 and in Wallis, Gilbert &

Partners' own booklet *Industrial Architecture* of 1932. Identical copies of the ground floor and a 'typical' upper floor plan appeared in the first three of the above sources.

The building stands on The Vale road, opposite a park and faces north. In 1917 the site was already built upon and occupied by Napiers so that the space available for the extension was of a shape into which a correctly rectilinear building did not easily fit. The plans show the oblique lines followed by the frame, with corner columns at acute or obtuse angles. The building measured roughly 120 feet by 150 feet, divided into six or seven bays of 20 feet 'square' and was constructed wholly of concrete reinforced with Kahn Rib Bars by Truscon.

As occurred at Tylors, New Southgate, and Albion, Glasgow, geological difficulties were encountered in placing adequate foundations to support, in this instance, a large four-storey building with basement. *The Architects' Journal*[34] reports that 16-inch diameter concrete piles of varying lengths were driven in groups of one to seven, depending upon the load, and generally to a depth of 12 feet. Each group was capped with a heavy reinforced concrete platform as a base for the columns. Owing to the close proximity of the main sewer, the basement, which contained the furnace and coalstore, was totally enclosed on one side by a reinforced concrete retaining wall.

Here, too, production processes were arranged in a downward flow, and the building was designed to accommodate lighter work in the upper storeys. Internal stanchions decreased in section in ascending order, from 22 inches at the first floor to 10 inches for the top two storeys, to meet superimposed loads of two and a quarter hundredweight per square foot and one and a half hundredweight respectively. During construction, 'Rigifix' slotted inserts were cast in the underside of beams for attachment of mechanical equipment and the building was heated by low-pressure hot water with a radiator in front of each window.

At the Napier site, there was insufficient space to accommodate the previously-employed hollow-square/rectangle unit plan. Here it was turned inside out, with glazed-over single-storeys, each one bay by three, placed each side of and penetrating the main block. Thereby, all floors were open to natural light. Access to the building was from the road front, by two vehicular entrances with sliding doors for goods traffic and two footways, separate for men and women, at their flanks. Stairways and sanitary facilities were placed forward of the single-storey areas, with goods lifts to their rear, leaving a considerable open space on each floor for production and other purposes. The despatch section was positioned at the eastern rear of the ground floor, with access to the yard and a gateway onto Warple Way.

Facilities for employees were, again, of a high standard for the period. There were cloakrooms, lavatories and drinking fountains on each floor; rest rooms were provided for women workers and first-aid wards with nurses in attendance. Space was also given over to recreational and athletic amenities. One large kitchen serviced separate canteens for workers, apprentices and staff; directors had a 'tastefully furnished dining room'.

The architectural treatment accorded to the Napier building again shows the adaptability of Wallis' repertoire. In this instance, the variation on his original theme was dictated by the plan and by the nature of the client. David Napier, then the senior member of the company and very much in charge, had a personal abhorrence of advertising and overt sales techniques. It was also intended that, after the war, the company should revert to the production of large, expensive, customised motor cars. No kind of popular exuberance or flamboyance could therefore be entertained in the aesthetic treatment of the building. The rebating of the upper floors at the sides of the building produced a ready-made frontal block, six bays wide by two in depth, and also governed the placing of the main entrances for goods, one bay in from each corner. What might then have constituted 'corner towers' were, at two bays square, too large in proportion to the remaining frontage. As a production unit, however, it was appropriate to accentuate the vehicular entrances—with colossal pilasters, pediments, decorated and ribbed cornices and a balustered 'balcony'. The vertical elements of the frame—the pilasters, corner piers and narrow lights—were here subdued, as in other designs, by an illusory setting back of the attic storey and the blocking of its corners by the horizontal relationship of the heavy, stepped cornices and the coping and plinth.

In reflecting the nature of the company, Wallis contained the decoration within an expression of the plan, to present a dignified and prestigious piece of architecture overlooking the park. The concrete work on the vertical elements was scored to suggest traditional stone; a few of the now customary nail-heads acted as end-stops on string-projections and on plain doorway architraves. Plain discs with pendant supporters appeared only on each pilaster below the balconies. The visual illusion of a stone building with stone carving and balconies overlooking parkland is reminiscent of the style assumed by factories a century earlier when the Industrial Revolution was in its infancy and the Napier family was already famous in engineering and industrial circles. Although recognising its antecedents, the factory at Acton was wholly modern, constructed of reinforced concrete, its technology the most advanced, its planning and layout representing the most up-to-date methods of production as well as conditions that were beneficial for the workforce.

Napier's reversion to motor car manufacturing after the war was not successful; the last Napier car was sold in 1924. Instead the company concentrated upon designing, developing and manufacturing aero- and marine-engines, for which the firm became famous. But almost complete reliance on government orders and a dislike of entrepreneurial management led to the company being taken over by the English Electric Company in 1942, and later merging with the General Electric Company in 1968.[35] For a company that so tenaciously held to its historic philosophy whilst manufacturing and developing very progressive equipment, Wallis' design was not so contradictory.

In both the Tilling-Stevens and the Napier buildings, although the ground plan dictated the composition particularly in respect of the placement of vehicular and pedestrian access, the result was a symmetrical façade. In both cases, the static classicism of the façade made a company statement that could be immediately perceived, but interest and lively visual scanning were induced by the arrangement of ornamentation. From Wallis' limited range of decorative motifs, selection was made to suit the composition and the nature of the client. But, in being integral to the structure and material, the decoration contributed to an overall effect of historical reference (albeit oblique and/or stylised) and traditional masonry that humanised and articulated an otherwise new and alien form. The limitation of the number of decorative motifs employed also made economic sense in the time and effort saved when similar form-boarding could be used for different buildings. In published sources, the Napier factory was adjudged an 'excellent instance of investing the strictly utilitarian building with architectural interest'.[36]

War casualties

In 1918, Wallis, Gilbert & Partners embarked upon a large-scale commission for the General Electric Company of Birmingham but, in that year also, four proposed designs (as well as the proposed wings for Albion at Glasgow) were aborted. All of them could be described as 'war casualties'. Although the United States of America entered the war in 1917, most of its army equipment and munitions were supplied by the Allies, thus increasing production demands in Britain. A major (final?) offensive by the German army into France and the Low Countries in mid-1918 also called for greater Allied supplies to repulse the attack, so that factories already over-burdened were looking for extra floor space. By the time, however, that their applications for licence to build could be processed, negotiations for armistice were afoot and government commitment would have been on a reducing scale.

Evidence of the unexecuted buildings mentioned below is reliant upon published sketches and the survival of plans on microfilm; of their non-execution, information has been obtained from the companies that still exist or their one-time employees and by investigation of the proposed sites.

All of the designs adhere to the formula being established by Wallis, Gilbert & Partners but they do include other permutations.

Jones & Shipman Limited

The building proposed for this company, machine tool manufacturers of East Park Road, Leicester,[37] was to be four storeys high and ordered on a grid of six by three bays of 18 feet 8 inches square, with stanchions 20 inches in section. The abutment of a single, four-storey bay at the rear served as the main stairwell to the production parts of the building. A row of three bays co-extensive with the Green Lane Road side housed, on each floor, sanitary facilities, a lift shaft and offices, and another stairway leading from the front door to the top floor. The top floor was given over to offices for senior management and typists; waiting rooms disposed at each of the narrow ends of the building were joined by a central corridor that separated drawing office from general office at each side. As companies enlarged their premises, increased and rationalised their production, there was a concomitant expansion of administration, for which separate accommodation became necessary.

Articulation and decorative treatment of the plain frame was particularly simple in this instance but nevertheless followed the pattern of colossal piers, heavy cornice and attic storey, with only minimal formwork ornamentation as capitals and a ribbed architrave with nail-heads around the main doorway. The then (and still) existing Jones & Shipman factory was brick built with plain stone lintels and arch over the main door. Wallis' restraint in the decoration of his proposed design suggests clients of very conservative temperament who may, in the end, have preferred not to venture into a reinforced concrete building anyway! Almost all Leicester factories are very restrained in their ornamentation. The corner site where the Jones & Shipman building was intended to stand is still occupied by houses and shops built in 1895.

Rubery Owen Limited

A design for Rubery Owen Limited, manufacturers of constructional steel and other steel products, of Darlaston, Staffordshire, was rather more complex. The proposed plans are dated August 1918 (Fig. 6) and were for the initial construction of a single-storey production building of 14 bays by 3, each 20 feet square, as the main workshop, with three adjacent small blocks for specific purposes, including an office block. Later extension was intended to be upwards by two storeys each for the offices and workshop, only partly so over the block to the rear, with the frontal annexe remaining as single-storeyed. In final form, the main block, again a long-fronted design, was articulated only by corner towers decorated with disc-and-pendant capitals, nail-heads as vertical stops on the cornices, a stepped pediment above, and some emphasis on the doorway. The office block was intended to be much more ornate, with probably even greater attention being paid to the main

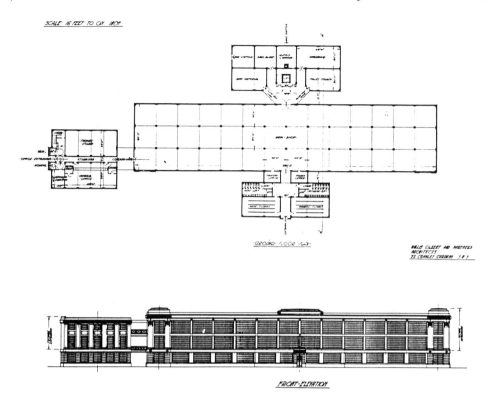

Fig. 6 Rubery Owen Ltd, Round Oak Steel Works, Darlaston, Staffs (unexecuted): plans—
ground floor, front elevation, 1918

entrance on the side. In 1918 it was still common practice to include office space within a production building but, as firms grew larger and/or manufactured a diversity of products on one site, the centralisation of administrative functions within a separate building became part of the rationalisation process in industry. Whereas differentiation of function within a multi-purpose building was usually shown in special treatment of areas occupied by management and open to visitors, different architectural vocabularies became necessary where the functions were in separate buildings. The latter arrangement gave greater opportunity for self-advertising display as well as practical advantages in operation, but it also reinforced class distinction between management, staff and manual workers.

During the First World War, the Rubery Owen company had been fully engaged on orders for the War Department;[38] it may have been caught in the increasing demand for armaments early in 1918 or was expecting a building boom when hostilities ceased. The firm's application for licence to extend its premises came too late in the day. The present company confirmed that the design was never executed.[39]

Singer & Company Limited

This firm, of Canterbury Street, Coventry, was one of the many vehicle and cycle manufacturing firms (including Rover, Raleigh, Rudge and Hillman) spawned by the Coventry Machinists Company founded by Joseph Turner and James Starley in 1863 to manufacture sewing machines. George Singer was recruited from Penn & Company, famous ships engineers of Greenwich, London, when the machinists diversified into building velocipedes and needed engineers with a broader knowledge than the fine precision work needed for sewing machines. Singer left the company in 1876 and established his own business at Canterbury Street, first to manufacture cycles, then in 1905 to produce motor cars under licence from Lee Francis and, in 1908, to produce his own models.[40]

Over the years the company's premises were extended in a piecemeal fashion and the commission to Wallis, Gilbert & Partners was probably intended to facilitate total integration of production when state assistance was available for the construction of a large building. Possibly Singer was also too late with his application; the plans are dated 24 August 1918. But post-war expansion, until the company was acquired by Rootes in 1956 (and later by Chrysler [UK] Ltd) continued by takeover and deployment of activities into a disjointed network of factories throughout Coventry—running true to the original manner of progression.

The aborted plans show a five-storey building with part basement, again long-fronted, but also forming an L-shape to fit into the available space on site, and on a consistent grid of 19 feet 5 inches square bays. An annexed five-storey bay at the elbow of the L was to house stairs, lift and sanitary facilities, following the pattern employed at Tilling-Stevens. The ground floor was intended for car finishing and storage; first and second floors for machine and fitting shops, and the third floor as a tool room. The fourth floor was to be added later and given over to amenities—that is, separate dining rooms for male staff and female staff, and a private dining room for management. A central kitchen, with store room and washing-up area, was to run centrally through the top floor, effectively segregating male and female workers' canteens.

In size alone, the building achieves a measure of monumentality; Wallis' treatment of the façade was simply to enhance that impression by framing the large area of unadorned structural frame and glass. The heavy string course at the first floor levelled off the rectangle to the rising ground of the street, so that the ground floor acted as a plinth. Only the outer pair of the four entrances received emphasis. The projecting colossal piers flanked each of them as familiar 'corner towers' to complete a frame capped by an attic storey, with broader mullions and stepped pediments. At the same time, the framing firmly delineated and gathered in the outer edges of the building to prevent its total domination of the street and the late-Victorian buildings beside which it was to have stood. Once again, nail-heads on the cornice provided vertical stops, while disc-and-pendant capitals and tasselled nail-heads on the doorway and name fascia acted as unpretentious ornament.

Clayton & Company Limited

Another unexecuted design of similar style and even larger bulk was projected in 1920 for Clayton & Company Limited, motor vehicle manu-facturers of St Thomas' Road, Huddersfield, Yorks. The company had been established in 1904 to manufacture commercial vehicles to Clayton's own design, bearing the trademark 'Karrier'. It machined its own component parts and assembled chassis; engines were supplied by Tylors of New Southgate, London. Considerable expansion and a move to new works took place in 1916, with commitment to wartime orders for lorries and tank components. After the war Clayton entered the highly specialised field of manufacturing municipal vehicles, to which it contributed many innovations of its own, including the first trailer coupling in the world, which still forms the basis for articulated lorries today.

Clayton was floated as a public company in 1920, under the new name of Karrier Motors Limited.[41] The plans for the proposed new building are dated March 1920, coinciding with the company's public flotation but only a month before the great slump descended. That, in itself, would have been sufficient cause not to continue with the commission, and the company's persistent trading difficulties over the next 12 years would have prevented any possible renewal of the proposal.

The building was to occupy land on the opposite side of Colne Road (now St Thomas' Road) to the existing works. It would have faced north, directly onto the road, and fitted into a triangle of land bounded on the rear (south side) by the steeply-rising Hope Street, and to the west by other premises. The design proposed a three-storey, long-fronted building of reinforced concrete frame, 14 bays by 3 of 22 feet by 21 feet 8 inches square. Two bays extending from the south-east corner were to serve as fuel stores and a heating chamber; future extensions were envisaged as similar units attached at the rear where a portion of land would still be available. The building was very simply planned within its area of approximately 310 feet frontage by 65 feet in depth. It was intended wholly for production purposes, except for a canteen, kitchen and stores which were to occupy the part of the top floor not used by the woodworking shop. A very large lift shaft, situated at the right rear, served each floor, suggesting a downward flow of processes. At one bay in from each of the front corners of the building, were stairs and lavatories and a doorway onto the road at the east corner.

The plan was clearly expressed on the façade, where the works area retained its almost northern-mill-like austerity, relieved only by tasselled nail-heads at the junction of base and column and a reeded cornice. The stair towers are treated as towers, standing some 10 feet in from the corners, rising above the skyline and capped and pinnacled above projecting piers with nail-head capitals. On the corners, blank spandrels protected the lavatories from view. A central pediment—presumably for the firm's name—would have provided a break in the long, plain skyline of the works section. The writer is assured that no building of this like ever stood on the site shown on a block plan, nor within the vicinity of that site.[42]

After the heady days of wartime profits, Clayton was one of the many companies which over-capitalised with a view to meeting post-war demands for products that had not been available during the war. The company may not have been so badly affected as some motor vehicle manufacturers by the release of used army equipment to public purchase, but it committed itself to municipal orders and, while the need for public transport, road-sweepers and refuse collection vehicles and such like would be there, once the economic slump occurred local authorities would not have been in a financial position to fulfil those needs. So, despite so much invention and development, the company's financial position deteriorated. Decline was attributed to the Government's devaluation policy, rising material costs, wage increases and the general reduction in trade. Eventually, despite capital write-down and rearrangement, the company went into receivership in 1934; it was purchased by Rootes and all work was transferred to Commer Cars Limited at Luton, Beds. Richard Clayton, son of the founder, moved to Tilling-Stevens. As with other motor vehicle companies purchased by Rootes, Karrier became part of Chrysler (UK) Ltd.[43]

It is difficult to assess what would have been the visual impact of these three long-fronted unexecuted buildings or their effect upon a street scene. Nothing of that ilk was in fact built and, when Wallis, Gilbert later designed large rectangular blocks with long fronts, they were introducing a very different kind of aesthetic. But even without the benefit of a means for true comparison, it is doubtful if the unexecuted designs would have had quite the handsome presence of the narrow-fronted version.

One other casualty of 1920, the last of the unbuilt designs in the Daylight/Masonry group, was for a firm that had also profited from wartime orders but whose product, irrespective of the economic down-turn, was least likely to find an expanding market in the post-war years. Which is a great pity: this design was narrow-fronted and, unusually, asymmetrical. It is truly a little gem and the construction engineers might well have enjoyed the challenge presented by its site and potential fire hazard.

Cambrian Candle Company Limited

This company, of Marine Square, Holyhead, Anglesey, Wales, was founded by a Mr Keegan and operated by him and his eldest son J. P. Keegan at the disused Marine Hotel, to manufacture candles of all kinds and sizes, which were in demand from all parts of the United Kingdom. The company just managed to survive the 1920s slump but was unable to pay for expansion. By the 1930s, electric lighting was replacing other domestic means, horse-drawn carriages were giving way to motor vehicles and pedal cyclists found battery-operated lights more efficient. The demand for candles, probably little more than those for religious purposes, was insufficient to sustain the business. The firm was wound up some years before the Second World War and the ex-Marine Hotel candle factory was demolished.[44]

The block plan of the site is dated February 1920, and shows the proposed building adjoining the existing works, facing south-east to Holyhead Harbour and running north-west co-extensive with the obtuse angle of North West Street on ground rising in that direction. This was a complex design, partly because of its shape and the inclination of the site, and partly because of the operational functions of the factory. On plan, the building spans 30 feet in width and extends nine bays to the rear with stanchions at 16 feet intervals. The only internal stanchion is placed centrally at the rear of the front two bays which house respectively, the main stairwell to the left, proceeding from the main entrance on that side and, on the right, cloakrooms and lavatories on each floor. The remainder of the building was intended for production purposes. Only the first and second floors run through the whole space of the factory, the front three bays being four storeys high, with a basement to house a future boiler house and the top floor allocated to the box-making department. Otherwise production was organised on a gravitational flow; wax barrels were to reach the second floor by an external lift at the outer elbow (west side). On the second floor, wax melting and mixing occupied the forward two bays, the wax and acid stores the three bays behind them, and a canteen filled the remaining three bays. The first floor was to be taken up with machines for candle-making, the produce then being stored and packed on the ground floor, the rear three bays of which were void over rising ground (Fig. 7). In view of the highly inflammable nature of the material and product, precautionary measures included an external fire escape attached to the furthest rear bay and the whole of the flat roof behind the fourth storey of the front block was to be used as a 40 000 gallon water tank.

Most of the exterior of the building is fairly plain and related to internal functions. The narrow frontage, however, is treated asymmetrically, with major emphasis given to the stair tower and doorway (Fig. 8). The entrance itself is fairly routine 'Wallis, Gilbert' in character but the upper reaches of the tower are most unusual. Ribbed bands are deeper on the capping (which forms a skylight) over the third-storey windows and on the capitals where the pendants drape discs with some suggestion of ancient Egyptian headwear. Between the capitals and adding even greater verticality to the upper sections of the narrow windows, are Roman fasces similar to those that appeared on the drawings for the administration building for the General Electric

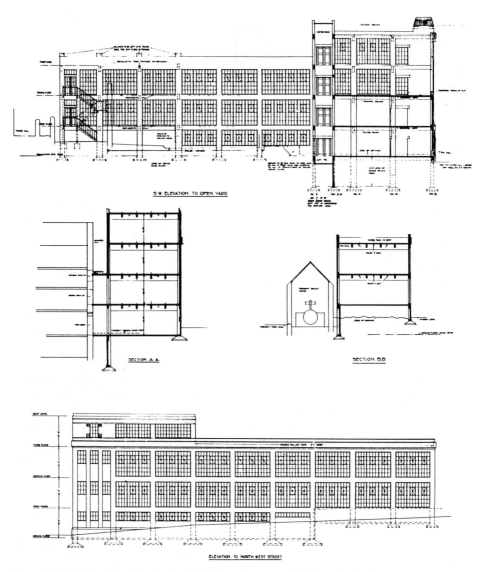

Fig. 7 Cambrian Candle Co Ltd, Marine Square, Holyhead, Anglesey (unexecuted): plans—side elevations and sections, 1920

Company before that design was revised. They were never used again as decoration.

Whether the proposed design for Cambrian Candles bore any relation to its Victorian neighbour is not known. It has no direct relevance to the maritime location or to the company's product, but this would have been an attractive building to grace Marine Square and the resolution of its complex structure and planning arrangements would have paid tribute to the architects'

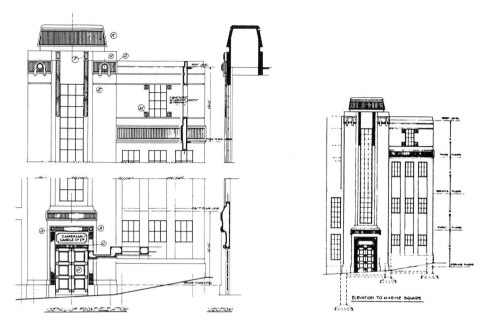

Fig. 8 Cambrian Candle Co Ltd, Marine Square, Holyhead, Anglesey (unexecuted): plans—front elevations, 1920

professional expertise. The name of Trussed Concrete Steel does not appear on the plans but, in 1920, the consulting engineers would have had to be very expert to ensure the future stability of the building. This design is another example of the adaptability of the frame building to even more unusual circumstances but it is a singular one in respect of Wallis' catalogue of decorative motifs and arrangements. Roof-top water tanks appeared in another design built some years later.

An interesting feature of the non-built designs of 1916, 1918 and 1920 is that all of them were for firms located in the more northerly parts of the country, before the southward drift of industry had begun. In each case, some overriding reason can be conjectured for non-execution, but it may also be the case that some element of philosophy traditional to the old industrial areas of the north played a part.

General Electric Company Limited

The loss to Wallis, Gilbert & Partners of so many commissions in the first years of the partnership's existence was, however, offset by a substantial appointment as architects for the expansion of the General Electric Company Limited (GEC) works at Witton, Birmingham from 1918 to 1922. There, rather different constructional techniques were required, largely contributed by Truscon, and different planning requirements from hitherto. At GEC too, Wallis introduced Egyptianised styling.

The client company had been founded in 1886 by Hugo Hirst (later Lord Hirst) and Gustav Byng as an electrical goods wholesale business at Great St Thomas Apostle Street, London, but moved to Manchester three years later to manufacture electrical products.[45] To meet the growing demand for electrical equipment for commercial and industrial as well as domestic purposes, and to supply an expanding international market, a new factory was built at Witton, Birmingham, in 1900. The 100-acre (later 130-acre) greenfield site, intersected by brooks and bounded by the Tame Valley Canal and the London Midland & Scottish railway, was acquired from the Deykin Estate. The intention was, ultimately, for it to be a self-contained manufacturing community with houses, shops, recreational and social amenities all within its boundaries, for the benefit of all the employees. By 1902 45 acres were covered by the engineering works, foundry, power house, test and despatch departments and the carbon works—although, ironically, lighting had to be generated from power produced by a threshing machine until the Tame River was suitably bridged to allow permanent steam boilers to be brought in.[46]

Further extensions were built, new products introduced, and operations in other locations were transferred to Witton. Increased production of electrical carbon and large-scale production of munitions during the First World War did not prevent the pursuance of normal functions or the addition of new products. Expansion plans laid down during the war were instigated in 1918 and entailed the doubling of manufacturing space, with facilities for the production of heavy plant. Amongst seven large projects, the machine shop extension, a new switchgear works and a new administration block were designed by Wallis, Gilbert & Partners.

The GEC machine shop extension, 1918–20
The building of turbine-driven alternators was becoming an important section of the electricity industry. In 1916 GEC obtained government sanction to build an extension of its existing machine shop but with certain reservations as to constructional material.[47] As it was, construction was not commenced until early in 1918, with a builder's contract dated 25 February. The building of generators needed to be separated from the manufacture of ordinary electrical machinery and the extension was designed to accommodate a production line of raw castings entering at the rear directly opposite the foundry, and flowing uninterruptedly through single-station operations until released, duly assembled and checked, at the front of the building.

In accordance with government licence restrictions, the building was constructed throughout of reinforced concrete; its longitudinal dimensions were governed by those of the existing steel-framed machine shop to which it was to be attached, and where the bays measured 26 feet 3 inches. The new process bays show a sectional width of 36 feet 9 inches for the turbo bay on the inner side and 35 feet 6 inches for the winding bay on the external side.

Overall, the building measured 448 feet long by 72 feet wide, with a double-storeyed height of 41 feet 6 inches. A row of single-storeyed buildings was attached to the free north side for lavatories, offices, ambulance rooms and small machine processes. A single tower, on the north-west corner, housed stairs and lifts and extended beyond the height of the main building to provide access to the intended later upward extension of a second floor. Although designed in conjunction with Truscon in respect of construction, and from experience gained in Manchester at British Westinghouse, this early venture into heavy engineering required considerable cooperation between the architects and works managers in planning a structure relating precisely to production operations.

The external bay of the extension was to carry an electric travelling crane of 25 tons lifting capacity; the internal bay, two similar cranes operating together. The differential loadings were reflected in the structure. The external columns, on bases measuring 9 feet by 6 feet, were 2 feet 6 inches in section to gantry height where they supported, on integral concrete brackets, crane beams 30 inches deep by 15 inches wide. From there, the columns narrowed to 1 foot 3 inches square. The centre columns show a double profile to carry cranes on either side. They rested on bases 14 feet by 6 feet, were 4 feet 6 inches by 2 feet in section, but with central perforations to carry shafting to drive machinery on the ground and to economise on constructional material. At gantry height, they supported crane beams 30 inches deep by 18 inches wide, with concrete troughs to carry power and lighting cables. Above that height, to roof level, the stanchions measured 2 feet square. The attachment of a crane beam on the internal wall, then opened up to the existing machine shop, was facilitated by anchoring reinforcement to the steel frame and concreting over. The internal faces of all columns had slotted inserts to which other mechanical equipment or shafting could be bolted. It was only after some 60 years of use that additional supports had to be inserted under the central beam.

The most unusual feature of the building was the construction of the roof. As the roof was later to support and become the floor of a second storey, the problems presented by the height of the building, the strength required and additional costs involved were overcome by a daring and advanced solution. The three longitudinal beams were poured in situ (like the rest of the building). Secondary beams, 21 inches deep and 12 inches wide, were placed at 8 feet 9 inch intervals and covered by reinforced concrete slabs. The slabs measured 8 feet 1 inch by 4 feet by 21 inches deep with a 9 inch flange at each edge. These secondary beams and slabs were all pre-cast on the ground and hoisted into place. The side interstices were filled with concrete reinforced with Kahn Rib Bars that were secured to stirrups already set in the beams. No unforeseen difficulties appear to have arisen in the execution of the exercise.[48] Existing plans date from 6 March to 22 May 1918, although the building was not completed until the end of 1920, when a final payment was made to the contractors, W. J. Whittall & Son of Lancaster Road, Birmingham, on 24 December 1920, just in time for the workmen to receive their Christmas bonus!

Plans for the second-floor extension bear dates from 27 July to 5 November 1919 but their execution appears to have been delayed for a few years. A photograph of 1920 shows the building as originally designed (Fig. 9). The need for extra floorspace in the machine works may not have been as pressing as that required for other developments, planned before the war and then taking place on site and at other company locations. The post-war slump seems not to have unduly affected the expansion. The company was fully occupied in meeting increasing demands for electrical equipment for public utilities in transport and telephones, for factories and domestic appliances, and for generating and distributing electricity. A sketch of the works dated 1923, which appeared on a broadsheet celebrating a visit by the Prince of

Fig. 9 General Electric Co Ltd, Witton, Birmingham: machine shop extension, front view, 1918–20

Wales to the works and also reproduced in the company's centenary publication, is sufficiently erroneous in regard to other buildings as to be disregarded in respect of the machine shop extension with the second floor already added.

Aesthetically, the building is almost wholly expressive of its plan, structure and function. Enhancement has been dedicated to both emphasising differentiation of those determinants and to integrating them into a total composition. This is a powerful building that reflects the product, the processes and the grandeur of the interior. Differentiation of function can be seen in the expression of the gantry beams at the side and rear, which also relieve the large expanses of glass necessary to provide adequate natural light in a building without windows on the roof or at the south side. The tower is expressive of itself as staircase and lift shaft; the double doorways and narrow, central vertical lights at foot and rear of the building reflect the two separately-operating interior bays. The front of the building is identified and made more visually impressive by the projecting piers, marked off at plinth level, and the Egyptian pylon-like treatment of the doorways—battered, ribbed framing, orbed corners and inverted cavettos—which also express the monumentality of the building's structure and function. While differentiation, to some extent, articulates the building, the compositional features and decoration that integrate the design also stress the articulation and introduce a degree of rhythm. The narrow vertical lights on the tower, in groups of three at the north and off-centre at the front, add interest to the basic symmetry of the design. Repetition of the narrow lights at front, side and rear act as unifying features, along with the all-embracing cornice with its nail-head decoration and the external string course effect of the gantry beams. The whole building was cement-rendered, in which the colour of the sand component produced a pleasant ochre colour, declaring a building in its own right with a function separate from the brick and steel machine shop to which it was attached.

Most of the visual impact of the building has been destroyed through alteration, particularly of the single-storey attachments on the north side, and the addition of wiring services. Difficulties have been encountered in colour-matching the rendering for repair work and making good after alteration. Lack of maintenance after the building was taken out of use has led to weathering effects and some spalling of horizontals. Whenever it was that the second storey was added, the addition did little to enhance the building's appearance. The heavy, blocked-in attic storey, with its nail-heads as pseudo dripstones, destroys the compositional balance and the addition to the top of the tower detracts from its essential verticality.

In view of its utilitarian purpose, the building could have been left severely alone, devoid of ornamentation. In 1918 that would, however, have been unusual. The existing buildings were in brick, gabled and windowed in the nature of north-country Nonconformist chapels. With the launching of new, important products, the large-scale development and consolidation of the site and an expansion of overseas custom, the introduction of concrete buildings for specific purposes would have called for a means of self-identification and a statement of how the company saw itself in a post-war future. The two other buildings designed by Wallis, Gilbert for GEC at Witton tend to bear this out.

GEC switchgear works, 1919–21
Plans for the new switchgear works were drawn in January 1919 while the machine shop extension was still in course of erection and, though larger and more complex, the main receiving bays have a more than passing resemblance to the earlier building. The 1923 bird's-eye sketch of the works shows the switchgear plant as a three-storey hollow-square with glazed-over central well and single-storey, north-light sheds to the west. The northern front of the main building has defined corners and two enlarged nail-head capped central towers. At first sight it is very obviously a design that conforms to Wallis, Gilbert format and style.

   The built works, which ranked as 'one of the most carefully planned and well-arranged workshops in this or any other country',[49] was of a very different arrangement. Truscon was involved in the construction but, again, the planning would have called for close collaboration with company experts. Measuring 240 feet by 390 feet and partially fronted by an office and service block, the production units alternated between double-storeyed workshops with north-light roofs and gantry beams, and single-storeyed, flat-roofed sections, which could be extended upwards should the occasion arise without denying light to other buildings and presenting a converse arrangement of the unit system until then in use by Wallis, Gilbert & Partners. (The possibility suggests itself quite forcibly that, when a proposed version of the unit system in hollow-square was presented, the works managers realised that a different arrangement of units would better suit their needs.) Internal glazed partitions, area walls and some top-lights ensured adequate natural light to the office block and the production unit to its rear. In the former, a large main room, behind the central projection, was housed an exhibition of the plant's products and other items of interest to visitors. A further unusual feature of the GEC development was the provision of an underground subway linking the switchgear works to the general administration block and drawing office across the road to the north-east, through which papers etc. were transported by a Lamson endless-wire conveyor.

   The main operations of the production section flowed from a centrally-placed stores, to which materials and parts were delivered via overhead cranes from the receiving entrances at the north-east corner. From the stores, material was fed through the relevant bench operations, to finishing rooms and then to testing and despatch sections at the south-east corner. With all operations on one floor, two-ton electric trucks were able to convey goods and parts from process to process without unnecessary handling or cross-circulation.

In addition to natural light in the building, special GEC lighting units, on the semi-indirect principle with gas-filled lamps, provided an illumination of seven-and-a-half feet candles over the whole working area. A semi-plenum system of heating and ventilation was installed, in which air was drawn from outside and then passed through a wet filter for purification and a steam range for heating. The air was then blown into the works through ducts built into the main structure. In summer unheated air was blown through. Offices and lavatory blocks were heated with hot water pipes, with a special system under clothes lockers for drying purposes and general comfort.

The whole of the switchgear plant was constructed of reinforced concrete, with power shafting attached to beams and columns. Now wholly demolished, the only illustration of the plant is not sufficiently clear to enable comment upon its 'architectural' treatment. As the office block part of the building faced to the main road of the site, it is safe to assume that there would have been ornamental formwork on the façade. By and large, however, the planned conception of the works appears to have been its main forté, expressing the coming together of minds—of experts in a new form of power who would expect advantage to be taken of every constructional and operating method or appliance as efficient and up to date as the company's own products, with architects who were now well versed in the needs of industry, and with constructional advisers who had even longer experience of the field.

GEC general administration building, 1919–21
The GEC contract represented for Wallis, Gilbert & Partners not only designing for heavy industry but also their first large-scale administration building, separated from other works buildings but also housing extensive drawing offices. The ground space available for the three-storey-and-basement building was to front and then wrap around the existing central stores. That arrangement and the requirement for regularly-shaped rooms for offices with a straightforward circulation plan account for the E-like shape of the building, its axial planning and overall symmetry.

Other than steel stanchions in the centre of the rear projections, all uprights were of brick, with concrete-covered rolled steel joists as horizontal beams. The front block measures approximately 212 feet by 24 feet, has a central hall, stairway and lift shaft and a longitudinal corridor. The main rear projections measure 41 feet wide and 80 feet deep, that on the south side extending some 20 feet over a three-bay, single-storey garage. Provision was made to extend both arms further to the rear should the necessity arise. Smaller projections, 14 feet by 31 feet 6 inches, at the inner rear, housed lavatory facilities and were clad in white, glazed brick to overcome lighting problems in the buildings with which they were co-extensive. A set-back projection, 15 feet by 18 feet, on the north side of the frontal block is a stair tower and gives access by a bridge attached at first-floor level to existing offices and the machine shop. The semi-basement housed store rooms, cycle stores, locker rooms and the strong room. At the south-west corner, a three-storey stairway to and from the drawing office on the top floor connected with the ramp into the underground tunnel to the offices of the switchgear works.

Infill consists of small-paned glazing with brick spandrels. The building was also rendered in pale, sand-coloured cement and may well have been scored to represent stone. Fireproof floors/ceilings in the rear arms were fashioned from hollow clay blocks, patented and supplied by the Klein Patent Fire-Resisting Floor Syndicate Ltd of London, and gave very satisfactory service until lack of building maintenance allowed water to seep into reinforcing bars, which then expanded and explosively detached an area of ceiling.

The building's dominance of the site, in uninterrupted vista at the end of the central roadway from the main gate on Electric Avenue (Fig. 10), contributed to its primary aesthetic concept of the expression of power—indicative, that is, of the seat of management, the company's product and the international status of the company. The design detail of the front elevation was different in plan from as-built and has since been changed again. But the basic structural form of heavy framing, by projecting corner towers and attic storey, of a 'colonnade' with important central doorway, has remained constant. In its built form, the basic structure was more reminiscent of pre-First World War German state architecture, with references to Schinkel and early Behrens than of a conventional, British palace front. There is no direct evidence of German influence, although the coincidence of the company's products with those of the German electrical-equipment company, Allgemeine Elektricitäts-Gesellschaft, Berlin, may be significant. Peter Behrens' designs for AEG in the early years of the twentieth century, which produced a recognisable 'company image' and logo and initiated influential new ideas of factory design, were published in America in 1913, in a journal that was generally available in Britain.[50]

The initially-proposed design certainly had Roman reference. The supports of the Egyptianised doorway represented Roman magisterial fasces—bound sticks, the symbol of strength and unity, and lictors of power and discipline—and were repeated horizontally below the clock. Wallis' own motifs were disposed in classical fashion: nail-heads in abundance as door and doorway ornament and, larger and tasselled, as bases at the junction of columns and plinth. Ridged bands and small plain discs were also used in a variety of places. The company's name was proclaimed by its initials GEC and the magnet logo on the corner towers. The company's products were referred to in the overlapping wheel motifs on the architrave and the head of 'Electricity'—goddess of light, frequently seen in electricity advertising at that time—on the central tower.

Fig. 10 General Electric Co Ltd, Witton, Birmingham: administration building, detail of main entrance, 1919–21

For the discussion of the decoration of the as-built version, reliance has been placed on published sources, as most of the first revision has been obliterated, the central tower has been decapitated, and the whole building has been refaced in a darker shade of rendering than the original. The revised plan of 2 February 1921 and photographs published in *The Architect*,[51] in Wallis, Gilbert's own *Industrial Architecture*,[52] and in *The GEC and its Engineering Activities*,[53] all show the replacement of ridged bands in the spandrels with rather grotesque, bronze-coloured, moulded plaster medallions which, other than perhaps representing a larger version of the wheel/magnet motif and corner nail-heads, bear little relevance to the overall design. The capital nail-heads were replaced by tasselled discs, separated by alternating-wave symbols. The head of 'Electricity' was replaced by a porthole (for a clock?) surmounted by the serpent and staff emblem, and all encased within the pediment. The Egyptianising of the doorway was taken still further, by changing the fasces to papyrus columns, with bud capitals and bound palm bases. A winged disc with uraei decorated the reveal below the inverted cavetto. The doorway thereby related more directly to the entrances to the machine shop extension, a short distance away to the north.

Over the inner doors of the administration building, the company's name and the magnet logo surmount a fanlight, of which the glazing bar pattern was repeated in the glass partitions to the porter's lodge on the left and the telephone booth on the right. The external framing of the entrance is in carved Portland stone; a suggestion that such intricacies were achieved by the use of pre-cast artificial stone was confounded by cleaning which revealed fossilised marine deposits common to Jurassic limestone. The steps are of grey marble, and lead to huge, double doors of cast iron, bolted in sections.

Decoration of the interior of the building was largely confined to places seen by visitors and, in the repetition of external features, marks off what is effectively a processional way, from the main gate to reception room, by a conflation of classical and Egyptian sources and mien. Although the hall ornamentation is composed almost wholly of 'Wallis-type' and GEC-related motifs in moulded plaster or terrazzo, the arrangement is of a lighter, more Robert Adam style of Neo-classicism, particularly in the complementary nature of floor and ceiling (Fig. 11). Views along the side axes showed corridors with piers and stepped cornices and a geometric treatment of doorways, relating to the glazing bar pattern embellished with nail-heads.

The way forward, however, is by the stairs or lift directly opposite the entrance, to the first floor and the 'inner sanctum' of the reception room, which is superbly panelled in walnut inlaid with ebony. That the room belongs to the route is shown in the similarities of the ceiling with the moulded-plaster elipse of the hall, the fretwork decoration of hall floor spandrels repeated in the panels, and the prevalence of nail-heads and ridged borders. But recalling that, in setting out on the processional way, the most emphatic feature seen from the main gate and on actually entering the building is the Egyptian doorway, the conclusion of the journey is signalled and celebrated by equally emphatic Egyptian features. Characteristically, these are found in the sense of enclosure created by the panelling, the pylon-like treatment of doorways and the bookcase, and the battering of panel frames; in the gilded, winged serpents and staff with royal cobra heads and minor uraei; and in the lotus sunbursts on the ceiling (Fig. 12). The door furniture was specially cast over standard bases. The escutcheons are pylon-shaped but the finger plates and doorknobs bear Wallis' personal imprint—

Fig. 11 General Electric Co Ltd, Witton, Birmingham: administration building, entrance hall, 1919–21

the former with stepped, ridged borders and nail-heads. The doorknobs, however, appear to bring together the emblems of Egypt, GEC and Wallis himself, with perhaps some oblique reference to the bronze medallions on the external spandrels. As the only part of the room which one literally takes in one's hands, perhaps the doorknobs also represent the offer and acceptance of the triumvirate shown in the design. However esoteric that suggestion may be, and although Wallis took designing for industry very seriously indeed, it would be typical of the impish sense of humour that occasionally bubbled through his work.

The discovery in Egypt of the tomb of Tutankhamun in December 1922 and the later exhibition of some of its contents excited very considerable public interest and led to a revival of Egyptiana as a fashionable and highly commercialised style. Some of the items from the tomb were expensively copied as *objets d'art* but, in general, Egyptian motifs were used indiscriminately as applied decoration. Wallis, Gilbert's contract with GEC was completed prior to the publicity and popularity engendered by the Tutankhamun

Fig. 12 General Electric Co Ltd, Witton, Birmingham: administration building, reception room, 1919–21

phenomenon; Thomas Wallis' use of the Egyptian style cannot therefore be attributed to that influence. The partnership's own offices at 29 Roland Gardens, which had been fitted out in 1918, bear more than a passing relation to the reception room at GEC.[54] As the Egyptian influence became more overt in Wallis, Gilbert designs, a retrospective eye suggests that the apparently Neo-classical decorative motifs—discs, pendants, tassels and ridged or ribbed borders—had their symbolic source as much in the emblems of the Sun god and the Moon goddess, the head-dresses, spade-shaped artificial royal beards, and bound reeds or papyrus stems that figure in ancient Egyptian painting, sculpture and jewellery, as in triglyphs, metope and patera. Wallis' personal feeling for Egyptian art and architecture is demonstrated by its most emphatic references being in the more expressively significant areas such as doorways, fireplaces and chimney breasts.

In the 1980s the GEC site at Witton became virtually moribund. Some buildings were leased out, others demolished; Witton Estates, occupying the administration building, had some expectation of future development of the site. The General Electric Company plc is presently, however, a major international concern that has many other electrical companies subsumed within its title; the Witton site was vacated as no longer suitable to its requirements.

The manner in which Wallis incorporated the idiom of Egypt into the GEC buildings was perhaps as pretentious as its 'post-Tutankhamun' application by others, but there was at least some indication, in the processional way at GEC, of the more meaningfully abstract and architectonic Egyptian influence that was to appear in Wallis' later designs and was, indeed, already emerging at another factory designed in 1921–22.

Caribonum Limited

When administrative procedures were being transformed by new technologies and more sophisticated organisation, Caribonum Limited became suppliers of office materials as an off-shoot of the Lamson Paragon Supply Company Limited of Canning Town, London, printers and manufacturers of check books. When venturing into making its own carbon paper, as interleaved in each check book, the Lamson Company set up a plant at Etloe Road, Leyton, London in 1907–08; the new company's name, Caribonum Limited, was made up from the first letters of 'carbon' and 'ribbon', with 'bonum' (Latin for 'good') added on.

Much of the success of the new company and its development were attributable to the managing director, Charles Frederick Clark. He was a member of the Plymouth Brethren, a firm believer in Victorian self-help, and a man of wide interests and many talents.[55] Clark instituted a system of direct sales to users, bypassing the established retailers, with a well-turned out sales force. He encouraged his employees to regard themselves as members of the 'Caribonum family' and, in return for one of the widest ranges of amenities, benefits and recreational facilities likely to have been initiated at that time, expected loyalty, strict moral behaviour and utmost tidiness.

When need for expansion of the company arose, Clark himself designed a factory complex to be built on 22 acres of land at Harrow, Middlesex, but town-planning permission was refused. In consequence, the home site at Leyton was extended and the layout reorganised. Plans for a factory extension and boiler house were drawn by William Stewart, architect of Aldgate, London, and approved for construction in 1920–21.[56] The layout was similar to the as-built version but Stewart's exterior accorded more to contemporary, masonry Baroque than did the revised design by Wallis, Gilbert & Partners. Why the commission was transferred to Wallis, Gilbert is not known but, given the nature of the client, the architects' brief would undoubtedly have been knowledgeable, detailed and very firmly organised. A watercolour perspective of the Caribonum works by L. H. Bucknell[57] and an original artist's impression of the building to the right on Bucknell's picture, show a Wallis, Gilbert design of 1921 that was not executed. It appears to have been intended to stand on the site occupied at the time by Shenstone & Company.

The site at Leyton fronted Etloe Road on its eastern boundary and the Dagenham Brook at the rear, western side. To the south and north were adjoining properties, but vacant land was purchased on the north and west, and land and buildings on the south side were purchased from the Shenstone Company, thereby including Laurel Road and forming an enclosed site. Two gateways onto Etloe Road gave access to the site; the one facing Wiseman Road was the main works entrance and that onto Laurel Road the main exit. The building constructed in 1908 for the company's move to the area sat centrally on site, thereby leaving space for the new extension to form an L-shape, outwardly facing Laurel Road and Etloe Road. Goods entered from Wiseman Road to a docking area at the junction of the old and new buildings on the south side, serviced by centrally-placed goods lifts at the junction of the two buildings and facing to Laurel Road.

The new factory was three storeys high with future extension envisaged in an upward direction; a fourth storey was added in 1952. The building was of steel frame encased internally in concrete, with chamferred columns of 14-inch section; externally, vertical encasement and spandrels were of brick, with a glazed brick plinth. Horizontals, lintels and sills were of concrete, surrounding metal-framed, small-paned windows. The corner tower, which contained stairway and lift shaft, and the exit gateways on Laurel Road, were of reinforced concrete, with metal gates (Fig. 13). Floors were also of reinforced concrete of extra thickness to carry the high superimposed load occasioned by the ink vats, and were covered in oak blocks in staff areas. All conduits for gas, electricity, telephones, water and steam pipes were enclosed in the structure to avoid dust traps and cleaning problems (but were not easily accessible for maintenance).

The production sections of the new building were concerned with the manufacture of ink. Organised on a gravitational system, ink was manufactured on the top floor, fed by pipes to storage vats immediately below on the first floor, and thence piped to filling stations beside the bottle stock department on the ground floor, for filling, finishing, packing and despatch. The remaining floor space on the first floor housed the printing and box-making department and, on the second floor, were the laboratory, general office, showrooms and executive offices. A spiral staircase beside a glazed court in the crook of the L-shape connected all floors, provided an additional fire escape and gave access to lavatories and cloakrooms.

In contemporary terms, the laboratory was very modern. In order to accommodate future demand, it was of an area in excess of immediate requirements. All benches were fitted with gas, water, electricity and some with steam, compressed air and vacuum induction. There was a fume cupboard, a 'daylight' lamp for matching colours, a dark room, a separate room for 'dirty' work concerned with ink and carbon dopes, a miniature glass furnace for experimental and testing work in connection with the bottle factory at Alperton and a reference library.[58]

The general office was also designed with a view to efficient operation, on open plan with long rows of standardised desks, at which all employees sat

Fig. 13 Caribonum Ltd, Leyton, London: corner tower and gateway, 1920–21

with their backs to the entrance to avoid distraction. All the furniture was of uniform height, including a wooden fixture, for stocks of office stationery, fitted around all four walls, its top inclined inward at a 45-degree angle to avoid untidy accumulations on the surface. On either side of the entrance were the cash and order departments; at the far end were the filing offices and switchboard rooms.

Interior decoration throughout the factory (and its branch offices) was of uniform buff colour walls, brown dadoes and white ceilings; a chequered pattern of green and white rubber floor tiles was used in corridors. The entrance hall continued the Egyptian styling of its exterior.

The power house in the north-west corner of the site, also designed by Wallis, Gilbert & Partners, provided an entirely integrated system. The electrical switchgear board was fed by a 430 horse-power steam engine and dynamo which supplied the electric lighting and power throughout the plant, with a gas engine and generator as auxiliary. In the same building, two large boilers and stoke hole, with an 80 feet high chimney, supplied a complete steam circuit. Below were two water tanks of 4000 gallon capacity; water was piped from them through a feed heater, then forced through the boilers to drive a steam engine, then passed through an oil separator to remove impurities, and on through a system of pipes to heat all the buildings and drive machines, after which the steam passed through calorifiers to provide hot water for dressing rooms and then back to the water tanks for re-use.[59]

A 'very friendly relationship' was established between Clark and Thomas Wallis, and their close collaboration in the planning and layout of the factory could have added to Wallis, Gilbert's expertise in factory and office design, since the meticulously-planned layout at Caribonum clearly owed much to Clark's attitude to business management and operation. It was Clark, too, who asked for the 'incorporation of the Egyptian style for the entrance gates, the main entrance and hall and his office on the second floor'.[60] Approval of the style also extended to Clark's son, C. A. Clark, who became managing director on the death of his father in 1945. Proposals for a new factory designed by Wallis, Gilbert & Partners in that year had the same 'elegant style with Egyptian traces'.[61] That design was not executed owing to failure to obtain the necessary land; a fourth storey was added at the Leyton site instead.

Most of the exterior of the 1922 factory at Leyton was of brick to sit comfortably beside the 1908 factory and the Shenstone building opposite. Decorative elements in the new building were, as at GEC, confined mainly to areas seen by visitors, with the stair tower as the company landmark. The same assemblage of recognisable Wallis, Gilbert features appear in the ribbed borders, nail-heads, discs, tassels, projecting cornice and set-back attic storey. The glazing bars and interior ironwork were of a pattern similar to those at GEC, Witton. The Egyptian element was more restrained and appeared in the pylon-like gateposts, the battering of the main entrance and stair newel post in the hall, and in the panelling of Mr Clark's office, where there was also a pylon-shaped chimney breast. More unusual, was the treatment of the corner tower, where a battered, horizontally-lapped formation was recessed into the angle of the piers.

A design for a bottle-making factory at Alperton in 1922, when the company ventured for a few years into making its own containers, is recorded in Sheds, section (d) of this chapter. Wallis, Gilbert & Partners designed the glass works and also a house for Mr Clark.

In the design and construction of the buildings for the Caribonum Company, the collaborative influence of the client is very marked but reveals too Wallis' ability to adapt to and interpret the nature of his client company and/or person with whom final authority rested in arriving amicably at an acceptable design. For instance, to compare Napier with Clark, while both were martinets in respect of the quality of their products and the behaviour of employees, Napier abhorred salesmanship and advertising, but these were Clark's greatest talents in obtaining his post at Caribonum and in making the company successful. The planning and appearance of their buildings were intended to suit their very different personalities. At this period too, Wallis, Gilbert & Partners were commissioned to design buildings for companies wherein the absolutely plain or very minimally adorned frame was preferred (or was dictated by economy) and which came closest to the concrete block at Albion, Glasgow.

Commercial Cars Limited

This manufacturer of motor vehicles, based at Biscot Road, Luton, Beds, only marginally escaped elimination in the slump of 1920. In 1905 a group of engineers had been experimenting with an innovative gear box designed by C. A. Linley, which they had developed so successfully as to decide upon full-scale production of a four-ton truck to their own design. A site fronting Biscot Road on the outskirts of Luton was chosen principally for its nearness to London but also because it had 'low rates, freedom from fog, cheap land and little [sic] restrictive building regulations'.[62] A well-equipped plant was in production by 1907; by 1911 facilities were doubled and 'Commer' had become the largest heavy-motor vehicle manufacturer in Britain. Four thousand vehicles were supplied to the armed forces during the First World War. At the end of the war the Luton works covered five and a half acres and further extension, designed by Wallis, Gilbert & Partners, added a further 37 000 square feet of floor space.

   Until that time, the Luton works were all brick-built with pitched roofs, fronting Biscot Road. The full site is bounded at the rear by the railway, to the south-east by the rear of domestic property facing Curzon Road and, to the north-west, by the works of George Kent Limited, engineers who had, as makers of motor vehicle steering gear, moved from Holborn, London, in 1907 'because electricity in that area was cheaper'. Most of the early Commer expansion was by way of single-storeyed, north-light sheds, so that the three-storey, reinforced concrete extension was an unusual addition. Of the surviving plans, two were for a single-storeyed building. The architects' name is shown as Wallis, Gilbert & Partner (partner in the singular), which suggests the commission was originally mooted in 1916 or 1917. Later plans, dated June 1919, by Wallis, Gilbert with Partners plural, are for proposed extensions by two floors, suggesting the ground floor was already built and was being added to for post-war expansion. What appears to be the case, however, is that the full three-storey building, without attic storey or cornice (marked 'blocked out' on plan) was built all of a piece in 1920. A Commer prospectus seeking increased capitalisation in July 1920 shows the 'new extension in course of erection'.

The new building was 'aeroplane' shaped and sited behind three single-storeyed sheds, with the main entrance facing north into the works. What was its intended purpose is not known, but a photograph of 1944 declares the building to be the spares stores. At the time of construction the company was already in financial difficulties.[63] In late 1919 the workforce 'had been on a three-day week for some time' but work on the new extension was reported to be continuing—'as the buildings are being erected in concrete, it is necessary to make the most progress possible while frost does not interfere with the work',[64] even though, by January 1920 the manufacturing works had closed down because of a strike by moulders. Unless Commer was to radically modernise its vehicle design it would shortly be competing with its own-built trucks when the War Office released them onto the public market. But if Commer needed such a large building for spares, then perhaps it was anticipating possibilities of future need.

Apart from a few nail-heads as terminals to piers, and possibly some emphasis on the doorways on the north side, the concrete building was quite plain. This may have been because economies had to be made (including omitting the decorated attic storey) or because a company whose board comprised engineers preferred an 'engineer's-type' of building. But planning was of a very precise order and is reflected in the shape of the building, which also demonstrates the adaptability of the frame to corridor junctions as proposed at Rubery Owen. And certainly the building was well-made. It had stood for 24 years when, on 6 November 1944, an enemy V2 rocket exploded at the crossroads of Biscot/Curzon/Landsdown. Nineteen people were killed, 196 injured, a crater 12 feet deep and 30 feet across resulted in damage spreading to an area of almost 2000 square yards. Domestic property and the recently erected Commer canteen and despatch shop took the brunt of the explosion, while the reinforced concrete building absorbed the blast, suffering only broken windows and buckled glazing bars. The opinion was voiced that, without the protection of the concrete building, the works would have been laid waste. There was, perhaps, something to be said for the composition and over-stressing of early concrete buildings except, of course, when demolition was intended.

Hayes Cocoa Limited

The other plain building was for Hayes Cocoa Limited of Nestlés Avenue, Hayes, Middlesex, a company founded by Eugene Sandow, a famous circus strongman who attributed his powerful physique to the drinking of cocoa. In 1912, Sandow established a cocoa-producing company in a Georgian house in Hayes, surrounded by acres of orchard land and chosen because of its proximity to the Great Western Railway and the Grand Junction Canal (the latter still used for transporting bulk supplies until the mid-1930s). As a German national, Sandow was registered as an enemy alien in the First World War and was thereby forced to stop trading. The business was taken over by a Swiss chocolate-making firm—Peter, Cailer, Kohler—which changed the Sandow firm's name to Hayes Cocoa Limited and built a large extension of the premises.[65]

In Wallis, Gilbert's aerial photograph published in 1932, the extension is shown to have swallowed up the Georgian house within a large three-storey block. There are two open wells within the block, giving increased floor space without interfering with light to other areas and representing a system Wallis, Gilbert were to employ again within the decade.

The cocoa company is now owned by The Nestlé Company Limited (hence the address at Nestlés Avenue) which still holds a complete set of the Truscon drawings for the building. Truscon was, in fact, responsible for the design of the building and Wallis, Gilbert for the planning, which may account for its unadorned state. But, for all its affinity with the Albion building, it appears less aggressive—or at least so whilst the column stumps on the roofline remain unfulfilled in supporting other storeys. In open, flat land, it does not tower above or compete with other buildings. From a distance, it seems almost to hug the ground. The new company, in 1920, had to sell off some of the surrounding land to pay for this building, so the avoidance of unwarranted expense may also have contributed to its plainness. As Europeans, the new owners may simply have preferred it that way.

Many alterations and additions have taken place over the years, including a large spray-drying tower, that have changed the visual aspect of the plant. When Nestlé made Hayes its British headquarters in 1949, a sculptured, concrete entrance was added on the west side of the building, to face down the long driveway that passes through landscaped grounds to the road which bears the company's name. The company also protects its processes and production very securely so that no photography or other kind of illustration is permitted.

A winning formula

By 1921, the practice of Wallis, Gilbert & Partners had been in existence for five years and had achieved a not inconsiderable success. Despite aborted commissions, profits must have been fairly substantial, even if fees were at a lower figure than the, roughly, five per cent charged by Wallis & Bowden in 1912 for the Stoke-on-Trent Town Hall extension. Although no precise figures are available for the built designs and there are no surviving accounts or like material from the practice, some indication emerges from the quoted figure of sixpence per cubic foot for Tilling-Stevens,[66] which gives a total of not less then £70 000. The sum of £60 433 13s 5d was paid to the contractor for the GEC machine shop and, during 1920–21, GEC paid the contractor Sir

Robert McAlpine an amount of £439 386 for a group of contracts, which included the administration building at Witton; that building was entered into the GEC accounts for 1925 at an asset value of £85 000.

These first five years reveal Thomas Wallis' perspicacity in taking advantage of Truscon's Daylight unit system. It had shown itself to be suitable for a variety of industries, of holding its value, of being adaptable to changes in methods of production, company reorganisation or expansion. The concrete aesthetic devised by Wallis showed respect for the medium in the nature of the frame and the materially-integrated decoration. The obvious modernity of the fabric had been tempered by observing traditional masonry concepts of articulation to express structure and plan. Permutations of a range of decorative motifs had allowed for individuality of expression, whilst restriction of the range to a fairly small repertoire of motifs idiosyncratic to the designer was economic in practice and also contributed to a self-advertising identification of the building as a 'Wallis, Gilbert production'.

A philosophy of approach also emerges that is intent upon raising the public status of industry with a prestigious form of architecture intrinsic to itself, upon enhancing industrial performance by well-thought-out planning, and upon lightening the burden of the workforce with better working conditions and amenities and something to gladden the eye in an otherwise harsh milieu. The formula proved equally successful in the ensuing five years, attracting commissions from a greater diversity of sources, in a greater diversity of materials and different types of buildings.

The 1920s were a bleak period for many industries. The dominant feature of the earlier years of the decade, particularly in the old staple industries, was a determination to return to the pre-war situation. But companies whose products contributed to or reflected social change were most likely to be in a position to seek expansion. By mid-decade, a feeling for 'modernity' was becoming more pronounced, particularly among the younger members of the public. Despite the industrial turmoil of the time and, for many, the lack of work, a greater sense of freedom was expressed in entertainment, clothing fashions and opportunities for travel. There was a marked change in Wallis, Gilbert designs from mid-decade that reflected an awareness of these changes in the cultural ethos. But factories designed for four companies whose products would contribute to that new ethos and which found need to expand in the first half of the decade adhered to the established formula. Two were of the long-fronted variety, to which the formula was applied more successfully over two storeys than the earlier, aborted multi-storey version, and two were narrow-fronted, multi-storey blocks.

Houghton-Butcher Limited

A factory for Houghton-Butcher Limited at Fulbourne Road, Walthamstow, London, was designed in 1919–20 and thus rightly belongs to the 'first five years' but the only surviving illustration, of 1928, shows it with the addition of a part-first floor—that is, as had been originally intended in the early, but only partly executed plans. The building deviated only slightly from the deposited plans, which explains why a company specialising in such a modern and popular product as photographic equipment did not reflect the kind of stylistic treatment common to 1928. The building is still standing but has been almost totally enveloped.

The company had been established by George Houghton in 1834 as makers of stained glass but, in 1840, in cooperation with Anton Claudet, had secured the patent rights to process Daguerrotype photographs in England and was thereafter engaged in the production of photographic equipment. In 1906 a factory was built at Fulbourne Road, Walthamstow, where, amongst other items, the 'Ensign' camera and daylight-loading roll film contributed to the company's prosperity.[67] William Butcher & Sons Limited was founded in 1895 and developed cinematographic equipment and the 'Empire' projector;[68] a merger of the two companies was arranged to cover the full range of photographic pursuits and became Houghton-Butcher Manufacturing Company. In consequence, an expansion of floor space was required, hence the building designed by Wallis, Gilbert & Partners.

The building occupies land between the earlier factory and Fulbourne Road; it faces east and measures 280 feet 9 inches on frontage and 75 feet in depth. It is constructed of reinforced concrete, 14 bays by 4 of 20 feet in width and 18 feet 6 inches in depth. Infill consists of metal-framed, small-paned windows with brick spandrels. As built circa 1920, four bays at the south end were two storeys high, of which the upper floor housed managerial and general offices, drawing office and staff lavatories and cloakrooms. On the ground floor, the south-east corner contained the main doorway, hall-porter's room, stairwell and lift shaft. The full run of the frontal bays included rooms for works offices, planning and tool-making. Most of the remainder of the ground floor was taken up by a machine shop and stores; when the first floor, of ten by four bays was added, that too was for production purposes. All works entrances, fire escapes and the despatch bay were at the rear. The disposition of sanitary facilities appears to have been governed by the needs of the workforce rather than the simplicity of drainage arrangements, since lavatories and cloakrooms are contained within the floor space at points convenient to the persons working in that area rather than, as at other sites, in annexed bays.

The façade was largely unadorned, except for the main doorway, where discs and pendants act as capitals to projecting piers, and a ribbed cornice and ribbed architrave with nail-heads follow a familiar pattern. Projecting brackets were to be inserted in the south elevation at both floor levels for the attachment of a future extension over Clifford Road, which was proposed to be relocated further south. Had that been realised, it is doubtful if an equivalent number of bays could have been added to obtain a symmetrical façade with corner towers and the main door as the central feature. As it stood, however, the distance between the two end bays prevented their disparate treatment giving an unfinished appearance to the façade; the north 'corner tower' simply acts as counterbalance to the more ornate entrance at the south corner at the junction of the two roads.

An interior view of the plant showing 'Rigifix' slotted inserts to carry power shafting (as at the Napier factory) was shown in an issue of *Kahn-crete Engineering*,[69] indicating that Truscon was the reinforced concrete engineer. In 1930, the commissioning company's name was changed to Ensign Limited. The building was later taken over by Fuller Electrics Limited, subsequently by Hawker-Siddeley Power Transformers Limited and most recently by Spring Steel Productions Limited.

William Stannard & Company Limited

A similar arrangement of the main door at one end and a balancing, but purely aesthetic 'corner tower' at the other was repeated in the concrete frontal block of a design for William Stannard & Company Limited at Buxton Road, Leek, Staffordshire in 1923–24. Large, single-storeyed, north-light sheds formed the main part of the production area at the rear. The sheds have since been demolished but the concrete block that fronted the road is still standing, albeit with alterations and additions. The whole of the interior has been changed to office accommodation and is presently occupied by the Britannia Building Society which purchased it from the previous owners, Adams Foods Limited.

The Stannard company was established in 1845 as makers of silk thread; the company is still in operation at Biddulph, Staffordshire, as a manufacturer of children's wear, but all its records and archives were destroyed by fire in 1966.[70] At the new factory at Leek in the 1920s, the sheds produced yarn and fabric; the frontal block was used for making and finishing garments, for stores, sample room, sanitary facilities and offices. A corridor ran between the two buildings, with access for males at one side and females at the other.

On the façade, treatment of the corner towers differs from earlier work in that, instead of projecting classical piers, the brick corners throw into relief the concrete pylons that are so remarkably akin to the Egyptian-styled chimney-breast in Wallis' own office (Fig. 14). The stepped capping of the towers and ribbed cornices are familiar but nail-heads appear only on the architraves and plinth. Discs are in greater profusion—in a row on the doorway cornice, set in squares as capital and end-stops, and on the inner doorway. The fanlight glazing bars are of a like pattern to those at GEC and Caribonum. In its as-built form, the powerful appearance of the Egyptianised corner towers would have had greater visual impact against the large expanses of glass, but all windows have been replaced, extra mullions have been inserted, cornices and copings have been covered by corrugated

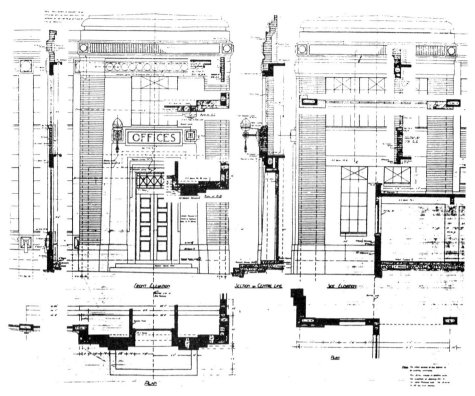

Fig. 14 William Stannard & Co, Leek, Staffs: plans—end tower, doorway, 1924

aluminium and the building has been rendered in light, sand-coloured cement. The original contractor was Henry Willcock & Company, but there is no evidence of Truscon involvement.

Babbage, Friendship & Hicks Limited

A factory designed for this firm at Devnit Works, Plymouth, Devon, returned to the narrow-fronted version of the Daylight/Masonry design. Although also for manufacturers of hosiery and knitwear and designed in 1923, this building was quite different from Stannard's, less straightforward in plan and located on rising ground on an awkwardly-shaped site. Fronting to Regent Street in a built-up, residential area then bordering on the suburbs of the city, it was surrounded by North Street, Seymour Street and Beaumont Avenue. The plans are dated October 1923 and the building was erected in 1924 by Wakeman Bros, now defunct.

The commissioning company was established in 1895 as Babbage, Friendship Company Limited at Vintry Works, Plymouth. When Hicks joined the company circa 1922, new premises were commissioned at Regent Street. The economic depression at the turn of the decade appears to have hit the company rather badly, as the premises were vacated in April 1932 and purchased by Underhills, a family of printers. The building was in use as a printing works for many years, the occupants trading as Underhill (Plymouth) Limited, and becoming part of the Terry Printing Group which purchased the factory in 1971. When economic depression occurred in the early 1980s, demolition was already imminent.[71]

The three-storey building faces south, with a frontage of 87 feet. It is basically four bays by four, each of 19 feet 8 inches square, and is stepped laterally to three bays, then two, on the west side where the site boundary narrows. To the rear, the rising ground was cut into rather than built over as intended at Cambrian Candle. The factory is built of reinforced concrete, infilled with brick spandrels to metal-framed, small-paned windows. All brickwork, including the parapet surrounding the flat roof, was left as such, possibly for reasons of economy or in deference to the brick-built environment, but was later rendered over as protection for bricks that were becoming porous.[72] Columns on the front elevation are at different intervals from the main grid to accommodate two double-doorways leading, on the left to sales room and works areas and, on the right, to offices, kitchen and dining rooms as well as sanitary facilities that are communally plumbed on each floor and show in the window patterns on the east elevation. A side door on the east acted as a staff entrance, while an external spiral staircase on the west side gave access for works people. A director's room on each floor beside the spiral entrance provided supervisory observation. A part-basement under the south-east corner housed waste storage and the furnace. Workrooms occupied the upper two storeys; and a large warehouse to the rear of the sales room on the ground floor completed the organisation of processes, storage, sales and despatch.

To the east, west and north, elevations concurred with the structure. On the road front, structure again articulates the façade, chiefly in the disposition of the piers, since they are not projecting. Decoration is restrained, with discs set in squares as capitals. Tasselled nail-heads act as bases above the plinth, on the central, stepped pediment that carried 'Devnit Works' against the sky, and over the doorways. The doorways themselves differ slightly from the plan. The fanlights were dispensed with and the entrances made more important by a battered line and projecting head that again introduces a touch of Egypt in being reminiscent of stylised uraei. In the economic climate of 1923–24, the Babbage factory would have been designed within a tight budget with scant room for frills. It nevertheless follows in line from the Tilling-Stevens and Napier factories.

S. G. Brown

Around the 1922–24 period Wallis, Gilbert & Partners designed buildings for S. G. Brown as his own-named company and as Telegraph Condensers

Limited as a factory complex at North Acton, London. They included separate office blocks, warehouse and production sheds; the roadside buildings are/were (some have been demolished) of such unusual design that they are discussed in section (d) below.

Barker & Dobson Limited

Apart from later extensions in 1934, the last of the Daylight/Masonry factories was designed by Wallis, Gilbert in 1926 for Barker & Dobson Limited, at Whitefield Road, Everton, Liverpool. Although contemporary photographs exist in published sources for one of the two buildings, other sources are negligible.[73] All the buildings have been partially demolished. The company was established in 1834 at Paradise Street, Liverpool, by Joseph Dobson who incorporated his wife's maiden name Barker as a 'partnership' cognomen. After expanding into the manufacture of confectionery at Hope Street, the company purchased the disused Liverpool tram depot at Whitefield Road in 1926, where a new factory was built, followed by further building in 1934 and other extensions. Barker & Dobson Limited became famous for chocolates, sweets and the equally well-known 'Everton toffee'.

There are no surviving plans. The Wallis, Gilbert publication describes the 1926 building as the 'despatch department' but that surely did not refer to the whole structure; the upper floors may have been used for box-making and packing, but some part of the building contained a laboratory.[74] The four-storey building faced south-east, fronting directly on to the street with two large vehicular entrances in the centre bays. It was constructed of reinforced concrete, infilled with metal-framed windows, on a grid plan of four bays wide by six in depth, to which further bays were added at the rear at a later date. The interior was largely open space, with circular columns, and perforations in the beams to carry machine shafting. Offices and other small process rooms appear to have been partitioned off on the north-east side. The fourth, or attic storey, later bricked in, was of lower height and was recessed on front between the corner towers. The towers are particularly solid-looking, with their narrow sidelights and heavy attic capping made more prominent by the space between them on the skyline. They contained, on the left, a large service lift and, on the right, the stairs with doorway to the street. On the façade, the projecting cornice and piers were decorated similarly to Tilling-Stevens and Napier, with ribbed banding and discs-with-pendants as capitals. Nail-heads acted as end-stops on corners and, larger and in layered form, as bases above the stepped plinth. Entrances were marked off by rustication of the architraves. The despatch entrances have since been filled in and loading bays have been inserted on the west wall. The decoration has been rendered over or removed. Originally, the exterior appears to have been rendered and then covered in cement paint. So little remains of the later buildings on site that description becomes impossible, except that one of them appears to be of brick-infilled steel frame. A surviving doorway has battered architraves, a stepped cornice and tasselled nail-heads below a narrow light between projecting piers, capped by ribbing and more tasselled nail-heads.

The company was purchased by Scribbans-Kemp in 1952 which changed its name to SK Holdings in the early 1970s. Eventually, however, reversion of the title was made to that of its best-known subsidiary, Barker & Dobson Limited, with headquarters at Bury, Lancs.[75]

James Hunt Limited

As the Daylight/Masonry period reached its closing stages, mention must be made of a relatively minor work that must have presented the architects with intriguing problems. For an extension of the premises—the addition of two storeys over two sides of a small court in 1924 for James Hunt Limited, Atlanta Road, Fulham, London—there was the need to marry old building with new, of cast iron and brick construction with reinforced concrete, and to arrange execution within a very small space hemmed in by domestic property, over a difficult access route.

James Hunt Limited was a paper merchant and is no longer in existence; the premises are in multi-occupation. Wallis, Gilbert's resolution of the brief included the use of *pre-cast* reinforced concrete beams and floor slabs, the chasing out of existing work to take reinforced concrete columns, and of matching original London fletton bricks. Whatever the difficulties of construction of this extension, the architects achieved a successful and compatible result. As presently used, the site is very well kept, for which some motivation must arise from perpetuating the atmosphere of the place. With its tunnel access, hide-and-seek alleyways and near-Dickensian peculiarity, the little complex reveals a charming surprise for the visitor and is a pleasure to its occupants. From the roadway, the rising block is now less formidable above the Victorian houses than it may have appeared in 1924, since the modern eye is more accustomed to such disparities, but there appears to have been no major objection at the time of its construction.

Finishing, standardization and individuality

The factories in this group seem not to have been left in their raw state, but whether they were left as rendered is difficult to discover. Most of them have been resurfaced on more than one occasion. At GEC, Witton, a strongly-coloured sand was responsible for the ochre hue; but for the rest, the method is not known. A paper on colouring for concrete works, published in 1912,[76] on the recommendation of an 'American authority', includes very strong colours of red, black and blue, but it is doubtful if Wallis, Gilbert would have entertained such a range. In his talk at the Institute of Structural Engineers in 1934,[77] Wallis discussed many ways of finishing concrete surfaces but made no reference to his early works. In the partnership's publication, *Industrial Architecture* of 1932, all the advertisements were by firms with whom Wallis, Gilbert commissions had been associated. Since they include the Concrete Marketing Company, it is possible that some Wallis, Gilbert buildings were treated with the products marketed by that company, such as 'Snowcrete', a white cement supplied with white aggregate, and 'Snowcrete No. 2' a 'delicate cream colour'. 'Colourcrete' was supplied only in buff and red. Other colouring products and special paints for concrete surfaces were available by the 1930s, but it is not clear how concrete buildings in the 1920s were dealt with.

Daylight factories by Wallis, Gilbert & Partners in the 'Masonry' style, in the decade from Tylors of 1916 to Barker & Dobson of 1926, had run through many permutations of the shapes and sizes inherent in the frame/unit system. That the architects' adaptations of the system met the needs and preferences of manufacturers is confirmed by the increasing demand for Wallis, Gilbert-designed factories. As the architects' reputation and status increased, ownership of such a building added to the status of the commissioning company.

The partnership's early recognition of the economic advantages of reconciling standardisation with individuality was exploited later in, for example, speculative house building (Wimpey & Company provided 26 interchangeable elevations for every standard plan);[78] Leicester City Council, at its Braunstone Estate Number 2, interchanged a small number of plans, roof styles, roofing tiles and colour of bricks within a set style; the furniture makers Parker Knoll produced a few basic shapes of chairs and settees which were then made up in the customer's choice of wood and upholstery.[79] The earliest version of a custom-built object arising from a basic form came from the motor industry, where manufacturers entering volume production built standard engines and chassis which were then fitted with the customer's own choice of body. Wallis' first designs were for the motor industry and he may have culled the notion from that source. In an article of 1926 devoted to 'The Industrial Works of Wallis, Gilbert & Partners', Eric Bird described Wallis as a 'lone hand' in understanding and meeting the needs of industry.[80]

Transitional designs

The 'Masonry' factories were sufficiently modern buildings in both architectural and industrial terms not to lose face in ensuing years even though, by 1926, times were already changing and Wallis, Gilbert factories were changing with them. The last of the true 'Masonry' style buildings appeared in 1926; the first of the 'Fancy' factories was designed in 1927. But overlapping those dates, that is from 1925 to 1929, some proposed designs were of Masonry form but, when revised to as-built, introduced a new kind of framing of façades and a new kind of decoration—faience tiles. These could be regarded as 'transitional' designs. In 1925, a factory that faced directly onto a major thoroughfare in central London, was steel-framed to overcome height restrictions imposed on reinforced concrete by the London County Council, and was the first up-dating from established orthodoxy.

Solex Licensees Limited

The design for Solex Licensees Limited at 223–31 Marylebone (now Old Marylebone) Road was commissioned in 1925 when Gordon Richards obtained licence from an American company to manufacture Solex carburettors in Britain and needed new premises for that purpose alongside his existing business. The five-storey building faces north-west on to (Old) Marylebone Road, with a small forecourt between the building line and the public pavement. There is adjoining property on both sides. Access from the front was by a double-doorway in the centre to the 'public' area and by large, collapsible doors on each side for vehicles to enter or leave the works. At the rear, sliding doors opened on to Watson's Mews.

The building is constructed of steel frame encased and faced in brick, with concrete-covered beams. The flat roof was intended to take an upward extension; plans for a proposed fifth floor are undated but it would appear that the forward part of an attic storey was included in the original design and has recently been pierced by a row of seven small windows. The westerly, rear portion of the building was single-storeyed only, with a pitched, trussed roof covered by corrugated asbestos and lit by Mellowes' patent glazing either side of the ridge. Ground coverage measured roughly 82 feet wide by 94 feet deep, plus a small abutment to the east over an existing yard entrance at the rear. Apart from the stair and lift wells, all floors were open plan and used mainly for production purposes. Space for other functions, lavatories etc. was simply partitioned off, as was the public area at the centre, ground-floor front, where a granolithic kerb protected the partition from damage. That section contained a waiting room and works manager's office to the left, a telephone booth and cashier's office to the right, with the public counter and hall between them.

As proposed on plan, the façade was fairly close to Wallis, Gilbert's orthodoxy—a suggestion of capped towers connected by a heavy parapet, ribbed cornice and plain spandrels; tasselled nail-heads as capitals to the twin piers of the towers and bases of the centre piers. As-built, however, the design changed from a concrete style to one of brick, with a broad 'picture frame' of attractive thin rustic bricks surrounding a large glazed area. On the outer edge of the frame, the bricks are of a brownish hue, inset with narrow vertical lights. A narrow band of black and white faience tiles was inset in the slightly projecting inner frame of dull, mottled red bricks. At ground level, a second frame, in concrete with battered uprights, surrounds the entrances, which are marked off by twin pairs of Doric columns horizontally banded at capital and base. Nevertheless, familiar identifying marks persist—nail-heads, tassels and discs, but the introduction of faience is new, as also are the motifs at the bases of the piers—stylised ram's heads in concrete to link the picture frame with the pylon frame.

On the street scene this building does not say 'factory'. It could well pass as car-showrooms, offices or even a shop-front appropriate to the metropolis. Its location, the fact of public access, the change from reinforced concrete to steel frame and brick, the American connection of the product, and the general feeling for something 'more modern', could all have contributed to the variation in pattern. Recently, all the windows have been replaced and the vehicular entrances have been glazed over so that the balance between frame and framed has been lost, but the building still has sufficient character to enhance the modern street scene. It is presently occupied by a very security-conscious American electronics firm and named Edison House. Access to the interior is not permitted.

American companies wishing to expand their overseas trade in the mid-1920s had a number of routes available to them by which to reach the European and Imperial markets. They could establish trading depots in Britain under their own name for the distribution of imports (often subject to import duty); as at Solex, they could grant licence-to-manufacture to British or European citizens; they could establish factories in Canada to gain entrée to the British Empire and, via Britain, to Europe; or they could build their own manufacturing base in Britain, thereby gaining tariff-free access to British markets and to Europe.

Wrigley Products Limited

Wallis, Gilbert & Partners' first commission from an American client building in Britain came in 1926 from Wrigley Products Limited at East Lane, North Wembley, London. The American company of William Wrigley Junior, manufacturers of chewing gum, entered the UK market in 1911 with products imported from an associate company in Canada. In 1925, Wrigley purchased a large tract of land at North Wembley on which to build his own factory and for resale of plots to other American firms that might wish to follow suit.[81] Directors of the firm visited England early in 1926 and, in their first week, interviewed a number of architects, finally selecting Wallis, Gilbert & Partners. They acquainted Thomas Wallis with their disappointment as regards 'pep' in Britain and asked him if he could prepare all plans, drawings, quantities and specifications for the proposed factory within one week. Mr Wallis was assured that this could be done in America and he promised to undertake the task if all particulars and requirements could be delivered to him then and there.

By parcelling out the necessary tasks into the four departments and by working day and night, the partnership fulfilled the promise, with every smallest detail worked out. The visiting directors were able to see all contracts signed and the first sod cut on site before their return to America shortly afterwards. Thomas Wallis and Frank Cox received a letter of congratulation from the company's Vice President saying that '. . . the most up-to-date American architects could not have made a better record' and praising Wallis for so competently 'assimilating our ideas'.[82]

The factory was built with similar expedition, and was opened in 1926. It remained the UK base of the Wrigley Company until the move to Plymouth in 1970 to take advantage of cleaner air. The 1926 factory has been considerably extended, also to designs by Wallis, Gilbert & Partners, including a four-storey block at the rear in 1954. More recently—and not by Wallis, Gilbert—an attic storey has been added to the main block and other major changes have been made to convert the block to multi-occupation. These have included a rather garish over-painting of the building that has completely destroyed its original character. The premises are now owned/administered by Waite & Son Limited as its Wembley Commercial Centre.

The four-storey building of 1926 faces due west toward the railway. The nearest main road, East Lane, bridges the railway some distance to the

Fig. 15 Wrigley Products Ltd, Wembley, London: mushroom pillars, 1926

south and a side road slopes down to what is now an industrial complex. The road shown on the original plan at the rear, east side of the building may not have been constructed since that part of the site was used for extensions. In 1926 access to the building was gained from that side through doorways into each end block. On the southern corner, the door was protected by a porte cochère of reinforced concrete, over which a one-storey general office was lit from three sides. A new door has been inserted in the side elevation as the abutted part has been built over. On the west side, loading bays were inserted and have since been extended to run the full length of the building.

The two end blocks contained, on each floor, stairs, lifts and lavatory facilities, with offices on the first floor and a kitchen and rest room on the top floor. The remaining floor space was devoted to manufacturing processes, organised on a downward-flow system, with the packing and despatch areas on the ground floor, above the refrigeration section and boiler house in the basement. Partitioning was inserted where special processes needed separation from the main floor. On the flat roof, a large water tank took central position, without benefit of aesthetic disguise. The building is constructed of reinforced concrete by Truscon, its most radical feature being replacement of post and beam by 'mushroom' columns supporting floor slabs (Fig. 15). Whence came the engineering know-how? Truscon must surely have been engaged in the four-day deliberations and design processes; or did the Americans opt for and include mushroom column engineering in their particulars? These metal-clad, circular columns, of 27 inch diameter, have inverted-cone caps and were placed on a regular grid that permitted the floors, measuring 220 feet by 75 feet, to cantilever beyond the outer row of columns. Since no allowance had to be made for depth of beams, floor-to-ceiling dimensions could be reduced and there was also greater flexibility in the placing of overhead services. Even so, the columns, being larger in section than the usual frame, consumed more floor space and the system precluded the infinite variety of annexed bays, court wells and abutments. Extension was intended and, indeed, only possible, by a repetition of similar units.

With the dead load restricted to the weight of the floor slabs, cantilevering and emancipation from load-bearing walls meant that infill could consist solely of glazing, uninterrupted by vertical supports—a layer-cake of solid and void. The basic format of the Wrigley building was Le Corbusier's *Dom-Ino* writ large. But, although the freedom of interior planning was exploited by the use of moveable partitions, Wallis seems to have decided against exposing to public view the visual fiction of floors floating in air.

The Architects' Journal described the design as 'courageous', but saw the innovative structure as a 'first attempt' in which 'these conclusion would not necessarily be final'.[83] Factory premises designed by Louis de Soissons and Arthur Kenyon at Welwyn Garden City, Herts, reported in 1930[84] had windows 'going round corners' but, nevertheless contained offices, stairs, lavatories and the water tank in a more solid structure in the centre-front of the building. Much earlier, in Germany in 1914, Walter Gropius had excited the modernists with a glass corner at the Fagus factory and, in his factory administration building at the Deutsche Werkbund exhibition of 1914, had shown a cantilevered staircase encircled with glass. While the latter design was applauded for its radical form, the vertiginious implications of its practical use seem not to have been considered. In Britain in 1926 reaction may have included other thoughts: when women formed an ever-increasing portion of the workforce and skirts were at their very shortest (prior, that is, to the 1960s), Mrs Grundy would not have approved such exposure. And there were many male Mrs Grundys among company owners.

Other problems arising from total inter-floor glazing would have been the placing of rainwater and flat-roof drainage pipes and the blanking on the exterior of sanitary facilities. Containing all services within a central core, a solution reached by Owen Williams at the Boots' factory, Nottingham (1931) and by Mies van der Rohe in his Lakeside flats, Chicago, Illinois, was not a wholly practical measure in factories, where production lines of machinery could have been interrupted by a centralised structure. Later at Firestone and Burton's, Wallis solved that problem by inserting a mezzanine but at Wrigley he closed off the short ends of the building very substantially. Extra stanchions were introduced to support the enclosure of space for specific purposes. The solid ends and mullions of the long elevation delineated the reaches of the building and reduced visual shock. What might be construed as a craven lack of courage to exploit the potential of the mushroom format should best be seen as Wallis' informed pragmatism and a realistic appreciation of British conservatism. Comment on the Wrigley building approved its simplicity but noted, even so, that it was free of the 'barrack-like bareness' that characterised many early reinforced concrete buildings and 'marred so much German work of the same class'.[85]

In any case, Wallis seems to have been wedded to the notion of monumentality as a symbolic and status-bearing vocabulary for manufacturing industry, most often manifested in the inclusion of 'corner towers'. At the Wrigley building, these were represented by the solid ends, where vertical piers and glazing offset the horizontal lines of the rest of the structure. On the long elevations, a moulded pylon shape defined by a thick line of dark tile framed the lower three floors and bore the decorative motifs of tasselled nail-heads at the corners, with discs in reeded boxes intersecting the uprights at each floor level. The lightness of the long façade was, however, maintained by leaving the, then, attic-storey lights completely free. That, in itself, drew attention to the building as something interesting and different. The only other decorations were Wallis' familiar signature of reeded cornices, end-stopped by nail-heads. But here, the framing technique departs from the hitherto heavy enclosing by towers, attic and projecting cornice. The battered moulding accentuates and brings forward the building's most unusual structural feature as expressed externally, and differentiates between the types of structure and function. At the same time, it introduces a suggestion of parallax that binds the 'towers' to the main body and, by introduction of a diagonal line, relieves the ostensible separation of horizontal and vertical lines.

The extensions to the rear were of normal frame construction. Brackets inset into exterior walls suggest that wings were intended to be joined across the open end to form a centre court. Many alterations have taken place over the years: an attic storey has been added, windows have been replaced and mullions introduced across the front. At the rear, the outer bays have been opened up as an external promenade without glazing and a wall built one bay in from the outer edge to accommodate 'shop fronts' to separate industrial units. At the ends of the building, many windows have been bricked in and rendered over. The present decor has little to commend it.

Young, Osmond & Young

The existence of another 'deviant' of this transition period—a factory designed and built for Young, Osmond & Young, electric heater manufacturers, at Broad Water Road, Welwyn Garden City, Herts—was discovered purely by chance. In the archives of the India Tyre & Rubber Company of Inchinnan, Renfrewshire, Scotland, was a copy of a letter dated 17 December 1929 from Frank Cox to a sub-contractor, H. P. Wilkinson & Partners of London, asking for an electric water heater to be installed in the directors' lavatory at India Tyres. In suggesting an appropriate appliance, he wrote

> Messrs Young, Osmond & Young have a very efficient type in the factory we erected for them at Welwyn, and if you ring them and ask for Mr Petrie he will give you full information.

The Young, Osmond & Young factory is still standing, albeit now unoccupied. It is fast becoming derelict and is not accessible to internal inspection. It is set well back from Broad Water Road (a recent building now stands on what would have been its forecourt) and lies between plots occupied by the Shredded Wheat building designed by Louis de Soissons and what were the studios of British Instructional Films Ltd. The site does, however, back onto what was then the London North Eastern railway, with nearby station and bridge over the line leading to the town centre. Unfortunately, no plans, deposited plans or contemporary illustrations have been found of the Young, Osmond building; a precise date of the design thus cannot be arrived at. The design itself and its construction accord more closely with the mid-decade transition, but local records have Young, Osmond first occupying the factory in 1928, and trading there as Unity Heating Limited, manufacturers of tubular electric heaters.

The building is L-shaped, faces east and consists of a two-by-six bay block of two storeys, with an abutted bay at the south-west corner. What at first appears to be a routine reinforced concrete daylight/unit production building, with internal partitions for administration or separate processes, is most likely of steel frame with brick infill encased in concrete rendering. The windows are wide—pier to pier, with small-paned glazing in thin metal bars. But the front of the building is something new! Not new in being radically modern, but new in being a first appearance in the Wallis, Gilbert catalogue. The loading bay is on the righthand side of the factory, so the doors in the slightly projecting, full-height half bays at the outer edges of the front are for pedestrians. Each of these bays has a moulded panel indented at the top corners, leaving only a narrow border. Within each panel is an upper storey window, below which another half-height moulded panel curves to a central, bordered disc, and provides the doors' surrounds. Between the two door bays, the central feature has seven colossal, flat piers that override the stylobate with a prehensile grip, and reach up to a broad frieze that carries a narrow band of dark red bricks. Another broader band of dark bricks ties the frontage at roof level from end to end, and matches the basal plinth which levels the building on ground sloping gently to the right. Rebated windows intersecting the piers have a broad band of brick at first-floor level. Against the dark red brick and the transparency of the windows, the cement-rendered piers, door bays, frieze and stylobate stand out sharply and impressively. Here, perhaps, is the forerunner of colossal mullions and free-standing pillars that grace the more unusual of the designs of the 1930s.

An enlargement of the Young, Osmond factory is attached adjacent to and extends back from the abutment on the south-west side of the original, and is similar in style and construction. This was probably built when a firm producing confectionery took over the building at a later date. Innovative as tubular heaters were in the 1920s, advances in space heating eventually overtook them. Presently the site is part of a much larger area leased to Polycell Products Limited (which is part of Williams Holdings). Only the film studio (a listed building) is used by Polycell, which moved to the area in 1962 to its newly-built premises—such a quintessentially 'Sixties' design that it is worthy of protection.

The Gramophone Company Limited

The mid-1920s saw the beginning of a number of commitments by Wallis, Gilbert & Partners for works for foreign nationals, which are dealt with in section (d). During 1927–29, however, the final 'transitional' designs were undertaken for The Gramophone Company Limited of Hayes, Middlesex, a company that had been operating in Britain since 1898 but which had its origins in America and Germany.

The National Gramophone Company, manufacturers of gramophones and disc-records, was founded in New York, USA, in 1896 and formed the London-based Gramophone Company in 1898. At Maiden Lane, London, gramophones were assembled from imported American components; the company made its own recordings but the records were pressed in Hanover, Germany. By 1901 the company was unable to meet demand. In 1906 a 50-acre site was purchased at Hayes, Middlesex, part of the Dawlish Estate. A factory for pressing records was built in 1907, a gramophone cabinet shop in 1911, a machine shop in 1912, and other auxiliary service buildings;[86] the company marketed its products under the label 'His Master's Voice' (HMV).[87]

Demand fell after the First World War, when the popularity of jolly or sentimental war songs declined, but with the new 'Jazz Age' business was booming; by 1926 new buildings were required at Hayes. These were designed by Wallis, Gilbert & Partners. Competition with other record companies became very fierce and, circa 1930, the Gramophone Company merged with its closest rival, Columbia Records, to form a new company, EMI (Electric and Musical Industries Limited). In 1931 three large recording studios were built at the rear of a house purchased in Abbey Road, St John's Wood, London, to become the first ever custom-designed recording studios in the world. They, too, were designed by Wallis, Gilbert & Partners.[88]

The company is now owned by Thorn-EMI, manufacturers of electronic equipment at Hayes; the manufacturing of records and tapes is carried out by EMI at 2 Uxbridge Road, originally the factory of R. Woolf & Company (Rubber) Limited and also designed by Wallis, Gilbert & Partners, in 1936.[89]

In 1926–27 when large expansion plans were afoot, the Gramophone Company had become disenchanted with its current architect, R. Layton Coles (Appendix B(2)).[90] The machine shop built in 1912 by Truscon and designed by (Sir) Arthur Blomfield, had proved more satisfactory, although problems had arisen. Blomfield had designed in reinforced concrete at Friars House, Broad Street, London, for Holland & Hannan in 1909, in which the Kahn system of reinforcement had been used.[91] At Friars House the concrete frame was encased in Portland stone, but the Gramophone machine shop made no such pretensions to beauty. The exposed concrete frame bore no decoration and was relieved only by brick spandrels and glass infill. The water tower is particularly ugly and does nothing to enhance this very austere building. It now has a new owner; the building and its later extensions and additions are painted a uniform and unattractive grey.

But the Gramophone Company appears to have been content with Moritz Kahn's advice and assistance. Perhaps in 1926 when the need for extensive additional building became necessary, the company thought to have something more stylish than plain concrete or the rather ordinary brick buildings of earlier years. The buildings designed by Wallis, Gilbert & Partners for the Gramophone Company were as follows: January 1927—cabinet department extensions; November 1927—record store; 1927–28—research laboratories, the administration building extension and the power house; November 1928—evaporating plant extension; May 1929—shipping department. The

Fig. 16 The Gramophone Company, Hayes, Middlesex: aerial view of site, *c.* 1970s

location of the evaporating plant is not known, nor were the dates of the designs shown, but all had been built by 1930 (Fig. 16).

The cabinet department extensions
The existing cabinet building appears to have been a five-storey rectangular 'horse shoe' closed only at single-storey height at the north end of the glazed-over central well, but since built up at that end to the full five storeys. The extension by Wallis, Gilbert was, initially, to add on in similar form to the west wall, to form another hollow rectangle. The second part of the extension, when built, was sheared off at the south-west corner to make way for, or come up against, the shipping building, to which it was later joined by a bridging section. The door and stairway marked 'A' on a redrawn plan of 1980 appear on the elevation as a corner tower with narrow triple lights. Two corner towers on the north elevation, of similar outward appearance, house stairs and lift shaft. The building is of reinforced concrete, supported on a regular grid pattern, in which only stairs and lifts are walled up; other sectioning is by partition. Apart from the Wallis, Gilbert towers, the building is undecorated, to match the existing one. It thus accords most closely with the machine shop of 1912 and, thereby, with the plain Truscon format.

The record store

Although the building was eventually bridged to the cabinet department, it was originally designed in 1927 as a free-standing new build. The architects were therefore allowed a freer rein in respect of styling. The building faces south, outward from the main site. The space available was roughly an elongated triangle and was hemmed in by the record manufacturing section (now demolished) to the north, the cabinet building to the west, other manufacturing plant on the east, and the Great Western railway on the south. The building itself follows the shape of the site, rising six storeys to 85 feet at roof level. Behind the parapet, services housing, the ventilation plant and the corner towers rise above that height. The grid pattern of stanchions is aligned with the south wall, the only internal solid walls being those that encase stairwells, lift shafts and sanitary facilities. All of those, except the main goods lift, are contained within the corner towers. Administration offices, divided by partitions on the fifth floor, also made use of rooms above roof level in the corner towers.

On the inner, north side wall, at ground level, large doors to three-bays' width gave access to the goods lift, the goods-in and despatch areas. All remaining floor space was given over to storage of the various categories of records. The two stanchions on either side of the goods access are of larger section than the others to support the wide opening, and they rise to the full height of the building. Otherwise, stanchions decrease in section in ascending order. At the fifth floor they are sufficiently narrow to be placed inside the windows, so that uninterrupted glazing on that floor runs the full length of the building on the south side and contributes to the aesthetic appearance of that elevation.

The north walls, largely hidden by other buildings at the time of construction, are utilitarian and reflect the structure. So the building turned its public face to the outside world. The corner towers form part of the framing of the south wall but, in this instance, are real, functional entities. The west tower has small, square windows in sets of three to ventilate and light the lavatories on each floor, with solid spandrels for privacy. The narrow tower that forms the whole of the east end contains the main entrance for visitors and staff; above that, a tall, narrow light illuminates and expresses the stairway. As presently standing, replacement windows are blanked out at each floor. The decorative formwork on that side remains as originally built— but not as originally proposed. In an architects' impression the east tower is very much in the Masonry style. The south elevation, however, brings the building into the 'transitional' stage, with a lighter form of framing. On the outer edge, moulded concrete, stepped, battered and highlighted by a line of black and white faience, surrounds the framing section of the fifth-storey windows and the narrow vertical lights. Within an inner band of stepped concrete, the 'daylight' windows form a chequered pattern of columns and spandrels, expressing the structure. Decorative formwork extends the horizontal line of the innermost frame into a string course that straps the framed area to the corner towers. The form of this decoration differs in various illustrations of the south front. Surviving plans and a sketch in *Building*[92] show a more elaborate ornamentation and a new curved motif. The architects' impression of the façade and an illustration in their *Industrial Architecture*[93] appear to show nail-heads at each end of the ribbed section. The illustration accompanying Douglas Wallis' article in *Architecture*[94] and a company photograph of the early 1940s show no formwork decoration at all. The true, as-built version appears to be that shown in an advertisement for Mellowes' windows and has short, ribbed bands, each terminating in a single nail-head, to complete the run of smaller nail-heads at the upper end of each column. The building as now standing supports this view, although the faience line has been painted over.

In the years prior to the purchase of land that extended the Gramophone site to the railway boundary, the company had been conscious of its public view to passengers on the Great Western railway. The company's title had been boldly displayed on the south side of the boiler house and the HMV symbol stood high on the weather vane over the administration building. These were hidden by later building, but the identity and prestige of the company would have been enhanced by the proud façade of the record store and recognition that such buildings were necessary to the company and affordable by it.

Further to the north, on what was the original Gramophone site at Hayes, intersected by Blyth Road, other buildings designed by Wallis, Gilbert & Partners were erected in 1927–28. Apart from Blomfield's concrete block of 1912, all the buildings in that area are/were of brick. The most outstanding of the early brick buildings is the administration block, to which Wallis, Gilbert added an extension fronting to Trevor Road.

The administration building extension
The original building is of brick with stone dressing, has gabled pavilion ends and a marked central doorway. It also has some unusual features: patent *triple* glazing to the directors' offices on the first floor, to ensure draught-free ventilation and suppression of factory noise; a large panelled room on the top floor has a ceiling that can be lowered or raised as required acoustically for recording purposes. All of the buildings gradually became obsolete and edged on to dereliction, but the ceiling mechanism still exists among the wooden rafters of the roof. The clock lantern bore a weather vane upon which the dog 'Nipper' and his gramophone proclaimed HMV to the surrounding area.

Earlier extensions had repeated the hipped roof format, with two blocks at the rear in London stocks, and leaving two walls closed off at the east side by similar buildings of two storeys. Wallis, Gilbert's commission was to build to three storeys across the open west end. No plans have survived, but the interior of the building is still arranged in offices of various sizes with a central staircase and lift, reached across the hall from the central doorway. The architects' impression is different from as-built, but only in regard to the corner towers and the treatment of the doorway. In Wallis' illustration in *Industrial Architecture*[95] the second-floor corner windows are also different, but the now-standing version does not appear to be a later replacement.

Even so, the administration building extension is a handsome building, well-matched in style and materials to its neighbour, and more so when the top hamper of the towers in the proposed view had been abandoned. Patently, difficulties arose in linking into the hipped roofs of the three- and four-storey buildings to which it was to be attached. Viewed from the upper storeys of taller buildings, the connections seem a little odd, but have given no trouble with leakages. The stone quoining, the doorway pediment over a Venetian window, the console porch and patera decoration have a Baroque tinge reminiscent of Wallis' very early designs for public buildings, still rather 'bitty' and incoherent. Indeed, the extension could have been the work of any medium-talented architect of the period. Only the battered door surround and the nail-heads terminating ribbed strips on either side declare it to be a Thomas Wallis building. Remarkably, despite the failure in detail, the building does present a very satisfying and successful composition. Across from the administration building facing to Blyth Road, the company renewed its power house.

The new power house
This was styled more in the spirit of the buildings to the south. Its date is not known but the need for additional power would have coincided with the general expansion of 1927–29 and the major conversion to electricity. Changing technology and the possibility of cleaner operating are revealed in the shape and the large glazed areas of the new concrete building, in contrast to the design of the older, brick-built boiler house beside it (but now over-painted to match). Nothing is remembered on site, beyond its being noted in plan files, of the extension to the evaporating plant. It has to be assumed that, when the building and its extension came to the end of their purpose, they were demolished or brought to different usage. One other building designed by Wallis, Gilbert in the original part of the site was the research laboratory, which probably dates from 1928 and was sited on Trevor Road.

The research laboratory
An industry overwhelmed by demand for its products at home and overseas needed to find ways of fulfilling the demand economically and technically and of developing its products to compete for and maintain its share of the market. A decision for total manufacture, as opposed to buying in com-ponents, broadened the range and number of topics for research and

development, but meant that with the provision of a purpose-built facility, a more integrated and cooperative approach could be achieved. The Gramophone Company decided that investment in a separately-housed research department was worthwhile.

The research laboratory faced on to Trevor Road to the north of the administration building. It was demolished some years ago; the only available plans are re-drawings of 1980 and include later extensions. The original building has, on each of six storeys, workshops and laboratories placed each side of a corridor running the length of the secondary axis. There was access at both ends to stairways and sanitary facilities on each floor. The central entrance was to a hallway that contained the main stairway and lift, and then led directly to a double-storeyed auditorium projecting from the rear of the main building. There, equipment was installed for experimentation and testing recording and acoustic control.

The building was (probably) of concrete-encased steel frame, with brick and glass infill. Wallis, Gilbert's artistic impression and a published illustration show a larger building with corner towers. The as-built version is shown in *Industrial Architecture*[96] and on the site view in which the building extends only to the inner brick verticals. With the brick-faced attic storey and plinth, they produce the 'picture frame' effect seen some three years earlier at Solex. The framed area is marked off at base by a concrete string course and, at its head, by a narrow projecting cornice and ribbed band. The skeleton structure is expressed on that part of the façade but the concrete verticals, stopped at base and head with tasselled nail-heads, are more emphatic than the broader, recessed horizontals and add visual height to a building so strongly defined by the frame of darker and different material. The enclosing nature of the frame is relieved by the battered, faience-trimmed doorway that repeats the framing effect. By drawing the eye to the centre and away from the large, outer frame, the doorway visually collects and stabilises the variety of punctuation surrounding it. The as-built version is much more compact and less grandiose than the one proposed. The use of brick was clearly appropriate to the older area of the site, but the revision of the styling has the more modern aura of 'transition' building and provides a coeval link with other Wallis, Gilbert buildings on site.

The last of these, for the shipping department, completed a trio of reinforced concrete buildings on the south side. Seen from the railway and the new road, they form an impressive and memorable group. The shape of the buildings was largely determined by what land was available on an already cramped site, their size by the demand for the company's product— the huge and fast-growing popularity of gramophones and records. The impact of this group of three monumental creatures just over the brow of the incline is considerable today; in the 1930s it would have been even more so (Fig. 17).

Fig. 17 The Gramophone Company, Hayes, Middlesex: view from Dawlish Avenue—(left to right) shipping building, cabinet building, record store

The shipping building
This building sits to the west of the cabinet building, to which it was joined by a single steel bridge at the sixth storey. Later connections are at lower floors. On the ground plan, the building represents a rectangle 213 feet by 75 feet, arranged on a grid of 22 feet centres, with columns decreasing in diameter through the upper five storeys. On the north side is a loading bay, serviced by a railway siding and glazed over at single-storey height with a rebating of the upper floors. The six-storey projections on either side of the loading bay and the south-east wall, are of normal reinforced concrete frame structure, with brick and glass infill. The radical feature of the bulk of this building is that, like the Wrigley factory, it is supported by mushroom columns. One advantage of building beyond the boundaries of the London County Council was that innovations of that kind and of building over three storeys in reinforced concrete could be carried out with impunity. On this occasion, unlike the case at Wrigley, Wallis achieved the all-glass corner on the north-west end of the building, but only because this was a temporary end awaiting future extension to 950 feet overall. The extension was never built, but would undoubtedly have terminated in a solid wall to accommodate services, as in the built section. Thus the problem with mushroom construction again presented itself: of shielding sanitary facilities and supporting stairways and lift shafts—the latter not only for decency's sake, but because, when open and in the event of fire, they provide a hazardous chimney draught. The writer of an article devoted to this building regarded the 'frame-like decorative motif' on the south side as a 'sort of huge architrave which is similar to the one on the older building fronting the railway' (record store) and so 'foreign' to the rest of the structure that association with the older building 'seems not worth while'.[97]

The need for new buildings at Gramophone was sudden and rapid, so that their placing on site was not part of an overall development plan. As demand urgently occasioned, buildings were fitted in as best they could be. Management was more concerned with adequate water and power supply, fire hazards, routes on site and the satisfactory, economic and speedy construction of the new buildings.[98] With the benefit of one firm of architects designing the triple group, some kind of association of style was both practical and aesthetically sensible. In criticising such association, the commentator omitted to suggest how access and servicing needs to all floors could have been met in a rectangular glass tank meant for storage and despatch. But he did admit that this group of buildings 'has a certain striking beauty, specially on the side facing the railway'.[99]

Given the structure of the building, however, the cantilevered floors could, where appropriate, have been curtained wholly in glass but, in the interests of safety, a low breast wall was built into the base of each run of windows. That increased the dead load on the floor edges. Floor projection therefore had to be limited to the extent that the narrow space between floor edge and outer row of mushrooms was largely unusable.

Within the building, storage space and the many offices for referencing and shipping documentation were partitioned off, some glazed, some solid. Mushroom construction lends itself to large, open span but partitioning of that kind of structure for offices and reference stations is neither simple to erect nor pleasing in effect (Fig. 18). Most of the upper floors of the shipping building are no longer in use and the partitioning is being dismantled. In altering internal arrangements or reorganising operations, mushroom

Fig. 18 The Gramophone Company, Hayes, Middlesex: shipping building, problems presented by mushroom columns on reorganisation

Fig. 19 The Gramophone Company, Hayes, Middlesex: shipping building, roof reservoir

construction does not offer the flexibility for re-use found with conventional reinforced concrete frame. Further, in attempting to attach rechannelled services and power lines, penetrating the essential hardness of the concrete slab floors has often defied the best of tools and craftsmen.

Figure 19 shows another unusual feature of the shipping building: the flat roof was constructed as a huge reservoir, surrounded and crossed by narrow catwalks. The quantity of water stored and available for purposes other than fire-fighting has, over the years, proved an invaluable investment. Here the architects were able to carry out this innovative practicality, projected but unexecuted in the Cambrian Candle design of 1920.

Decoration of the solid end of the shipping building is fairly minimal. The composition expresses the structure and its internal use. Plain, stepped pendants form capitals to projecting piers, a ribbed band extends around the plain tower heads and recessed service housing on the roof. The general appearance strongly resembles the south elevation of the Wrigley building. Further similarities occur on the long southern elevation, although only one part of the ultimate framing can be seen on the shipping building. There are the same discs in reeded boxes terminating the low-wall horizontals on the battered, moulded concrete frame, and there are similar ribbed cornices. But the extra two storeys provided room for a second, outer frame—and there are no mullions to interrupt the long runs of glazing. The shipping building is therefore more in line with the Modern Movement than was the Wrigley factory, but where its decoration differs from Wrigley it comes closer to the 'Fancy' style of Wallis, Gilbert & Partners. Before being painted over, the inner frame showed two lines of coloured tiles and, on the upper corner of the outer frame and on either side of the logo pediment, are the ram's-horn motifs, already used to great effect on a Fancy factory that predates it. The asymmetry of this south elevation, as standing, supports the view that the fully-extended building would have been completed in like manner at its south-western end. By itself, the framing may well have been insufficient to visually hold together the very long façade; what kind of central feature may have been envisaged? In its standing form, very little has been made of doorways. As suggested in respect of the unbuilt designs of 1918–20, in the heavier, Masonry form, Wallis was not at his best in designing elevations of tall, long-fronted buildings. Most of the Fancy factories were long-fronted, but low, with more powerful framing and a lot more colour. The prototypes were already off the drawing board when the Gramophone record store was commissioned, but it was never a style for six-storey buildings. Hence only gestures in that direction were made for the Gramophone set.

(b) The Mid-term Period 1927–35—The Fancy Factories

By the later years of the 1920s, the general ethos was brighter, more daring; the 1925 Paris Exhibition had introduced Art Deco; the Egyptian style was still very popular. English vernacular or the Arts and Crafts genre were still preferred for private housing, to differentiate from Georgian 'council' houses, but places of entertainment were more numerous, more colourful and, above all, glamorous. American influence on public and private life was more marked and Americans who invaded British industry to circumvent the 1927 Tariff Act brought with them their own ideas of factory planning. Business was picking up. New trunk roads leading out of London were opening up new areas for development; the distribution of electricity was being rationalised, encouraging more extensive use of a more reliable source.

There was an increase in large-scale manufacturing. Companies moving to, or setting up on new and larger sites were considering lateral-flow production in preference to the gravitational system of multi-storey buildings. Constructional steel was more readily available and more economically competitive with reinforced concrete.

In their designs of these few years, Wallis, Gilbert & Partners responded to the many influences and, in celebration, produced the 'Fancy' factories. But not many of them. The flowering was brief but glorious, and withered with the frost of economic recession. A few in similar style were designed by other architects. Wallis, Gilbert & Partners—best known for the genre, and the genre for Wallis, Gilbert—designed only 10, of which nine were built. The last of them overlapped the 'later period' by three years.

The outstanding new feature was the introduction of coloured decoration. For the rest, there were new and unusual motifs, an elaboration of main entrances, and landscaping. There was something of all the styles then popular, as well as Modern, and there were new forms of layout. Mostly there was a new 'concrete' aesthetic, even when steel frame formed the building's skeleton. But there was no longer the kind of basic theme found with the Masonry type where, despite appropriate variations, a recognisable homogeneity existed. With so much that was new, however, tradition was not abandoned. The homogeneity achieved in the various Fancy designs was a coherent welding of old and new—and more successfully than in wide-spread attitudes of the time. The Masonry factory had produced a modern building out of Edwardian Baroque classicism. The Fancy factory, in looking backwards and forwards at the same time was, in accord with the contemporary ethos, the true Janus building.

The Shannon Company Limited

The first Fancy factory, in rather tentative form, was designed in 1927 for The Shannon Company Limited of Burlington Road, Kingston Bypass, New Malden, Surrey. This company manufactured office equipment and furniture under a 'Shannon' trademark. The eponymous principals of the firm were personal friends of Thomas Wallis in the circle that included manufacturers in a similar field, such as Lamson Paragon and Caribonum.

The building plans for a new factory and offices at 175 Burlington Road, Raynes Park (variously referred to elsewhere as Malden, Kingston, and now in the Borough of Merton) were handed over to the company in 1970 and appear to have been lost. But plans deposited with the local authority are still extant and are dated May 1927. They show a south-facing, long-fronted, two-storeyed block, nine bays by two of 25 by 20 feet, with a single-storey, north-light area adjoining at the rear, but of which only some two-thirds of the whole was to be built 'under present contract'. Many delays occurred before permission to build was granted, as amendments of (often minor) constructional details were pressed. Eventually, Frank Cox pointed out to the planning authorities the urgency of his clients' possibly losing their option on the land while having to evacuate their existing premises at Dalston when the lease expired on 31 July 1928. They had expected, said Mr Cox, to occupy the new building at that date; time to build was becoming a vital issue.[100]

When the building was constructed in 1928, the design was executed *in toto*, not in the projected consecutive parts, but the ground plan was re-arranged. In the built work, the proposed western-end main doorway was transposed to the eastern end of the façade. There were three central loading bays shown on the elevations of 16 May 1927 not the two vehicular entrances flanked by footways as on the ground plan of the same date. The goods entrances/despatch bays presumably still led directly to the assembly and warehousing sections at the rear, but the relocation of the main front entrance and the inclusion of the proposed cabinet factory must, however, have caused the transposing of internal functions from west to east, particularly affecting the office layout.

The north-light, single-storey building attached at the rear of the frontal block was constructed of reinforced concrete columns, steel beams and roof trusses, 'Daylight' windows with stone lintels and brick spandrels. Sanitary facilities, coal store and boiler house were proposed to be annexed to side elevations, leaving uninterrupted floor space for production purposes. The relocating and partitioning off of internal functions would not, therefore, have been difficult. This area terminated in a thin wall, for future extension. Wallis, Gilbert were responsible for extensions in 1957.[101]

The front block, of reinforced concrete by Truscon, has some kinship with the buildings for Houghton-Butcher and Stannard—that is, long-fronted, two-storeyed, with corner towers, one of which contains the main doorway, the other acting as compositional balance. But, unlike the orthodox Masonry style, there is no attic storey or penultimate, heavy cornice to join corner towers into framing an area of glass and piers (although there are identifying nail-heads to signify the designers). At Shannon, the framing is not formed by the structure, but is a separate decorative element that projects forward of the towers and surrounds a 'colonnading' of the structural piers. The battered line of the frame acts, as at Wrigley, as a suggestion of parallax to tie in the corner towers.

In reproduced photographs of the Shannon building, the low walls at the bases of the windows, albeit recessed, do produce rather too-emphatic horizontal lines. But, as the main block was faced with *white* concrete,[102] the interplay of light and dark—white concrete against dark, reflective glass, the variation in shading produced by projections and recessions—would have incurred a rhythmic effect in which neither plane achieved constant dominance. All that was checked, however, and contained, by the colour and different material of the faience trimming, throwing the moulded, stepped frame into prominence. The role of the faience strip was to define and accentuate the main features of the building—framing the façade and logo pediment, the doorway, the end windows and tower caps. At the same time, it projects a feeling of cheerful lightheartedness of which concrete by itself was rarely capable.

Like most of the Fancy factories, Shannon was its own advertisement, striking the eye of the passing motorist. The modern man, whirring by in his motor car on the new, fast bypass road, would remember the unusual, modern building and the name of its product. But more than that. Once the viewer became the customer and passed through the pedestal gateposts, the curving path turned him to where more pedestals, shorter and bearing fancy metal lamp standards, and a distinctively-marked architrave, indicated the building's entrance. The rebating of the doorway, the stepping back of its framing above quarter-round plinths, drew the customer into the building.

This processional way is more than just signposted by decorative motifs, as at GEC; it is planned as an almost relentless path. Its like was to be elaborated still further at later Fancy factories, of which Shannon was the prototype. The kind of framing effect, first seen on the Wrigley factory and later on the Gramophone building, was a means of treating the appearance of large, tall buildings—a more modern way of relieving the mass of concrete and glass. In the Fancy factories, framing found its natural milieu, becoming a live element in the total concept of what the building was all about.

The Shannon factory is still standing. Unfortunately, it has been totally enveloped in silver and coloured corrugated aluminium by the owner Queensway Carpets, being rather more interested in the prime location than the appearance of the original building. Only the gateposts and fence are visible survivors. The object of the public face of the Shannon building was to attract and capture the customer. The object of the planning and layout was to enable the customer to, there and then, deal with all aspects of the transaction. Now, however, the building has been disembowelled and acts wholly as a large retail shop and warehouse. Shannon occupied the building until the mid-1970s; the company name still exists as a subsidiary of Twinlock plc, Beckenham, Kent.

A second factory of this ilk was also designed in 1927 but exists only on plan and, so far as can be ascertained, represents the only one not built. This was for Graham Amplion Limited, Crofton Park, London.

Graham Amplion Limited

The block plan for this scheme shows a site extending west from an opening onto Perry Hill between Crofton Park and Lower Sydenham, on which an office block, laboratory and main factory were to be built. Surviving plans, referring only to the laboratory, are dated 3 October 1927 and show both a single- and a two-storey version (Fig. 20). Both are for front elevations and show a battered frame and an elaborate doorway, set against corner towers.

'Amplion' was the trade name of wireless loud speakers produced by Alfred Graham & Company Limited. In 1911 the company was described as 'electrical engineers' at Crofton Park Road, Brackley and, in 1924, as telephone manufacturers at Caxton House, Tothill Street, London (Wallis, Gilbert's founding address). In November 1926, a new private company of the same name was registered, possibly with a view to building a new factory at Crofton Park. The site shown on the block plan is now a residential area but the houses are of late 1920s style. Perhaps the company was not permitted to purchase the site for manufacturing purposes; a few years later it is found established at St Andrews Works, Slough, Bucks.[103]

The two-storey building proposed to be built at Perry Hill shows a

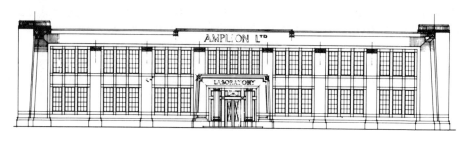

MAIN ELEVATION
LABORATORY BLOCK.

Fig. 20 Graham Amplion Ltd, Perry Hill, London (unexecuted): proposed two-storey laboratory, front elevation, 1927

colonnaded front with dressed capitals within a battered, ribbed frame set against corner towers. A line of faience defines the frame, the pediment, possibly the tower caps and the central doorway. The relation with Shannon is clear, but here the conflation of classical and Egyptian is more pronounced. The doorway is more complex and more ornate than the Shannon entrance; centrally-placed and almost a duplicate of the façade, it offers a two-fold invitation to enter. Not since the GEC administration building had so much been made of a main entrance. Presumably the entrance halls of Shannon and Amplion would have been equally as attractive and welcoming as at GEC but no data have survived.

It may be that the Graham Amplion commission was aborted before plans were drawn for the office block and main factory, but a commission from the Firestone Tire & Rubber Company of Akron, Ohio, USA, for a new factory beside the Great West Road at Brentford, Middlesex, gave occasion to implement and develop the ideas contained in the Amplion elevation.

Firestone Tyre & Rubber Company

So many myths have arisen and been perpetuated; so many contradictory judgements have been passed, that the historical importance of the Firestone factory has never been realised. So many things came together at Firestone, revealing attitudes to work and profit-making, the nature of advertising and consumerism, the philosophy and capability of the architects, attitudes and beliefs about industry/trade/factories—in both contemporary commentary and subsequent architectural history in relation to the building. It was Firestone that revealed the paradoxes, Firestone that brought down opprobrium on the architects' heads.

The client was an American company that had operated a distribution agency in Britain since 1915 at Tottenham Court Road, London. In 1927 foreign trade was increasing rapidly, but the shipment of tyres to Britain and the imposition of $33\frac{1}{3}$ per cent import duty was costing the company US $15 000 (around £4000) per week. The decision was made to manufacture in England. The commission to Wallis, Gilbert & Partners was the company's first overseas factory. The character, and what may have been the expectations, of this client are illuminated by a brief reference to the company's existing plant in America. Harvey Firestone founded the Firestone Tire & Rubber Company in Akron in 1900. The company prospered by virtue of aggressive salesmanship and continual improvement of merchandise and manufacturing techniques. To accommodate a move into volume production, coincidental with the rapid development of the automobile industry (an order from the Ford Motor Company for 10 000 sets of tyres), a new factory was built in 1910. Towards the design of the new plant, Harvey Firestone 'concentrated for many months on ways of arranging the most effective layout', studying the movement of processes with the aid of a small model and a piece of string.[104]

The new factory was designed by Osborn Engineering of Cleveland, Ohio, and stood on a 15-acre site on the outskirts of Akron, near to four railway connections. It was set back from the roadway with an intervening railed-off lawn and organised in layout as a central passageway extending back from the main entrance, with four wings on each side. The proposed view was not dissimilar from as-built. The arrangement ensured optimum natural light and ventilation and the design allowed for further extension of any of the wings without interruption of production. The 'most modern principles of hygiene and fireproofing' were incorporated. The structure is of steel and concrete, brickfaced, and with three-quarters of the external surface glazed. Auxiliary buildings for power, cement mixing, and so on, were adjacent and a pumping station to ensure an independent water supply from a lake one mile distant. (The many other tyre manufacturers in Akron relied on the unreliable source of leasing rights to water from an old canal.) Recreational, canteen, medical and other worker facilities were added in 1915.[105] A fifth storey and a clocktower were added later. Wallis, Gilbert & Partners would have understood their client's views on factory design; they were very similar to their own.

The site chosen for the British Firestone Tyre & Rubber Company factory was west of London at Brentford, 28.3 acres of the Syon Estate, formerly farm and orchard land, with a frontage of 1260 feet to the Great West Road—a new six-lane arterial highway opened in 1925. Bounded by road, canal and railway (to which new sidings were laid), the site was awkwardly-shaped but the dimensions of the original factory left space for future extension. The surface of the site was very uneven; levelling began in December 1927 and excavations for the foundations and basement in March 1928.

The initial plans were submitted in February 1928, with revisions and plans for ancillary buildings in the ensuing months. The main block consisted of a south-facing, two-storeyed administration building, behind which was adjoined a single-storeyed, north-light production factory, backed by a four-storey block for storage, repairs, intake and despatch. The flow of operations took a different path from all previous Wallis, Gilbert designs. Materials entered at the rear of the multi-storey building via a loop road from the highway; manufacturing processes followed a U-shaped layout through the single-storey building with a double, parallel line of machines, returning to the multi-storey block with finished goods for storage and despatch. A four-storey cement section jutted forward from the west corner of the south wall of the multi-storey building. Beyond the top curve of the loop road were the power house and chimney, the water tower to feed the sprinkler system, three sunken water reservoirs, pump houses and the garage (Fig. 21).

Down the centre of the whole building, from south to north, a mezzanine floor projected over the production area from the first floor of the administration building (Fig. 22). On the same line below ground, a tunnel containing all service lines and power supply ran forward from the power house, permitting convenience of maintenance and access to the basement rooms.

It is as well here to correct some contemporary and subsequently repeated reports. It is true that, after informed discussion, *contract* plans were drawn within three weeks.[106] Wallis liked to be known for the speed with which the practice could submit a design—the office was organised to that end and it was persuasive in getting a commission. It was perhaps politic therefore to omit to mention that plans for Firestone continued to be drawn and redrawn over the following six months. The story lingers, however, in comments such as '. . . they [Wallis, Gilbert & Partners] designed the Firestone factory in

Fig. 21 Firestone Tyre & Rubber Co, Great West Road, Brentford, Middlesex: view from Great West Road, *c.* 1950

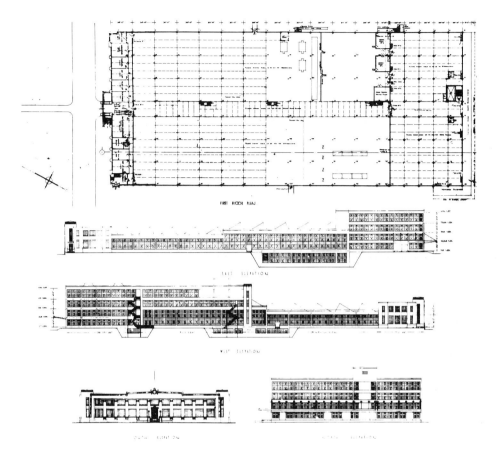

Fig. 22 Firestone Tyre & Rubber Co, Great West Road, Brentford, Middlesex: plans—
ground floor (American first floor), elevations and sections

three weeks and got it built in eighteen'.[107] The report that only 18 weeks
elapsed between the arrival on site of the main contractor (Sir Robert
McAlpine & Sons) and the production of the first tyre,[108] is also true but refers
only to the building of the superstructure and again bears the mark of
publicity-seeking. What was done in 18 weeks was indeed a considerable feat
for which acknowledgement is owed to the remarkable organising of
construction by the Progress Chart system around the future flow-of-
production plan. Railway lines were laid on site to facilitate movement of
materials; tyre manufacturing machines were installed in progressive order
as each section was completed. But a considerable amount of construction
work had preceded the arrival of the 'main contractor' in June 1928 and the
factory was not complete when the ceremonial production of the first tyre
took place on 16 October 1928. Work on the foundations and basement, due
for completion on 5 June, was a separate contract from the superstructure—

although Sir Robert McAlpine & Sons was the contractor for *both* sections. Photographs taken fortnightly throughout construction show work already done by June and work still awaiting completion in October. But, as Frank Cox pointed out somewhat forcefully at India Tyres, first the building must be ready for use.

Published sources in 1929 also state that the purpose of the mezzanine floor was as a supervision gallery. Its purpose on plan, in the specifications and bills of quantities of May 1928, as built and in subsequent use, was always to house lavatories, washrooms and cloakrooms and personal lockers.[109] Here was another solution to the placing of essential facilities—not abutted, not outdoors, not taking up working floor space—but up in the air, bothering no one and yet in clear view of supervision from the floor! The factory was, and continued to be reported, as a 'reinforced concrete building'. The foundations, basement and floors were of reinforced concrete by Truscon. All the superstructure was of steel frame, mostly concrete clad with brick and glass infill.

The main building measured 200 feet on frontage by 467 feet in depth, of which the administration building accounted for one bay's depth at ground level and two bays' depth at the first floor. Most of the building was constructed on a grid pattern of 30 feet square, except for the mezzanine supports at 20 feet wide and the multi-storey building of 20 feet in depth. The main entrance was on the centre front of the administration building and reserved for management and visitors. Staff and production workers entered on the east side of the office block, where a small hallway gave access to a corridor running the full width of the building at the rear of the offices, and to the works area. From that hall, a metal stairway led to the canteen and kitchens that occupied most of the east wing of the first floor. Unusually, the main canteen was 'integrated', in the sense that it was open to men and women, staff and works personnel. For the canteen staff, convenience of operation was worked out in minute detail. A 'hospital' on the ground floor provided first-aid facilities until an independent medical centre was built at a later date.

Dining rooms for directors and senior management were also on the first floor, to the east of the double-storeyed central hall and were reached by the stairway from that hall. Works managers' offices were on the ground floor of the west wing, a laboratory on the east side, both with direct access to the works area, while the Superintendent of Labour had his office immediately adjacent to the works entrance in the east tower. Managerial offices and the conference room, both wood panelled and artistically decorated, were at the further end of the first-floor west, with showroom and general offices nearer the hallway, each side of a central corridor.

Working conditions in the production area were superior to those found in most north-light buildings of the time, certainly so far as light and ventilation were concerned. At that time tyres were core-built by hand, requiring much heavier physical labour than the drum-built system introduced within a year or two. There were opening lights in the roof and on the side elevations, to ensure cross-ventilation. Most north-light factory gables were pierced only by small porthole windows but, at Firestone, the 'Daylight' glazed infill not only gave more natural light but also visual access for the workers to the outside world. The raised portion of the north-light roof towards the rear was to accommodate taller machines such as calenders and mixers. The four-storey abutment in the west, rear corner contained the cement section, with a gravitational feed system to the works floor. Fabric storage and spreading rooms were glazed like the rest of the works area but the cement-making section was walled in to prevent air pollution; it had a separate fire escape. A sprinkler system was installed throughout the factory and offices.

Planning of the layout, servicing lines and circulation pattern was very complex indeed. But, once organised, the operating system within the plant was very simple and efficient. Apart from people who worked in the ancillary buildings, once an employee entered the east door, the pattern of his/her working day was laid out under one roof—including access to all facilities. The production system benefited piecework employees, progress chasing, resolution of hold-ups and breakdowns, and supervision at both factory floor and office level. And, given the state of the art, all in the healthiest working conditions, with the best of amenities and in more salubrious surroundings than many industrial plants of the time.

Firestone was completely new build, on a prime site in a semi-rural area, but fronting a new, major highway. Here there was no need to reach a compromise with existing works methods or buildings, or with adjacent premises. All of the architects' experience and philosophy could be enmeshed with the client's requirements and very similar approach. And whatever might be the purely American influence on the design (certainly the integrated canteen was not a product of the British class system) this was a British factory where the architects' knowledge of the milieu and the contemporary ethos would be important to its success. The comprehensiveness of the design is such that no part can be faithfully discussed in isolation; the appearance of the factory is therefore as integral as any other aspect.

The structure of the buildings as a clothed skeleton frame is indicated by the planes of support and the large areas of glazing. The variety of structural forms expresses the buildings' functions and differentiates between them. The single-storey, north-light section traditionally typifies a manufacturing section of open floor space, housing machines that needed to be anchored to a solid foundation, but the unusual expanse of glass suggests a more modern approach to improved lighting and ventilation. The multi-storey block suggests lighter weight machinery and, in the restricted ceiling heights and long loading bays, storage, intake and despatch. Its flat-roofed, undecorated, rectilinear form is the steel-framed version of Kahn's Daylight unit system; at the same time, it is characteristic of the Modernists' interpretation of a 'machine age' industrial building. The chimney indicates the location of the power house, the controlled massiveness of which expresses its internal purpose. While not appearing too unfinished, the thin ends of the administration building forecast extensions by a company with confidence in its own future. The structure of the building displays a logical distinction between manufacturing and business functions. But more than that, advantage was taken of its face to the road for the company to make its most public statement.

Profit making was the object of the enterprise but many other things combined in that pursuit. The company had to be seen as a good company, as viable, stable, confident, up to date and forward-looking; also as a good employer; as a purveyor of products people preferred to buy—product-selling followed on-line from product-making. In the art of salesmanship and advertising, a company is 'selling' itself—its standing and its mark becoming integral to the commodity. For a company like Firestone, which regarded quality and reliability as major selling points, a public statement by way of its British headquarters building had to be more than a superficial gloss.

The designer's task, in presenting the statement three-dimensionally, was to relate all parts to the whole in a corporate identity that expressed how the company saw itself and how it wished to be seen and understood. For an industry that was part of the new machine age and with no tradition of its own, the Modern concrete idiom might have appeared eminently suitable, especially when located beside a new arterial road on which its products were intended to be used. But that style lacked favour with the British purchasing public and it was too noncommittal, too anonymous for a firm that wished to catch the eye and the favour of the passing motorist. Something with a municipal flavour, as introduced by Sir Bannister Fletcher in the Gillette factory in 1935 when the area was largely built up, was also inappropriate to the first industrial occupant of a near-rural landscape.

Alternatively, classical language still held unequivocal status, prestige and meaning in contemporary architectural design, and came naturally to Thomas Wallis. Further, Modern Movement disciples asserted that their style derived from classical sources; Traditionalists regarded an updated version of classicism as appropriate to the times. As the chosen style, it would be a fitting gesture to the historical origins of the Firestone site, provide a means of relating to each other the variety of functions expressed in the structure and also form the basis of 'good shape and proportion' that Wallis considered essential to industrial buildings.[110] But enlivened, nevertheless, with *eclectic* detail (related that is, to the word's classical etymology—'to choose' from the best of everything) for what Wallis called the 'necessary cunning introduced for some purpose just where its value is most desired'.[111]

Full advantage was taken of the building's position on site. Set back from the roadway on rising ground, its first impact was that of a white temple sitting high and proud between green lawns and the clear light of an open sky. Engaged columns were recessed into a well-defined rectangle and decisively framed by a white-concrete architrave and stylobate, set against Wallis' familiar corner towers. By day, contrasts of colour and materials, of light and dark, of stillness and movement engaged attention. Within the huge, static form of the white frame, a bejewelled colonnade was captured by a line of blue faience. In blue, green and vermilion, ceramic lotus-petal capitals were joined to bound-palmleaf bases by vermilion-beaded arrises on artificial stone-faced columns, set against a dark plane of glass. Seen from the roadway, the three-dimensional modelling of the façade and the progressive recession in form and tone created a depth that intensified the invitation presented by the causeway from road to threshold.

The processional way at Firestone was a masterpiece of invention, ostensibly modelled on the ascent of the Acropolis in Athens to the Temple of Athena, goddess of arts, crafts and mechanical skills. There, after ascending the ramp, celebrants passed through the white marble colonnade of the Attic Propylaea, then through a high, dark hall, richly painted in blue and gold, to emerge into the blinding light of sacred places—here, presumably the temple of industry. It all fits very well. There were the ramp and the colonnade. The Firestone hall was cramped, double-storeyed and poorly lit, but mysterious in blue and gold, with reflected light making the white marble floor and the black marble trimming glisten. Egress was directly ahead to the brightly lit factory floor or, by the narrow stairway that turned a short, quick 90 degrees at the right rear, climbed steeply, clockwise around the room, across a half landing over the doorway and then turned upward to the first floor, directly forward to the works mezzanine arm or aside to the company showrooms.

But all that begs the question of the Egyptian influences, of Wallis' predilection and, historically, the ancient path from pylon to shrine of the ancient Egyptian temple. Mostly, in fact, the references here were Egyptian. From the splayed arms at the gateway, where little plots shaped like the [Wedjat] eye of Horus, blessed the journey to the building's entrance—signalled by the timepiece and company's name in the centre of the pylon frame—the way marked off by sphinx-like pedestals and ornamental lamps. By the stepped pathway, of consistent width, the visitor arrived at the doorway—pylon-framed in dark blue faience and deeply recessed between quarter-engaged columns (Fig. 23). Despite the classical patera and guttae, and the emphasis of the company identity in monogrammed shields, the detail in path and doorway announce the entrance to the temple of Amun-Ra. Ram's-head sphinx, ram's horns on the heraldic device, beside the clock, on the final pedestals and the lamp standards above them, stand for Amun—the most powerful of the gods of ancient Egypt (or Zeus-Amun or Jupiter-Amun to include a conflation of Greco-Roman-Egyptian reference). The many circular motifs denote the sun and the sun god Ra. His rays burst forth in the fanlight, in the bronze filigree of the doors and again above the round face of the clock—time being eternal as the diurnal progress of the sun. When Ra assumed the

Fig. 23 Firestone Tyre & Rubber Co, Great West Road, Brentford, Middlesex: main doorway, 1929

deity Amun as his begetter, the two aspects were combined as Amun-Ra or Ra-Amun. That the doorway represented a major staging post is noted in what is actually a minor feature (but once more an example of Wallis' impishness) that signifies under whose auspices those who enter are allowed to do so. The wings of Horus, the sun of Ra, the horns of Amun and the gothic F of Firestone are all contained within one motif at the base of the lamp standards.

Wallis would not have expected the people who trod the processional way to understand its connotations. Rather the use of Egyptian motifs would have been appreciated for their fashionable popularity—and are still regarded as superficial novelty. But if there was any significance in the symbols and stages noted thus far, beyond the door had to be a long, straight path, passing through light and dark, with hypostyle halls on either side where the grid pattern of columnation did not match that of the corridor path, and terminating in the seat of ultimate power. Interruptions along the path would be merely stages on the way.[112] Fanciful as that may be (and these were Fancy factories), the ground plans display a fair consistency of analogy that links aesthetics, plan and structure. The power house, where the path ended, was the source of power (hydraulic, electric, gas, compressed air, steam) without which the plant could not operate. For all its distance from the beginning of the path, the power house was decorated with concrete formwork that matched the motifs on the administration building; thus a connection was established—and not inconceivably also a mischievous pun, connecting managerial and motive power.

The concrete decoration on the administration building was less conspicuous by day relative to the contrasts of form and colour. By night, however, floodlighting threw into stark relief the reeded edging of the battered frame, pediment and tower caps, the ram's-horn terminals on the pediment, east door architraves, the curved corner motifs on the towers (Fig. 24). Floodlighting of buildings was very popular in the late 1920s and throughout the 1930s; it produced a similar result to the photographic technique used in picture postcards of film stars and was part of the 'modern technology' form of advertising that included sky-writing and neon-strip lighting.

The new forms of concrete decoration introduced in the mid-term buildings were more clearly of Egyptian origin. Reeded edges were no longer contained within borders, ram's horns replaced the ubiquitous nail-heads of

Fig. 24 Firestone Tyre & Rubber Co, Great West Road, Brentford, Middlesex: factory floodlit at night, 1930

former buildings (although they were still to be found, but much less obviously) and sphinx and pedestals like cut-off obelisks defined entrances, as landscaping became possible and popular. The new decorative forms were much more stylised, assertive and cleaner-cut than the classically derived motifs of the earlier buildings.

The classical formula of the basic structure of the Firestone factory was rather more evident in the massing of buildings. On the east elevation, for instance, the antique language of the colonnaded office building was gradually diluted in the thin ends. Stripped, modernised and thrust north-ward by the 30-degree angle of the saw-toothed roofs, the idiom rose to its Modern version in the multi-storey block, only to be re-established in original form in the power house. While Egyptian references symbolised the status and importance of industry, in its capacity to provide and as an eternal source of regeneration, classical influences provided the building and its occupants with an unearned but better understood respectable historical dimension and a sense of continuity. Transposed into Modern form, the advanced level of the company's attitudes and technology was made evident. The combination of past and future modes typified the ethos of the here and now.

Reinforcing the fact that the building was representative of its time, were suggestions of Art Deco, the influence of Hollywood and the techniques of advertising that were also part of the contemporary culture; that is insofar as they contributed to building an 'image' of the company in which consumers could see reflected the image to which they themselves aspired. Luxury-oriented Art Deco found its way from the salons of Paris and the staterooms of transatlantic liners to Woolworth's teacups and powder compacts, pro-ducing an illusion of luxury for the many. It has been called a vision of the world in which 'every man is as handsome as a film star and every woman as well turned out as a millionaire's mistress'.[113] The forms of Art Deco were many-angled, multi-coloured, gilded and silvered, and culled from 'primi-tive' sources. It was intended as an exotic, dramatic and purely decorative—but exclusive—art form, but became commercialised into the 'last univeral art form'. Much of that could be ascribed to the decoration of the Firestone building and suggests a similar appeal but the precise instances that are Art Deco and nothing else are remarkably few.

Closely related to the age of electricity and the new leisure ethic was the seductive fantasy of the cinema, where exotic ornament and advanced engineering combined to achieve a precise physical and psychological function. What the cinema offered was vicarious rather than voyeuristic, but the atmosphere created by design was not only warm, comfortable and luxurious, it was mysterious and fanciful and glamorous. The films and their stars influenced fashion and behaviour. Hollywood 'sold' its stars to the public by building enviable images of glamour in published as well as cinematographic form. Entertainment was as much an industry as was tyre-making; the Modernists, however, regarded manufacturing industry as wholly to do with machines, which should be expressed in its buildings. Decoration did at least recognise the human dimension; decoration of a kind that echoed the leisure ethic suggested similarities of quality and character in work and play. Wallis believed that money wisely spent on some form of decoration, especially colour, had a 'psychological effect on the worker, if he is a good worker, and good workers look upon their buildings with pride'.[114] Ex-Firestone workers have confirmed that they were proud of the building and enjoyed its colour and unique qualities.[115] For many of them, the colourful company image contained in the motifs and logos, the products and the advertising, and as projected in composite form in the buildings, put a name and a face to anonymous machine-made products and mechanised production, and suggested that they too were an essential part of a team.

Advertising was not so very different in the pursuit of image-building, aiming to sell goods by appealing to aspiration, dreams and the desire for upward mobility. Thomas Wallis believed that an attractive building and a 'little money spent on something to focus the attention of the public' was not wasteful. In his view,

> a properly conceived and well-defined façade on a main thoroughfare will give proportionately better results than that obtained from the large yearly expenditure so often incurred in usual advertising.[116]

But the aim was very similar. Speeding past the Firestone building, the young man on his motorcycle and the flapper on the pillion were, in imagination and experience, in the same situation as the wealthy man-about-town and his sleek, exquisitely-gowned companion. The company image was designed to beguile them all.

All in all, however, the quality of the Firestone design was too well thought out, had too great an integrity and social understanding to be charged with the kind of gimcrackery that pervaded much of the Hollywood and advertising media. Firestone appealed to social memory, inspired confidence in the future and recognised the ancient appetite for embellishment as well as upholding exploitive capitalism. In any case, Greek classical architecture was not all of unsullied, noble, white marble, as extolled by eighteenth-century neo-classicists; it was often highly coloured and the aims or ideals so expressed were just as base or as lofty.

The quality of workmanship and materials has some bearing too in contributing to the dignity of the Firestone factory. It is revealed in the prescriptive clauses of Specifications and Bills of Quantities, as carried out in construction, realised in the limited need for subsequent maintenance and in the difficulties encountered in demolition. Costs were substantial: £21 166 6s 6d was paid to the contractor (who was also responsible for sub-contractor costs) for the office block, and £91 427 13s 6d for the north-light and multi-storey sections, making a total of £122 594 for the super-structure. Excavations, foundations and basements added another

£26 577 10s 7d. Extension of the multi-storey block became necessary within a year. Further extensions were carried out in 1934–35 and 1939–40; many other single buildings were added to the factory and the final extension was to the frontal block by wings on each side in the late 1950s. Douglas Wallis was responsible for the later additions and forebore to emulate the pattern of the original façade. Nevertheless, as standing at the time of demolition in August 1980, the Firestone building was quite magnificent, a powerful edifice with great dignity and self-assurance.

Initial response to the building in 1929 was very favourable. High praise was accorded to the planning and layout, and commentators welcomed the happy coincidence of industry and attractive appearance.[117] One commentator enjoyed the building as the 'most refreshing note on the westward journey out of London',[118] while another noted the combination of extreme efficiency with a strong, almost dramatic sense of design.[119] A few sour notes were introduced, such as the view that although the 'ceremonial front towards the road is vigorously conceived' the design 'lacked artistic unity'[120] and that, while the main elevation 'bows to no convention . . . but has considerable merit in its simplicity and fine scale . . . the moulded ornament is, however, somewhat coarse and uninspiring'.[121]

The charge of 'façade building' made its most damning impact in the discussion session after Thomas Wallis' address to the RIBA in 1933.[122] The opening remarks of the speaker chosen to move the vote of thanks summed up the general attitude to factory design in Britain. 'When we think of factories we are apt to think chiefly of what has been done in America, Germany and Holland' but, only after hearing Mr Wallis did they appreciate, he said, that 'there has been a terrific amount of work put into our factories in England since the war'. Much of the discussion was devoted to practical questions but, in regard to 'the architecture', C. H. Reilly observed that in Liverpool they did not give a factory 'an Egyptian façade' and, whilst congratulating Wallis on the 'fine series of factories on the Great West Road', felt that they made domestic architecture for miles around 'look absurd'. Reilly had hoped to hear more of Mendelsohn's designs because 'there is no façade making about the Mendelsohn-type of design in America and Germany'. H. Goodhart-Rendel hoped that 'we shall soon outgrow the making of veneers to factories' and that 'all such veneer will disappear shortly'. Hans Williams was concerned about the effect of soot and dirt on white cement, fearing that '. . . in four or five years' time the beautiful building looks like a painted lady in the morning after her face has been divorced for some time from her vanity bag'. Since Modern buildings in white cement were equally susceptible to soot and dirt, the implication of the painted lady suggests an aura of immorality about adding colour to industrial buildings.

In 1934, E. Maxwell Fry regarded the factories beside the Great West Road as vulgar and childish, displaying 'all the worst sentimentalities of uncultured commercialism'.[123] Other writers remarked upon the stridency and questionable taste of the buildings, seeing them as pompous and vulgar. Leathart asserted that the simple elevation of the function of a factory building was more akin to suitability of purpose than the 'larger magnificence of the industrial palace overloaded with advertising appeal'.[124] This lack of understanding of what industry was all about, its rôle at that time in revitalising the national economy, overcoming fierce competition and attracting customers, has not diminished even in most recent times. In consequence, the contribution of Wallis, Gilbert & Partners to major improvements in factory design has been relegated to the fringes of architectural merit.

How little was known, understood, or already investigated about factories or about Wallis, Gilbert & Partners was revealed in the outcry over the demolition of the Firestone factory in August 1980. Suddenly, the building was a 'masterpiece', a 'crowning glory', a 'shimmering palace of white columns, pediments and brightly coloured tiles stretched out luxuriously on the lawns beside the Great West Road'. The loss of the façade was regarded as a 'work of art . . . hopelessly mutilated', but still no-one looked beyond the façade. The mistakes made in reportage in 1929 were repeated verbatim and further mistakes were made. Thomas Wallis was confused with his son Douglas as the designer and in quotations from their respective publications. The estate agents handling the sale of the property invented a new architect named 'Wallis Gilbert'—a mistake as uninformed as the reference to the practice as *Wallace*, Gilbert & Partners by Gavin Stamp as editor of *Britain in the Thirties*, and which he described as being pre-eminent in designing the showy, vulgar, *moderne* factories on the Great West Road and Western Avenue.[125] Marcus Binney spoke about the demolition as the great tragedy of the loss of this 'rare example of façadism'; to modern commentators and architectural historians, only the central façade had meaning.[126] It was not seen as integral to the total composition nor was its purpose understood; Wallis, Gilbert & Partners were known only as the designers of flashy factories beside the Great West Road and Western Avenue.

In 1974, Bevis Hillier described the object of the Firestone causeway as to instil 'suitable awe in the visiting commercial rep'.[127] But no commercial rep would even have thought to enter by that path. There was neither commodity buying nor retail selling at the factory door. The aim of the causeway was to impress important people on pre-arranged visits to tour the factory, such as motor manufacturers with large orders for original equipment or the principals of municipal or private transport undertakings seeking mileage contracts, famous racing or record-breaking drivers, film stars and other popular figures who would endorse the product, and royal personages whose visits provided free press publicity.

The historical importance of the Firestone factory lies in the totality and comprehensiveness of the planning and design in relation to what was achievable at that time and what that said about contemporary attitudes and beliefs. The Firestone factory was like a book in which every page was significant in itself but had meaning only in the total context. Most critics, then and now, seem to have ventured no further than the front cover and their own personal prejudices about factories and industry.

But manufacturers understood the language of the design and appreciated the advanced planning and layout. Early in 1929, the managing director of another tyre manufacturing company, The India Tyre & Rubber Company, of Inchinnan, near Renfrew, Scotland, saw the Firestone factory and immediately commissioned Wallis, Gilbert & Partners to design an administration building and warehouse for his company in like mode.

The India Tyre & Rubber Company

The initiative for British-built 'India' tyres came not from America, where the founder firm was located, but from an enterprising Englishman. In 1926 John Cooper visited the India Tire & Rubber Company at Akron, Ohio, USA, with a view to establishing manufacturing rights in Britain. After abortive attempts to site a factory in England, he joined with the India concessionaires in Glasgow, Scotland, to acquire, in 1927, 68 acres of land at Inchinnan that had been relinquished by William Beardmore & Company, when the Air Ministry decided against future development of airships that Beardmores had been building during the First World War. Labour was abundant in the area—Scotland had a huge post-war unemployment problem, although at the India factory, special transport facilities had to be arranged for employees to reach the rather isolated site on the Clyde estuary.[128]

Share capital was raised in Britain and, with staff seconded from India in Akron, the surviving Beardmore buildings were converted to tyre production, the first of which came off the line in June 1928. The company became wholly British-owned in 1930, when India of Akron withdrew its holding after the 1929 Wall Street crash, but the Inchinnan factory prospered. Plans for a new two-storey office block parallel with the road and a single-storeyed, wedge-shaped warehouse between the office block and the existing production area were drawn by Wallis, Gilbert & Partners and approved in May 1929.

The construction contract was awarded to a local builder, John Train & Company Limited, on 4 June 1929, with a required completion time of 16 weeks. The builder's own estimate of six to eight months proved to be more realistic. John Train could have had little experience of frame and concrete construction, his main claim to fame at the time being the rebuilding of the Kelvin Hall, Glasgow, although some years later he advertised his firm as 'Reinforced Concrete Specialists'. At India, there were problems with quality, with sub-contractors and suppliers, with materials and, inevitably, as time went on, the Scottish winter. The warehouse section was completed on time, by 16 September 1929 and, despite delays, the administration building was complete and in use, with roads made up and the whole ceremonially opened on 30 April 1930, but this was only because of the prodigious efforts of Frank Cox and the architects' insistence on speed and quality.[129] The builder was frequently urged to make greater use of overtime working; Cox visited the site to 'prepare and agree with you a schedule of completion of each trade *room by room*', insisting that completion of the outside of the building could wait, 'what we want is occupation inside'.

One sacrifice to speed was conceded when the owners preferred to ignore the mismatch of colour between the white tiles and white glazed bricks in the women's lavatories rather than incur further delay in replacement but, after problems with external rendering, the builder was brought to London to see and learn from the surface of the Pyrene factory, that was '. . . infinitely better than at your job'. Samples of internal plastering were sent to the builder to show what kind of surface was required and the means of achieving it. On another occasion, he was instructed to '. . . hack up the granolithic floor of the Girls' Cloaks and Rest Room and re-lay with wooden blocks . . . as intended by us'. Cox's visits had invariably coincided with wet weather that obscured one particular defect but, discovering one dry day that the lettering of the company's insignia on the parapet 'in no way matches the red in the lower part of the building', he insisted that new lettering be put in.[130] The spacing of the words remains, however, a little unfortunate. Although these and other defects were not always due to the contractor's work, he was responsible for sub-contractors and supplies and was subsequently penalised under the terms of the contract, chiefly as to completion date.

The India factory stood in open country, some 21 yards back from the Glasgow to Greenock highway, on the section at Inchinnan known as the 'straight mile'. The buildings faced north on land falling away from the road. There were four entrances to the site, each 30 feet wide—two at the outer edges of the site for works personnel and vehicles, and two inner openings leading to the new offices.

The two-storey office block was constructed of reinforced concrete to the design of Truscon, with brick and glass infill and rendered in 'Atlas White' cement. The building measured overall 255 feet in width and 42 feet in depth. The grid pattern of columns was arranged to suit the interior layout, primarily to accommodate a corridor running east/west, crossing the main hall in the centre. Rooms of one, two or three bays for administrative and servicing purposes were disposed on each side of the corridor, some with brick walls, others with wood and glass partitioning. Space for lavatories, cloaks and rest rooms was on a generous scale. On the first floor, where managerial and executive offices occupied a central position (and a higher one, with a commanding view of the countryside), the corridor was shorter, terminating in large open-plan offices for sales and stock control respectively. The corridor was extended and partitioned off to the full length of the building when two-storeyed wing extensions were added in 1956.

Office staff entered by doorways in either of the end towers, both of which contained stairways to the first floor and to rooms above in the tower. In the third storey of the east tower was the caretaker's flat, with access to the flat roof; equivalent space in the west tower was used for bulk stationery storage. On the ground floor, doorways in the rear wall gave access to the warehouse and works area. Only directors, managers and their visitors used the main entrance; at one time, no one else was even allowed to enter the hall from the works floor. On the ground floor, the hall and attendant services occupied the central bays. Space was taken in the corners by two showrooms, two display cabinets, a waiting room, enquiry desk and telephone switchboard; directly opposite the doorway was the main stairway, flanked by short passages to public telephone booths tucked beneath the stairs. And there still remained a hall floor space of 42 feet by 9. At a half landing, the stairs returned on each side to the main large landing and reception area.

The warehouse was fitted into the wedge-shaped space between the rear of the office block and the front of the main production section, co-extensively with the latter. Built of steel frame with brick infill and metal-framed windows, the warehouse has three runs of glazed and slated pitched roofs, the one nearest the office block tapering off to an acute angle.

Although, clearly, there are family likenesses in Wallis, Gilbert designs, every building was in itself unique. So that, when Andrew Melville of India Tyres asked for an 'office block like Firestone', he could not have expected an exact copy but more of a 'fraternal twin'. There were, in any case, different determinants to be taken into account. True, the India office block was a white concrete building that framed a recessed colonnade and an impressive central doorway, and was decorated with coloured faience. It was situated in a rural area, set back from a main highway and 'landscaped' in the intervening space. But it was designed for Scottish clients, a Scottish location and the Scottish climate. Further, the office block and warehouse were additions to an existing works, rather than a complete new-build factory. Although the functions of the two new buildings were differentiated in their structure, a link was established throughout in the relation of the utilitarian appearance of the warehouse to the existing production area, and the relation of the brick-faced piers, gabled 'pedimented' roofs and concrete cornice of the warehouse to the formal classicism of the office block.

The end towers of the office block appear as substantial buildings in their own right, with Horus-eyed plots marking the path to their own respective doorways. Their powerful build was intended to support future extension by way of a third storey to the main block, thus further enhancing the building's commanding position in low-lying open country. The owners purchased the surrounding land on both sides of the roadway to prevent any Great West Road-style colonisation. Fields not taken up for works housing and later extension were leased to local farmers; the company steadfastly resisted attempts by the local council and property developers to acquire the land for other purposes. Since extension was intended upwards, the side elevations of the towers were aesthetically complete, with ram's-horn ornaments on fore and aft corners and a rhythm of triple windows, diminishing in size in ascending order, linking them with the three slit windows on the front, and expressing internal usage.

But the towers did not stand in splendid isolation. Part of their interior plan was contained within the framed colonnade that projected forward by some four feet; their assimilation into the main body of the building was externally reinforced by the continuous bands of green, red and black faience and reeded edging on parapet and plinth. Red, green and black faience also decorated the caps and bases of columns and the main door architrave. But less exotically than at Firestone. There were no lotus petals, no heraldic devices, and fewer ornaments on the doorway. Metal work for the railings and on the doors themselves was more similar to that at GEC and earlier factories; as well as the cross pattern and patera, there were reeded borders, nail-heads and tassels. Finger plates on the doors in the hall were identical to those in the GEC reception room.

If somewhat sedate in detail, a trifle solid in its classically inspired form, the major impact of the India building was somewhat different and changed with viewpoint; at its best, white and sparkling against a glowering sky and distant, purple hills. In the Clyde Valley, the isolated works could be identified from miles away by the white glazed brick INDIA on the factory chimney. Seen from a fast-moving vehicle and closing in on the site, the white columns set up a mobile rhythm against the battleship grey window frames and glass reflecting the northern light—a massive portico against impenetrable grey; red, green and black faience beside the flickering chequer-board of small-paned windows gave an impression of tartan trimming—that was diminished when the glazing was replaced with large panes in 1961.

For the visitor at the gate there was something else. Entering from the side, between stumpy pedestals and directed along level ground past the colon-nade to the Horus-eyed plots, splayed railings and lamp-topped pedestals to the main door, this processional route owed most to Roman influences. At the wide entrance way, the doors were not deeply recessed but derived their importance from their position between two massive, free-standing columns (Fig. 25) that mitigated between the still, almost two-dimensional effect of the columns at close quarters and the restless patterning of the hall behind them. In the hall, between two proscenium arches inlaid with black and red faience—one over the doorway (Fig. 26), the other over the stairs directly opposite—the terrazzo floor of the hall, with Art Deco borders and central logo, set up a syncopated rhythm with the Art Deco glazing bars in the inner doors, in the fanlight, the glass partitioning and the jagged lines and dots of colour. Amongst all that, the wooden-tiled roofs of the showcases were a little

Fig. 25 India Tyre & Rubber Co, Inchinnan, Renfrewshire, Scotland: main entrance, 1956

'cottagey', but gave an indication of the Arts and Crafts references to be found in dark oak panelling, the hand-crafted appearance of the light fittings, door furniture and radiator casings along the route to the managerial offices or board room, and the country view towards the River Clyde that greeted the visitor through the large window of the main landing.

Perhaps, in this remarkably eclectic assembly of ancient and modern, Wallis was realising not only the backward- and forward-looking attitudes of the day but, as well, a contiguity of the country's long and turbulent history and the aggressive competitiveness of modern times. And, in setting the eye dancing in that lively hall, something like the skirl of the pipes after the slower, tartan-trimmed rhythm of the exterior. If Wallis was involved during the First World War with the munition factory at George Town (and his daughter states that the family lived in Paisley for a while when she was very young), he would already have known something of the place and the people. Did he try to put too much into the India building? But neither the people nor the place could be known or understood all at once. Perhaps the most intriguing fact about the India building was the way it could change: actively glittering in the rain, still and cool in sunlight, changing with perspective and distance and, as in an excellent narrative painting, there was always something else to be discovered that one had not noticed before.

The office building was extended in 1956, not by a third storey, but by the addition of wings designed by in-house architects (the company and the

Fig. 26 India Tyre & Rubber Co, Inchinnan, Renfrewshire, Scotland: entrance hall, 1980

building then belonged to Dunlop Limited) in which the faience trimming was repeated. Many other buildings were added to the site after the Second World War and the India office building lost something of its solitary splendour. Still standing, it has reached an awful state of dereliction. In 1932, Dunlop Limited acquired a controlling interest in India Tyres, effected a complete takeover in 1936, and operated the factory at decreasing capacity until it closed in 1982. Application for listing of the building was notified in 1981 but not served. It is understood that listing has now been achieved.

Pyrene Company Limited

While the India buildings were dragging on to completion, another larger commission had been started and finished, much nearer to home for Wallis, Gilbert & Partners and directly opposite the Firestone factory. This was for the Pyrene Company Limited to be sited beside the Great West Road, at Brentford, Middlesex. The company was founded to manufacture fire extinguishers to a design invented by a Scottish engineer in 1907 and later expanded into other forms of fire protection apparatus, metal finishing and chromium plating of car bumpers, exhaust pipes and non-skid chains. As the company outgrew its base at Stoke Newington and additional premises around London and with the acquisition of an operating licence from the American Parker Chemical Company for rust-proofing of manufactured articles, the decision was made to build a new factory with everything under one roof.

The site beside the Great West Road was chosen for its proximity to London, convenience for delivery and despatch by road or either of the two nearby railways, and for the 'prestige afforded by a commanding position on a superb highway' in the company of other buildings of 'fine design'.[131] Construction commenced in May 1929 and the completed building was ceremonially opened in May the following year.

The three-acre site faces north and rises sharply over a short distance from the road. At the east end, ground was cut away for the gateway and a road that circled round to loading bays and the demonstration ground at the rear of the building. The ground floor at front is aligned with the top of the embankment, with a lower ground floor for garage and boiler house built into the step-down on the east. Parallel to the main road, steps led to the works entrance. The skeleton is of steel frame, mostly on a grid of 20 feet centres, with brick and glass infill; it was rendered in white cement. Floors are of reinforced concrete. The building measures 480 feet overall on frontage.

The ground floor was devoted to manufacturing processes. The plan shows a basic rectangle with a corridor along the secondary axis. From the rear, south side, a one bay's depth projection was co-extensive with the loading bay. On the east, a two-storey projection (over the garage) contained the works entrance, lavatories, first-aid room and a covered entrance to, and including, the Parkerising department. The built version appears to have had an intermediate set-back between the main block and the works entrance. Changes have been made to that part of the building, so that the original shape is no longer distinguishable. The frontal block, to two bays' depth and including the corridor, is two storeys high, as are the corner towers that return as wings to enclose a single-storeyed, north-light section. Opening on to the loading bay, the warehouse and despatch department occupied central place in the north-light section and were flanked by stores and receiving areas that served the variety of product processes disposed in the separate rooms about the corridor.

The first floor was taken up by offices, board room, canteen and private dining room, to which access was gained by the main door (placed centrally on the façade), hall and main stairway. Between the two flights of steps leading to the main entrance, a small blockhouse with a door onto the pavement, contained electrical switchgear and fuse box, floodlighting control and water supply cocks. Above the main door, a tower rises to 110 feet; on its top floor was the drawing office, receiving natural light from all sides and, below it, the Pyrene powder processing department, reached by external stairs beside the loading bay or a spiral staircase in the receiving department—perhaps one way up and the other way down. Another spiral staircase led from the corridor to the works manager's office on the first floor.

The flat roof of the main two-storey section is surrounded by a substantial parapet and was drained by iron pipes of square section let into the structure and releasing to the land drain at inspection boxes. Other innovations included a system of call bells for distance contact throughout the works, chromium-plated drinking fountains in the corridors, electrically-operated blinds in the canteen to convert the room to a cinema, exhaust ventilation of sections producing fumes, and a constant supply of fresh air that was warmed in winter by heated coils in the intakes. The building was centrally heated from the boilers that supplied steam for manufacturing and processing purposes.

The Pyrene building was another 'Daylight' factory, laid out in units appropriate to operating functions. But once it is said that the north elevation is a recessed colonnade framed against corner towers and that, as a member of the Fancy group, it is decorated with coloured faience and Egyptian formwork, relation to previous designs ceases. The main verticals are piers not columns—and thus not so amenable to the fulsomeness of Egyptianised botanical ornamentation but essentially straight lined in keeping with the Modern rectilinear forms of which the building is composed. It is a not very happy mix of classical influences and Modern forms, rather than a progress (as at Firestone) linking one with the other, more a conflict between past and future that finds no resolution in the present. Again, it is a mix of verticals and horizontals between which the interplay is not well orchestrated. More successful is the Dudokian cubic massing at the east end and in the centre, but the eye has to leap from one to the other over unrelated space rather than wander among related planes.

The Pyrene solution may have initiated the demand for tall towers on industrial and municipal buildings, but here it was not the isolated, equilateral version that became so popular in the 1930s. The Pyrene tower is more robust, rising from the full depth of the frontal block and purposefully out of an ascending order of supporting blocks. More romantically-inspired than the Modern format of the rest of the building, this centrepiece can be said to represent the company's flame symbol in its upward surge from pavement steps to the high-placed logo. In concert, the bands of faience trim suggest rows of lighted candles. There is, too, more Egyptianising in the reeded borders, battered architrave, ram's-head sphinx and the ram's-horn corner motifs—even a touch of tartan (in reference to the inventor of the company's chief product) in the chequered squares on the architrave faience. Towndrow regarded the centre part of the building as a 'piece of sheer architectural indulgence' of which 'Mr Eric Mendelsohn would not approve', but which he himself did.[132] As an individual feature, the tower section is successfully handled and wholly Wallis in spirit. It should, however, have been securely bound to its wings by the broad band of figured faience, but the hyphenated short runs and breaks in the long bands do not fulfil that rôle, nor do they form a well-defined encasement for the colonnade.

The public impact of the building was meant, again, to be the view from a moving vehicle. Thus, the staccato effect of the banding, the reeded or faience-capped set-backs and the constant exclamations of the less-than-powerfully decorated piers would, when allied to the nervous angularity of the Art Deco doors, gates and standard lamps, add an up-to-date art form to the plainer geometry of a basically Modern building and, in setting up a kind of rhythm, contribute an overall concept to arrangements that lack cohesion. Perhaps this was what was meant by Jazz-modern.

At the centre of the entrance, the rake of the embankment was too sharp and the distance from the pavement to the doorway too short for any kind of processional way. Rather the visitor was swept upward to the narrow vestibule and precipitated into an extravagantly furbished hall. There, a double staircase swept around the room to the first-floor landing and corridors. The influence of the leisure ethic was pertinent and clearly 'up-market'. With decorated columns and pilasters, fancy metal balusters, Art Deco chandelier and wall lights, the Pyrene hall could well have been the foyer of a luxury hotel. For the workforce, there was a sort of ceremonial passage stepping up to a triumphal arch in the projecting block on the east end. Taken by itself, the geometry here was very effective, powerful indeed in respect of the works entrance and much more welcoming and prestigious than was usually the case.

The company certainly considered its new building of great prestige value. The building was floodlit at night (the original lights were still there and about to be replaced). As a means of high quality advertising, the company produced a beautifully designed folder about it, written by Howard Robertson and illustrated by Joseph Pike. In 1949 the north-light section was extended further to the rear of the main building but, 20 years later, the company was taken over by Chubb Limited, which occupied it for a few years; then it fell on troubled times. It was eventually taken over by a property developer who, after attempting to change the building into wholly office accommodation, went into receivership. It stood empty from 1974 to 1979, when it was bought by Tarmac Construction Limited, which has since sold it to Glaxo Pension Fund, but retained occupation on a 35-year lease-back. Various refurbishments and alterations over time have included demolition of all of the north-light section and its replacement with a free-standing, pitched-roof shed. Other additions have been made to the main building. A new heating system has been installed, all ceilings have been lowered and windows replaced. The central entrance was blocked up and the hall ripped out—the present main entrance is at the east end near the old Parkerising unit. At one stage, the exterior was painted over but the local council insisted the faience trimming should be uncovered, most of which has been carried out, although the piers are still over-painted.

Some of the earlier alteration work was of very poor quality. In 1984 Tarmac began a complete overhaul, repairing past defects and reinstating the central entrance doors with as near a match as could be obtained, but the hall remains an empty shell. Problems frequently encountered with the flat roof have been remedied. The building is now wholly office accommodation; it is known as Westlink House and is the present London headquarters of Tarmac Construction Limited. The metal finishing part of Pyrene has become Pyrene Chemical Services Limited and, together with the fire-extinguisher part of the business under Chubb, is part of Brent Chemicals International plc at Iver, Buckinghamshire.

George Kemp Limited

Wallis, Gilbert & Partners found 1929 a fruitful year, with continuing work as consulting architects, a factory in Paris, another in Cape Town, South Africa, public works and a commission for a biscuit factory beside the North Circular Road at Cricklewood in North London, for George Kemp Limited, then of Brewery Road, London N7. Construction began in April 1929 and the building was completed in October 1930. The factory has been demolished and the site redeveloped as an industrial estate known as 1000 North Circular Road, Staples Corner in the Borough of Brent. Source material for the Kemp factory is scarce, with only published photographs and deposited plans for reference. The company is now defunct, having closed in 1962.

The site of the Kemp factory, between Staples Corner and Coles Green Road, faced north to a curve in the North Circular Road. The ground rose sharply to south and west; a decline to the east was cut away to allow access for vehicular traffic from the road and to insert a lower ground floor in the building. There are similarities with the Pyrene building in terms of form, but here the frontage was much longer—some 650 feet, with an overall depth of 138 feet. The unit system was employed in a most unusual way—three multi-storey blocks were separated by two single-storey, north-light sections. The format was dictated by operational functions: that is, continuous, direct-line processing of materials entering at the west end and goods despatched at the east end, which also accounted for the off-centre placing of the middle multi-storey block (Fig. 27). There was a basement below the west block, a tunnel for the works entrance below the middle block and an exposed lower ground floor to the east block that contained stores, despatch department and the entrance to the offices situated in the upper storeys.

The building was constructed of steel frame and reinforced concrete, with glass infill, arranged for the most part on a grid of 30 feet depth and 25 feet width; both end blocks were supported at 18 feet : 30 feet 6 inches : 18 feet—a structural pattern that was expressed on the façades. At the rear of the building, across its full width, a corridor connected lavatories, rest rooms, cloakrooms, lift, stairwell and small processing, all contained in bays 18 feet deep. An abutment at the east/rear is noted on plan as 'Temporary Tin Washing Department'.

In a food-processing plant, hygiene is important. As well as the usual well-arranged sanitary facilities, each north-light section had six washing fountains placed and shown on plan by solid circles. Processing also produced considerable heat and fire hazard. There were thus three banks of opening lights and an inner ceiling of insulating, pre-cast gypsum panels on the south angles of the roof. The gypsum panels also absorbed condensation and, with an outer covering of asbestos cement tiles, reduced the amount of flammable construction material.[133]

There were offices above the despatch department in the east block, presumably dealing with orders, accounts and general administration and to accommodate managerial functions. The west block was probably for bulk storage of materials-in, perhaps fed gravitationally to the manufacturing floor, with some office accommodation for receipt and storage records. The purposes of the middle block are even more a matter of surmise. As an integrated, volume-production factory, the company may have produced its own packaging, printing and advertising material on the floors above the 'cooling room'. Alternatively, or as well, that building could have contained the canteen, recreation rooms and so on, although it was an extraordinarily large building to dedicate to amenities. One photograph of the entrance to the middle block is captioned 'The main entrance is at basement level and leads to offices and staff room by a subway'.[134] That adds up to a great deal of office space. In Wallis, Gilbert & Partners' own published illustration,[135] that entrance is designated 'Works Entrance' and the doorway to the east block as 'Office Entrance'—both also as shown on plan. The entrance to the middle block was, nevertheless, very imposing. Metal double gates and two porters' lodges led to faience-trimmed colossal columns in a battered frame. But all there was behind them was a tunnel, 20 feet wide, 120 feet long, built according to the 'Truscon system', terminating in 'employees' stairs' at the

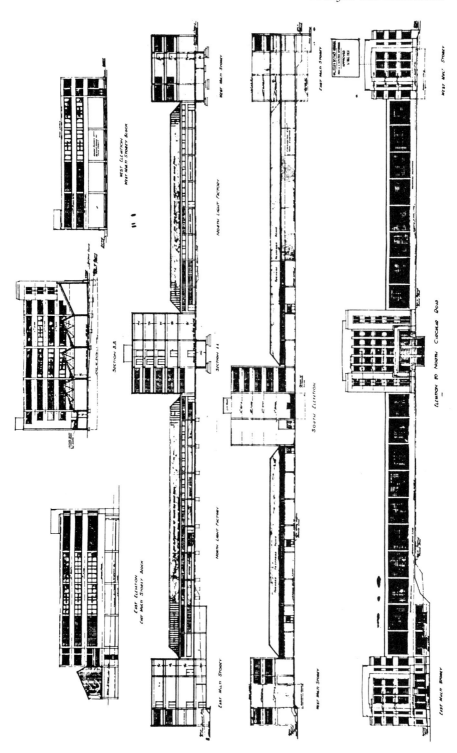

Fig. 27 George Kemp Ltd, North Circular Road, Cricklewood, London: plans—elevations and sections, 1928–30

back of the building, and releasing into the works corridor. The stairwell continued upwards to the upper storeys but, given its position, it may safely be assumed that the stairs were very utilitarian in treatment and appearance. The design of the entrance in the east block has more to commend it as the 'office entrance' than picture captions and plan designation, but the commentator who described the way through the middle, largest block as the 'main entrance' could be forgiven for misinterpreting its grandeur.

Since the designing of Firestone, the architects had paid more attention to works entrances, elevating their status above the traditionally plain, not-for-public-view door at the side or rear. Part of Wallis, Gilbert's design philosophy was to improve conditions for employees. The move to improve their status and express that on the elevations may have been extrapolated from ideas expressed in the Firestone design. The entrance and canteen jointly used by staff and shop-floor workers at Firestone and the mingling of gender, the company image and totality of composition that sought to ensure overall team spirit and, too, deliberate play with the very obvious fact that, without motive power, the factory could not function, may well have sparked greater realisation of the importance of the workforce in the scheme of things. Not all employers would have yielded to such a suggestion but, at Kemps, the token recognition of the importance of the workforce was at least to tell the public 'this is where our people enter and leave'. Certainly it somewhat invited the charge, 'Queen Anne at the front and Mary Anne at the back' but, at that time, shop-floor workers were still regarded in Victorian terms of 'hands' operating machines. Even the socially-minded Modernists saw factories as containers of mechanised production. Public recognition of the existence and importance of the workforce was not only, architecturally, more accurate an expression of function than a 'machine aesthetic'; there was commercial benefit to be derived from a workforce that appreciated a gesture of respect.

Access to the east end of the Kemp site was at road level across the cut-away ground to the lower ground floor of the building. Furthest east, a vehicular entrance served the despatch department and, some yards to the west of it, were a separate gate and path to the office entrance at the front of the east multi-storey block. In comparison with the huge overall size of the Kemp factory, the office entrance was quite small, but derived its importance from its solid pylon shape set against the transparency of the hall windows.

Flanked by very Modern glass corners, the battered lines of the concrete architrave stepped forward to a pylon crowned by a band of faience and a crenellated pediment, then stepped sharply back to the recessed doors. Of interest here was the combination of ancient and modern, solidity and flimsiness, and of progression and recession. All slightly overdone, but it works quite well in drawing attention to itself in so large a building.

Only on the two doorways to Works and Offices was any decoration or antique reference to be found in this very Modern building. But some slight reminiscence of the country-house style—main building, low wings, end pavilions—may have contributed to its air of superiority and distinction. Chiefly, however, the design rose out of the operating lines and was truly an example of form following function. The result was an unusual resolution of the problem Wallis found with long frontages, and this solution was much better than the mixture of horizontals and verticals of the Pyrene factory. Here the geometry was simple and clear. Strong verticals on the fronts of the multi-storey blocks; perpendicular to them, strong banks of horizontals on the side elevations that were visible above the two long, low, but clearly-defined horizontals between them, and each making its own powerful statement. No cubic massing, no build-up of solids and voids, no interplay of planes, but clear separation of each set of lines, made more explicit by the large amount of glass infill. Yet, paradoxically, it was the tension created by the fragile glass skin that unified the structure, binding the opposing skeletal lines into one coherent, very self-assured building. Hence, another reason for the Fancy doorways—to pierce that aloof independence with some display of human involvement.

Hall & Company Limited

During the summer of 1929, Wallis, Gilbert & Partners had been engaged in designing an engineering workshop at Salfords, Surrey, for a firm of building suppliers and coal merchants, in which the company's vehicle fleet would be maintained. Despite some minimal faience trimming of the main entrances, the workshops were a single-storeyed, north-light building more appropriately dealt with in the Sheds section of this chapter. There was continuing work at Hendon, Middlesex, for Papercraft Limited, a subsidiary of the Lamson Paragon Supply Company, with large north-light extensions in 1929; in 1930, a shed-like structure for H. J. Mulliner & Company Limited at Bedford Park, London; an office extension for Pressed Steel (Great Britain) Limited and an office block for the British Paint & Lacquer Company, both serving local motor manufacturers at Cowley, Oxford—all of which were either minor works or are dealt with in later sections.

Late in 1930, however, Hall & Company Limited, the builders' merchants for which the workshop at Salfords had been designed, commissioned Wallis, Gilbert & Partners to design its new head office at Cherry Orchard Road, East Croydon, Surrey. Although not really a factory, the building has greater claim to Fancy designation than perhaps the Kemp factory, of which it was the complete antithesis, but to which it was related by the main criterion of decoration with coloured faience.

This family business of builders' suppliers and coal merchants originated in 1824, moved to Croydon in 1842 and converted its company title to Hall & Company Limited in 1918. Over the century many new products were added to the company's range of manufactured and factored goods, with an increasing number of depots and manufacturing bases set up throughout the southern counties. From 1924, the national housebuilding programme had produced a phenomenal rise in sales; the existing head office, extended over time from two small cottages, became both inadequate and inappropriate, but road-widening operations in the area had precluded new building until late in 1930.[136] The new head office building, completed in 1931, was demolished a few years ago after the company's headquarters moved to Redhill, Surrey, as part of the RMC Group.

The building faced south onto Cherry Orchard Road and had a large products yard at the side and at the rear. Rectangular in shape, the building was three storeys high, with usable roof space and a part-basement for stores, strongroom and boiler room. It measured overall 90 feet on frontage by 43 feet in depth and was constructed of steel frame with brick walls. There were Truscon reinforced concrete floors (including the third floor, which suggests that future extension was perhaps intended upwards or that the roof space was to house heavy equipment), reinforced concrete foundations, basement stanchions and stairs, steel roof trusses, and a tiled, hipped roof flattened at the ridge. Some internal walls were of brick, others of glazed wood partitioning.

Despite its decoration, this was a traditional building in Georgian style with Beaux Arts planning on primary and secondary axes. The main entrance at centre front led to a hallway and, directly opposite, stairs to the upper floors; the stairs hugged the walls, leaving a centre well for men's cloakrooms on the ground and second floors, and a tea kitchen on the first. The hall was crossed by a central corridor, running east/west, the full width of the building, with offices on each side on the ground and first floors but blocked on the second floor by offices at each end. The lift shaft was at the corner junction of stairs and the west corridor. Sanitary facilities occupied the same position on each floor, to the right of the stairway, but with no external evidence of plumbing or, indeed, of rainwater pipes. Some constructional material had to be bought in and some services sub-contracted but, as far as possible, the building was meant to advertise the company's products, hence its construction in brick, tile and concrete. Only on the east side was the elevation obscured by existing property, and so the building had three public faces: the main frontage to the road; on the west to the yard, but also visible from the highway; and the rear elevation that overlooked the Croydon railway station. Unusually, it was the rear face that was floodlit at night, not only because the front of the building rose directly from the public pavement, but it was felt that the north façade would be seen by more people—the daily commuters at the railway station that served this dormitory town. Hence, around the tall, narrow stair lights on the rear façade, a colossal, rectangular, blind arch, stepped at its upper reaches to exhibit the company's name, punctuated by narrow slit windows, and flanked by many-windowed wings, was magnificently eyecatching.

All three public faces were different, but bound together by the broad, plain concreted bands at plinth and cornice and the long run of windows alternating with green tiled panels between the cornice and the string-course sills. On the west side, below the 'attic' storey, similar windows and panels were accented by lintels of red faience and dentilated bricks rendered in white cement. Below them, a rendered porch, with battered uprights, projected forward of the flanking, small-paned windows and protected the entrances for 'outside' employees to the departments dealing with yard activities. This elevation works reasonably well, given the diversity of materials and patterns. The suddenness and solidity of the porch was relieved by the block-like build-up from the side plinths, and given a sense of belonging by the white surround of the corridor window. Although this elevation had a public rôle, being visible from the road, the works entrance has again been made a dominant feature.

It is difficult to know what to say about the front elevation. There was a resemblance to the west side in the enclosed span of windows and tile panels on the first floor, but the pattern of the glazing bars was different—from other upper and lower storeys—and perhaps a little too active. Some verticality, lacking elsewhere on this elevation, was introduced in the tall side windows. The details plan shows faience spandrels behind the tall, rendered mullions; as built, these were white rendered panels, but it might have been better to have left them plain brick, with less interruption of the vertical line. Intended faience ornament was, fortunately, also omitted from the corner inter-ruptions of the upper string course. Even as executed and with the reduction in decoration, the building has difficulty in finding a coherence within itself or of expressing its Georgian brick format, with which the Fancy entrance was completely at odds. A massive, white-rendered pylon framed a row of columns—two engaged, four free-standing, faced in Portland stone over blue brick cores, and ornamented at cap and base with green, red and black faience. On the fascia, the company's name was inserted in glass and lit from behind. Recessed behind the columns were small-paned sash windows, over faience-clad spandrels and, in the centre, the main doorway. That was further recessed within a faience-decorated architrave. The bronze glazing bars in the doors and fanlight were sprightly Art Deco in style, but the bronze bordering and the door furniture were altogether too heavy, almost gross, in comparison. The originally proposed design for the door was more coherent and less aggressive. Unusually for a Fancy main entrance, here there was no irresistible invitation to enter—even the side pedestals sat solid and square. Since the building as a whole was meant to say something about the company's products—a three-dimensional catalogue?—the entrance seems to say more about its history.

Separated from both product and history were, however, the company's factoring activities, the buying-in and reselling of such merchandise as bathroom wares, domestic stoves and boilers, for which showrooms had been established at Redhill, Surrey, and Hove and Bexhill in Sussex.

Salesmen travelling in those areas were dealt with in a room set aside at headquarters, situated on the left of the vestibule. The buying customer intent upon building materials would first be reminded, on entering the hall, of the company's operations as coal merchants by the brick fireplace and brightly-burning fire directly opposite the main door (although the rest of the building was centrally heated). But the customer's path was to the right, by the enquiry desk, thence to the waiting room and finally to the showroom 'containing an interesting display of building materials'[137] at the end of the right-hand corridor.

The historical path celebrated the company itself, its longevity as a family concern and its progression into modern times. The founder, George Valentine Hall, was born during the reign of George III. In 1824 he set up business extracting stone and lime from Merstham Quarries in Surrey and sent them to London by the Surrey Iron Railway; the trucks returned with coal for local sale. More than a century later, the new head office building was formally opened on 9 December 1931 by Joseph Hall, George Valentine's descendant.[138] Thomas Wallis attended the ceremony. The principals of the firm and informed, eminent visitors would have appreciated the indications en route of the company's historical progress. On this basically Georgian building was a monumental entrance copied from the architecture of a culture ruled by dynasties. On it were stone-faced columns, beyond it a coal-burning fire and, on the wall of the entrance hall, a brass tablet recording important dates in the company's history. The decorative terrazzo of the hall floor was continued only over the first flight of stairs, indicating ascent to the first floor landing, around which the offices of chairman and directors were assembled. Immediately opposite the head of the stairs was the oak-panelled board room, sited directly over the entrance. There, family descendants and more-recently recruited, non-related directors jointly decided upon the present and future activities of the company, with reminders from the past in the pictures on the walls.

The whole of the building was about building—materials, construction and history—but lacked the controlling discipline of effective building design; none of the concepts portrayed was sufficiently dominant to instil cohesion. But then, the company was there to sell building products not building design, and the headquarters was well liked; people grew fond of it, which might well justify the existence of buildings that do not conform to architectural purism.

The Avon India Rubber Company Limited

In the same year, 1931, a more congenial marriage of brick, faience and white cement was achieved in the design of an offices, service station and warehouse building in London for a firm of tyre manufacturers. The Avon India Rubber Company Limited was founded in 1885 in Limpley Stoke,

Wiltshire and was taken over in 1890 shortly after moving to Melksham, Wiltshire, where its present headquarters and manufacturing base were in operation as Avon Rubber plc. Rapid expansion, with the introduction of pneumatic tyres at the turn of the century, led to the founding of depots in many large cities. The company built a five-storey block on Euston Road, London, in 1903, to serve as its main London depot and to house advertising and export departments. Despite the slump of 1920–24, the company prospered sufficiently to decide upon new and more modern premises for the London depot.[139]

The site chosen in 1930 at Mabledon Place, London, was a triangular plot at the corner of Mabledon Place and Flaxman Terrace. The ground sloped down toward Euston Road, some yards to the north. The building was L-shaped, 40 feet in depth, and aligned with the pavement on both fronts, so that the northern arm was at a slightly obtuse angle. The flat-roofed, three-storey building measured approximately 87 feet to Mabledon Place on the east and 127 feet to Flaxman Terrace on the south. It was constructed of steel frame, with brick walls and casings, reinforced concrete floors and pre-cast concrete stairs and sills. Stanchions were disposed around the external walls, most at 20 feet centres; the only internal stanchion was that supporting the cross wall of the stair tower. Most of the ground floor was used for delivery and despatch of tyres and for garaging the transporting fleet, hence the large vehicular entrances on the south side. A trade sales section in the north arm was entered through a door placed centrally on the east, Mabledon Place, front. At the far south end was a stairway to the first floor, between the main building and the petrol station and thus an extra fire escape. Inside the main ground floor, a beam and track travelling hoist, an external lift in the crook of the L, and a tyre shute moved tyres up and down, and/or directly to the trade-sales counter, from the tyre stores that occupied the whole of the first floor. Beneath the outer corner of the building was a fuel store and 'heating chamber' and a blue-brick flue rising through the corner tower.

The second floor contained offices; those for managerial staff, including advertising, sales and export, were partitioned off immediately within the exterior walls and a large open-plan general office was accommodated around the internal angle. Access to the offices and, for staff, to other floors, was by stairs or the centrally-placed lift in the tower at the far north end of the east front. Taking advantage of the sloping ground, the base of the tower was dropped to a lower level than the main ground floor and a mezzanine floor was inserted between ground- and first-floor levels. The top landing led directly to the main second floor and to a large reception room on the left, with a room for travellers and/or staff lunches on the right. Behind the stairwell on ground and mezzanine floors were the men's lavatories, finished with a flat roof; the women's lavatories on the first floor and those for the directors on the second floor, were all within the main structure.

The only true faience trimming of the building was the company's name lettering in red on the fascias at ground floor and 'pediment'. It could be argued that the Avon building rightly belongs with section (c) designs, in which the stylistic norm arises from structural geometry and the introduction of sculptured decoration. But the form does not speak for itself; rather, the decorative treatment that makes the form more visible and interesting speaks for it, in striking patterns of glossy black and matt white that follow the structural lines, but too boldly and in too artistically contrived a way to deny the Fancy label.

Most emphatic are the broad, horizontal bands of white cement rendering, bordered by black, glazed bricks, at each ceiling level. Between them, the pattern of windows and light brown brick mullions is almost dissolved away, to confirm the open span of the floor space behind them. Interrupted by recession of the brown brick walls and glazed corners of the main external angle, each façade is complete in itself—slightly projecting, slightly battered, contained by the ram's-horn motifs against the 'corner towers'. At the same time, a connection is made and the horizontal lines maintained by the black and white bands at lintel and sill of the corner windows, the grasping fingers of the black-and-white stripes on each ground-floor corner, the black and white string course below them, and the plain brick plinth that levels the base above which these horizontals are stacked (presaging the layer-cake version of 'modern architecture'?). On the east façade, the ground-floor section is made even more lively by the chequered pattern of the white glazing bars of the large windows and the Egyptianised treatment of the trade entrance. That doorway presents another of Wallis' evocative metaphors, accenting the importance of the selling section with the twin-plumed crown of the all-powerful Amun[140] pointing to the company's name; and again, by the flanking pylon effect rising from the rounded edges on the corner blocks to the horns of Amun that contain the band bearing, again, the company's name—high, but directly over the entrance.

A more clearly defined verticality is expressed by the corner towers. Less pronounced perhaps at the main corner, where elegant brown brick walls, intercepted only by clear glass, provide a still moment between the bold contrasts of the two façades, but more explicitly on the stair tower, in representing its internal function. Narrow lights, bordered by stepped white rendering, rise through the brown brick wall, from white, sculpted architrave to white stepped tower caps. The incomplete symmetry of the architrave is unfortunate and, whilst the zig-zag effect over the door relates to the Art Deco style of the bronze metal glazing bars of the door itself and the lamp later installed above it, there is in that entrance design an absence of relevance to the tightly-knit format and arrogant self-possession of the main block.

The claim that the building was constructed in three months has some substance. The only extant plans are dated between 31 December 1930 and the end of February 1931. Photographs showing the building completed and in use were published in June and July 1931.[141] Two years after completion of the building, Avon became a public company. The building appears to have been in active use until the mid-1960s, when it was converted to an air terminal by Sky Tours. Ten years later, the whole block was demolished to make way for a new National and Local Government Officers' Association (NALGO) headquarters building.

Hoover Limited

The Avon building does offer intimations of the 'geometric-sculptured' style of the later works from 1931 onwards, but two more Fancy factories were built after the Avon commission. For Hoover Limited, from 1931, Wallis, Gilbert & Partners began a lengthy commissioning of some 10 buildings at Western Avenue, Perivale, Middlesex. The company originated in North Canton, Ohio, USA, as manufacturers of leather goods and harnesses. A relative of the principals, one Murray Spangler, was a school janitor who suffered from asthma; he designed a suction cleaner so that his work did not exacerbate his respiratory condition. In 1907, Hoover manufactured the cleaner as a sideline but, when the decline in horse transport seriously reduced the company's business, the cleaner was improved, developed, and brought into full production in 1914–15.[142]

Export of Hoover vacuum cleaners to Britain began in 1919, via a manufacturing base in Canada, to avoid tariffs and, later, to take advantage of Imperial Preference. A small manufacturing unit was established in Britain in a second-hand factory in London but, as demand increased and entry was gained into European markets, a new and more salubrious base was considered necessary. A year was taken over the choice of site. Land on the corner of Bideford Avenue and Western Avenue at Perivale was decided upon because, according to the European Managing Director, C. B. Colston, it was

> . . . magnificently placed for road and rail transport and for the housing of our workers, . . . we overlook Ealing golf course, which will never be built on . . . we could get good playing fields at a reasonable price . . .[143]

and the site was large enough for expansion. Mr Colston also believed that a 'dull, drab factory is a definite handicap'. There was no such handicap in the designs produced by Wallis, Gilbert & Partners.

The first building, known as 'Number 1', was designed in 1931 but the only surviving floor plans in the architects' archive bear the date 1934 and were drawn when extensions were carried out and internal uses were reorganised (see Fig. 28). Number 1 building faces south, was two-storeys high, flat-roofed, roughly rectangular in shape and stood well back from the road for later landscaping. It measured approximately 220 feet wide by 120 feet in

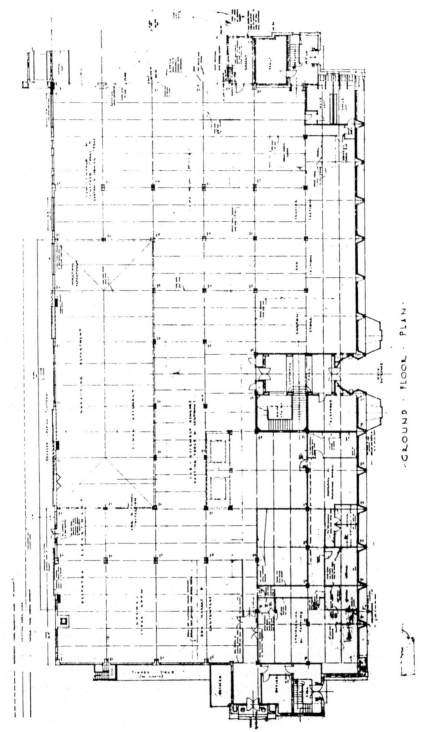

Fig. 28 Hoover Ltd, Western Avenue, Perivale, Middlesex: plan—Building Number 1, ground floor, 1934

depth, with set-back projections on the west and east sides. The floors were open plan and separated where required by movable partitions. On the north side, a central area five bays wide by two deep was of single-storey height, with a hipped, glazed and Trafford-tiled roof. It opened on to a long loading dock across the back of the building. The first floor was consequently a frontal block with returning wings on the east and west sides—a similar format to that at Pyrene.

At first, operations consisted only of finishing, repairing, servicing and packaging vacuum cleaners made in London or part-assembled from Canada. The work took place on the ground floor. The upper floor was largely office space but also had a canteen and kitchens on the north side of the west end. Access for office staff was through doors at the front of the set-back stair towers; the workforce entered through a door in the west elevation; for kitchen and canteen staff, there was a small staircase beside the loading bay at the rear. The main entrance, for directors and visitors, was placed centrally on the south front, with hallway and stairs leading to a large landing and waiting room on the first floor.

The Hoover building was undoubtedly the fanciest of the Fancy factories, but by no means the most attractive (see Fig. 29). So many colours, so many shapes, so many bits of this and that; all beautifully designed and executed but with no meaningful pattern or controlling concept. The lack of any kind of coherence in the basic composition is partly to blame. The battered framing of a recessed colonnade flanked by corner towers follows in line from the Egyptianised classicism of earlier Fancy designs. But here, there is no relation between the towers and the projecting façade. Unlike the India building, which was also designed to gain height by the addition of a third storey, here

Fig. 29 Hoover Ltd, Western Avenue, Perivale, Middlesex: as-built, 1932

the towers are set too far back, are barely integrated into the main structure, and are too tall in relation to the main block prior to later extension. Further, with the Poelzig-cum-Mendelsohn type windows serrating the outer edges of the towers, the building's silhouette is neither satisfying nor well delineated. The straight-cut lines of the tall windows on the towers, the lumpy contours over the doors, the Art Deco treatment of the doors themselves, the fragmented transom and the narrowing of the long window at its base, to which the faience trim does not extend, and the triple indents below, are all at odds with themselves and with the curving lines of the Expressionist windows. There is complete alienation between the vocabulary of the towers and that of the main façade; there is no binding feature, such as a string course, an association of geometrical forms, or a consistency of decorative elements. When a third storey was added to the main block in 1935, it provided a direct link between the towers—set back in line with them, repeating the faience strips, but with a different pattern of windows. The combination of towers and third storey creates the impression of an interesting but wholly separate building, which stresses the lack of relation with the main block.

Even standing alone, however, the composition of the main block façade is not integrated within itself. Some reaching for height is apparent in the vertical raking of the V-section columns and the absence of breast walls in the windows. But, against the powerful white concrete framing,[144] the narrowness of the frontal plane of the columns, the difference in shade and surface of their artificial-stone facings, and the blank void of the windows, produce neither an effective rhythm nor a balancing of rectilinear lines. The jagged, vertical stepping of the columns, with their chevron-like blue and red faience trim, and the plethora of green, rectilinear glazing bars strike a discordant note with the stronger, calmer lines of the white frame. The red faience line, set into the frame, fails to control the colours. It is too weak against the lines of the towers and is not all-encompassing, being dissected from the blue baseline by slabs of red, black and blue faience at the outer edges. Further confusion is wrought there by the winged horns of Amun; they have green and red keystone-shaped tiles in the inner curve, from which a line of green faience extends round the corner—but only to the junction with the towers' plinths.

The recessing and shade-contrast of the framed area, which should contribute to drawing the visitor into the building, is too busy with itself to do so. Thus, the central entrance is able to dominate only by being even more frenetically active. Recessed deeply between the centre columns and two similar piers, the main doors have Art Deco glazing bars and are protected by highly decorated, monogrammed, metal gates that close to an outwardly-pointing V. Above them a band of sharply contoured concrete, with vertical tubular lamps in the valleys, is surmounted by a great flare of colour. This exotic fan-shape is comprised of red, black and green faience, white stucco, gold and black metal and plain glass.

Writers have described the decoration of the Hoover factory as culled from the art of Central and North American Indians, such as frequently appeared in Art Deco jewellery, and other artefacts.[145] Here the decoration is very extravagant; nevertheless, Wallis' ornamentation of his Fancy factories always contained some relevant comment or programme. Hoover Limited originated in America, but the decoration of the British factory bears no resemblance to the art of the Iroquois territory from which the family came, although there are some similarities perhaps in the doorway motifs to the beadwork of the Potowatami Indians further west. The gold fir tree designs (that do not appear on the drawn plans) have some relation to the Indian art of the south-west of the United States and, possibly, to the animal and vegetable designs of ancient civilisations of Central America.[146] How knowledgeable was Wallis of these possible sources one is not able to say. On the other hand, the nervous angularity of much of the Hoover decoration is certainly Art Deco; it is indeed, the only Fancy factory to which 'Art Deco' as a general decorative description can be sensibly applied. Such a modern fashion may have been seen to coincide with an American inflection taken from the popularity of 'Western' films where historical accuracy was not important and the 'Red Indians' mostly portrayed by Hollywood were an imaginative composite taken from Plains Indian tribes. Their feathered headdresses and war paint designs do have a little stylistic kinship with the Hoover doorway, but Wallis' sources were rarely so trivial.

It is difficult to make sense of the Hoover building as a whole but the owners and employees always considered it to be 'Egyptian'. The most powerful structural feature is the battered frame; the most decorated feature is the main access to the building. In accepting the relation of an Egyptian frame terminated by horns of Amun to an Egyptian doorway, it is possible to find a relevant underlying programme. In ancient Egypt, the confidant most close in body and second only in rank to the king was the king's fan bearer. The colourful, long-poled, semi-circular fans were of vulture feathers. The vulture symbolised the goddess Mut, protector of the king. As well as the fan shape over the Hoover doorway, there are Horus-eye (Wedjat) shaped pavings at the main gateway to the factory, battered pedestals to the metal-framed lamp standards and the pathway from gate to door passes between other fan shapes, of rose beds set in spacious lawns. The vulture and the Wedjat snake together symbolise the protectors of the 'Two Lands' of Egypt. This Egyptian symbolism comes closer to a representation of the close relationship between the Hoover parent and its first overseas base than, say, thunderbird feathers worn by an Apache chief.

The visitor to the factory, guided along the path, is drawn into the fluted arms of the doorway columns by a downward tilt of the faience line and the black banding of the grey terrazzo floor, to pass beneath the favoured symbolising of the entrance. The floor pattern of the hall matched that of the entrance way—grey terrazzo, black banded and skirted. Walls of deep beige and a white ceiling were moulded, at pier and cornice, in steps, flutes, curves and cofferings, with tall metal-framed lamps set into the wall.[147] Via a stairway to the left, with its polished metal handrail and metal balustrading marking the way with a repetition of the fan pattern, the visitor would reach a palatial landing/waiting room, decorated like the hall, from which access was gained to the directors' offices at the front, west side of the first floor (Fig. 30). The abrupt change at the threshold from a highly coloured to a neutral decor and the sudden change of direction are startling, but the visual activity created by twitchy lines and moulding is sustained. Possibly the coloured exterior was designed to excite the senses, attracting the visitor to come close, whilst the internal pathway, palely elegant but still disturbing, was meant to stimulate the mind—for business deals ahead?

As was usually the case in Wallis, Gilbert factories, the visitors' route was the most decorated and the most eloquent. The staff route to the first floor offices, via the stair towers, was less extravagant but apparently dealt with the same concept. Beyond the doors are, again, neutral colours; but here in smooth, rounded, plainly Modern forms. Yet the journey upward passes so many shapes and sizes of apertures of incoming light that, en route, attention would be alerted and the brain awakened.

Fig. 30 Hoover Ltd, Western Avenue, Perivale, Middlesex: Building Number 1, upper hall, 1987

When the third storey of the main block was added in 1935, office space was expanded to accommodate records, mailing and a print shop. Because of the set-back in line with the towers, there was interference of natural light by the original parapet. A hipped, glazed roof was therefore placed over the forward portion of the third storey. Windows on the front elevation are in groups of three, with painted concrete spandrels and beams, where the lines of faience were inset. Presumably white concrete, as used for the rest of the building, was then too expensive. More recently, an extra floor has been inserted to raise the ground floor and insert a semi-basement. In 1981, windows on the façade were replaced, having been specially made to match the original ones. But glazing at floor levels was over-painted, further exacerbating the surfeit of colour and lines. At the same time, many faience tiles were replaced, which may account for the insertion of pink where one would have expected red.

As was the practice with many commercially-important buildings, Hoover was floodlit at night. At Firestone and India, floodlighting revealed more clearly the superior quality of the building's form and composition; at Hoover it brought the deficiencies into focus. But the building was well-liked and enjoyed by clients, their business associates, the people employed there and the general public. Locally, there was some curiosity about why the building contract was awarded to Higgs & Hill and not to Percy Bilton & Company who were responsible for almost all other construction, including houses, in the Perivale area. The Hoover factory was built as a 'monument to advertising', a showpiece headquarters. It was pictured on sales ephemera, such as jigsaw puzzles, penknives and ashtrays. Linked with the erection of the building, a salesmen's contest was held and charted in terms of 'brick-by-brick' achievement; a trowel was given as a souvenir. The company slogan, 'Hoover beats as it sweeps as it cleans', was illuminated in neon lights at the rear of the building where it could be seen from the railway.[148] Thus, although exceeding the bounds of decorum and failing in compositional merit, the Hoover building served its purpose well. With aggressive salesmanship and constant advertising markets expanded; within two years, more floor space was required.

The first of a number of building extensions and additions (Fig. 31) was designed in January 1934 and known as Building Number 3. Sited to the east of and perpendicular to the existing block, the four-storey building of reinforced concrete measured 100 feet by 80 feet on a grid of ten by four bays and was designed on the frame and glass 'Daylight' principle. A single-storeyed, quarter-circle bay infills the junction with the main building. On the road front, glazed V-shaped projections rise through the storeys and break the reeded skyline in a semblance of corner towers, echoing the shape of the columns on the main building façade.

It was at that stage that full manufacturing processes began at Perivale. The ground floor of Building Number 3 contained the raw material stores, manufacturing plant, a diesel engine and generator plant, sanitary facilities

Fig. 31 Hoover Ltd, Western Avenue, Perivale, Middlesex: factory complex and head office, *c.* 1970

(in a similar position on each floor), stairs, goods lift and a loading dock to the yard at the rear of the main block. The motor department was on the first floor; production office, reconditioning section, bag and Bakelite moulding sections on the second, with a doctor's surgery alongside the lavatories and cloak-rooms. Part of the third floor was walled off for the engineering department, testing and the storing of paint and overalls; the rest of the floor space was given over to the transfer of the canteen and kitchen from the main building. A 40-feet-square water tank, lift motor housing and lantern ventilators extended above the otherwise flat roof. This was a straightforward manufacturing building of Kahn-inspired design. The enhancement of the roadside elevation is attractive, with good, clean modern lines. By itself, it is very pleasant; the single-storeyed arc is very pleasant too; but the juxtapositioning of both with the already self-alienating towers and façade of the main block is awful.

Within one more year, more floor space was needed. Another four-storey 'Daylight' block, ten bays by five, was erected to the north of the site, abutting Building Number 3, parallel to the original main block but with an open-ended court in the centre. This was known as Building Number 5. A single-storeyed loading dock and a goods lift, below which was the basement boiler house, opened on to the yard. Through the full height of the building, a projection at the south-west corner contained stairways, lavatories and cloakrooms serving each floor. On the west elevation, V-shaped oriel windows lit the stairwell; these small casement windows on the outer corners of the lavatory bays opened outwards towards each other on spragged hinges, reinforcing the idea of the V-motif but dangerously so to the passer-by. The building was devoted wholly to manufacturing and the servicing of processes, with stores sections as appropriate to processes on each floor. The engineering and drawing offices were on the third floor.

Between 1932 and 1936, various other smaller additions were designed and executed by Wallis, Gilbert for Hoover, such as those for petrol storage, cellulosing, scrap and waste disposal; there was also a neutralising tank, a fire brigade building and a garage. The last major addition of the interwar years was that of 1937 for a garage and canteen (Building Number 4). This was a free-standing building to the west and slightly forward of the original main block. It was rectangular in shape, eight bays deep by three wide, at 20 feet centres, and was constructed of reinforced concrete and steel, with concrete and glass infill. The garage and car-wash section, on the ground floor at the north end of the building was entered through the end bay facing Bideford Avenue, which also gave access to the works yard. Beside it, one bay in, was the main entrance—to hall, stairway and lifts. Two projecting bays on the east side of the building were also stair towers, for access from the works side. At the main entrance on the west side, from Bideford Avenue, the stair tower is expressed in the tall, faience-edged window that rises above a moulded, many-faceted architrave inset with vertical, tubular lamps and flanked by narrow hall windows. Gates to that entrance and the vehicular way beside it are of Art Deco pattern metal, with battered concrete pedestals supporting metal-framed lamps. A similar double gateway, further south on Bideford Avenue, provided vehicular access across the front of the building.

On the east side, tall windows in the outer walls of projecting towers light the stairwells, the uppermost storey of each of which has fully-glazed walls. The towers are capped by flat roofs, faience-trimmed at the edges in line with the string course that surrounds the building. Very substantial architraves around the east-facing doors are centred with vertically-raised oddities of fluted concrete; above them are small, bowed windows with scalloped caps. Fancy metal brackets support external lamps high on the chamfered corners of the towers. (The rear of the building was altered in 1958 to include a fire station and security office.) As more floor space became needed for the production area, the mailing room, print shop and stationery store were transferred to the ground floor of this building. Employment and personnel offices and interview rooms filled the forward bays with access by four single doors on the south front. On the first floor, progressing from the rear forwards, were cloakrooms and dressing rooms, the rest room, staff and management dining rooms, kitchen, lavatories, the manager's office, and a lounge with external balcony. The second floor was wholly occupied by the works canteen, cafeteria and kitchen, with ancillary services. Over the central bays of the canteen, the roof was raised to provide clerestory lighting and ventilation.

All outer-wall stanchions were placed internally, which permitted glazed corners and an external appearance for most of the building as an uninterrupted stack of layers of white concrete alternating with long-paned windows with green glazing bars. The windows were trimmed only at the level of the uppermost lintels, with a string course of red and black faience. By and large, the Hoover canteen building represents what, in Britain in the late 1930s, was an acceptable form of Modern architecture, albeit here compromised by some very quirky bits of decoration. The front of the building, however, incorporates features that were more popular at the time, a sculptured geometry of curved windows and doors and a central 'tower' piece that would have been happily at home on a restaurant at a seaside resort. The lower portion of the façade, framing the windows and doors of the employment section, is faintly domestic. Since much of the building was for off-duty activities, the 'recreational' treatment of the rest of it was reasonably appropriate, but its debonair spirit is quite put out by the over-heavy hanging balcony.

The V-shaped window in the centre of the upper façade, with its moulded, stepped capping and chequered faience, is not unexpected as an identifying and associative feature. But, even with its supporting concrete 'candles', the modicum of verticality it introduces into the largely horizontal form of the building, is overpowered by the presence of the balcony. Whatever upward thrust the central feature may have achieved against the insweeping grasp of the long windows was nullified by the unduly heavy decoration on the lower edge of the balcony wall. The significance of the reiterated V-shapes and motifs throughout the Hoover complex has not been discovered; it appears to have no specific relation to Hoover as it was also used at Freeder and Ault & Wiborg (discussed in (c)).

Mr Colston, European Manager, was well pleased with it all. In an item in the *Financial Times* he expressed his delight that

> . . . it has increased the health and happiness of everyone concerned. A dull drab factory is a definite handicap . . . The new factory, in short, has proved a good investment . . . It has enabled us to increase our business and we are prepared for all eventualities.[149]

Hoover plc vacated the factory in 1987, moving headquarters to Merthyr Tydfil in Wales and manufacturing to 'a more modern factory' at Cambuslang in Scotland. The premises were taken by the Mountleigh Group plc. Then came the problem of deciding upon re-use or demolition. With thoughts of the loss of Firestone, that the Hoover façade had some protection from listing but that the local planning authority preferred demolition, there was another rush of praise for the design. Already in a press release of May 1984, Hoover had quoted from Snowdon and Platt's 'Great West Road Style'—'This is the building for which Thomas Wallis must principally be remembered and marks the high point of his personal style',[150] and from a 1975 RIBA guide to selected buildings in London of the interwar period

> Unquestionably the finest of Wallis, Gilbert factories: Egyptian Art Deco and modern movement faience adding up to the Granada Tooting [interwar cinema] of the factory floor. Not a foot is placed wrongly in this extraordinarily happy blend of styles.[151]

By 1989, referring to the 'major planning row' to which the building could be subjected, Kenneth Powell, in the *Daily Telegraph* of 31 January, described it as 'Wallis' masterpiece'. Contemporary comment was less appreciative. A poem, backed by a sketch that leaves no doubt to whom or to which building it refers, condemned the decoration in nine verses, a few of which are

> Leave no space undecorated;
> Hide those ugly wheels and pipes.
> Cover them with noughts and crosses,
> Mess them up with stars and stripes.
>
> Now for curves and now for colour,
> Swags and friezes, urns and jars.
> Now for little bits of faience,
> Now for giddy glazing bars.
>
> What the country wants is beauty,
> Art's the thing for industry.
> Who'd suppose such curves and zig-zags
> Could conceal a factory.[152]

Hoover Number 1 was overdecorated but the depiction of an absolutely plain 'engineer's design' above the zig-zag one tends more to the concern that factories should be decorated at all rather than the lack of architectural merit of this particular example.

When Thomas Wallis was designing Hoover Number 1 he was experiencing considerable domestic turmoil—estrangement from his wife, involvement with Doris Rudland and, in 1932, the death of his second son. All of these may well have affected his creative concentration in producing the hotch potch that resulted. Even if the motivation was provided by American pressure for sheer eye-catching kaleidoscopia, there is no real excuse for the lack of cohesion or harmony in the basic composition. One is moved to wonder how those who should have known better allowed themselves to be blinded by so much colour and Babel vocabulary.

Freeder Limited

The last of the Fancy factories was designed and built in 1934–35 for Freeder Limited, paper manufacturers, at Brimsdown, Essex. Freeder was a name long established in paper making in north London; in the early 1930s, the company at Brimsdown operated from north-light sheds set back 50 feet from Mill Marsh Lane. The commission to Wallis, Gilbert & Partners was for three buildings: an office block facing south to the road and attached at the rear to an existing production shed; a long, narrow, single-storeyed building for ancillary purposes, along the west boundary of the site; and, 50-feet to the rear of the existing works on the north side of an open concrete yard, a new production unit.

The last mentioned of the new buildings was of steel-frame construction and measured 125 feet by 125 feet, with external stanchions at 25 feet centres on concrete-encased ground beams. (The presence of a nearby canal and the name of the road suggest that the area was marshy and that building foundations needed special attention.) A central row of stanchions, from front to back, supported the trough of two pitched, trussed roofs, top glazed and Trafford-tiled, with special ventilators on the ridges. Access was by four double doors at the front which, like the two side walls, were fully glazed while the rear gables were blank walls. Infill throughout was of rendered brick. Apart from walled-off rooms for various stores, the boiler house and a small despatch section, the whole of the floor space was devoted to manufacturing purposes. This building was simply a straightforward, nicely-finished production unit.

The single-storeyed, flat-roofed ancillary building on the west boundary measured 102 feet by 15 feet. It was constructed of steel frame, infilled with rendered brick, small-paned, metal-framed windows and wood-panelled doors to each facility. These comprised a garage (nearest the road), an oil store, canteen, lavatories and cloakrooms, employment office and time-keeper's lodge, all conveniently grouped in a free-standing building, to leave the production areas free from encumbrances. Covered access ways for the workforce moving between the amenity block and the works would have improved general conditions, but were not possible because of the road and yard having to provide access and turning space for vehicles.

The flat-roofed, two-storeyed office block was constructed of steel frame infilled with concrete, rendered brick and glazing, and had reinforced concrete floors. It was rectangular in shape, measuring 110 feet on frontage and with an overall depth of 25 feet 9 inches. In the centre of the ground floor was the main hall, walled off from storage rooms to the rear and open-plan wings to east and west. The intended use of the wings is not shown on plan but, as they were to have granolithic floors, they were presumably for storage, some manufacturing process or showrooms. Both wings and storage rooms had communicating doors in the wall shared with the existing production building. The main entrance on centre front led to the hallway, which had a terrazzo floor, black banded and skirted; on the left was the enquiry office, on the right a waiting room. The stairs rose along the east wall and turned across the rear wall to return to a first-floor hall/landing. A corridor, aligned with the rear wall of the first floor, gave access on the west to directors' offices and sanitary facilities, and to general offices and staff sanitary facilities on the east. Over the ground-floor hall was the shipping office.

The side walls and those on the front, for some 15 feet from the corners, rose above the roof line and were stepped and capped in ribbed concrete and a line of vermilion faience, suggesting corner towers. Tall, narrow lights, edged with vermilion faience, on the front walls appear to light stair towers, but floor plans confirm that the appearance of towers was purely aesthetic with no internal relevance. Projecting three feet forward of the 'towers' and set six feet in from the outer corners of the building, was a battered, concrete-faced pylon frame, ribbed on the outer edge and with a line of vermilion faience on the inner edge that returned at the bases. Within the frame a colonnade of V-section, vertically-stepped, engaged columns, with black and vermilion faience bands at heads and bases, was intersected by long-paned, steel-framed windows that had fluted breast walls at first-floor level. On the fascia, below a stepped, rib-edged pediment, the company's flag and the date of the building were inset in vermilion faience.

Access to the site for the workforce and transport was by the wide, double-gated road on the west side. For the principals of the firm and for visitors, a path led directly from the road, through centrally-placed metal gates flanked by battered pedestals, and then between green lawns to the main entrance, the importance of which was demonstrated by pairs of twin columns intersected by narrow lights. The deep recession of the doorway drew the visitor into the building; within a broad, white concrete surround, whose fluting terminated in feather-heads, were double doors with sun-burst glazing bars. Above, rays of glass and white glazing bars fanned upwards, through a broad chevron of black and vermilion vertical stripes on fluted white concrete, to a crown of feather-heads intersected horizontally by bands of black faience on white concrete.

Here there are similarities with the Hoover Number 1 building, in the shape of the columns and the treatment of the doorway. But, with its more overtly Egyptianised classical form and the limitation of decoration to a defining of parts, the Freeder building has a clarity and simplicity that were absent from its larger predecessor at Perivale. Here, too, despite the pretence of corner towers, the composition is more integrated and presents a visual entity. How well it was composed would have been more obvious when the building stood in its original white rendering than would have been the case with the stone-drab colouration it acquired later. As the smallest of the Fancy factories, this last among them had a compact dignity and sturdiness, made the more attractive by well-placed shafts of colour.

Assessment of the Fancy factories

It was the Fancy factories that brought upon Wallis, Gilbert & Partners the charge of façadism—an epithet that became an epitaph. Although H. Goodhart Rendell had hoped veneers would soon be outgrown, he did concede that, whilst the demand existed, Wallis, Gilbert's were the best of their kind and had been done with scholarship and skill.[153] Other professional peers were less kind. Criticism of the Fancy façades not only ignored the relevance of the façades to the factories behind them and what the façades had to say in that context; there was, indeed, concern that factories should be decorated at all, although no good reason emerged as to why they should not. The general debates that ranged around 'machine' neo-Georgian and stripped classical aesthetics seemed oblivious to the need for a commercial aesthetic, identifiable with manufacturing industry *per se*, and serving its many requirements.

The *Oxford English Dictionary* defines 'façade' as the face or front of a building towards a street or other open space, especially the principal front. On the other hand, 'façadism' as defined by Gardiner, for example, is where 'an external kit of styles is pinned on as a decorative front to conceal internal emptiness'.[154] The front elevations of Wallis, Gilbert & Partners' factories were composed of a number of styles but the resultant façades were not purely and only decorative. They were part of the meaning and function of the building, they were representative of their time and were an integral part of a total composition. They were never, therefore, an indication of 'internal emptiness'. Behind each façade or front elevation, planning and design were apposite and of a very high order. Differentiation of function was expressed on each building (including the façade) and within a factory complex, all being brought together into what Wallis himself prescribed—a 'harmonious design throughout a group of factory buildings'.[155] Form and content were closely related.

In his Introduction to *Façade*, Bevis Hillier described the buildings illustrated therein as 'slang architecture'.[156] No argument is raised here in respect of the American buildings instanced; they are not sufficiently known to this writer, but 7 of the 12 British buildings were designed by Wallis, Gilbert & Partners. 'Slang', as defined by the *Oxford English Dictionary*, refers to a low and vulgar type of speech, a jargon peculiar to low or disreputable characters, highly colloquial but below the level of educated speech. If that applies to the language of Wallis, Gilbert Fancy factories, it can only be out of prejudice and superficiality of judgement that looks no further than the pretty face.

Contemporary criticism has been perpetuated into present times, hence the repetition of unconsidered statements, incorrect reports and the making of new mistakes. Hillier is at pains to establish American attribution of the Fancy designs; that does not stand up to analysis. In any case, an overt display of American origins, proclivities or infiltration would not have been commercially sensible in the British industrial world at a time of economic depression when tariffs were in force to protect the home market and indigenous manufacturers. As pointed out above, the Firestone causeway was not designed to 'instil awe into the visiting commercial rep'; Hillier's comment could not have been made if he had had a better understanding of the industry and the architecture—or even of the building. One could search in vain in the Firestone design for Hillier's 'tiled walls' and the 'touch of Gothic in three-sided bay windows'.

The view that the Hoover building was the best and most representative of these so-called Art Deco factories serves only to bring the others into disrepute. Hoover was the only Fancy factory for which the Art Deco description was remotely possible, but to quote it in those terms as the 'prime' example amongst the rest, is to make another superficial assessment. The lack of coherence in the Hoover composition and the incongruity of its incorporated styles offer no exemplar by which to judge the rest. Only Firestone could justly stand as a prime example but not as 'Art Deco'. To compare one with another serves no useful purpose. Each was designed to suit the particular circumstances of the client, the location, site, product and all other determinants of design. Some results were excellent, others less so. But each should be judged individually on its own merits and not hierarchically within the group.

Different as the whole Fancy group is from what came before and that which followed, the philosophy of the partnership remained constant. The buildings therefore reflect the cultural ethos of the time—brighter, more colourful and more 'modern' but clinging to the past. The styles employed, ranging from very ancient to very modern, express the Janus symdrome of looking in both directions at the same time, which was a very prevalent public attitude in those years.

The Fancy designs were, however, apposite in other ways. Some of the factories were for new industries, where an implied lineage was a stabilising adjunct to an expression of forward-looking modernity; for older industries, able to expand or enter upon new ventures, the factories were an expression of both pedigree and advancement.

In more general terms, as company images, the Fancy factories were both symbols of success and talismans to conjure up success. For the general populace, they appeased social memory, fed the appetite for ornamentation and sustained myths against the clinical objectivity of science that threatened to overwhelm. They were also colourful beacons of hope in darker days and evidence of cultural continuity in rapidly changing times. In accordance with Wallis, Gilbert philosophy, these buildings were a means of elevating industry to a more acceptable civic and social status and, thereby, of elevating the workforce—by better working conditions, by offering a building worthy of their labours and of an individuality and presence with which they could be proud to identify. As Wallis pointed out in his talk to RIBA, contempt for society could too easily be bred in the minds of workers whose factories were no better than 'pig-sties': 'it is up to the architect to cultivate ideas in the minds of the leaders of industry'.[157]

Wallis' use of colour was not without precedent. The original Classicists and the Egyptians used colour in their architecture. Colour and form expressed the meaning of their buildings and identified their social role in a manner that was representative of their period and was thus well understood by the populace. What Wallis was doing in concrete and tile was what the Greeks and Egyptians did in stone and paint—and for much the same reason.

Most of the earlier works of Wallis, Gilbert & Partners were designed as variations on an original theme. Although some of the Fancy factories adhered to a recognisable format of battered framing of a colonnade flanked by corner towers, each was in itself thematic, something to be experienced, and to which decorative elements often gave the key. There were some similarities of detail in the faience work, but many of the tiles seem to have been specially designed for each building in accordance with the theme to be expressed—such as lotus blossoms for the Firestone Egyptian temple and the 'zig-zag' for Hoover. Unfortunately, there are no relevant surviving archives of Carter & Company Limited, which supplied most of the faience; the more detailed working drawings by Wallis, Gilbert & Partners that followed from more generalised colour-washed drawings have not survived.

Of the 10 Fancy factories designed by Wallis, Gilbert & Partners, one was not built and five have been demolished. Of the four still standing, one has been enveloped, one is unoccupied and rapidly becoming derelict, one has become the front elevation of a supermarket and the remaining one, Pyrene, is in use only as offices and has been much altered.

In their day, the Fancy factories were successful, popular and profitable. But they were expensive to build. Even during the few years of their commissioning, times were changing; architectural styles were becoming less idiosyncratic, more uniform, in a British version of Modern.

(c) The Later Works to 1939—The Sculptural-Geometric Phase

Economic recession reached its nadir in Britain in 1931. The slow climb to relative prosperity was encouraged by the example of a 'National' Government which, with its all-party but largely Conservative composition, projected a sense of national unity, of everyone pulling together toward a happier future. This was reinforced by the communications media which, although providing the populace with access to a wider world, were the direct means of forming a homogeneity of public opinion. British achievements and successes were widely publicised; the popularity of the Royal Family generated the notion of one large national family. There was greater concern for personal and social well-being; unemployment remained a major problem but less so in the southern regions of the country, where opinion was mostly listened to, and to which new industrial development continued to migrate.

Gradually, 'being modern' took on a smoother, sleeker, more sophisticated air and was measured by that degree. Derivatives of Art Deco and Arts and Crafts remained popular for some years. Public buildings and those for the higher reaches of commerce still favoured a classical or Renaissance appearance. An architectural style began to emerge, however, that was not Modern in the continental or international sense, although the influence was there, but in rendered or exposed brick, with long-paned glazing of long windows. The strong feeling for horizontality was most often counterbalanced, particularly in the more widely-used brick construction, by cylindrical towers that bore the stamp of 'Odeon' architecture, or by singular, rectilinear towers, generally placed at centre front, that tended toward a municipal mien. The hard lines of geometric structures were often offset by curving or sculpted dressing. It was a style so favoured for schools, hospitals, offices, local authority buildings, shopping centres and factories, that the purpose of one building was barely distinguishable from another.

Coty (England) Limited

For Wallis, Gilbert & Partners, designing in the new style was overlapped by the Fancy factories but the forthcoming transition was already evident in the factory for Coty (England) Limited, beside the Great West Road, to the west of the Pyrene factory. Information about the company or its building is limited. There are no surviving plans, except those published in *The Architect and Building News*,[158] and no archive material in the possession of the present-day company. All of the main manufacturing area of the original factory has been demolished; the frontal block is still standing but has been converted wholly to offices. The Coty Company is now part of Beauty International Fragrances Limited, a subsidiary of Rigease plc, and occupies Harbour House, next door on the west side, designed for Coty by Wallis, Gilbert & Partners in 1952. So far as can be ascertained, earlier in the twentieth century, Coty (Paris) was a French manufacturer of perfumes, whose wares were distributed in Britain through wholesale agents. In about 1930, when the product range had been extended to toiletries and cosmetics, the company decided to build a manufacturing base in Britain.

The site chosen beside the Great West Road was awkwardly shaped, so that the two-storeyed, flat-roofed frontal building faced north on to and co-extensive with the highway, while the single-storeyed, main manufacturing area at the rear was angled toward the east. The latter building was steel framed on a regular grid four bays wide by six bays deep on the west side and five bays deep on the east. It abutted the two-storeyed building only at the eastern part of its obliquely angled end. Dimensions are estimated at 120 feet wide by 150 in depth (east) and 180 feet (west) overall. The steel-framed roof was flat, with a raised central portion that had clerestory glazing. Was it Thomas Wallis' personal variation[159] of the east/west roof described by Douglas Wallis as an American improvement on the north-light[160] or was Douglas involved in this design?

Entrance gates on each side of the site gave access from the highway to the service road that encircled the building. Personnel entrances on the west side of the works building, separate for men and women, opened to cloakrooms and lavatories and thence to the work floor. Work stations were disposed around the outer wall and in the centre, with aisles around the centre part. On the east side of the site, through a wider gateway and road, vehicles delivered raw materials to the back of the building and collected finished goods from a loading bay on the east side. The production line was oriented as far as possible in the same direction. Processing, however, consisted of a number of small departments, for example, 'cologne', 'powder', 'soap', which were separated by partitions.

The two-storey building at the front of the site appears to have been of reinforced concrete by Truscon, and is of estimated dimensions 130 feet wide by 60 feet in depth. Entrances are by the main doorway in the centre front and a rear door in the wedge-shaped space between the two buildings. In *The Architect and Building News* report, this building is described as an 'office block' but most of the ground-floor space was devoted to storage: on the east for finished goods, with through access at the rear to the despatch section; to the rear of the central hall for bottle washing and storage; and on the west side, the essence store and mixing department. On the first floor a corridor led from the main stairway landing eastwards to the directors' and general offices, staff lavatories and tea room. On the west side of the landing were sections partitioned off for 'creams', 'rouge', 'brilliantine', 'fats', 'sundries' and also a laboratory.

Externally, the major impact of the building arises from the emphasis on horizontality. Layers of white concrete and darker, recessed glass are accentuated by long-paned windows with glass corners, a string-course effect of continuous, projecting sills and lintels, horizontally ridged, and a line of red faience with uneven, open triangular ends on the fascia (the faience has since been rendered over). Raised, stepped end blocks on the fascia seek to contain the elevations on the skyline but any pretence to corner towers is thwarted by the glazed corners beneath them, that cut down even into the plinth. The external wall stanchions offer little in the way of verticality, acting only as widely-spaced mullions, or visual props, to inspire confidence that the weighty concrete will not crush the flimsy glass.

The major vertical treatment comes with the monumental main entrance. The building is set back from the roadway on rising ground, landscaped with grassy plots and shrubs, so that ingress has an upward as well as an inward progression. From pedestals at pavement level, low baluster walls rose by stepped blocks to the level of the building, and then swung out around the entrance landing. To effect a narrowing of the way to the doors, the black skirting to the steps was matched by a similar line along the base of the building that angled inward and upward at the base of colossal, vertically-stepped splays to the recessed doorway. From a more distant view, the eye is drawn still further upward to the company flag by piers that curve in and up at lintel level to flank the taller stairway window in the centre. As if to legitimise this temple-like entrance, the door lintel carries a row of scarab forms and is capped by a cavetted cornice. But, although the entrance is given its due importance, its verticality is terminated and the overall horizontality of the building is maintained by the overhang of the fascia, the open-ended streak of red faience and by paired sets of rounded quadrants, that give visual continuity to the long lines of upper-storey windows.

In the recessed entrance, the [originally] glazed doors opened directly into a double-storeyed hall, which has not been too drastically altered. Lighted by the central window, the sharper angles of this square room—the stepped cornice, arrissed newel and thin baluster rods—are softened by bowl-shaped wall lamps, the sweeping curve of the stairway and the continuous, rounded, metal banister rail. Beginning with curved steps, at the rear left corner, the stairway spirals along the east wall, across the front wall and rises along the west wall to a landing with a curved balcony, facing the window. Originally, a reception desk was set into an alcove on the right of the main doorway.

Most of the Coty building was concerned with manufacturing production. Administrative functions occupied only the east wing of the first floor. It was therefore appropriate and economical to limit space for the internal pro-cession route to that section. Wallis' treatment of the compact space was elegant and successful. Assuming that the presently naked walls were originally decorated with, at least, equally elegant pictures of the company's products, the hall expressed the stylish intimacy of a smart, modern beauty salon, in which the products would be used or could be purchased. The effect was therefore product-oriented, imaging the luxury of self-indulgence—once, that is, the visitor had passed the portals. The products were primarily for women, the workforce was mainly female, and buyers for salons and departmental stores were often women, but there is nothing feminine about the external appearance of the building. As things were regarded then, it reflects the bolder, thrusting, more masculine world of industry and com-merce. There is no delicacy in the sculpted curves; opposing structural lines are counter-weighted rather than counter-balanced. But there is a small warning of the change of gender at the threshold and a reference to the company's products. Those little scarabs on the door head are amulets, symbols of new life, light and warmth, images of self re-creation.

The Coty 'office' building was originally finished in white cement; light and shadow would have been more pronounced than appear in the present beige render. The tendency to top-heaviness may have been relieved by the streak of red and the company's flag on the fascia. Despite the faience trimming, however, the Coty building had none of the romantic splendour of the Fancy factories. In 1931, it was a very modern building, not aggressively so, but with a distinctly determined air.[161] Its layered geometry was characteristic of the Modern style in concrete that began to appear in the 1930s in Britain, and with greater frequency after the Second World War. The separation of horizontal and vertical planes, with sculpted finishing, was indicative of a more moderate version, often in brick with concrete dressing, that became much more common in the later interwar years.

Pasold Limited

A factory designed by Wallis, Gilbert & Partners for Pasold Limited at Langley, Buckinghamshire, in 1932 followed the latter mode. It is rare to come upon a first-hand account of the raising of a factory, still less one that includes an external but involved view of British industry in the 1930s. In his autobiographical account of his company, Eric Pasold states that, when travelling along the Great West Road, he was so struck by the beauty and magnificence of the Coty, Firestone and Pyrene buildings that he immediately determined that Wallis, Gilbert & Partners should be the architects of his new factory.[162]

The Austrian family of Pasold had been knitters and weavers for 10 generations at Fleissen, Bohemia, and had produced knitwear since 1870. On the dissolution of the Austro-Hungarian empire after the First World War, the Pasold family was not pleased to find itself redomiciled in the new state of Czechoslovakia, with a new nationality. Eric Pasold was, however, a convinced Anglophile, although it was not until he became principal of the family firm on the deaths of his grandfather and father in 1930, that he was free to set up a manufacturing base in Britain. But there was one surprising discovery about Britain that, so contrary to continental attitude, in Britain 'anyone engaged in manufacturing was looked down upon'.

From Christmas 1931, an exhaustive search was made within a 30-mile radius of London for a suitable site for the new factory. Pasold refused to consider second-hand factories or a location in more northern, established hosiery-manufacturing areas where commerce and labour were 'tainted by tradition'. Great West Road sites at Brentford and beyond were much too expensive at £2000 per acre, or at Greenford or Perivale at £500 per acre. Pasold visited Slough Trading Estate and was disappointed to find that, in comparison with Great West Road factories which he regarded as the 'industry of the future', those on the trading estate were 'tightly packed' and 'looked like barracks', with no prospect of expansion other than moving, when necessary, to one of the larger factories. The greenfield site chosen by Pasold, at Langley, facing Station Road and with Langley railway station immediately on the north boundary, was discovered only because the driver 'lost his way'. On 17 March 1932, the purchase of 17 acres was concluded for a total of £4500.

Pasold had already decided upon the layout of his new factory. In the USA in 1929 he had found that American hosiery factories were as old-fashioned as the mills at Fleissen, but a visit to General Motors and, later, to the Bata shoe works in Czechoslovakia, had convinced him that a 'conveyor belt system' of processing was most rational. His travelling companion in Britain, Czech architect Helmut Amoratico, had sketched out the required layout plan for Wallis, Gilbert to convert to imperial measurement, standardised dimensions and working drawings. The buildings were constructed of steel frame with brick and glazed infill, and placed centrally on site to allow for future extension at sides and rear. They consisted of a two-storeyed, flat-roofed 'office block' measuring 88 feet 6 inches in width by 21 feet in depth, facing west on to, and set back 75 feet from, Station Road. Attached at the rear was a single-storeyed manufacturing area. This was the same width as the office block and 136 feet 6 inches in depth, with granolithic floors and steel-trussed, north-light roofs of glass and Trafford tiles. It provided three long work bays, 29 feet 6 inches wide, with stanchions at 19 feet 6 inch centres. 'Hollow' (cavity) walls were externally rendered and glazed in continuous 'steel sashes'. The temporary rear wall, with centrally placed double doors, was of four and a half inch brick to allow for ease of future extension. All facilities were external to the rectangular, open floor space to permit uninterrupted production lines running in parallel, although the extra stanchions in the two bays on the south side, to support special shafting for certain machines, may have proved problematic on reorganisation into building expansion.

The boiler house was abutted on the north side, to accommodate an automatic oil-fired boiler serving a *Calique* heating system, 'the first of its kind in Britain'. (Note: This German heating system was installed at British Bemberg Limited in 1929–30.) *Calique* was a permanently sealed system; water was raised high above boiling point but remained as a liquid, passing through unflanged, narrow-bore, drawn-steel pipes welded together. There were thus no traps or possibility of leaking joints and no exhaust steam. The water was returned to the boiler for reheating; where steam was required, for example by the calenders, small calorifiers were installed.

The works entrance, cloakrooms, lavatories and clocking-on devices were sited on the north side of the ground floor of the frontal block, and were directly open on to the works floor. A solid wall separated this section from the central hall. The south side of the ground floor contained a store room with rear door and a workshop open to the works, again separated from the hall by a solid wall. The main entrance was centrally placed on front, leading to a partly double-storeyed hall. The stairs began at left rear and were protected at the well sides by a solid concrete baluster to circle around the walls in an anti-clockwise direction to the first-floor landing, across the rear side. Pasold intended the hall to be 'lofty' and 'impressive'. Amoratico had sketched fitments seen at the Strand Palace Hotel, London, for incorporation into and to 'glamorise' the factory hall, but these were not described by Pasold and there are no surviving photographs. To save time and money, however, the offices were not plastered or decorated until long after occupation, which took place on 13 June 1932, but the scheme was probably similar to that used for the manufacturing area—white ceilings, eggshell blue upper walls, 'battleship-blue' (grey?) for the dado and all exposed steel— even the machines were painted to match. Brackets were fitted to stanchions in the works area for hanging flower baskets.

The layout of the first floor of the frontal block also appears to owe much to Amoratico, since it lacks the usual clarity of circulation expected of Wallis, Gilbert planning. Offices to the north and south of the central landing led from one to the next with no wasted-space corridors. Lavatories were placed to the immediate north of the landing, for male and female to west and east respectively of a small vestibule that led to the first of the northside offices.[163] The exterior of that building followed the modern, horizontally-layered format but here the solid layers were of red-brown facing brick to 'tone with the trees and cottages of Langley village'.[164] Each layer edge was string-coursed by on-end bricks coming up to concrete lintels and sills of continuous, uninterrupted vertical casement windows. Repeating that verticality were the twin, colossal brick piers on each side of the main entrance. The company name, in large, free-standing letters, was raised above the roof line.

In the 1930s attracting foreign firms to manufacture in Britain was not actively encouraged, even for the employment they offered. There were strong currency regulations which Pasold managed (illegally) to circumvent, but only to an absolute amount—hence the economies in the factory building. He also had difficulties persuading local women to become factory workers and, again within strict regulations, had to bring in Czech workers to train them; the foreigners were allowed only a six months' stay.[165]

Thus, for all his regard for the Great West Road factories, a design of that kind was beyond the pocket of Eric Pasold; the chosen site was in an agricultural area where there was strong opposition to industrialisation. Hence, the choice of building materials, the lack of decoration and the restrained modernity of the built design. Continental influence may have ensured that the layout took advantage of every inch of usable space but that too was governed by funding. With a freer hand, Wallis may well have given the building a little more character. Extensions to the manufacturing area were carried out at the rear of the existing building in 1935 and 1936, to the north in 1937 and 1938, and another section was added to the office block on the north side in 1939. There are no surviving plans or photographs of these buildings except as they appear on a site plan and aerial photograph of *circa* 1962, which include many later extensions and additions. Chessums Limited were the contractors for all the 1930s buildings and Wallis, Gilbert & Partners were retained as architects. Pasold mentions that all engineering matters were discussed with, and advised upon, by Ingenier Kock, a 'very able young German engineer in the architects' employ'. The only surviving Pasold plans in the Wallis, Gilbert archive, other than those mentioned above, are for extensions in 1952.

Pasold's original aim to manufacture in Britain had been to base success upon the production of a single, therefore cheaply produced and cheaply sold, product—women's fleecy-lined, marl-coloured *directoire* knickers. The factory had been designed for that specific purpose, with long production lines that required no resetting to cope with a diversity of designs, trimmings or colours. But sales were not high. Then for the first time, and very much against the stern principles of his upbringing, Pasold visited the West End of London and saw from the shop windows that his product was very out of date. Women in the 1930s were looking for lightweight, fashionable under-wear in a choice of fabrics, styles and colours. Thereafter, considerable success was achieved by Pasold with a diversification of products, direct-to-retailer selling and the invention of the 'Ladybird' mark series of children's clothes. Pasold eventually took over many other allied companies, but finally merged with Coats, Paton, Baldwin Limited. More recently, most of the factory complex has been demolished and redeveloped as an industrial estate. The original office block, now vacant and much altered is still standing.

Roberts' Capsule Stoppers Limited

The designs for a factory and offices in 1932 for Roberts' Capsule Stoppers Limited at 159 Peckham Rye East, London, were also affected by financial and locational restraints. The manufacture of printed metal closures for bottles and jars was at a fairly primitive level when the company was founded at Southwark by E. C. and F. C. Roberts in 1887. Gradually, with improvements in production, in-house innovations and the introduction of lithographic printing, the company expanded, moving to two factories at Peckham. Tin plate was printed at one factory and then taken to the other for stamping and forming. A very wide range of closures was produced as there was then no standardisation of container sizes, but the major problem was that of transport between the two factories. Tin plate was so heavy that only small loads could be carried by the vehicles then available. By 1930 it was clearly evident to the company that a new, custom-built factory was needed, where all operations—art work, design, plate-making, printing, stamping, forming, the manufacture of sealing wads, tool design and making, and administration

—could be rationally organised and housed under one roof. But the factory had to be located in Peckham in order to retain trained employees.

A site that had been garden land attached to a large house was purchased; the factory faces south-west on to Peckham Rye East and extends northwards along Solomon's Passage. It is constructed of reinforced concrete frame, by Truscon, with brick and glazed infill, on a grid of 14 bays by 3, and of estimated dimensions of 280 feet in depth (aligned with Solomon's Passage) and 70 feet on front. Most of the building is of two storeys, flat-roofed on the front bays. A trussed, pitched roof, two bays wide, runs front to back over the inner south-east side; a shallower, trussed, pitched roof of one bay's width that extends along the north-west side is interrupted by a flat-roofed third storey over five bays. A single-storeyed section, abutting the south-east side, contained works lavatories, cloakrooms, switch room and boiler house. Other than the solid-walled stair and lift wells, the ground-floor space was partitioned into three large areas for printing (at the south-west end), warehousing, loading docks and works entrances (in the centre) and the press shop at the rear, with a run of small process rooms in the south corner.

The first floor contains offices, walled off in the front bays. Along the north-west wall, between the two stairwells, were other offices, the canteen, lavatories, cork drill and glue rooms; the remaining large open space was given over to other production purposes—drilling, aerography, and so on—and divided between stopper and metal-cap manufacture. The second floor was used for storage of wood tops and corks.

The elevation to Solomon's Passage is impressive, with rendered frame, large daylight windows to the ground floor and dark brick spandrels below the upper storey windows. The three-storey section has two vehicular entrances flanked by footway doors. Its height breaks the skyline and its access points interrupt the long run of ground-floor windows, so that structural enhancement, by broader stanchions and additional mullions, articulates the rather austere Kahn-like façade with a palace front effect.

On the plan of May 1932, the front elevation is in character with that of the north-west side. The as-built version is, however, in a much more Modern style. All of the frame, the extra intermediate stanchions, parapet and breast wall are rendered in concrete. A vehicular gateway on the right of the site led to the central double doorway, which was retained in the as-built. That doorway, with metal bars protecting glass in oak frames, leads directly into the factory area. A new entrance to the offices was placed in the far left bay. In line with a narrow footway gap in the boundary fence, the main entrance has a recessed doorway between plinths curving inwards and downward, and an inward-curving, vertically-stepped architrave. Above the small canopy over the doors, a clock is set in a stepped, diamond-shaped frame. Further above, a narrow, horizontal window with ribbed cornice lights the stairwell; above that, a small projecting cornice and the window to the staff lavatory are capped by the broad fascia that runs the full width of the façade. The fascia, with its centrally raised pediment above the gold-coloured lettering of the company flag,[166] binds together a façade that has lost its originally-planned symmetry. A projecting double lintel and infilled recess at the opposite corner makes some small effort to balance the interesting, but rather bitty and indecisive treatment of the main doorway.

The window placings and sizes do, however, reflect the internal plan—a prescribed feature of Modern design. On the other elevations, the windows are of the standard, small-paned variety but the long-paned ones on the front of the building, in the new 1930s style, had to be specially made.

The entrance hall has none of the opulence of other Wallis, Gilbert factories. Two circular steps at the left rear begin a stairway that curves round the walls to a small landing against the rear wall. It gives access on the right to a corridor across the rear of the first-floor frontal bays, leading to the directors' offices and giving access to the general and typists' offices. The route is not abundantly clear as, from that first landing, the stairs rise more convincingly to a corner turn along the north-west wall and then to an upper mezzanine (as shown in the window placings). But the rooms at the terminal are staff cloakrooms and lavatories—not the expected destination. The contrived planning of fitting the lavatory into the half floor is very odd. Had someone forgotten it? There was no other plumbing in the vicinity with which it had to connect; there was space on the first floor just inside the production area, where other offices were sited. It just adds confusion to the front elevation and to the processional route to the directors' offices.

Situated in a residential area, overlooking the mature trees and grass of Peckham Rye, the building's frontal block suggests a Modern-style house in parkland surroundings, and it is not in too great a conflict with its Georgian neighbour in whose grounds it has been raised. Nowadays, the observer's view of this attractive building has been spoiled by later changes. These include the retention of an air-raid shelter in the forecourt and the consequent transfer of the double gateway from right to left of the frontage; the unmatched replacement of the upper windows and insertion of a central mullion where the general office has been divided; and the loss of nearby trees through encroachment of other less-well designed industrial buildings. The slightly oblique angle of the front to concur with the building line on Peckham Rye and the street line on Solomon's Passage is not at all noticeable.

The factory and offices were first designed in May 1932; it was probably soon afterwards that the design of the frontal bays was changed, although there are no surviving plans. When the building was completed and/or occupied is not known, but the company held its annual general meeting there on 8 June 1933. It would appear that as much time was taken over the choice of design as the means of construction—building costs in relation to present and future operating requirements being the prime factor. Reliance upon the sale of the old factories to part-fund the new one and the demolition of houses at the rear of the plot to provide building space exacerbated the problems. Possibilities of where savings could be made were examined, costed and scribbled in notes addressed to the architects. The stark anatomy of the originally-planned front elevation may well have been less expensive and more quickly built but the as-built version was better suited to its location and was a more up-to-date expression of a forward-looking and innovative company.

The company is still in occupation, still includes members of the founding family, and recently celebrated its centenary. The range of products in printed tin and aluminium has been considerably widened.

Reid & Sigrist Limited

It is unfortunate that the rather 'Modern' factory designed for Reid & Sigrist Ltd, at Shannon Corner, New Malden, Surrey is now no more than a photograph in *Architecture Illustrated*.[167] Extensive search of planning offices, record offices and libraries has produced no plans and none exists in the architects' collection. Even the precise location of the building cannot be determined and it is thought to have been demolished.

The clients were manufacturers of aero-instruments and of some stature individually in the history of aviation. George Hancock Reid DFC served during the First World War as a Major (pilot) in the Royal Flying Corps, and continued thereafter as a Squadron Leader in the Royal Air Force, until his retirement in 1927.

Frederick Sigrist MBE joined Thomas Sopwith in 1910, became his Works Manager and later General Manager of Sopwith Aviation & Engineering Co Ltd, and designed some of the Sopwith aeroplanes, demonstrating and testing them in the USA. When that firm was taken over, he became Managing Director of the new owners Hawker Aircraft Ltd and of Hawker Siddeley Aircraft Co Ltd. Sigrist was the originator of the Hawker system of metal construction for aircraft.[168] Together, Reid and Sigrist set up in business at Canbury Park Road, Kingston upon Thames, testing aeronautical apparatus.

The new factory at Malden Way was to house the designing and making of aeronautical instruments (including the gyro-horizon compass and other aids to night flying). It appears to have been built in 1933 although much of Reid's work from 1935 was at Desford Airfield, Leicestershire, training civil and RAF pilots, and reconditioning aircraft for tropical use and target tugs, later for final assembly of Spitfires. Sigrist was probably a non-involved partner in the later years.[169]

For such clients, a Modern building was appropriate. The first impression is of cubic white concrete with slit windows and glazed corners. This was a two-storeyed building, with a central entrance and a set-back tower. It was most probably of steel frame encased in rendered brick. The ground floor was some seven bays wide by two in depth, with the outer bays open and ungated for vehicular traffic. Set into the area between plain, deep plinth and plain, even deeper, continuous fascia, were four recessed windows each side of the entrance. The sides of the entrance were vertically ribbed above sill level, each with a slit window. Two stocky square pillars, with the corners more sliced off than chamfered, led into the entrance beneath a straight, black-tiled lintel. The black band matched that at the lower edge of the plinth and the recessed band just below the tower cap. The pillars had black and red faience cappings.

The upper storey was in two blocks set each side of the recessed tower, with single slit windows near the inner edges, matching those below, and four windows set into each block below a similar deep fascia. These upper blocks extended only to the outer edge of the ground-floor windows, but they do have glazed corners. On the upper side elevations are four vertical slit windows that match the single ones on all sides of the tower, these latter being set within slightly projecting concrete panels. The tower itself has the same severed corners as the doorway pillars. All glazing bars were painted apple green.

Solid takes precedence over voids; the windows seem almost not to be there. The powerful horizontals and low doorway are barely offset vertically by the chunky tower. This is nevertheless a quite striking building, all straight geometry made more prominent by the added colour. But for an aviation-related building it sits very firmly on the ground. In 1946 the Desford connection was closed. In the mid-1950s Reid & Sigrist joined with Decker Ltd, but then went out of business.

Sir William Burnett & Co (Chemicals) Limited

Also very much in the Modern idiom is a factory for Sir William Burnett & Co (Chemicals) Limited at 891 Great West Road, Isleworth, Middlesex. Sir Wm Burnett & Co Ltd were timber merchants and wood preservers at Nelson Wharf, Millwall, London. The firm made its own brand of wood preserver and also soldering fluid and soldering paste. In 1933 chemical manufacturing was separated from timber and a new company formed for that purpose, with a new factory commissioned in the same year.[170]

The front building is of white painted, cement-rendered brick, two-storeyed and low slung, but with beguiling asymmetry and unusual curving elements. The building faces south and is set back a short distance from the roadway, with the production area attached at the rear. The site is rhombic-shaped, veering in depth to the west, and dictates the overall shape of the factory. Incomplete copy plans (expensively obtained from Hounslow Borough Environmental Services Department) show the front building to measure some 93 feet in width overall and 20 feet in depth. From a paved yard at the rear east, the production area extends westward some 60 feet at its widest point and beyond the end of the front building, to fit into the site. It is some 50 feet in depth, with a rectangular 'temporary saw mill' attached at the rear.

The ground floor of the frontal block has a porch, vestibule and hall, off centre, to the east of which is a private office with sanitary facilities, and a large general office which terminates at the triangular east end to contain the filing room, check room and stairs. To the west of the entrance is a kitchen, a rest room and, also triangular but with an internal right angle (rather than on the outer edge as at the east), cloakrooms and lavatories. The partial upper floor contains only a three-bedroomed 'caretaker's apartment', with living room, kitchen and bathroom.

Stanchions throughout are of reinforced concrete. The production area has an east/west pitched roof, steel trussed and clad in asbestos tiles and patent glazing. The frontal block has brick cross walls but rolled steel cross beams over the open plan general office; secondary joists are of wood. External walls are of rendered brick, painted white, windows are steel framed, and floors are of concrete covered with granite, granolithic or wood blocks as appropriate.

Externally this front building is almost a piece of sculpture, with a touch of Expressionism, a faint remembrance of the Einstein Tower and a strong suggestion of the upper decking of an ocean-going cruise liner.[171] The east end is curved, has narrow vertical stair lights and a band of green faience just below its flat roof. Thrusting westward from a solid beginning, between plinth and fascia on the ground floor, is a row of windows with concrete mullions and continuous, projecting concrete lintels and sills, intercepted at one bay in from the west end for the entrance, and curving obliquely round to the rear at the terminal point. Above, a similar section reaches out from the east 'tower', stopping at the second bay to curve round to meet its rear companion that progresses one bay further westward. Both are flat roofed and have windows, lintels and sills identical with those below. The remainder of the distance to the west is the flat roof of the ground floor, pierced in appropriate places with lantern lights, and backing up to a parapet that screens the factory roof, but permits the obelisk-shaped, white-rendered chimney, with its green tiled band near the capping, to add verticality as of a ship's funnel. All glazing bars and front railings were painted bright green. And very pretty it is, too! Thomas Wallis often took advantage of the shape and fall of a site to enhance a building; here, where the shape of the site could have presented a major problem, it has been creatively exploited. And the very Modernity of this frontal block tends, again, to suggest the hand of Douglas Wallis.

C. W. Martin & Sons Limited (Alaska)

In 1934 C. W. Martin & Sons Limited of 61 Grange Road, Bermondsey, London, demolished its 'K' building and replaced it with a large, multi-purpose, six/seven storey building of reinforced concrete and encased steel, designed by Wallis, Gilbert & Partners.

Martin's dealt in fur. In the eighteenth century seal skins were used for oil extraction and leather, the fur being sold for manure. Early in the nineteenth century a Chinese method of removing the long top hairs was discovered, and seal fur became a high fashion fabric for all sorts of garments and purposes. Furrier John Moritz Oppenheim founded his business in 1823, concentrating upon importing and processing Alaskan Furseal skins. In 1869 the business passed to the owner's sons and moved to a new, specially-built factory in Grange Road, Bermondsey. Charles Walter Martin was their Managing Director; he took over the firm in 1873, was joined by his sons in 1880, and the firm became C. W. Martin & Sons Limited at the Alaska Factory in 1911. Although in that year the wholesale slaughter of seals was curbed and brought under international control, quotas remained high and the firm prospered.[172]

GOAD Insurance maps of the area[173] show an awkwardly-shaped site, that extends narrowly and some distance back from the road at the north to a much larger, roughly square area at the rear, south end. Around the walls and within the yards, numerous buildings for different usages and processes were built, becoming even more tightly packed as the years went by. The 'K' building crossed the site from the east on the north side of the larger area and projected a short distance into the narrow part.

An embargo in the early 1930s on the importation of dressed and dyed furs into Britain permitted the home fur trade to expand into international markets. To handle the increased volume of work, the Martins rebuilt 'J' building in 1932 and 'K' in 1934. The latter's six/seven storeys were used as a dyehouse (ground floor), laboratory (second), drum shop (third), finishing (fifth), sorting (sixth), with a sawdust store in the basement. The new building extended across the full width of the site. To facilitate access to the large area at the south of the site, part of the ground floor had to be left open. No original plans are available, but there appear to have been 12 bays in width and roughly two bays in depth at the west end, one-and-a-half at the east. The rear and side elevations are straight-lined and rectangular. At the front the set-backs and projections take advantage of the space available.

More recently the building was purchased by Charterhouse Estates and altered to office accommodation. Various alterations were made, including extension of the east rear wall by half a bay outward and upward from the first floor. When that company went out of business in the late 1980s, the building was redeveloped by London Buildings plc in conjunction with the Marmot Group into residential use as the Alaska Apartments Building.[174] The invitation to the opening of the building in 1993 describes it as 'a fine example of Art Deco industrial architecture', which is nonsense, as too is much of the 'Thomas Wallis story' in the accompanying brochure.

The apartments are excellently planned, and reinforce the view of how well vacated factories lend themselves to domestic habitation—all space and light, particularly when, as here, the building originally conformed to the Kahn 'Daylight' formula of frame, glass and white rendered brick.

It is pleasing too that the exterior has retained its integrity. Its most impressive feature is the seven-storey tower facing the entrance driveway from the road. The original broad opening through the ground floor of the building has been filled in across the rear bays, so that the tower rises above pilotis. A central, double set of recessed, narrow vertical windows rises through five storeys, and is thus broadly framed at top and sides in white concrete. At the seventh storey, the tower is stepped in, four times, at its outer edges, with a central stepped gap on front which gives sight of the small building set atop. Its flat, flying roof and sun deck and the walled sun deck behind the top storey are very Modern and very attractive. This small building probably housed the lift machinery, but its form was part of the original design.[175] The original four-bar railings around all the seventh-storey roofs on the west side have been replaced by a single projecting, white rail, anchored (and netted) a short distance below roof level. Where once, writ large above the uppermost windows, was the name MARTIN'S, is now ALASKA in red lettering. The bay to the right of the tower is set back, with windows across its full width; further to the right, a projecting bay echoes the tower with its double row of tall, narrow windows, but here they terminate in a small cross window in the top storey.

This is a wonderful building, beautifully restored. The whole of the factory site has been redeveloped to provide a rather more salubrious setting, but the original brick and stone monumental gateway at roadside of the 1869 Alaska factory has been rebuilt, providing a historic vista of considerable stature.

Wallis, Gilbert & Partners continued to receive a regular flow of commissions, their status secure as experts in factory design, and for a diversity of non-industrial building types. Those include domestic property, public transport work, petrol stations and garages, waterworks, the first-ever custom-built recording studios and such well-known designs as the Great Portland Street car showrooms, the Daimler Hire building and the London and Country [Victoria] Coach Station, as well as an increasing number of commissions from the London Passenger Transport Board for suburban depots and garages.

Glaxo Laboratories Limited

In 1934 Wallis, Gilbert & Partners received enquiries from Joseph Nathan & Company in connection with the designing of new premises to house its Glaxo Department, which eventually led to a substantial commission. Shortly before occupying those new premises, the department was incorporated on 16 September 1935 as Glaxo Laboratories Limited, at Greenford, Middlesex. The 'Glaxo' trademark was registered by Joseph Nathan & Company in 1906 for a pure and nutritional infant milk food as a new venture in its business of importing bulk dried milk supplies for the civil service and armed forces from its own sources in Australia and New Zealand. With the growing interest in child welfare, particularly after the First World War, the company expanded rapidly, moving twice to larger premises and, in 1920, to the newly-built Glaxo House in Osnaburgh Street, London. By 1932, with a wider range of food and pharmaceutical products, Glaxo House was outgrown and expansion into satellite units was proving unsatisfactory. New, specially designed premises were needed, located outside London in cleaner air and with sufficient acreage for future expansion.

The site chosen in 1934 was some 10 miles west of London at Greenford Green—15 acres facing east to the newly constructed Greenford Road. On the southern boundary the Grand Union Canal was a link with the London docks and the Midlands for the shipment of bulk supplies and fuel. Two railway stations were within easy reach and the surrounding area was opening up to new housing estates, providing accommodation for present and future employees.

In simple terms, the commission to Wallis, Gilbert & Partners was for a three-storey office block and a laboratory fronting the site, with a manufacturing area to the rear. But the brief was a very complex one: for each of its many products the company required separate production flow lines, each with room for future expansion that did not impede other departments.[176] Concern for better health, both nationally and individually, was a major feature of the 1930s. As Glaxo products were devoted to that end, it was reasonable to assume a rising market; many of the products were, however, new—the result of research and discovery, whose future development could not be predicted; hence the need for flexible expansion space. In the interests of strict economy and utmost efficiency of construction and subsequent operation, discussions, reports, acquisition of operating data from other companies, revisions of space allocation, location of departments and services, and recasting of costs took place over nine months. Decisions were arrived at and then revised—for instance, whether to generate electricity or take supplies from the mains.[177]

For the elevation of the new building, the architects suggested a 'nicely designed brick building', since the clients were anxious to have a 'very sober appearance' with an entrance similar to 'what is provided in an important banking establishment'. But they were prepared to meet the costs of a 'distinctive entrance hall' that combined a 'reception office and two, or if possible, three interview rooms, so placed that visitors do not have to enter into the main body of the offices'. Contemporary protocol had also to be observed in that the departments on each side of the central hall were to 'link up without making the entrance hall a passage way' and, since it was not desirable for 'staff to use the main staircase', a secondary staircase and a staff entrance at the rear of the building had to be added in the plans.[178]

In March 1935, the General Manager, Harry Jephcott, reported that 'work in connection with the Greenford scheme has been continuously heavy and exacting. It has frequently involved excessively long hours on the part of all concerned.' In that connection, he expressed appreciation of

> the work of our architects, their staff and their consulting engineer, who have been unsparing in their efforts to press forward with the maximum speed and have been particularly helpful . . . in seeking jointly every possible means whereby the cost of this scheme might be reduced.[179]

Assiduous attention to client's requirements was not unusual for Wallis, Gilbert & Partners and had contributed to their success; they were ever ready to assimilate new ideas, to learn from their clients' experience, and to advise from their own. But the Glaxo commission really did drag on—the clients could never make up their mind. Eventually and finally, the architects managed to see a group of works managers, discovered what was really wanted, and from then on were able to move forward (see Appendix B(1)).

The construction contract for the Glaxo building was awarded to Richard Costain Limited. The 'first sod' was ceremonially turned by the company chairman, Alec Nathan, on 18 March 1935 and attended by Thomas Wallis.[180] The new complex of offices, laboratory, factory production areas, warehousing, despatch and loading bays, workshops and boiler house, was completed and ready for occupation within eight months.[181] The site sloped down to the south side, which permitted the insertion of a lower ground floor into the southern side of the building; there are, however, no surviving plans of the ground floor or notes of its dimensions. A first-floor plan and an aerial view of the completed factory in 1936 show the basic 'aeroplane' shape of the two-storeyed part of the building. To each side, between fore and aft wings, were single-storeyed sections, including the canteen and despatch bays.

In the office block, a corridor bypassed the projecting, central, double-storeyed hall and connected to open plan offices on the ground floor, which were used for sales, advertising, export and ancillary departments. The upper floor was separated by a long central corridor, forward of which were offices for the directors and senior management, the upper hall and stair hall. The conference room and accounts section were at the south and north ends respectively; partitioned offices completed the floor plan to the rear of the corridor. Behind the front 'wings' block, the 'fusilage' section contained the postal department and cashier's office on the ground floor, the analytical laboratory, sanitary arrangements and other services on the second floor. In the 'tail' wings, the food processing and pharmaceutical departments on the first floor were separated centrally by cloakrooms, lavatories and various small processing rooms. The departments were fed from the ground floor from a bulk store of raw materials; their products were returned to the packaging department that was in the opposite section of the ground floor. Externally, to the rear, are the power house and chimney.

The experimental laboratories, animal house and similar departments were housed separately in a building on the north side, in line with the office block and connected thereto by a first-floor bridge. To the far rear of the site, on the north side, three single-storeyed buildings with trussed, pitched roofs housed oil extraction, Farex drying, chemical sections and other similar specific functions. The main manufacturing buildings were top-lit from trussed, hipped roofs and from glazed walls, whilst the remainder of the buildings were flat-roofed.

The layout plan of the central section, running from front to back, with wide wings perpendicular thereto, not only allowed for future expansion of individual departments, but the intervening, fully-glazed walls ensured maximum natural light to all sections. The front building is set back some 80 feet from the roadway, on the industrial building line. The unbuilt-on ground was landscaped with lawns, flower beds and trees. Some space was devoted to sports facilities but, in more recent years, much of that land has been taken up for major building extension.

All the original buildings are of steel frame, with brick and glass infill and facings. The 'very sober appearance' required by the client precluded a fancy design or anything spectacularly Modern. But the style then achieving reputable popularity—featuring planar geometry in brick and glass—had a restrained modernity and dignified anonymity that was eminently suitable. Horizontality is stressed by long bands of buff-coloured bricks, continuous concrete lintels, sills and plinths, and string courses of on-end bricks. Separating the solid layers are reflecting bands of long-paned windows with glass corners and window piers faced in black glass (Fig. 32). The main vertical elements appear in the central feature, where the main entrance is recessed between two-storeyed projections, each a full bay in depth and width. Each of these bays rises above the general skyline with a stepped brick capping. On the fronts are colossal, stepped brick piers, their heads joined by a band of on-end bricks to match the recessed spandrels. Between these projections, the half bay, in which the main entrance is centrally placed, rises still higher above the skyline, with a crescendo of verticals pointing to the company flag on the capping.[182] Leading to the doorway, wide stone steps rounded on the lower treads draw the visitor in by a gradual narrowing of the way. The skirting is in stone; above it sculpted pedestals and low walls in concrete curve inwards and upwards to single-storeyed 'tower' shapes, also in concrete, on each side of the doorway. Between tall narrow lamps on the 'tower' fronts, a moulded architrave with Egyptianised centrepiece frames the double, glazed doors. Above, within a broad, brick frame, is the tall, narrow hall window, deeply recessed between vertically stepped concrete reveals, that rise from quadrant arcs on the inner sides of the 'tower' heads. Although horizontal lines are accentuated throughout the façade, the main visual impact of the building is provided by this central discontinuity. There is a lot of detail in this centre section; Wallis had yet to learn how to leave well

Fig. 32 Glaxo Laboratories Ltd, Greenford, Middlesex: front elevation, 1936

alone when tackling a more Modern design, but somehow it works. By its powerful forward and upward thrust, the centre block becomes the major feature; in consequence, the remainder of the building forms subservient wings. Entrance to the site is from the right side front, so that the parade of black glass mullions, as minor verticals, mark passage along the horizontal lines to the rising pile in the centre. Hence the breadth of span of the lower steps and the over-abundantly sculpted flanks that converge on the doorway. Moreover, the arrangement is also an external manifestation of the hierarchy of the plan and the operation of the business. The central block contains the hall, stairway, reception rooms and directors' offices, segregating the principals and visitors (customers) from the manufacturing and administration areas, as stated in the brief.

The entrance hall also met the clients' brief in being very distinctive; but it is not at all warm or inviting. Extravagant of space and reaching majestic double-storeyed height, it relies upon structural form for effect. And, as befitted the image of a company engaged in the production of food and pharmaceuticals, it is light, airy, cool and clinically white. Heralded by the sculpted curves at the entrance, attention is drawn to the reeded, rounded pillars, curvilinear corners and staircase by black skirting and black bordering of the white stone floor. Light and shadow created by the structure were made more effective by high windows and a central, tubular pendant lamp in

Fig. 33 Glaxo Laboratories Ltd, Greenford, Middlesex: entrance hall, 1936

chromium and glass. That the room itself is square is apparent in its upper reaches, where bare expanses of wall, a stepped cornice and coffered ceiling echo the rectilinearity of the exterior of the building and the layout plan (Fig. 33).

As an essay in space and form, the hall lacks a dominant or integrating factor that would aid instant comprehension or, more appropriately, a coherent visual mobility. For the individual, the room could be intimidating—there is no explicit processional way, since the reception and waiting areas are unconnected and the stairway is too narrow, disappears too quickly and does not impose itself. The visitor is captured and probably nonplussed. The entrance to the lower ground floor at the south end is more effective in adding to the bold stature of the building. Powerful, sphinx-like blocks terminate the thrust of the plinth and beams of the inserted floor; stout, dwarf columns and a deep fascia are unyielding in their support of the elevation. This is concrete expressing its inherent puissant qualities, and doing it very nicely. Later extension has, unfortunately, almost obscured this unusual feature.

Whatever aesthetic inconsistencies may be found, however, the clients were well pleased with the buildings, appreciated their 'functional unity', celebrated the accomplishment of that 'primary aim of modern industrial architecture', namely, 'fitness for purpose within an aesthetically satisfying framework'.[183]

The new Glaxo research building

Designed shortly afterwards by Wallis, Gilbert & Partners and sited to the north-west of the main block beside a new road, this is closely related in style and materials. The plain, concrete-framed entrance, recessed between curving brickwork, shows a more successful handling of the two materials. The blanked windows on either side of the door are an unfortunate intrusion and the unfinished appearance of the raised central bay is distracting in an otherwise very pleasant building.

The Glaxo milk-drying factory

The design of this factory at Driffield, Yorkshire, in 1937 also bears some relation to the parent building in the choice and dispositon of materials and in steel-frame construction. Set back from the road, the building is part single-storeyed: a flat-roofed, frontal block with receiving bay, weighing facilities, laboratory arrangements for the testing of incoming liquid milk, and a despatch bay on the north side. Part double-storeyed—attached at the rear of the frontal block and perpendicular thereto—is the manufacturing area, brick-walled sheds, one with top-lit, trussed, hipped roof and two with north-light roofs where, on a gravity feed system, the milk was processed into powder. The sheds are distinctive only in their internal arrangements and their forest of roof ventilators.

The design of the frontal block, mainly in brick and glass, with a continuous concrete canopy, concrete-edged parapet and raised central section, is reminiscent of a local railway station. The incurving pillars of on-end brick that flank the doorway and the long-paned windows do, however, add a touch of contemporary sophistication, a modest echo of the trabeated style of some of the new London Underground stations. Richard Costain Limited was the contractor; the building was erected and ready for occupation in only three weeks. It is still standing and is presently occupied by Twydale Turkeys Limited. When the Wallis, Gilbert partnership was dissolved in December 1945, Glaxo opted to become clients of Elliott, Cox & Partners, who were responsible for most of the considerable later expansion on the Greenford and other sites. Greatly as the Glaxo principals were impressed by Wallis' design, the eventual success of the very long discussion and reworking of the original brief was largely owed to Frank Cox's inestimable patience; later Stanley Elliott would face the same sort of trial with costs and quantities. Both appear to have reaped their reward.

Reliance Cords and Cables Limited and Murray, Sons & Company Limited

Two further commissions in 1935—for Reliance Cords and Cables Limited, Fingal Works, Staffa Road, London[184] and for Murray, Sons & Company Limited, tobacco manufacturers at Whitehall Works, Linfield Road, Belfast, Northern Ireland—were for extensions to existing premises. In both cases, these led to further work for the partnership during the rest of the decade, and both companies became clients of Elliott, Cox & Partners in 1945.[185] The Reliance buildings of 1935, 1936 and 1939 appear to have been steel-framed with trussed roofs and cement-rendered walls. The first Murray extension was a three-storey building (extended by two further floors in 1944) and followed the increasingly accepted pattern of concrete-edged brick and glass layering.[186] A smaller extension of May 1938 added a single-storeyed section to the front of the orginal factory (built in 1900, architects: Watt & Tulloch) with little regard for aesthetic harmony. Extension works of 1954 and 1968 were carried out by Elliot, Cox & Partners. Although, over the years, the work for the Reliance and Murray companies reached quite substantial proportions, it is doubtful if further, detailed investigation would reveal any major contribution to constructional or architectural history.

Lamson Paragon Supply Company Limited

The company for which Wallis, Gilbert designed a major extension in October 1935, the Lamson Paragon Supply Company Limited of Canning Town, London, generated a considerable amount of work for the practice. The Lamson company had spawned Caribonum Limited of Leyton, London, Papercraft Limited, Hendon, Middlesex, and had entered into association with The Shannon Limited, New Malden, Surrey, in 1926. Wallis, Gilbert & Partners also designed houses for the principals of these firms; they were Thomas Wallis' personal friends. There were commissions for new buildings at Canning Town, at Cambridge, and at Johannesburg, South Africa, further extensions at Canning Town and a continuation of commissions after the Second World War.

The company as such is now defunct, having been assimilated into Moore Paragon UK Limited, which is part of the Canadian holding company, Moore Corporation Limited. The Canning Town premises were vacated in 1982 and have since been completely demolished. Archive material in respect of the actual buildings is minimal. The Lamson name and the company's early financial support were American and the company's founders and early management were of Anglo-Canadian origin,[187] but the Lamson Paragon Supply Company attributed its growth and success as much to efficiently 'solving the problems of modern office administration', with new kinds of methods, forms and stationery, as to the influence of its transatlantic sources.

All the company's products were produced by machinery invented by and exclusive to itself. Constant development, market research and analysis and direct selling to customers enabled the company to exploit the rapid expansion of administrative work after the First World War. The efficiency of Lamson methods was demonstrated by the company's applying them to its own organisation; its leadership as a 'good employer' was shown in the provision of a wide range of facilities, amenities and benefits for its staff.[188] When there was such empathy of views in both business and design between these companies and their architects, no wonder that such close personal friendships ensued.

The factory extension designed in 1935 was a four-storey block facing onto an internal roadway at the rear of the existing works. Standing four and a half bays wide by four bays in depth on a grid of approximately 20 feet centres, the extension was built southward of and attached to an earlier building constructed of cast-iron frame, with a tall, campanile-like corner lift tower. The new building was of steel frame with stanchions enclosed in brick. Beams were cased in concrete and exposed on the exterior as continuous, string-course lintels, above small-paned, bay-width windows. On the front elevation intermediate brick mullions were inserted; sills were of artificial stone. All spandrels were of brick in cavity wall construction. The forward part of the frontal bays was flat-roofed, the remainder covered by north-light trusses, with Trafford tiles on the southern aspect. The doorway at the south end of the front gave access to the stair tower, expressed by a tall, uninterrupted narrow light above the door and a blank wall on the south elevation. On each floor to the right of the stairs were men's and women's lavatories and cloakrooms; otherwise, the floors were of open plan to allow for free disposition of machinery.

In the nature of the client's business there were many separate production processes. With adequate lifts and an existing array of loading bays, floors could be used differentially; a multi-storey building was thus a rational choice and a saver of ground space. The existing factory had been developed over some 40 years on that site and was of traditional construction and appearance, with which the new extension, albeit of more modern materials and construction, was not too overtly at variance. The opening of the new building coincided with the company celebrating its golden jubilee. At a special party held at the Olympia Ballroom, London, guests included Mr and Mrs Kahn and Mr and Mrs Wallis.[189]

Designs for a row of garages for the factory extending 120 feet along Dartmouth Road, were drawn in August 1936 and May 1937. These were of steel construction, with brick infill, trussed, pitched roofs and an array of sliding doors across the whole of the front elevation. Two further designs of the late 1930s for Lamson Paragon are of greater interest, but it is not known if they were executed. There appear to be no surviving plans and only coloured, artistic impressions exist. One of them, intended to stand long-fronted to Dartmouth Road, is shown as a concrete 'Daylight' factory of regular grid proportions in the Kahn manner. On the symmetrically designed front elevation, however, are slightly inset end pieces with recessed doors below tall windows. The stepped and battered outer edges curve outward at the bottom, standing forward of the 'corner towers', which have glass corners and stepped, reeded copings. A vocabulary of geometric structural lines enhanced by sculpted finishings entitles the building to a place in this group. In essence, however, the design has evolved, stripped and modernised from Wallis' original concrete aesthetic via the basic form of some of the Fancy factories. The other Lamson design was also long-fronted and was destined to be sited at Cambridge. The apparent intention was to build in brick with concrete dressing on steel frame. In appearance, the rather sudden central massing up to a very tall, slender tower, is compatible with the form that became so common in the late 1930s and gained municipal credence. Most usually, such an emphatically vertical feature was flanked by wings of equally emphatic horizontality. In this design for Lamson, however, the verticality of the wing piers is accentuated by recessed areas of tall, uninterrupted glazing. Thus we have here not an evolution, but more of a nuptial—a central feature of 1930s municipal Modern wedded to the framed colonnade with corner towers and Egyptianised doorway of Fancy origins. In these designs of the 1930s Wallis seems willing to accept the increasingly popular format of 'British Modern' but to be unwilling to relinquish entirely the earlier styles that were so much his own invention.

Richard Klinger Limited

Conformity reappeared with designs first drawn in January 1936 for a complete factory complex for Richard Klinger Limited, at Ruxley Corner, Sidcup, Kent. Unusually, the factory is still occupied and still privately owned by the originating company, which is headed by a fourth generation member of the Austrian family of its founder. In 1886 Richard Klinger invented a safe water-level gauge for boilers; in 1850 his invention of 'Klinger-it', a calendered mixture of natural rubber and asbestos, became a household name for sheet gasket material. A factory was built at Gumpoldskirchen in Austria in 1890, another in Berlin, Germany, in 1913. Further inventions and developments in the 1920s, to solve problems arising from advances in engineering and innovations in the motor vehicle industry—a wide range of compressed moulded friction materials for brake and clutch linings and cylinder head gaskets—permitted greater overseas expansion, beginning with a move to Britain in 1936.[190]

The site chosen for the new factory faces north to the Sidcup Bypass, in what was then a wholly rural and undeveloped area. In the absence of drainage and other mains services, septic and anaeroid tanks had to be provided, wells sunk for a water supply, and power and light self-generated. Planning of the factory was governed by efficient process routeing of the variety of products and by the flammable nature of the materials and processes involved. The layout was, therefore, complex but very compact. At the front of the works is a flat-roofed, two-storeyed block, 232 feet wide, with a four-storey central tower with basement, part of which rises above ground level as an insertion to fill the slope of the ground from south to north. The building's wings return around a single-storeyed area that has two trussed, hipped roofs backed by a four-storey block of one bay's depth, for reception and distribution of materials. At its rear and at right angles thereto is a row of single-storeyed sheds with top-lit, hipped roofs. Across the west side of the central well, a block of flat-roofed buildings, stepping down rearwards from four and a half storeys to a single storey, is joined to the rear-projecting wing of the frontal block by a two and a half storey section. The well is closed across the east end by another single-storeyed shed with hipped roof.

Isolated from the main buildings on the west side of an internal road were the boiler and power houses, coal store and the now obsolete chimney, from which process steam was channelled to the manufacturing area. In the main building basement a second boiler acted as reheater, along with an auxiliary boiler for use during maintenance of the main supply. Detached from the main building on the east were garages, then used for fitting brake linings to customers' vehicles, a car wash, storage facilities and garages for company cars.

Apart from foundations and retaining walls in the basement, which are of reinforced concrete, all of the buildings are steel framed with brick and glass infill. Most of the manufacturing area is built of yellow flettons; the frontal block is of light brown and reddish brown bricks. As far as possible, all buildings are of fire-resistant construction; precautions against fire were elaborate for the time and included internal fire doors, guillotine shutters and flame-proofed electrical fittings.

The ground floor of the frontal block forms part of the manufacturing area; the first floor, with central corridor, serves administrative purposes and contains a variety of general and managerial offices, the drawing office and laboratory. Main access is by stairs from the central hall, with a secondary stairway on the west side, emerging beside cloakrooms and lavatories. On the mezzanine and first floor on the west side were rest rooms, kitchen, canteen and other facilities, which could also be reached from the works entrance and stair tower on that side. The main lift shaft is adjacent to the stair tower; a secondary goods lift on the east side served only the ground and basement floors. The central tower in the frontal block has entrance hall, landing, a four-roomed executive flat and storage facilities, respectively, on its four floors. The arrangement allows penetration of natural light to all areas[191] but the tightly-fitting jigsaw of separate sections does not permit of easy extension. When expansion became necessary, a separate building designed by Elliott, Cox & Partners was erected in 1957, on land to the west of the original block and is connected to it by a first-floor bridge.[192]

The horizontal lines of the frontal block wings are accentuated by bands of light brown brick edged with string courses of darker, on-end bricks and continuous lintels and sills of artificial stone. The plinth-like basement is faced in artificial stone surmounted by three courses of darker on-end bricks. Between the solid layers are long rows of windows, with pale brick mullions and white glazing bars, but there are no glass corners. To maintain the sense of compactness, the outer ends of the wings are delineated by a suggestion of corner towers, by slight recession, short parapets and shuttered vehicular entrances to interior loading bays. They also act as counterweight to the central tower, which rises over the full depth of the front block and projects a short span forward of it. Corner windows break into the precipitous height of the tower, so that the main vertical accent is provided by the pale brick surround of the central window, recessed between dark brick reveals that reach upward to the dark brick coping. Below, the stepped-forward surround of the main entrance, intersecting a continuation of the recessed window and stepped reveal, initiates the vertical rise. At the same time, however, the arrangement draws the visitor into the building. In contrast to the stone-faced basement 'plinth' and the stone steps, the way is marked off in concrete—in the flanking pedestals with shallow vases, in the slabs stepped upwards and inwards to the recessed concrete architrave, in the canopy over the doorway and the capping of the brick surround.

The geometry of the façade is wholly rectilinear, the only exceptions being the minor features of the circular vases and the concave arc of the plinth slabs on each side of the doorway. The reversal of linearity in the entrance hall is therefore unheralded. Fine black lines form a grid pattern on the marble floor and complement the geometry of the coffered ceiling and of the exterior; but they are quite overwhelmed by sweeping curves and circular forms (Fig. 34). There are similarities with the Glaxo hall: a decor of dramatic structural lines in black and white and a narrow, offset stairway. But here the way is made indisputably clear, signposted by circular pillars of black glass along a narrow path, compellingly directed by the glister of inward-curving chromed glazing bars and skirting on the drum-shaped corner kiosks and the sharply pointing angles and huge curve of the frieze. Underfoot, little stabs of black edge the round-ended steps to a low, stage-like landing and the stairway, which is right-angled to the hall and turns on itself to the full landing above. The contrast between the over-modernity of the entrance hall and the restrained colour and geometry of the exterior was symbolic of a company that was ahead of its field in engineering innovation yet concerned for its impact upon a countryside environment. Tightly-planned land use, green landscaping of the factory site with retention and further planting of trees and the choice of very pleasantly coloured bricks allowed this factory to sit comfortably in its

Fig. 34 Richard Klinger Ltd, Sidcup, Kent: entrance hall, 1938

rural surroundings. The one external concession to its fundamental role and place beside a major new highway appeared in the company flag on tower and fascia in red neon lighting (now replaced). The area has since been built up and further industrialised, but the Klinger building retains a decorous mien, attractively superior to those of later, adjacent commercial buildings.

Ault & Wiborg Limited

In 1936 Wallis, Gilbert & Partners designed a factory which, because of the nature of the production materials involved, was also subject to greater risk from fire. This was for Ault & Wiborg Limited, printing ink manufacturers of Watford, Hertfordshire. An ink-making firm had been founded by Americans Ault and Wiborg in Cincinnatti, Ohio, USA, in 1888. A British base was established in London in 1899 but later the American principals withdrew when the London base voted to become a British public company in 1934.[193]

At that time Watford was a flourishing centre of the printing industry. In 1936 the well-known firm Odhams Limited built a new factory two miles north of Watford beside the A41 road. Ault & Wiborg retained its London headquarters but expanded to build a new plant at Watford on the opposite side of the A41 to Odhams, for the sole purpose of supplying Odhams with printing ink. For many years ink was sent across the road in barrels carried by horse-drawn vehicles until a storage tank and piped system were installed. In the choice of site, however, Ault & Wiborg was unable to obtain land reaching directly to the road; a timber merchant occupied the intervening space and permission was never granted to build a roadway through from the Ault & Wiborg factory to the A41 roadway. Consequently, the factory is barely visible from the A41 and the main entrance to the site is at the rear from Cow Lane.

The factory faces south, is two-storeyed throughout and measures 170 feet on frontage and has an overall depth of 95 feet. Construction is of steel frame, with brick and glass infill and facing. Fire resistance was increased by extra thickness of concrete floors and the flat roof, the casing of external stanchions in four and a half inch brick and all beams and internal stanchions in concrete to a depth of two inches. All internal doors in the manufacturing area are large, heavy fire doors that close automatically along an inclined rail when the thermal link is triggered by suddenly-rising temperature. All other doors are of slow-burning oak. Solvent storage tanks were sunk underground at the rear of the courtyard and, further to the rear, a separate building houses switchgear and other power services, which were channelled below ground to individual buildings and machines.

The layout of the original factory consisted of two sheds, 50 feet wide by 90 feet in depth, standing parallel to each other, 70 feet apart on a north-south axis. They are joined across the south end by a flat-roofed building 70 feet wide by 30 feet in depth, which projects 5 feet forward on the front elevation and connects with the sheds to a depth of 25 feet. The buildings thus enclose an open-ended court yard. In the forward half of the centre block are, on the ground floor, the main entrance and hall, to the right of which is the manager's office and, on the left, cloak- and locker-rooms, showers and lavatories. To the rear of these rooms and facing into the court are two loading bays flanking the goods lift. On the first floor a kitchen, canteen and laboratory occupied the front half; the rear portion, with goods lift opening to east and west in the centre, provides a throughway between the two sheds.

The front 25 feet of the sheds are storage areas on both floors, for ink, varnish and other commodities. The rear parts of the sheds are the manu-facturing areas with mill rooms on the ground floors, lighted by windows on all sides, and charging rooms above; the latter have solid walls and are top-lit by glazed, trussed, pitched roofs. The roofs are gabled on the north but hipped over the south storage bays. Apart from a few rolled steel joists in the hipped ends, all roof trusses are formed of bolted angle iron. Originally the roofs were covered with sheet asbestos but this has been replaced by corrugated asbestos cement sheets, faced internally with plaster board for insulation. Dust extractors on the ridges tended to remove more heat than powder, but were not sealed off and a new system was not installed until the 1970s—this system now disfigures the front elevation. All the windows in the sheds are those originally inserted; only those in the offices have been replaced to allow double-glazing.

The factory walls are faced throughout in mottled, yellowish-buff bricks, with concrete dressing containing marble chips that glister in sun and rain and produce a slightly rougher texture on the surface to accord with the 'rustic' finish of the bricks. This choice of material was in recognition of the semi-rural southern aspect of the factory had it been visible through the trees that line the highway. Recently, however, most of the concrete work has been over-painted in light blue, resulting in an unhappy contrast with the colour of the brickwork and a negation of the original aesthetic concept. The front elevation and the returns around the hipped roof portions follow the popular layered principle, but they depart from the usual geometry with a greater intermixing of vertical and horizontal lines with the introduction of large structural curves and the absence of long, narrow window panes that generally graced the style. Above the rendered base, windows with narrow rounded brick mullions and continuous concrete sills and lintels are set into the brick façade, to leave broad solid corners to the wings.

On the projecting centre piece, robust rounded towers of 'Odeon' affil-iation appear externally for the first time in a Wallis, Gilbert design, and curved glass follows the line of the middle layer of brick that sweeps in to the recessed main entrance. On each side of this doorway, colossal V-section columns, vertically stepped from a narrow front plane reach up to the fascia soffit. These columns are similar to those at Hoover and Freeder. Whether they had faience inserts is not known, but sharply-angled facets are there, as though similar form shuttering had been used. The wide overhanging fascia may have required intermediate support; some strong, centrally-placed vertical emphasis may have been asethetically desirable; but the style of the columns is wholly alien to the overall grammar of the building. Moreover, the size of the columns detracts from the importance of the doorway; their placing obscures the upper side windows. Standing free of the insweep of the outer walls and the splayed curve of the base on one side and the stepped-in concrete surround of the doorway on the other, they gainsay the invitation offered by the surrounding structure. What possessed Wallis to cling to these Fancy elements? They were too different to pretend to another transition period. Or was he overruled by a client envious of the impact of the Fancy factories? The only excuse is perhaps that, since the front door was not able to act in its usual capacity when all access to the site was from the rear, something wildly extravagant was added to the original design to make some sort of impact through the trees and the timber yard to road users. Perhaps when the building was designed there was a prospect of a forecourt and a real face to the road. But if that had been the case, the insertion of those columns would still have been a grave error of judgement. More recent over-painting of the columns, the installation of a glazed vestibule and the removal of the ornament over the doors tend to exacerbate the fault.

In contrast to the monumentality of the round towers and the V-shaped columns, the visitor would find the entrance hall surprisingly small. It is single-storeyed, has stepped coving to the ceiling and ribbed columns in the corners. On the right are the reception desk, telephone room and door to the manager's office; on the left are staff cloakrooms and lavatories. But there are no stairs! Other than the goods lift at the rear of the central section and the external stairs at the rear of the sheds, the main access to the upper floor is by a stairway in the east tower. This leads to the wide corridor between the sheds to all parts of the first floor and, by metal ladder, to the roof. The round towers rise above the roof and parapet as single walls; the one on the east side once contained the water tank.

The layout of the central area is very compact, but has no obvious circulation pattern. Its design was determined by contemporary operational requirements, with an economy of space and cost, but with little regard for future expansion or future use. Except for the columns, as a variation of the accepted version of British 1930s Modern, the design is pleasant enough and, from a distance, well balanced. The building materials were well-chosen to meet briefing requirements and to harmonise with surroundings. The building is still in very good condition and has required a minimum of maintenance.[194]

As the company has grown and new products have been introduced, the site has been built up; expansion of office and storage space, canteen facilities, and so on, has also required new building. As a member of the Ault & Wiborg plc, the company at Watford was taken over by the Sun Chemical Corporation of USA but retained its own name.

The layered effect of the modified version of the Modern style provided a much simpler format for the long-fronted office or factory. The introduction of rounded walls, curved ornamentation and central vertical emphasis provided a means of relieving and adding interest to the trite geometry of the style. Conformity to style, however, tended to deprive Thomas Wallis of his much-loved corner towers and he was reluctant to abandon colour and classical reference to the dominance of form alone.

R. Woolf & Company (Rubber) Limited

The anomaly noted at Ault & Wiborg appeared again in another design of 1936 in an office block and factory for R. Woolf & Company (Rubber) Limited at 1–3 Uxbridge Road, Hayes, Middlesex.[195] The company was a family concern, originally operating as rubber waste merchants at Mile End Road, London and, from 1914, as manufacturers of rubber tyres and other rubber goods. The move to Hayes was for purposes of expansion in response to the growth of the motor industry. The company prospered at Hayes until the early 1960s when, during a period of full employment, labour was difficult to recruit. The problem was solved by privately-arranged subsidised immigration of a workforce from the Indian sub-continent. Within a few years, however, the company had no recourse but to close as a result of an enquiry into its working practices and levels of pay by the University of London; it was taken over by P. B. Cow & Company Limited.

The property was acquired by Brixton Estates plc in 1968. Strict governmental control of industrial development at that time forbade the proposed redevelopment of the site; in consequence, the factory buildings were reduced to structural steelwork. New walls, floors, roofs and services were installed and the existing office block modernised and refurbished.[196] In March 1971, EMI Record Manufacturing and Distribution Service occupied the premises on a 42-year lease. Further modifications were made to suit EMI production requirements. Considerable work, particularly on the office block, was carried out to correct previous sub-standard alterations; the site was extended and there is a large amount of new building. The only surviving original plans are those deposited with the local authority, from which copies, or even a sight of them, are not available.

In 1936 the site covered eight and a half acres, facing north to Uxbridge Road, with its main entrance on the east of the frontage. On the west of the site is the Yeading Brook, that forms the boundary between the Boroughs of Hillingdon and Ealing. Bulbrook Road formed the southern boundary and there is other property on the east. The office building that fronts the works is set back from the road. To its rear, and extending eastwards, the single-storeyed factory covered 164 262 square feet and was composed of steel-framed sheds with top-lit corrugated asbestos-cement pitched roofs, running north-south. The sheds immediately co-extensive with the office block terminated in top-lit, hipped roofs. Walls were of rendered nine-inch brick, with small windows, or wholly of corrugated metal. There were four smaller buildings on site—a garage, canteen, stores and the gatehouse.

The two-storeyed office block has a frontage of approximately 192 feet and is built largely of steel frame on a 14 feet grid, infilled with rendered brick, tile and glass. From the main central entrance and hall there was access to the wings, which were used for offices and storage and divided by partitions and some solid cross walls.[197] On the elevations horizontal layering of solid and void is very much in evidence. Above the black plinth, the continuous base, breastwall and parapet were rendered in white cement. Between these bands, slightly recessed windows of small, rectangular panes with cream-painted glazing bars were intersected by stanchions faced with light green tiles. The rather dramatic effect of apparently unsupported broad horizontal bands is intensified by the corners curving round, in glass and masonry, to side walls of similar design. Continuity is interrupted only on centre front, but not conspicuously so from the distant view, since the centre band, although curving boldly into the recessed entrance, runs on undeterred over the doorway. So the columns appear only as exclamation marks to identify the entrance and to point to the monogrammed fascia. The approaching visitor, on the other hand, might well have been surprised by the complexity of the entranceway design.

The rising curve and insweep of the white base and black plinth on each side of the shallow steps invite the visitor to enter. But the direction they indicate is confounded by two free-standing V-section columns that, from the narrow front plane, are vertically-stepped on both sides. Set back in the widest of the three potential entrance spaces, the doorway is lighted by a metal-framed lamp on chromed brackets to give some indication, but black and white horizontal striping of the architrave uprights tends to nullify clear definition of the entrance. Further, the V-shaped columns were decorated with bands of black, green and red faience, so that the eye is distracted upward from the coloured base, by vertical lines, to the coloured head. The columns support the overhanging fascia but, beside and behind them, is further confusion. The fascia rises in centre front but is set back from the uppermost horizontals; these turn in at sharp right angles not quite in line with the rising lines of the base. The upper glass and tile layer runs on behind the columns, curving inwards to cross the recess, in opposition to the convexity of the lower layers.

An entrance and processional way of almost unremitting clarity and attraction had become a forté of Wallis' designs in earlier buildings. With the onset of conventionalisation of Modern styling, however, there appears at times to be a certain wilfulness, a need to 'do something with the entrance' to unsettle the rigid geometry of Modern wings. The width of the Woolf entrance and the depth of its recession may, as at Ault & Wiborg, have called for intermediate support or a major statement to challenge the dominant horizontality of the wings. But here formalism is in conflict with Fancy at the expense of the user. Perhaps neither architect nor client regarded the anonymity of Modern as appropriate to industry, nor the alternative art form of playing about with planes as pragmatically useful. Without the added extra, Wallis was doing quite well with British Modern, working it as though he understood it, and producing designs much less dull and anonymous than many another of the time.

When Brixton Estates acquired the premises, some alterations had already been made to the office block. The parapet had been given a darker capping and a classical pediment on the centre fascia. The red lettering of the company's flag had been removed and a new one installed in the centre band; the coloured faience on the columns had been painted over. More recently, the owner EMI has squared off and glazed over the central entrance way; a pillared porch has been added and the pediment removed. The green tiling has been painted with brown 'preservative'. The Mendelsohnian gatehouse remains but the office block hall has been stripped out, leaving no trace of the original design, of which, so far as can be ascertained, there is neither record nor memory. Whatever criticism may be levelled at Wallis' ornamented

Modern, later 'modernisation' of this building has ensured that its original character and presence are now sadly absent.

Huntley & Palmer Limited

Nineteen thirty-six continued as a very busy year for Wallis, Gilbert & Partners. A further commission in that year for a large office block to an existing factory came from Huntley & Palmer Limited, biscuit manufacturers of Reading, Berks. The company had been founded by Thomas Huntley and George Palmer in 1841; like most of the best-known biscuit and chocolate manufacturers, they were members of the Society of Friends and part of the tightly-knit and mutually supportive community of Victorian Quaker entrepreneurs. From 1846 the company operated from a remodelled silk mill at Kings Road, Reading, which was ideally placed between the River Kennet and the Kennet and Avon Canal, and adjoining the Great Western Railway. High quality, unadulterated products brought spectacular growth to the firm and considerable extension to the factory. In the face of increasing competition after the First World War, the firm merged with Peak Freans in 1924, to form Associated Biscuit Manufacturers, and became part of Associated Biscuits Limited upon merging with W. & R. Jacobs in 1960. Production at the Reading factory ceased in 1977 and the expanded company was taken over in 1982 by the giant American firm Nabisco, whose British headquarters still occupy the office block designed by Wallis, Gilbert & Partners in 1936.[198]

Facing south to Kings Road, with a straight frontage of 304 feet and depth overall of 43 feet, the ends of the office block curve round to Forbury Road on the west and to Gas Works Road on the west. The building rises to four storeys and is flat-roofed. The steel-frame construction is infilled with brick and glass, with concrete-rendered dressing. A grey-green, stone-faced base decreases in depth toward the east, visually levelling the building against the incline of the road (Fig. 35). The layout of the building is simple and straightforward. Each floor of the core rectangle is partitioned off into offices on each side of lateral corridors. The only interruptions in the pattern are for purposes of access. On the far right a vehicular entrance—a 'tunnel', one storey high—passes the side entrance and the porter's lodge to emerge at the back of the building. In the centre of the building, the main entrance leads to a double-storeyed hall and stairway, with a secondary stair and lift in a tower that projects from the rear of the building. Each of the end sections contains, on each floor, cloakrooms, lavatories and more stairways that lead up from the side entrance on the east and from a street door on the west end. The circulation pattern is very clear on plan but the similarity of each floor layout called for efficient signposting and, with interview rooms grouped around the entrance hall, a well-organised communications system to minimise human travelling time and distance. Thus, departments were grouped in rationalised order, there was a 'book lift' near the main door, and an early

Fig. 35 Huntley & Palmer Ltd, Kings Road, Reading, Berks: view from Kings Road, looking east

survey plan shows evidence of a 'Lamson' pipeline for the transmission of administrative material.

By size alone, this building is impressive. Its bulk has been exploited aesthetically by highlighting the large-scale geometry of its internal planning. On the long, straight front, strong horizontals are connected by a parade of less-emphatic verticals; on the curved returns, pronounced vertical treatment expresses differentiation of function and ultimate containment of the building. But, so that size and scale do not overwhelm, a variety of materials and structural decorations has been employed to increase articulation and add visual interest. The threat of the sudden rise of the building directly from the public pavement is alleviated by the different treatment on front of the ground-floor exterior. Long-paned windows, alternating with equal-sized panels of red mottled brick, effect a slower, pedestrian-paced rhythm. The sharp angle with the pavement is mitigated by the colour and texture of the base and its narrow, gently curving run-off shelf below the top course. But the severance of the ground floor from the upper storeys by the deep, white concreted band of the lower fascia is not total. Red brick continues above, narrowed to colossal piers. Between them broader expanses of glass, large-paned and rising through the full three storeys, are blanked out in blue-green glass at second- and third-floor levels to colour-match the base. The broken horizontal lines of coloured glass and white concrete pier heads and bases punctuate the long line of piers and produce a faster rhythm for the more distant view. An ascending series of string courses in on-end brown bricks begins above the base, is broken to link the lower window heads, reappears above the concrete band and, as a deep roof-line fascia, gathers in and stabilises the mobile pattern of the upper storeys.

The side elevations are quieter, more restful as befits their usage. The west end is a true arc of 50 feet 6 inches on a set-back of the original building line to allow for road widening. Architecturally, it has been very elegantly handled—to round off the building and not to compete with the main façade. The east end curves only at the corner, and then straightens into alignment with the street. Further along, it cuts back at a right angle around an existing building; its sharper turn and shorter frontage are expressed in the closing up of piers and window spaces. Unlike the front elevation, the planar emphasis of the end portions is strongly vertical, but relation is established by a similarity of treatment at head and base and by the use of coloured glass. There is, however, a minimum of concrete dressing on the ends.

On the main façade concrete plays a major defining role. Its whiteness contrasts sharply with the darker hue of the other materials although, originally, many of the features described here as 'concrete' may well have been pale artificial stone facing. The parapet encompasses front and sides, tying the building into a composite whole on the skyline, but rising at the corners and centre front to identify primary elements. The broad band above the ground floor begins only where the front elevation is set forward some 27 inches, and so boldly directs the eye to the central entrance. There, similar material rises, in steps and curves, to the company flag. At closer quarters, ingress is signalled by Doric-style columns, faced and ribbed in grey-green stone, that flank the wide steps of York stone. Here, happily, neither the shape nor the placing of the columns interferes with the invitation to enter, which is extended by the rounded corners of the stone base, as it turns into and around the entrance way to the main doors. These are oak-framed and recessed beneath a fanlight that is fancifully decorated in gilt metal; the doors themselves are glazed in screeded glass, curved at the centre corners to accord with the metal foot guard and the extended handles. The extravagant, slightly Hollywood-Egyptianised styling of the main entrance and the incidence there of curved lines in an otherwise rectilinear façade anticipate the splendour of the entrance hall. Some more recent alterations have been carried out, but most of the lavishness of both features and atmosphere remain.

This spacious hall extends through the full depth of the building and is double-storeyed over the stairway. On the ground floor, beside the doorway, glazed partitions curve from the corridor entrances to the vestibule walls, to form an interview room on the right and the commissionaire's room on the left. In the far corners were, on the left, a lobby, a store cupboard and lift and, on the right, another interview room. Part-wall ends and internal angles are profiled by half- or quarter-round ribbed columns, in deference to the design of the free-standing stairway, which is centrally placed directly opposite the

Fig. 36 Huntley & Palmer Ltd, Kings Road, Reading, Berks: hall and stairway

main doors. Drum-shaped bronzed newels surmount round-ended treads that rise to the rear wall, narrowing to a half landing beneath a large medieval hall type of window with attractive metal glazing bars. Dark terrazzo skirting and borders define the floor space and the stairway (Fig. 36). From the half landing, the stairs bisect, climb in opposing course along the rear wall and the intersecting cross walls, to return to a full landing at the front of the first floor. Behind the intersecting walls, each of which has tall, decoratively glazed lights, are another lobby leading to the lift shaft on the left and, on the right, the secondary staircase that rises through the projecting tower on the rear elevation.

Originally the first-floor landing extended to the front wall and was lit by the window beneath the concrete uprights over the main entrance. There was another interview room on the east side and a strongroom in the west corner, but this section has been walled off, leaving only a broad path linking the corridors at each end. Some of the design features encountered in the Huntley & Palmer hall will be familiar: an intermingling of curves and straight lines to define space, to accent structure or as purely decorative motifs; ribbed pillars, coffered ceilings, contrasting floor borderings, little black stab marks on stair treads, an imaginative use of metals—all appear in earlier designs of this later period. But this hall is not at all clinical as at Glaxo; it is not ultra-modern as at Klinger or Hoover. The tone here is softer, more luxuriant— taking its cue from the gilded wheatears in fanlight and balusters. They represent the raw material of the company's product, perhaps too the fecundity of the enterprise, so that modernity is tempered by Nature. Walls were buff coloured with deep, moulded patterned cornices; floors were surfaced in cork. Metals have a subdued gleam rather than a hard shine; light from electric lamps is suffused through white and grey opaque glass and, from windows, through coloured glass and a pattern of dark glazing bars. The original design of the hall suggests it was meant as a comfortable and attractive meeting place; despite alteration, much of that sense has been maintained. After all, the company's product was very domestic indeed.

The Huntley & Palmer office block is large and self-contained, intended to accommodate all aspects of the company's administration. The amount of floor space required for such a purpose is indicative of the great increase in the numbers of white collar workers in the interwar years. Advances in office procedures, business forms and recording mechanisms and the departmentalisation of functions called for much closer attention to organisation, layout and working conditions. There was some borrowing from the rationalisation of manufacturing production lines, but the interrelated matrix of administration is not resolved by direct flow processing. Physical circulation paths for internal and inter-departmental contact are extravagant of time and space, albeit a means of relief in a largely sedentary occupation. The accepted belief in a hierarchy of accommodation also affected layout planning. Protection from noise conflicted with adequate supervision; companies such as India and Glaxo, which chose open-plan offices, later installed partitioning. But, whilst glazed partitioning seemed a reasonable compromise, it suffers from a goldfish bowl effect that is not conducive to mental concentration; and floor space has to be sacrificed for corridors. In more recent years, various modifications of both principles have been tried, but no really satisfactory solution of office planning has yet been arrived at.

Champion Sparking Plug Company

A factory and offices for the Champion Sparking Plug Company Limited at Hatton Corner, Great West Road, Feltham, Middlesex, were also designed in 1936. The company, whose product is implicit in its name, remained in existence, but manufacturing operations ceased at Feltham in 1982. The buildings were demolished shortly afterwards and the site has been redeveloped.

The building faced south on a greenfield site beside the Great West Road at its western terminus. It was basically rectangular in shape, steel-framed with brick and glass infill, and single-storeyed throughout apart from a tall tower over the main entrance. The manufacturing area was an open shed, with five north-light roofs and low brick walls beneath continuous glazing on three sides. Operational areas, separated by glazed partitions, were laid out in order from west to east, as two large processing shops, the receiving and storage section, and the shipping and stock rooms. The flat-roofed office block was attached along the east wall, the main entrance and hall set slightly forward and leading to offices on each side of a corridor running from the hall to the general office at the rear. Staff cloakrooms and lavatories were abutted eastwards from the far end of the east wall. The works superintendent's office, works lavatories and cloakrooms were contained within the centre shop, but the transformer, fuel store and boiler house, with external doors, more men's lavatories and the 'blueing' room were all accommodated in a narrow, flat-roofed block projecting from the front of the building, co-extensively with the workshop at the west end. This was a rationally planned and compact layout, largely determined by operating processes, but which nevertheless allowed for future expansion into the surrounding unused site, or upwards over the flat-roofed portions.[199]

The external appearance of the Champion building subscribes to the then equally-popular format of a long frontage surmounted by a tall narrow tower which, most usually, took a central position. Here, however, the building occupied a corner site with public façades to both front and east sides and was visible from domestic property on the west; unusually too the administration building did not front the factory but adjoined the side of, and shared frontage with, the production area. But, despite the irregularity of the building line and the asymmetry of function, the building was contained and identified as a whole by continuous banding. Base and parapet, in light brown brickwork, were edged with string courses of artificial stone at plinth, sills, lintels and copings, and separated by long runs of glazing. Differentiation of function was apparent to some extent in the windows—standard, small-paned industrial with narrow, stone-faced mullions for the production area; long-paned, with broader, brick-faced mullions for administration—and also in the treatment of corners—sharply angled on the former, rounded on the latter.

The major company statement was made by the one vertical emphasis—in the main entrance and tower. Attention was drawn to the doorway by a concrete surround rendered in granite aggregate; rectangular flower-box pedestals flanked shallow steps; a flat, upright facing stepped in to a canopy of peculiar and unrelated shape. The brick tower began its ascent above the pedestals, stepped in slightly to roof level, and then rose abruptly to a capping band of on-end bricks, top-edged in concrete. Centrally on each elevation, tall inset windows terminated in a clockface and contained the company's name, spelled vertically and back-lit at night through the windows.

In a review, Leathart praised the building for its 'simplicity and generally unaffected air', noting that it had 'none of the pretentiousness of the majority of industrial buildings' beside the Great West Road.[200] Presumably he was of the A. Tristan Edwards' persuasion that believed industrial buildings should be 'unobtrusive', since he did take exception to the main entrance. Yet, without the landmark proportions of the tower, the building has very little character at all—one of the problems indeed of British Modern—although one has to agree with Leathart that the tower is 'out of scale'. But his description of the entrance as 'lumpy' can apply only to the rather silly shape of the canopy, since the actual entrance is pleasant enough.

The later addition of another block projecting from the front and running westward from the shipping entrance to join the existing abutment, added more bulk and substance to the long, low frontage, and relieved the entrance feature of its isolation with an interesting display of shapes and shadows.

ASEA Limited

Also in 1936, Wallis, Gilbert & Partners were designing for ASEA Limited, Swedish manufacturers of electrical equipment, operating from premises in Fulborne Road, Walthamstow, London. The original contract appears to have been for offices and a canteen; there were further extensions in 1937 and, after the Second World War, by Elliott, Cox & Partners. The property was taken over by the Fuller Electric Company and later became part of a much larger development when acquired by Hawker Siddeley Power Transformers.[201] As much as can be identified as original Wallis, Gilbert in the standing buildings is of plain brick with horizontal bands of windows, but the doorway and entrance surround reveal a creative reconciliation of contemporary modern format with a remembrance of classical ideal, executed in very well-crafted brickwork.

Spencer Corsets Limited

The last of the Wallis, Gilbert commissions in the productive year of 1936 was for large extensions to an existing factory owned by Spencer Corsets Limited, at Britannia Street, Banbury, Oxon. The company was formed in February 1927 as the British subsidiary of Berger Brothers of Newhaven, Connecticut, USA, makers of women's made-to-measure corsets. It was privately owned by the two Berger brothers and Mr and Mrs R. Allen of Banbury, and named after Spencer Berger, son of one of the founders. The company purchased a disused cotton mill in Britannia Street, Banbury. There, lady corsetières were trained and then acted as independent agents, securing orders in the customer's own home or on a door-to-door calling system. The orders were then made up at the central factory.[202] By the early 1930s, as the health-conscious basis of corsetry gained ground—'better posture, better health'—there were two thousand Spencer fitters operating nationwide; larger manufacturing premises were needed. To avoid raising loans, the company established a building reserve fund in 1935 and it was possible for plans to be drawn in October 1936, but building did not commence until February 1937. The building was completed in May 1938, having exceeded its £40 000 initial estimate by £10 000.[203]

Dorothy Allen, known and addressed as 'Madame Directrice', was the driving force of the enterprise, a martinet who insisted upon strict segregation of sexes and on strict observation of personnel hierarchies. In the new factory, nevertheless, she had facilities installed that were unavailable to employees in their homes, such as clothes washing machines, baths, showers, a chiropody service and an in-house doctor.[204] Directors' meetings were held alternately in Britain and America; as a result of Mrs Allen's transatlantic journeys, the architects were required to design a factory that was the 'last word' in modernity, whose interior decor drew its inspiration from the liner *Queen Mary* but which, externally, was in accord with the existing buildings. The contractor, T. D. Kingerlee of Oxford, who had built the old factory, was appointed to build the new one.

The old mill is a rectangular brick building with cast-iron supports and a pitched roof with gabled dormers. Its narrow front faces east onto Britannia Street. The new factory was built in its grounds—lawns, gardens and a tennis court on the north side. Extra land was purchased further to the rear to provide a vehicular goods entrance and car park. The site and the street slope down from south to north. In configuration, the new extension consists of a large rectangular four-storey block and basement aligned east–west parallel to the old building and connected to it across a 61 feet gap by a crossing section of the same height, like the bar of a letter H. In the forecourt is a single-storeyed hall and main entrance, standing free at the front and sides but attached to the crossing section at the rear. The whole of the new building is flat-roofed and steel-framed, with concrete floors and foundations. It is encased in Gloucestershire redsand brick with artificial stone sills, lintels and copings and a Horton stone entrance way. Because of the steep incline of the land, most of the basement is visible and is glazed to match the upper storeys, but had to be treated with rock asphalt against water seepage from natural drainage. (As other factories in the area have closed, the water table has risen still higher; basement pumps are in constant operation.)

The main block on the north side measures roughly 38 feet on frontage by 136 feet in depth. Dimensions have been rounded to the nearest foot, as some measurements on plan are noted to half-inches. Stanchions at 12 feet 6 inch centres provide large uninterrupted floor spaces. The most forward bay is of slightly shallower depth as the brickwork to stanchions stands prouder than the rest as an aesthetic framing device. Manufacturing processes occupy the basement, the ground and first floors, offices the second, whilst the third floor, of only six-bays in depth, accommodates directors' and their secretaries' offices, lavatory facilities, dining room with porthole windows, rest room and lobby. Forward of the third floor junction with the crossing section, the flat roof provided space for 'taking the air' and *al fresco* meals. At the rear, bowed French windows led to a balcony over the final bay of the second floor—the whole of the directors' suite having some pretence to a liner's upper deck.

The crossing section, some 61 feet wide and 36 feet deep, has a passenger lift in the projecting front tower. Behind it, on each floor a 10 feet wide corridor connects the old and new blocks; behind that is the central stairway and, beside it on most floors, male and female lavatories. Cloakrooms were sited in the old building. In the basement area of the crossing section, the boiler house was served by automatic stoking and fuel control, the chimney being housed within the structure for appearance sake. Mains water for taps and central heating was assisted by an extra resource of water tanks in the basement, to improve upon the low pressure and to serve the sprinkler system in the event of fire. On the north side was the switchroom; electric power was drawn from the mains via a transformer housed in the yard at the back. On the side adjoining the main block is a goods lift which, on the ground floor, opens to a loading bay on the rear side. Also on the ground floor a first-aid room faces the doctor's surgery across the corridor, the doctor's room being sited to the right of the passenger lift; on its left is the staff entrance, which opens from the passageway between the entrance hall and the old building.

The rectangular hall, 37 feet wide by 46 feet in depth, occupies most of the forecourt. It has a parapet behind which another raised section gives additional height to the ceiling and contains a glazed lantern with electrically operated clerestory windows. On the front, a central projection with higher parapet contains the front entrance. Rounded steps lead up between Doric columns (with correct entasis) that support the arch, all in Horton stone. The lettering 'Spencer House' on the archivolt, and the architrave of the recessed door extending over an arched window, are both in polished gun metal. Enclosing a small vestibule, twin pairs of bronze doors have etched glass and dendritic glazing bars to match those in the porthole windows on the entrance flanks and in the new entrance attached to the old building.

In the large, terrazzo-floored hall, the forward corners have been walled off into small rooms but, originally, the under-hung side bays, separated by ribbed, plaster pillars, provided seating alcoves for visitors. Overhead, the raised central portion is framed by moulded, patterned coving and lit, below the lantern, by a centre-hung chandelier and a glass ceiling, etched to match the doors and paned in a rectilinear pattern of black glazing bars. Directly opposite the doors, the full length of the hall away, is the reception desk, originally built-in but now replaced; to its right is the lobby to the passenger lift and, to the left, a short stairway leading to the corridor.

Mrs Allen's concern for dust and fire hazard stipulated that, as far as possible, all doors should be flush and all corners and fitments rounded to avoid dust traps. Special fire doors were fitted to descend under temperature control. Many of the internal walls were left unplastered, the bare brick being painted with gloss paint. But the directors and visitors ascending by the passenger lift to the top-floor directorial suite encountered only luxury surroundings. A large, comfortably furnished waiting room led to the lobby and the directors' offices. These still retain many of their original fittings and furnishings. Elegant fireplaces surround 'Magicoal' electric fires; central heating radiators are encased in the walls. The adjoining bathrooms have coloured suites, and all wall corners are rounded. The floors are of oak block or maple strip. As the interior of the building retains so much of its pleasant 1930s atmosphere, one is happy to find that many attractive, original pieces of furniture are still in evidence.

Despite the use of brick and stone, the exterior of the building does not sit happily beside the original mill, and its somewhat gaunt lines are at odds with the cosseted luxury of the interior. On plan, the layout arrangements and circulation paths are rational and efficient but, to the external observer's view, the massing is incomprehensible, cramped and ungainly. Each section appears to belong only to itself but is denied space for complete self-expression or possibility of relation with its neighbours. Most of the original, small-paned windows have been replaced with modern large-paned ones but, in the surviving decorative windows, glazing bars are somewhat out of accord with each other and with the shape and archaic style of the entranceway. But one should be grateful that this unusual building— probably the best that could be done in the location and in the circum- stances—and its contents still exist, not just as a monument to 1930s stylistic delights but as able to function in full operative use without 'modernisation' for the sake of modernisation. Unfortunately, however, because of the rising water table, it is slowly and gently moving sideways down the steep hill. Fortunately, that is not the fate of its occupying company. When bespoke corsetry declined in popularity after the Second World War, the word 'corset' was removed from the company's title. Although becoming involved in made-to-measure surgical wear under contract to the National Health Service, the company was not experienced in volume production or able to compete with ready-to-wear fashion undergarments. In 1972 Bergers sold the com- pany to Ashborne Investments, which disposed of it in 1974 to Thomas Tilling Limited. When the latter was taken over by BTR in 1983, Spencer's managers and directors arranged a buy-out as Spencer (Banbury) Limited and expanded into the fashion market; the building remains the property of BTR.

Platers & Stampers Limited

The date of the design of a factory for Platers & Stampers Limited at Colne Road, Burnley, Lancashire, is indeterminate and of some small historic note. The decline of the cotton industry in the north-west of England caused massive unemployment. In November 1936 Burnley Corporation set up a Development Sub-Committee to look at the possibility of attracting new industries to the area. The sub-committee reported on 5 January 1937 that an arrangement had been arrived at with Platers & Stampers Limited for the erection by the Corporation of a factory fronting Colne Road, to be leased to the company, and requested that application be made to the Ministry of Health for permission to borrow £80 000 for that purpose. On 27 February 1937 the request was recommended by the General Purposes Committee; the amount was amended to £84 070; on 3 March 1937 the Council approved the application. Three months later on 2 June the Town Clerk reported that the Minister of Health had consented to the development of the land, to the erection of a factory to be leased to Platers & Stampers Limited, and to the Council incurring the expense by borrowing the proposed sum.[205]

Six months *prior* to that consent, however, on 9 January 1937 the local newspaper, the *Burnley Express*, had published a photograph of the chosen site, showing structural steelwork already in place.[206] Given that the site, on the rising curve of Colne Road, has a fall of 12 feet and that land had to be made up and retaining walls built before construction could commence, it would appear that the commission to Wallis, Gilbert & Partners was received some time in 1936. The illegality of the Council's 'desperate action to relieve unemployment' incurred ministerial threats of personal surcharging,[207] but these seem not to have been carried out. The factory was completed and handed over in November 1937. The company concerned, Platers & Stampers Limited, was formed as a British subsidiary of the Edward Katzinger Company of Chicago, Illinois, USA, with a view to expanding further into British Imperial markets. Its products, kitchen hardware, tinned ware and bathroom fittings, were marketed under the name 'EKCO Products', but the name was already in use in Britain by a well-known firm making wireless sets, so the title Platers & Stampers was chosen to indicate just what the company did. It was eventually changed in 1953—we now know it as Prestige Limited.

The site and buildings have been considerably extended; the original building measured 330 feet on front, facing east to Colne Road, and 275 feet in depth overall, stepping in on the north side in line with the railway embankment, to which new sidings were built. The factory is single-storeyed and steel framed on a grid of 25 feet centres in depth and 30 feet centres in width. It is infilled with brick cavity walls; some parts of the concrete floor are suspended over filled ground. A central, east/west mezzanine floor has a flat, glazed roof with clerestory windows; other than the pitched roof bay on its south side, all other roofs are north-light. They were fitted with louvred, anti-glare, frosted glass and covered on the south side with asbestos-lined insulating panels. The Government's rearmament programme was in being at that time; accordingly steel and other metals were not so readily available, so timber was used for gutterings, internal wall boards and the flat roof of the centre front two-storey office section. Covered loading bays were placed along the north wall, with access to road and rail; the boiler house, providing some power, the central heating and hot tap water, was placed in a separate building at the rear of the site. A special cooling system was installed for summer months.

Most of the factory floor was open-plan to accommodate rows of separately-motorised processing machines, and the assembly, storage and packing areas. Specialist departments for intermediate processes that required singular facilities were walled off; the enamelling section had a woodblock floor and fume extraction equipment; the drying room had constant temperature air conditioning; the plating room had an asphalt floor which meant that these department could not be very easily moved should there be need to reorganise. Also separated off were the hot tin processing section, the burnishing room and a tool-making room. The mezzanine floor contained sanitary facilities, cloak- and locker-rooms and a canteen, which were reached by stairways at each end.[208]

In the central, front two-storey block, only the entrance hall, stairway and a first-aid post encroach into the factory floor space. Above, the partitioned off stairwell turns around on itself to a small landing. On the first floor are two executive offices and an open-plan general office. The latter and the landing are top-lit from a lantern in the flat roof and a long window in the recessed main entrance. Surprisingly, the woodwork of the glazed partitions of the upper stairwell is decorated with almost-forgotten nail-heads. Behind the stairwell is the strongroom and, beside it, a corridor running out onto the mezzanine floor.

The entrance hall is spacious, light and self-consciously 'Modern', with a plethora of structural and decorative curves. Directly opposite the entrance, matching doors with curved, tubular handles are recessed between curving-in walls beneath a curved overhang. They open directly into the factory. The darker bordering of the grey terrazzo floor and skirting also gives precedence to that direction, suggesting the supremacy of the manufacturing area over administrative needs. The hall, however, extends to the right to reach the offset terrazzo-laid stairs. From rounded treads, the stairs rise along that wall, curve left to climb across the wall behind which is the production floor and then left again to the first-floor landing.

Curves appear in the right-hand newel and the stanchion to the cross beam; the chromed, tubular handrail rises over a curve. On the left, the newel is formed by the rounded column of a standard lamp, matched to engaged standards on each side of the inner doorway. The columns of the lamps, ribbed in the pattern frequently found in Wallis' pillars of that time, are of plaster painted to look like wood. They are capped by large, round metal vases containing electric lamps that diffuse their light upwards. A fancy, curved pattern in thin metal decorates the radiator cover and the fanlight; the ceiling has a moulded border of half-circles. The hall has been very well cared for and retains its 1930s glamour, but it does seem a little unsure of itself. Its planning is confusing and its decor, so unheralded on the exterior, comes as a surprise.

Externally, from the curve of Colne Road, the building presents itself as a broad expanse of brickwork dominating the landscape with powerful

Fig. 37 Platers & Stampers Ltd, Colne Road, Burnley, Lancs: view from Colne Road, 1938

horizontal lines and rectilinear forms, riding the crest on a concrete base trimmed to ground contours (Fig. 37). On the upper edge of the base, continuous string courses of dark red, on-end bricks and concrete are aligned to the true level of the floor and window sills. But the windows themselves, although rectangular and long-paned, are not part of the overall horizontality of the design. In the wings they are placed separately in each bay; the rounded concrete mullions and touches of quoining in rounded reveals do not anticipate the bold curves of the entrance hall. A certain fussiness in their treatment does, however, counteract the huge spread of brick that ingeniously hides the north-light gables. The red brickwork is stratified with bands of darker, on-end bricks and is capped by a rebated concrete cornice and overhung coping.

There are no end stops to these horizontal lines. The spread of the wings is controlled by the mass at the centre that breaks upward and forward of the elevation. There, the bands of concrete and on-end bricks are repeated, but the brick face of the projections changes from cavity wall to Flemish bond, to surround tall windows and to form a broad frame to the recessed entrance way. Within the recess are four vertical windows and, centrally, the doorway. Here, and on the framing, unadorned rounded reveals provide a nice finish; the vertically-ribbed concrete splays and cross beam relate to the mullions in the wings. A deep band of bricks above the lower windows and the long window below the overhang are coherent with the overall boldness of the structure. The simplicity of the arrangement is, however, defeated by unnecessary detailing—in the chequered pattern of the glazing bars in the upper window, the ribbing of the concrete cross beam and the on-ending of brick below it. Add to that a parade of huge, tall phallic candles anachronistically pretending to be a colonnade, and a well-balanced composition of broad planes, strong masses and subtle brickwork—stylistically more continental than American or north-country English—falls victim to a streak of wilfulness that emerges in Wallis' later designs.

Slough Trading Estate

In the late 1930s Wallis, Gilbert & Partners received commissions for designs at the Slough Trading Estate, Buckinghamshire. As industry continued to migrate to the southern counties, land values increased particularly on the perimeter of London.[209] With the extension of railways and bypass roads, however, relatively cheaper land became available further westward along the Thames Valley. The 1700-acre Slough Trading Estate, some 25 miles west of London, was owned and operated by Slough Estates Limited. The site contained a housing estate with many social amenities and, initially, 'standard' factories for rental with all services laid on and obtainable at reduced cost from bulk sources.[210]

In 1932 Eric Pasold had rejected this location for his new British venture because the factories on offer at the estate were too small, had no room for expansion and were architecturally dull. Between 1932 and 1939 the number of factories on the estate rose from 114 to 270. Most of the companies accommodated there produced consumer goods and consisted of newly-founded enterprises, those seeking relocation to a more salubrious and profitable area, and foreign firms seeking a British manufacturing base. But, as industry diversified and companies of proven viability moved to the estate, architects were employed to design their premises.

A factory by Wallis, Gilbert & Partners was published in June 1938[211] and was thus, presumably, designed in 1937. The design shows the increasing preference for buildings of brick-patterned brick dressed with concrete or artificial stone, its form in essence the massing of parts. More idiosyncratically, this building reveals manneristic tendencies and reminiscence—less wilfully than at Platers & Stampers but which interfere immodestly with the clarity of good basic composition. Tall, square corner block towers, flanked by projecting rounded supports, all in brick, are connected by a brick fascia above tall windows that match those on the side elevations and in the centre fronts of the towers. The windows have opaque glass at first-floor level, but that does not detract from their contribution to verticality in the design, which receives even greater emphasis in the elongated concrete mullions. They clip on to base and fascia like neon tubes or, more appropriately, as upright bars protecting the windows of a bastion-like structure. Horizontal treatment is shadowy and, except for the shallow concrete plinth, appears in the patterning of the brickwork. Long lines of half-headers form the tight curve of the tower supports; on-end bricks in a darker colour outline base and copings; they form a broader string course at lintel level and deep cappings to the towers.

Against that, the concrete surrounds of the doorways giving access to the towers are out of character. They are too reminiscent of Wallis' early concrete aesthetic and the stepping up of the cornice is too fussy, the rounded lines of the splays are at odds with the rectilinear reveals of the tower windows above them; nothing in their shape has any relation to the rest of the design.

The Entrance Gateway
Much more effectively handled in concrete was an Entrance Gateway to the Slough Trading Estate. The date of that design is not known but the strong curving lines suggest the late 1930s. There are, however, elements of earlier designs in the stepped V-section 'columns', although the Egyptianising of the flanking towers is more powerful and stylised than in any of the Fancy factories. The 'spirit of masculinity' that, to Leathart, embued the Slough factory with 'strength and solidity' is also evident in the gateway to the estate.[212, 213]

Simmonds Aerocessories Limited

The same vigour and bold stylization are apparent in a factory for Simmonds Aerocessories Limited, manufacturers of aircraft accessories, that faces north on to the Great West Road at Brentford. Oliver Simmonds, who founded the company in 1931, was also an aircraft manufacturer—Simmonds Aircraft Ltd, founded in 1928—and was an innovatory and influential engineer in the field of aeronautics. The Aerocessories company specialised in small components, some of in-house invention, and had an international trading range.

In 1935 the company took possession of a small factory built on this same site by John Laing & Son Limited. Two years later, Wallis, Gilbert & Partners were commissioned to design considerable extensions which, though conceived as a whole in December 1937, were to be built piecemeal over the following years, by the same contractors.[214] The first-built portion, with elevations to the Great West Road on the north and to Clayponds Lane on the east, was erected in 1938. Extension of that building, eastward along the frontage and making use of part of the foundations of the earlier building, was followed by a complete west wing of similar design; thereafter, the centre block and tower. Additional buildings were erected on land at the rear.

Simmonds vacated the premises at the end of the Second World War; the building was acquired by British Overseas Airways Company as headquarters, and converted wholly to offices. Further extensions and alterations have been, and are still being carried out by the present owners, SmithKline Beecham Group plc. The original building, however, although constructed over a number of years, appears to have adhered to plan.

The building measures overall 415 feet on front, increasing to 448 feet to take in the angle of Clayponds Lane, and 208 feet overall in depth. The central portion consists of two, flat-roofed, four-storeyed blocks flanking a tower, also flat-roofed, that rises a further eight storeys to 140 feet. Beneath this section a basement 'stronghold' was constructed as an air-raid shelter, equipped with hospital and operating theatre. The walls are two feet six inches thick with stanchions four feet six inches square, all in reinforced concrete. Oliver Simmonds was Chairman of the Government's Air Raid Precautions Committee and, with his understanding of the destructiveness of aerial attack, personally designed the shelter. Although the building never became a target, the experience of building the shelter was important to the architects and the builders when involved in other defence installations.

On each side of the centre block, flat-roofed, three-storeyed wings stretch out to circular corner towers and then return to encompass a single-storeyed, 400 feet-long manufacturing shed. The shed was top-lit, with pitched, asbestos-clad roof, adjoining parallel to and at the rear of the multi-storey buildings. The manufacturing area continued along the west side and across the back of the building, separated by open yards and attached to the main block by a stair tower that was part of the tower block. The ground floor throughout is of reinforced concrete; most of its floor space was given over to manufacturing and storage. On the front and side elevations, it appears more as a lower ground floor, with windows set low in the stone-faced base of the elevations. The floor above is described on plan as the 'main floor', to which access was gained from the main entrance on centre front, from both wing towers and, for works personnel, on the west side. The front bays contained offices and entrance hall; the remainder, at the rear of the site, contained small process sections, the boiler house and groups of lavatories and cloakrooms at east and west ends.

The first floor of the multi-storey part was also occupied by offices on front and in part of the west return; in the centre front, a gallery surrounded the double-storeyed entrance hall. At the rear were works and staff canteens, kitchen and catering services, which again joined the main block at the stair tower. First and second floors of the centre block, over the manufacturing shed, were also used for manufacturing purposes. Thereon upwards, in the further eight storeys of the central tower, are stairs and lifts; manufacturing processes occupied the lower storeys whilst the upper ones provided a suite for the company's directors that, on the topmost floor, opened out to a roof garden. The boiler flue was integrated into the tower, passing underground from the boiler house and rising through the tower to discharge above roof level. Heating was by high pressure water, with special floor panels in the hall. Above the ground floor, the building is of steel frame encased in concrete, with brick panelled walls and reinforced concrete floors.

Interior decoration of areas seen by visitors and for the use of the upper echelons of management was lavish and expensive. The Chairman's room had cedar-panelled walls, decoratively moulded plaster ceiling, oak strip floor and very modern electric light fittings in opaque glass. Oak-panelled walls in the conference room were decorated with the component parts manufactured by the company. Most elaborate of all was the double-storeyed hallway. Above the floor of Travertine marble, pale walls and a balcony frieze of carvings of various means of travel through the ages were of polished Pericot marble. In contrast, skirtings and fluted columns were of darker Ashburton marble; the free-standing columns supported pale bowls that diffused light from electric lamps set in huge discs in the ceilings. On the rear wall, between the lift shafts (that gave direct access to the penthouse suite) a fountain played over rocky outcroppings into a pool surrounded by live vegetation and edged with fluted Ashburton marble. Curved Travertine steps on each side led to stairways and office corridors.

Externally, the publicly-seen shape of the building is fairly simple and coherent. The verticality of grand, central massing—a huge rectangular tower flanked by projecting blocks—is balanced by the horizontal lines of the wings that reach out and then suddenly curve in, to grasp circular tower corners. Yellowish-grey Whitwick bricks provide a pleasing background to accentuation of the geometry by stone dressing—on the wings to stress the horizontal lines, with continuous sills, lintels, corniced copings and a parade of plain mullions. Curving balusters to the steps on the corners lead up to attractive stone door surrounds and canopies, combining with the end towers' tall windows, to add some sense of verticality.

On the centre portion, however, detailing in stone is much more bold and elaborate. Appropriately enough, given the change of scale, the bases and cappings of the supporting blocks are deeper, and more substantially so at the tower heading, their heaviness relieved by rebated and dentilated cornices. But the most outstanding features are the stone mullions, which Wallis employs here very imaginatively and to much greater effect, adding power and presence to an already impressive structure. As a reiteration of the masculinity found at Slough, these mullions, charging upward from base to cornice and differently shaped at head and toe, suggest more a congeries of stylised sphinx than the bastion bars at Slough; and they are not so overtly phallic as the candles at Burnley. In profile, they remind one of attenuated Ethiopian lions. Various motifs appear about the building, indicative of the company's interests. On the tower head is the sculpted figure of an airman beneath outstretched eagle wings; monograms set on spread wings decorated the end towers and still exist in the railings. A stylised aeroplane ornaments the balcony over the entrance. But the building itself has none of the elegance and grace of flight; it is powerful, thrusting, supremely confident, more expressive of the engines and engineering that lift the flying machines into the skies and manifested in the main entrance.

Although a series of sweeping curves draws the visitor, by broad steps and structural recession, to the doorway, it is only from the longer view that the entrance's contribution to a major statement becomes evident. Four short, fat columns, shaped like piled-up gear cogs and piston rings latched to the walls on the outer sides, support an over-massive balcony. Huge knuckles, the extension of broad mullion arms, grasp the underside of the balcony as though to heave the slim aeroplane motif aloft; the arms thrusting ever upwards, reach to the winged airman at the summit. Narrative though the design may be and, fortunately, less ornamented than shown on plan (where Egyptianising is more evident), the entrance is, sadly, a little grotesque. A similar balcony disfigures the elevation of the Hoover canteen building and was designed at much the same time. Certainly a building of such command-ing presence as the Simmonds' required an equally imposing entrance, one more dynamic than gross? But, however one may criticise Wallis' entrance-way, nothing can excuse Beecham's attempted modernising emendation, which is totally out of character and conspicuously unsuitable.

When BOAC acquired the premises in February 1947, very extensive alterations were carried out internally[215] and more were to follow by Beecham. The writer is informed that the original construction and design were so excellent that the building can withstand any amount of interior alterations.[216] The pity is that external alteration has been of such inferior quality.

John Laing & Son Limited

While the Simmonds building was under construction, Wallis, Gilbert & Partners became involved in another form of industrial development for the main contractors at the Simmonds site. In the mid-1930s John Laing & Son Limited purchased 470 acres of land at Elstree, Herts, to be developed as a 'garden city' of mixed housing, shops, public buildings, schools, recreation grounds and gardens set about made-up roads with all services laid on. The estate was to be bordered on its perimeter with the existing main roads by factories for light, clean industries, accessed by separate service roads so as not to disturb the residental areas, and plots were to be for sale, leasing or building privately by potential customers.

As Laings of Carlisle, the firm had been stonemasons and builders for over a century; under the newly registered title of John Laing & Son Ltd, a London office was opened in 1920, to service major government and municipal building contracts in the south of England. The company moved to new headquarters at Mill Hill, London, in 1926, with sufficient resources to finance speculative development of private housing estates in the London suburbs.[217] The estate at Elstree was one of a group that formed its 'third phase' of developments. Factory sites were advertised in glossy promotional brochures and on estate hoardings, but planning permission to erect industrial buildings on prime sites beside the new Barnet Bypass was refused. In 1939 the development was interrupted by war.

In *Semi-detached London*[218] Alan Jackson quotes from *The Estates Gazette* of 19 November 1928, that Wallis, Gilbert & Partners and C. M. Crickmer 'drew up plans' for the Laing Elstree estate, the former to be responsible for the estate to the west of the Barnet Bypass and the latter for land to the east.[219] No evidence has been discovered in support of that statement; the Laing archives show that Crickmer was never involved at all in the Elstree development and that Wallis, Gilbert & Partners were responsible for only one factory on the estate, known as 'Factory Number 1', for which no plans have survived.[220] In the Wallis, Gilbert plan archive, however, are plans for 'New Factory Number 3, Laing Estate, Elstree' dated 26 July 1938, which was never built.

Factories Numbers 1 and 3 were both designed as corner buildings, Number 1 to be built on the north side of the junction of Ripon Way with the Barnet Bypass and Number 3 to complement it on the south side. Dimensions and layout are identical, but reversed; each factory has a frontage to Ripon Way of 200 feet, an elevation of 100 feet to a service road running parallel to the bypass, and a main entrance and tower set obliquely across the salient corner. Each short elevation faces east. Both show steel-frame construction on a grid of 20 feet square bays, with brick and glass infill. The two roadside elevations of each factory are flat-roofed to one-bay's depth, with a second storey from entrance tower to part way along each side. Works offices and lavatories occupy the front ground-floor bay of each east-facing short end; the boiler house in each case, with flue directed upward through the tower, is placed on the ground floor, at the Ripon Way side of the tower. First floors contained offices and staff lavatories, the second and third floors of the towers provide a caretaker's flat and the fourth holds a water tank. The remaining floor space of each ground floor, including that under flat-roofed bays on the Ripon Way side, was for manufacturing processes; the bulk of those are covered by trussed, pitched, top-lit asbestos-cement roofs, oriented east-west, gabled at the west ends and hipped at the east ends behind the first-floor offices and tower.

Both buildings were prescribed to be faced in yellow 'Hunziker' bricks (a hard, engineering type) with concrete dressing, each roadside elevation having long rows of vertical, long-paned windows between brick piers, with continuous sills and copings. The corner units each contain a small vestibule and hall, a waiting room on one side of the doorway and a telephone room on the other, doors leading to the manufacturing area and a staircase leading to upper floors. It is in the corner units, however, that the similarity between the two designs ends. They are different in shape, plan and external appearance.

The built design, Factory Number 1, is by definition the earlier design. It is shown on a block plan of July 1938 for Number 3 as 'existing building', which places it at late 1937 or very early 1938. The corner unit has a five-storeyed tower of plain yellow brick, with an uninterrupted tall, narrow window on front, capped by a concrete canopy, and groups of single windows on the other elevations. Above the main entrance, the tower walls curve concavely to engage flanking, two-storeyed blocks, each angled back to its roadside elevation. In each, a tall, narrow window is framed by a slight projection of the brickwork. Recessed at the outside of each block, narrow secondary blocks, a few courses higher, have double slit windows to each floor. At ground-floor level, set across the corner and into the curve of the tower, is the main entrance. Plain wooden doors with glazed fanlights are flanked by short, drum-shaped walls of fluted concrete. On their lower part, moulded palm forms rise in the flutes from a plain base; two narrow bands are cut in around the tops. Above them, a deep convex concrete balcony is decorated with a deeper cutaway of geometric pattern on each side of a sculpted piece reminiscent of a Lalique dragonfly. The concreted entranceway is over-heavy and out of character with the rest of the building. The rounded walls are hollow and, internally, provide cupboard space for the telephone and waiting rooms, but the shape of the walls and the intrusion of internalised drainage downpipes negate any practical use. Beyond the tiny vestibule, glazed doors lead to a small hallway, with stairs at the left rear to a dangerously awkward landing and a narrow corridor at the back of the first-floor offices. Outside a corridor window, a precariously supported, wood-slatted walkway serves as a fire exit which, under later laws, was deemed an inadequate escape facility from the tower. The tower rooms then fell into disuse.

From the Barnet Bypass the traveller sees a building of grace and dignity, sitting comfortably on a corner site, with swept-back wings hiding the manufacturing area. A closer, stationary view, however, reveals a certain lack of quality. The number and arrangement of projections and set-backs at the corner are too great and too complicated for the size of the building and the space available. Internally, the complexity makes for difficulties and awk-wardness in layout and circulation. In a speculative venture, austerity of interior treatment and decor is not unexpected; here economy is very evident and ill-matched with the bravura of the entrance. The roadside elevations are straightforward and pleasant. Economy and simplicity applied to the design of the corners may have resulted in a more coherent building. When completed, the building contained 24 000 square feet of floor space and was offered at a rental of £1440 per annum; it was first occupied by Caribonum Limited in 1939.[221] The present occupant and owner, Carl Zeiss Jena Limited, has used the building as offices and warehouse for over 12 years. Mainten-ance has been neglected, concrete shows spalling, there are cracks in the brickwork and the Crittall window frames have rusted. When the company's new warehouse is completed, the Ripon Way building is likely to be demolished. Over the years, however, apart from a few of the usual problems with flat roofs, the structure has proved satisfactory—'considering it was not an expensive, custom-built premises, it has weathered well'.[222]

In the unbuilt design (Factory Number 3), treatment of the corner unit is bolder but still something of a hotch-potch. The outer flanks of the corner tower present to the roadside elevations two-storey projections, V-shaped in glass with brick bases and capping, and ornamented with moulded concrete shafts on the apex of the V. Across the corner, vertically-stepped brickwork blocks of two storeys support a five-storeyed brick tower that, again, has a tall, narrow light over the entrance. The head of the tower appears to be a lantern caged in horizontal concrete bars. The concrete doorway surround has ribbed splays and a heavy, stepped canopy and is flanked by fancy, concrete-capped, narrow, round pillars of brick. As if that were not decorative enough for such a highly complex profile, Wallis then added a single colossal mullion, thrusting upwards through the tower light from a prehensile toe gripping the door canopy to a backward curve—like a helmet crest—jutting into the sky. On a plainer background the glass Vs and bold mullion would have been quite magnificent, but still at odds with the simplicity of the rest of the building. Possibly the intention was to add glamour and stature to the anonymity of a plain brick, rented factory.

At this stage of the partnership's *oeuvre*, Wallis seems unable to leave well alone. He is not afraid of corner sites, but he had achieved better results in the past. In handling the modern idiom, he had juxtaposed planes and masses, balanced curves and straight lines, exploited structural forms to provide interesting space—often competently, sometimes with considerable confidence and masterly innovation. Some detail features had been inventive and successful as emphasis or decoration; others were ponderous, weighty, even gross. But all too frequently, and detrimentally, in too great abundance.

The design of Laing Number 3 factory was, in fact, a re-use of ideas that first appeared in a competition entry in 1936 for an Imperial Airways Terminal building to be erected directly opposite Wallis, Gilbert's Victoria Coach Station in Buckingham Palace Road, London, and probably designed by Douglas Wallis. It was then used with much greater success at a factory designed but a month or two before the unbuilt Laing factory for Montague Burton Limited at Worsley, Manchester.

Montague Burton Limited

When Montague Burton started his tailoring business in Sheffield in 1900, tailoring was a sweated industry. Burton's ambition was to improve working conditions and to establish an integrated enterprise, from purchasing all-British materials to direct selling to the public of finished goods. It was achieved by cash-only trading, precision processing and standardisation of equipment. Expansion brought the firm to Leeds, Yorks, and, in 1921, to the custom-built Hudson Road Mills on a 100-acre 'works estate', with every possible facility and service for the firm's employees. By the mid-1930s the company was the largest multiple bespoke tailors in the world, was producing its own cloth and operating more than 400 retail shops; served by its own transport fleet, it brought low-cost, made-to-measure tailoring to a wide range of public custom. By 1937 the company had exhausted the supply of suitable labour in the Leeds catchment area and also needed an expansion of floor space.[223]

In the late 1930s, although the rearmament programme provided more work, unemployment persisted in areas where old staple industries were still in a depressed state. Measures were taken by national and local government to attract new industries to those areas (as, for instance, had been the case at Burnley for Platers & Stampers Limited). Burton's choice of a site in Lancashire not only offered a new source of labour in unemployed textile workers but, in bringing new industry to the area, qualified for support from the Lancashire Industrial Development Control.[224] The 25-acre site at Worsley, presented by the local authority, was part of the Bridgewater Estate, five miles from Manchester. It faced south to the new arterial East Lancashire Road and was eminently suitable for the kind of 'garden factory' Burton desired. There was easy access for goods transport by road, rail and the Manchester Ship Canal and, by a network of omnibus and tram services connecting with surrounding towns, for personnel.[225]

Burton's Leeds headquarters factory had been built by direct labour to the design of elevations by Nathaniel Martin and plans by T. H. Rowntree, both members of the practice of Leeds architect H. Wilson, who had designed Burton's shop premises. In 1931 Montague Burton Limited had taken over Wilson's practice as the Burton Architects Department. For the new factory at Worsley, therefore, a complete in-house service was available. Nevertheless, Wallis, Gilbert & Partners were chosen as architects 'because of their reputation, as Montague Burton wanted a prestige building'.[226] They were, however, to work in association with Martin and Rowntree. Rowntree's contribution was an expert knowledge of the layout of Burton factories, which were organised so that all processes were segregated and each operated by groups of workers who were specialists in their particular sphere; on-line coordination relied upon a highly sophisticated system of routeing and reference filing. From Martin would have come an appreciation that 'Montague Burton held very positive ideas and, although no architect, would not accept a building that did not have a strong vertical emphasis'.[227] Since Wallis, Gilbert & Partners were known for efficiently planned working layouts and good working conditions and, in these later years, Wallis' designs showed a distinct predilection for a major piece of verticality, the choice of architect proved to be a happy one.

In the first instance, Wallis, Gilbert & Partners submitted drawings for a factory in reinforced concrete, thinking that would be more suitable to the kind of weather prevailing in the north-west. But, as the factory was to be built by a direct labour force more at home with steel and brick, Wallis converted the design to those materials without altering the style or form.[228] To clothe the steel frame, smooth bright red Accrington engineering bricks dressed with pale buff terracotta were chosen—as materials more familiar to the builders, as having historical precedent in the region and as having for many years proved suitable to the local climate. Terracotta ware and decorative elements in black, buff and red faience by the Middleton Fireclay Company are an instance of the choice of northern suppliers for many of the building materials used.

The factory was set back from the highway on raised ground. Access roads curved in and up from the east and west sides to the forecourt and the service road that surrounded the building. Parallel to the main road, the frontal block—253 feet wide by 40 feet in depth—contained the goods receiving department on the west side and the goods despatch department on the east, both with large, covered loading bays. Between them was the entrance hall, with commissionaire's office, four waiting rooms, telephone and valve rooms and a lavatory occupying the corners and side walls. Directly opposite the central, main entrance, two stairways, rising to east and west, curved round the rear wall to the first-floor landing. The first floor, set back on the front elevation, reached out to four bays on each side beyond the centrepiece and was glazed on all sides. It contained offices, storerooms, cloakrooms and lavatories, and access to the central tower that rose 80 feet above ground level. The second floor in the tower was used as a storeroom; the two floors above housed water tanks, one of which fed the factory-wide sprinkler system.[229]

Attached at the rear of the front block and angled westward was the single-storeyed factory area, with asbestos-tiled, north-light roof and glazed walls. It was of open plan, measuring 215 feet wide by 432 feet on the west flank and 496 feet on the east. Most of the forward space housed manufacturing processes; behind that, the pressing room was partitioned off. At the rear was a canteen large enough to seat 1800 people and to provide recreational amenities for them, such as table tennis, billiards, a library, and so on. The decor was in shades of cream and, on the south wall, were murals painted on canvas showing the stages of creation of the suit, from sheep shearing to finished garment, the work of T. E. Murphy of Leeds College of Art. On each of the flanking walls was a mezzanine floor, one bay wide which, from the exterior, suggested a two-storey building. Over the manufacturing and pressing areas, these floors housed lavatories and cloakrooms with clothes-drying racks; over the canteen were rooms for welfare and employment offices, the doctor's consulting room, surgery and medical clinic, a dental surgery, an opticians and a sunray treatment room. Access was by stairways at intervals along each wall beside the workers' entrance to the building. The whole factory was air-conditioned (the first of its kind in Europe) and centrally heated.

Standing separately at the rear of the factory were the maintenance and service block and an electricity transformer unit, both built of red brick with flat roofs. The former housed the boiler room with its 140 feet high chimney, fan room, pump room, switchgear, cycle store, main garage, sports club and workshops and storerooms for painters, engineers and joiners.

Beneath the centre of the front block of the factory, was a cellar in which all the mains services were metered. From the cellar and from fan rooms at the back of each end of the frontal block, three ducts, six feet wide by seven feet high and fashioned of reinforced concrete, ran underground to the service block at the rear of the suite. The central duct contained gas, water, electricity and steam pipes; the outer ones drew in air, which was washed, filtered and warmed in winter, discharged into the factory and extracted through ventilators in the roof. All these services were controlled, monitored and regulated from the service block, as also were the factory lighting, electrically operated opening and closing of the north lights, a system of coded signals to communicate with heads of departments, and the diffusion of music into the factory, directly or by relayed wireless programmes.[230] In the early days of construction, running sand had been found in the subsoil at the rear of the site; it eroded the concrete ducts before the walls were set and caused water seepage problems afterwards. These were dealt with by effective maintenance and no movement of the building's foundations was ever recorded.[231] A survey in 1951 found the building in excellent condition and well maintained.[232]

The object of raising personnel facilities to mezzanine level in the factory had been to ensure continuous manufacturing floor space into future sideways extension. More than half the total site had been given over to sports fields but, when extension became necessary, the canteen was taken over for production purposes and the only encroachment into the sports fields was for a new, separate canteen on the east side in 1966. Paternalism of the kind exercised by Montague Burton fostered a 'family spirit' in a total environment—the factory was named 'Burtonville'. Although in such circumstances, discipline was often strict (Caribonum was another such example), here expense was not spared in the enhancement of working conditions or in the construction of the building. Floors, for instance, were of oak block in the offices, terrazzo in the hall, oak parquet in the waiting rooms and maple strip in the factory.

The rather brash colouring of the building's façade was redeemed by the quality of its form and fabric. The horizontal lines of the ground and first floors were not unduly emphasised as such. Long lines of colour contrast were punctuated by vertical stripes of black and buff faience on the rounded window piers of the ground floor and the flat black tiles on those of the upper floor. Copings were of on-end brick, offering a solid skyline that rose by mass, from the long frontage of the ground floor via the mid-way step-up at the rounded flanking corners of the first floor, to the tall, brick tower and the company flag. Against the night sky, the profile was dramatically delineated by neon strip lighting (Fig. 38). By day, the building up of form toward central verticality was further accentuated by the decor. The reaching outwards of the wings was countered by the striped window piers marching inwards to meet their like in colossal form at the central entrance. There, four free-standing pillars, 25 feet high, vertically striped in black and buff faience, supported projecting, drum-shaped brick fascias. Capped in buff terracotta above the first-floor skyline, the fascias turned in, toward the tower. Set back 16 feet from the building line, built square on front with a tall, central light, the tower was rounded at the rear and capped with three stepped courses of buff terracotta. On its roof, a cylindrical glazed lantern was anchored by a great terracotta-faced arm that curved backward, like a helmet crest, from the disc of the

Fig. 38 Montague Burton Ltd, Worsley, Manchester: (a) view from East Lancashire Road, 1939; (b) factory floodlit at night, 1938

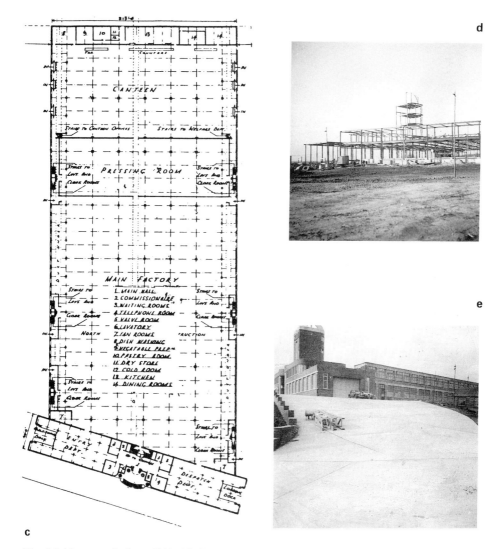

Fig. 38 (c) ground plan, 1939; (d) factory under construction, 1938; (e) access road, 1938

lantern roof to the rounded coping of the tower (Fig. 39). True panache!

Although the treatment of the entrance played a major role in drawing the eye upward to the tower and company flag, it also made for a very lively way of ingress. Invitation to enter began with the curving in of the wings to the two outer striped pillars and lamp standards—drum-shaped lamps on drum-shaped bases that flanked the rounded steps to the recessed entrance. As the way narrowed, the walls maintained the horizontal pattern of the wings, in square-angled, glass-cornered windows jutting out between the outer pillars and those on each side of the doorway. The doorway itself was relatively modest, its appearance tuned to that of the tower; plain, flush doors with

a

b

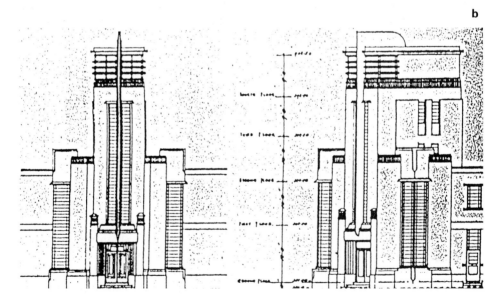

Fig. 39 Crested towers: (a) Montague Burton Ltd, Worsley, Manchester: tower lantern and crest, 1938; (b) John Laing Ltd, Building Number 3, Elstree, Herts, 1938;

Fig. 39 (c) Entry for Imperial Airways Headquarters competition

standard metal plates and handles below a ribbed and grille-patterned tympanum and a lintel in terracotta. The uprights of the surround extended into the vestibule; externally, they showed as circular pillars cut back concavely toward the door. These too were in pale buff terracotta to match the reveal of the tower window and the triple-decked, semi-circular canopy over the doors. The canopy and doorway sported soffits of red faience.

The factory was completed and ceremonially opened by the Earl of Derby on 24 October 1938. Successful operation over many decades of the production of men's made-to-measure suits came to an end, with final closure, in the early 1970s—'priced out of existence by cheap labour in the Far East and Eastern Europe and the refusal of the modern man to wear a formal suit unless compelled to do so'.[233] 'Burtonville' suffered the fate of other Burton factories in Lancashire; it was demolished in 1975 to reduce the company's rating bill.[234]

Cooperation and teamwork were the tenets of the Wallis, Gilbert practice, as too was working closely with clients, works managers and engineers. In this instance, collaboration with an enlightened client and knowledgeable in-house architects was a coming together of like minds to produce a very splendid building—there was elegance and modernity in the planning, lay-out and form and an exemplary advancement in servicing, working conditions and amenities. All of Thomas Wallis' canons for industrial buildings are apparent in 'Burtonville', including architectural status, landscaping, advertising value, quality of materials and the use of colour. Set against the moderation and acceptability of 'British Modern' in the 1930s, the choice and arrangement of colours at the Burton factory invite criticism. But, in a depressed area, the brazen confidence of this building and its cheerful whiff of the seaside resort, offered a beacon of hope, a raising of the spirit. When, as here, as much attention was paid to health, welfare and recreation as to commerce and industry, it was reasonable to express those aspects in the elevation. Physically a landmark in the area, the whole concept of this garden factory was equally a landmark in industrial architecture.

Elizabeth Arden

The final building in this group was designed in February 1939 for Elizabeth Arden, manufacturer and purveyor of cosmetics and beauty care preparations, at North Acton, London. Elizabeth Arden was born Florence Nightingale Graham at Toronto in Canada on 31 December 1878, the daughter of a poor Scottish-Canadian market gardener. By the turn of the century the use of cosmetics was becoming respectable in America; in 1907 Florence Graham moved to New York to learn the business. In 1910 she changed her name to Elizabeth Arden and, with borrowed capital, opened her own beauty salon on Fifth Avenue.[235] Despotic, imperious, with a hysterical temper, she was also an excellent businesswoman, a promotional genius and the first to popularise treatment and exercise as a major part of beauty care. By the 1920s she had achieved international fame, with salons established worldwide and direct sales of her own products to the best department stores. Unlike her almost-only rival, Helena Rubenstein, Elizabeth Arden had no personal interest in the laboratory or production side of her business but was more concerned with a relentless ambition to enter the exclusive circles of 'old money' American society.[236] Towards that end her salons were like grand drawing rooms, her advertising and packaging were refined, arresting and impeccably 'well bred'.

In Britain in 1939 war was a horrific possibility. Experience showed that, in such event, the importation of luxury goods would be curtailed and/or have heavy duties imposed upon it. To meet the expanding market in Britain and to ensure continuity of supplies, Wallis, Gilbert & Partners were commissioned to design a factory for Elizabeth Arden at North Acton. Given the client's lack of interest in manufacturing production, but with her insistence upon a refined image, the design of the factory is reasonably conservative. In an area of rapid development of industry and housing, not far from the new arterial road of Western Avenue, the factory faces east to, and is set back from, Victoria Road. It is within easy reach of underground and mainline railway services. Construction is of steel frame with brown brick and glazed infill.

The ground plan is a simple arrangement of two rectangles. The larger, 16 bays by 16, of mainly 10 feet centres on front and 12 feet 6 inches in depth, has a single-storeyed, open-plan manufacturing area, with north-light roofs, but the front bays are two-storeyed and flat-roofed. The forward part contained offices, entrance hall and stair tower, dining and recreational rooms. Set well back from the front building line and adjoining the south wall of the larger rectangle, a smaller, single-storeyed building, 13 bays wide by 11 deep, was used for storage, intake and despatch.[237] In recent years, activities have expanded and most have moved to a new, larger building on the south side of the site, now termed the 'Victoria Industrial Estate'.

On front, the overall form of the building presents a conventional arrangement of horizontally-layered, two-storey wings balanced vertically by a central, recessed, three-storey tower with a tall, narrow light above the main entrance. The disposition of building materials within the rectilinear geometry gives the wings an appearance of self-contained units. Each is completely and broadly framed in brick, with an inner narrow band of concrete. Across the centre, at first-floor level, a breast wall of on-end bricks, banded narrowly in concrete at upper and lower edges (as the lower-floor lintels and upper-floor sills) is terminated at each end by a hand-like shape in moulded concrete. White-painted stanchions, giving an impression of mullions are, in fact, free-standing behind the windows, so that the long-paned windows themselves are continuous within their assigned compartments at upper and lower floors.

In consequence, the central tower appears to have squeezed itself into an insufficient space between the two framed wing units, but never so far forward as to dominate them. The concrete dressing of the tower adds to its alienation. A heavy, moulded concrete door surround, with fluted half-engaged columns as reveals, is capped by two thick, projecting slabs to form the doorway cornice and the sill to the tower window. The fluted concrete reveals of the tower window are, again, too substantial for the thin fluted canopy at the window head. Certainly, the centrepiece needed very positive treatment to emphasise its importance, but this design was not well-conceived and bears little relation to the coherence of the wings.

Assessment of Geometric-Phase factories

In general terms, the most obvious differences between this group and its predecessors are the increasing use of steel and brick as constructional materials and a growing preference for manufacturing production to be housed in open-plan, single-storeyed buildings, suitably obscured from public view by a taller 'office block'. The expansion of administrative functions, their division into specialised departments and their segregation from manufacturing areas into a separate, and usually frontal, block, was already occurring prior to the 1930s. In this later group of factories, however, no matter how small a portion was occupied by administration, front blocks assumed the differentiated appearance of offices—although it has to be said that, frequently, with later expansion the whole frontal block would eventually become office accommodation. The appearance of these blocks could usually be characterised formally as horizontally layered wings with central vertical emphasis, often to tower proportions.

Wallis, Gilbert & Partners' works had always demonstrated their intent to enhance the face and status of industry. Their pioneering designs were dedicated to a recognisable industrial aesthetic and reflected a social ethos of which their establishment-minded peers disapproved or did not understand. In the 1930s, however, the national desire for greater unity and stability was as much an ethos imposed from above as rising from any common groundswell. It is therefore unusual to find such a degree of conformity in Wallis, Gilbert buildings at that time, with a style so universally accepted in the country and for almost any type of building. By the 1930s too, the influence of the Modern Movement was much stronger, so that uniformity and anonymity would be key features of even an anglicised version. And Wallis, Gilbert & Partners always adapted their designs to accord with cultural changes. In this group, too, there was a greater number of foreign clients and/or commissions funded by foreign money. When home industries were protected, conformity to indigenous stylistic ideas would have been important. Eric Pasold, for instance, encountered great difficulties in assuring authorities of the 'Britishness' of his enterprise.

But, given the similarity of many of their basic forms, as always in the Wallis, Gilbert *oeuvre*, no two factories were ever completely alike. In the main, differences were achieved with decorative treatment, means of articulation and colour. As brick and steel became more easily obtainable and possibly even less expensive than reinforced concrete, a much wider range of brick colour and finish was produced. Wallis' designs show some pleasing ideas in the use of brick—for example, at the Pasold, Burnley Platers, Klinger and Slough factories. There were innovations in decorative elements, such as the colossal mullions at Slough and Simmonds and the roof crests at Laings and Burtons. In this group, too, a different kind of 'programming' occurs: on a number of occasions, the façade presents the company's public statement while the hallways refer more to the company's internal essence. In criticism, however, the tendency to over-decorate, to over-articulate, cannot be ignored. But Wallis was not alone in that. Many architects of his generation, trained in the Beaux Arts school, had difficulty in reconciling themselves to the austere geometry of the Modern idiom.

Wallis' earlier problems with long-fronted buildings had been overcome and he had shown himself to be a master of the total, unified composition. In these later years, however, there are lapses in compositional integrity and instances of good designs impaired by strange and unrelated features. Such failure may be accountable to a reluctance to relinquish more satisfying styles for one with no inherent warmth or narrative appeal. Decorating the formal lines of British Modern was not an easy task. An architecture that relied upon its form as its essence tended to resist quite implacably the application of ornament. But Wallis believed that factories should be decorated, to express their importance as equal to public buildings, to resist the dominance of science and technology and to create buildings with which workers and the general public could find some sense of identity.

There is the possibility, too, that the failures were due to a diminishing creativity as Wallis approached old age. But that would indicate a general falling off, which is not the case. This group of buildings does, nevertheless, coincide with profound changes in Wallis' domestic life. The break with his wife and family and the social ignominy of unwed cohabitation with his erstwhile secretary may, at times, have affected his creative confidence. There was, as well, the fact that in his sixties his chosen female companion was little more than half his age; that may account for the overt masculinity of some of the designs in this group and for moments of harking back to earlier triumphs. At Burnley Platers, for instance, there is a parade of phallic symbols at the entrance and the unusual reappearance on the upper stairway of the nail-head decoration of Wallis' more youthful years.

But clients seem to have been well pleased. There was no diminution of the reputation of the practice and the workload was sustained at a very high level. Many other buildings as well as factories were designed and seen to completion.

(d) Other Designs

This section covers the total time span of the preceding sections of this chapter to include buildings that do not fit into any of them. There are three sub-sections, each with its own chronology: (i) designs that differ stylistically; (ii) with no disrespect to the buildings, is a miscellany of minor works, references and other oddments, collected together so as to complete the survey; and (iii) sheds—that is, buildings for purely manufacturing purposes.

(i) Different Styles

Liebig's Extract of Meat Company Limited

Construction of a six-storey office building for Liebig's Extract of Meat Company Limited at Place de Mier, Antwerp, Belgium, was begun in July 1924, which would date the design activity at *c.* 1923–24. No plans have been discovered. The only references are an illustration of the built work in Wallis, Gilbert's *Industrial Architecture* and a (slightly different) artist's impression published in *The Building News* of 4 September 1925.[238] The Liebig Company's product, forerunner of the Oxo meat stock cube, was developed in the 1840s by the German scientist, Julius Liebig. It was marketed in Britain after 1865 from a depot at Southwark, London, and, from the 1920s, at Thames House, Queen Street Place, London.

The office building in Antwerp was rectangular in shape and very narrow fronted in accordance with local design. It was constructed of steel frame with reinforced concrete floors and rose directly from the pavement presenting facings of marble and Beauville stone. Two steps up from the pavement, slightly recessed, glazed double doors with bull's-head roundels, were flanked by tall windows and capped by three fanlights. In front of them, four white marble columns supported a white marble surround that extended across the full width of the building. Skirting, column bases and lintel were of black marble. Torch-shaped lamps set on black marble squares, ornamented the uprights of the marble frame; tasselled nail-heads appear in its upper corners.

The five storeys above the entrance were faced with Beauville stone. The shallower first-floor front showed a long window, broadly framed in stone. The cornice was decorated with a winged orb containing a darker-coloured bull's head in the roundel in the centre, and tasselled nail-heads at the outer edges. Above it, colossal piers and mullions rose from tasselled nail-head bases, through four storeys, to a diamond-patterned band above the windowheads and a 'feathered' cavetto cornice. On the tall, narrow windows recessed between the mullions, floor levels were marked off by small moulded spandrels. The differences between as-built and artistic impression are minor and, apart from the broken/solid roof line, are concerned only with changes in decoration. It is not known whether the proposed reconstruction of the existing factory at the rear was carried out or, indeed, whether these buildings are still standing.

Across the Place, the Liebig building faced the King of Belgium's palace, which may account for the Liebig's extravagant facing materials and elegant appearance. The lower parts of the building are very nicely conceived and are Modern in feeling, but the strong vertical emphasis of the upper reaches might have been better served by retaining the solid capping to complete, and serve as, another taller frame. Although there are suggestions of a compressed version of Wallis' reinforced concrete factories of that time, and the moulded decorative motifs (presumably here in reconstituted stone) are similar, the 'framed colonnade' had yet to be introduced. And, generally, the whole character of the Liebig elevation presents a polished sophistication and urbanity complementing its setting.

Telegraph Condensers Limited

Factories designed by Wallis, Gilbert & Partners for Telegraph Condensers Limited and S. G. Brown Limited were for the same client and were probably coeval, *c*. 1924–25. They were similar in their unusual appearance and occupied parts of the same large plot of land at North Acton, London, bounded by Victoria Road on the west and north, by Wales Farm Road on the east, and by Western Avenue running diagonally across the south-east. The S. G. Brown premises, with subsequent alterations, are still standing; the Telegraph Condenser factory has been demolished.

The Telegraph Condenser Company, manufacturers of and dealers in telegraphic instruments and electrical equipment at Vauxhall Street, London, became a private limited company—Telegraph Condensers Limited—in July 1910. J. A. L. Dearborn, the chief London agent for John Lucas Limited, and S. G. Brown, scientist (and later Fellow of The Royal Society), were the original owners and directors. By 1914 Brown and his wife were the sole directors. Plans for a new factory at Wales Farm Road, Acton, were drawn by Wallis, Gilbert & Partners in October 1924, but planning permission was not granted until May 1925, delayed by contention over reinforced concrete loadings. Frank Cox argued that reinforced concrete regulations were 'in flux'; he pointed out that only a few years earlier plans for D. Napier & Son had been accepted by the same local authority under local regulations and that Trussed Concrete Steel had been contracted by the architects free of restriction. But Ealing Borough Council insisted in this instance on adhering to London County Council regulations.[239] It may well be that that decision was probably owed to Napier's being a wartime factory built under government auspices when steel was in short supply but, while peacetime building regulations remained unresolved, the planning authorities were unwilling to accept individual responsibility.

The office block at Telegraph Condensers was aligned across a curve in Wales Farm Road and faced south. The production area was sharply angled at the rear on land sloping to the north-east, and measured eight bays by four, frame-built at mainly 20 feet centres. The row of bays nearest the office block was two-storeyed; the remainder was single-storeyed with part flat roof and part north-light. In the intervening triangle, a works entrance on the narrow, west side led to single-storeyed cloakrooms and thence to a three-storeyed block, the lower two floors of which contained lavatories and the second floor a residential flat.

The office block, measuring some 99 feet wide by 32 feet deep, was single-storeyed. From a centre-front doorway and entrance hall, an east-west corridor gave access to various offices and a rear door to cloakrooms and works area. The surviving Wallis, Gilbert plans contain only sectional drawings of the elevations.[240] The building was brick-faced and had a tiled, pitched roof with east and west gables. At the centre front, the entranceway, with glazed double doors beneath a raised, flat-topped parapet, was recessed between flat-roofed projecting blocks that housed the small offices flanking the entrance hall. These had narrow lights on front; the long runs of standard, small-paned windows on the wings were intercepted by mullion piers. Parapet and projecting block copings were of on-end brick. This fairly ordinary design, almost cottagey in appearance, was then enlivened by a plethora of concrete dressing of plinth, sills, lintels, mullions, window reveals and door piers. Concrete nail-heads were added at lintel and coping levels to all corners of the parapet and projecting blocks, at the base of each mullion and at the head of terminal piers. Door piers and mullions had ridged, concrete 'capitals'; the entrance was surmounted by a concrete cavetto cornice patterned with moulded 'feathers'.

Had the whole façade been rendered, form would have prevailed over decoration, but a continuous parapet would have been necessary to alleviate disparity with the tiled roof. As it was, constant visual competition between materials gave nowhere for the eye to rest. At that time, Wallis' designs in reinforced concrete were unmatched for clarity and distinction. His handling of brick had shown an understanding of the medium and an ability to design accordingly. Here, however, there is a direct conflict of concepts. This fault was compounded by a repetition at the factory complex designed for S. G. Brown.

S. G. Brown Limited

No deposited plans appear to have been registered for the S. G. Brown building,[241] there are no plans in the Wallis, Gilbert archive and those obtained from the present occupants, BBC Television, are copies of later drawings of only the front and west side elevations of the office block. The company was not listed in the London Post Office Directory until 1934, and then as electrical engineers; in 1939 the firm is listed as nautical instrument makers. Garcke lists only Telegraph Condensers Ltd.[242] Wallis, Gilbert & Partners illustrated the office block in their *Industrial Architecture* in 1932 but, coming closer to the date of the Telegraph Condensers' factory, the built works for S. G. Brown Limited were illustrated in *The Architects' Journal* of 14 April 1926.[243]

The manufacturing area consisted of a long, rectangular, flat-roofed, single-storeyed building facing Western Avenue. It is constructed of reinforced concrete frame with circular internal stanchions and external brick walls. At the rear of the building, pitched-roofed sheds were built at right angles at the western end. When, later, more similar buildings were attached toward the east, lanterns were cut into the flat roof. Vehicular access on the south side passed the porter's lodge built into the flat-roofed building, and then turned across the back. On the further side of the internal road are a row of north-light sheds, loading bays and works offices with an access way to Victoria Road.

On the front elevation of the flat-roofed block are projecting end blocks and a stepped-forward central entrance. The building is set back from the pavement on rising, landscaped ground; metal double gates and a flight of stone steps give access to the main doorway. All the publicly visible elevations are of red, mottled brick above a white concrete plinth; the original standard, small-paned windows have been replaced. The concrete dressing on this building is startling, but a little more coherent than that at Telegraph Condensers. The Brown building has tasselled nail-heads in the upper corners. Concrete sills, lintels, mullions and reveals frame individual windows but in broad continuity on front as the lintels run on through the stepping forward of the entranceway and terminate in nail-heads. On the corner blocks the lintel line is interrupted by windows with brick sills, lintels and reveals but marked off beyond them with more concrete nail-heads. Despite the struggle for dominance between brick and concrete, this building is very *likeable*.

The office block, sited to the east on Western Avenue, is much more extravagant and of more serious mien. In 1926, it was single-storeyed, plus basement, and had many similarities with Telegraph Condensers, but no pitched roof. By, at the latest, 1932, a second storey had been added. Given the flat roof and Wallis' views on extension, one assumes that the finished design was inherent in the original part-built. There are some elements here, both formal and decorative, that appear elsewhere in Wallis' designs but, as brought together in this building, have no familiar counterpart. The building, also flat-roofed in the two-storeyed version, stands back from the road on ground rising to the east. It is levelled against the gradient by a basement and lower ground floor under the west wing, the walls of which are cement rendered beneath an all-round concrete base.

There is no simple way of describing the elevations. On the ground floor front are four, projecting, brick-faced blocks, each of one bay's width, that rise to flat, stepped roofs slightly higher than the first-floor level. Two of them flank the main central entrance; two stand at the far corners, flanking the ground-floor windows. They are brick-panelled on front to frame recessed windows. Behind the corner blocks, recessed brick towers with stepped roofs break the skyline. In the centre, over the entrance, a row of windows is set back beneath a brick fascia that also rises above the skyline. Accordingly, the rows of first-floor windows in the wings stand slightly forward in brick frames; in each frame a rebated line in brickwork has on-end bricks in the uprights and flat courses along the tops; the inner frames have on-end bricks with mitred corners along the tops and are edged with a concrete line. Copings throughout are of on-end bricks which, other than those on the tall towers and raised fascia, are also capped with a line of concrete. All the windows are small-paned with metal glazing bars and, except for those in the four lower tower blocks, have heavy concrete sills, lintels and mullions. On the wings, the breast walls are concrete panelled, so that two storeys of windows appear to be framed in concrete within a brick frame. Lintels to the ground-floor windows are shallower, but each mullion rises from a concrete tasselled nail-head. Plain concrete nail-heads are dotted about at every

Fig. 40 S. G. Brown Ltd, Western Avenue, Acton, London: view from Western Avenue, 1932

possible corner—of the projecting front blocks, of the wing frames, of the upper towers and fascia and at the head and base of each mullion in the wing windows. A rough count gives a total of about one hundred (Fig. 40).

A flight of stone steps leads from the roadway gates to the central entrance. Four square, concrete pillars with ridged capitals supported a diamond-patterned beam and a cavetted, feather-patterned cornice on the original one-storeyed building. The brick fascia above the cornice was removed when the second storey was added. Recessed behind the pillars, tall windows flank the glazed door to a small vestibule; glazed double doors beyond open to a double-storeyed hall and stairway. Most of the moulded decoration in the hall has been removed. Opposite the main doors the marble staircase, with fancy metal newels and balusters, rises to a half landing against the rear wall and then divides to climb around each of the side walls to a long landing that leads to corridors and offices in the wings.

The side elevations show brick framing of concrete framed windows similar to those on front. On the east, the mullions are differently spaced; on the west there are two loading bays to the lower ground floor and, above them, four large windows with narrow ones in the centre.

The buildings commissioned by S. G. Brown for his self-named company have much stylistically in common with those of Telegraph Condensers. The cavetto cornice and the diamond-patterned line above the entrance to S. G. Brown's offices are, however, the same as those at roof level on the Liebig building in Antwerp. But the latter building was a happier combination of old and new than the mixture of Victorian and rectilinear Modern of these office blocks at Acton.

In the forecourt of the S. G. Brown office building, steps with low brick walls and pedestals lead up to the centre *and* from the sides to the kind of terrace usually found on the garden side of a large Victorian villa. On such villas, too, windows were often heavily framed and mullioned in stone against brick walls, particularly when Elizabethan styles were part of eclectic historicism. Their like here, in concrete, against a modern, flat-roofed form in brick exacerbates the conflict of concepts found in the other buildings in this commission, particularly when further enhanced by Egyptiana and an unforgivable quantity of nail-head motifs. But perhaps that was exactly what the client wanted. Certainly Mr Brown was extremely pleased with the result and wrote on 15 April 1926 to tell Thomas Wallis

> We have received a copy of the 'Architects Journal' for April.14th., and may I congratulate you on the excellent article and wonderful pictures of your architectural achievements in Industrial Buildings. The old fashioned and ugly Works and Offices are replaced by your excellent designs, to be an ornamentation and *not* disfigurement as in days gone by. You are indeed to be congratulated, and we are proud to have Works, stamped with the obvious stamp of Messrs. Wallis, Gilbert & Partners, design.[244]

Fulsomeness in the client, fulsomeness in the design!

Michelin Tyre Company Limited

In 1926, Wallis, Gilbert & Partners were involved with a much larger factory complex for the Michelin Tyre Company Limited, tyre manufacturer of Clermont Ferrand, France, which was about to establish a manufacturing base in Britain at Stoke-on-Trent, Staffs. Thomas Wallis referred in his talk at the RIBA in February 1933 to 'our buildings for the Michelin Tyre Company'[245] but the architects' role appears to have been largely of a consultative nature. The buildings and layout were designed by the company's in-house engineers; the original plans still held by the British company are in French.[246] Some drawings were, however, published in Britain[247] and are shown in English and in Imperial measurement. Wallis, Gilbert & Partners may have only anglicised the plans for the contractors, Peter Lind Company of Westminster, and have overseen construction—mushroom construction was used in this same year that Wallis, Gilbert were using the medium at Wrigley. But one published drawing, showing a gateway in the 10-feet high, 3000 yards long wall that bounded the site, has a distinctly Wallis, Gilbert flavour.

As a French company, Michelin was restricted by licence and could only import tyres into Britain; these were distributed from the well-known 'Bibendum' building at Fulham Road, London. The location chosen for the

British manufacturing base, when such was permitted, was on an 80-acre site at Stoke-on-Trent, alongside the newly-built Campbell Road, beyond which on the east is the River Trent. The Newcastle-under-Lyme Canal formed the western boundary and there was railway access at the south end of the site. Thus, important requirements for tyre manufacture—a good water supply, effluent disposal facilities and good transport links—were already catered for. The geology of the site was less appropriate; in that respect, Wallis, Gilbert certainly earned their fees. Some parts of the land were of water-logged peat, others of river deposits of sand, clay and gravel. A system of land drains and rainwater and effluent culverts had to be installed, as well as the usual sanitary access to the local main drains. A huge amount of reinforced concrete was used to overcome foundation problems. Altogether 10 miles of piling were sunk; pits for heavy presses and petrol tanks were built inside coffer dams; basements required strong retaining walls; most ground floors of reinforced concrete were suspended.

Site layout was different from the direct flow system most often employed by Wallis. Buildings for specific purposes and/or processes were dispersed about the site, with the power house in the centre and a covered loading bay running the full 920 feet length of the elevation of joined Buildings 1 and 2, parallel to Campbell Road. These gave intake-despatch access to all sections of the very large building. Sufficient unused space surrounded each building for future, individual extension. The site has, nowadays, been so built upon, buildings have been demolished, altered and added to, that it is difficult to distinguish the original buildings.

Most of the buildings were single-storeyed of steel frame with north-light or top-lit, pitched roofs, which were made fire-retardant with hollow, terracotta blocks and separate, suspended ceilings of hollow tiles. Multi-storey buildings were constructed of reinforced-concrete frame, exposed against brick infill. Whether through French preference or the likelihood of excessive wind pressure, windows set in the brick infill were quite small compared with the 'Daylight' type to which the architects were accustomed. In complete contrast to the Bibendum building, the Stoke-on-Trent buildings were devoid of any decoration or ornamental relief—a distinction, perhaps, between 'selling' and 'making' images.

The probability is that Wallis, Gilbert & Partners were engaged not for their aesthetic creativity but because of their reputation and experience, their knowledge of reinforced concrete and ability to cope with difficult geology. It is probable, too, that the architects also learned something from this exercise.

British Bemberg Limited

Another consultative commission, for which Wallis, Gilbert were not the original designers, but for which they did not hesitate to take advantage of mistaken attribution[248] was for British Bemberg Limited at Doncaster, Yorks.

Here, however, there is evidence that their contribution was not inconsiderable. They redrew the plans of F. Flakowski, the German company's architect, transposing them from metric to Imperial measurement, were responsible for subsequent revisions and alterations, and advised in respect of geological and effluent disposal difficulties.[249]

In Britain, manufacture of artificial silk [rayon] was largely cellulose-based. In Germany, hard pressed by scarcity after Allied blockades during the First World War, a cupra-ammonia-based product had been developed.[250] J. P. Bemberg Actiengesellschaft of Barmen manufactured artificial silk by the latter method, distributing its wares in Britain from a London depot. A British manufacturing base was established when British Bemberg was founded in July 1928, to operate under licence from the parent and its associated companies. Of the seven stockholders, five were German and two were Dutch; two British directors were appointed in 1929.[251]

The site chosen for the new British factory was 50 acres of Wheatley Hall Estate on the outskirts of Doncaster, purchased from Sir William Weymss Cooke, and included parts of a farm and golf course previously held by tenants. On the west and north boundaries are the River Don and the Wheatley Hall Cut of the Sheffield Navigation Canal. On the south, a new road was built—Wheatley Hall Road; on the east were farmed lands of the estate. Private sidings were laid to connect with the London North Eastern railway. The Yorkshire location was probably chosen for its proximity to the woollen industry and its source of unemployed, experienced and retrainable textile labour. But the site itself was not without difficulties. It contained swamp and marshland, running sand, clay and an area of hard red sandstone. Six hundred feet below ground lay part of the Barnsley coal measures, which remained unmined as support for the river, canal, railway and the proposed factory. Leasing clauses for substantial subsidence compensation inhibited the proposal for leaving only coal pillars. The local planning authorities had forbidden the building of houses on the site.[252]

Manufacture of artificial silk required considerable quantities of clean, soft water. Seven boreholes were sunk to provide the required one million gallons per day and a water-softening plant was built. Problems arose when it was found that the system was depriving local farmers of their hitherto natural water supplies. No effluent could be discharged by the factory into existing waterways because of chemical pollution. In any case, the copper content was recoverable and saleable; acid cellars and copper settling tanks had to be constructed over three feet deep concrete rafts above the running sand. The spinning department and drainage channels were floored with one-inch thick acid-resistant tiles laid in bitumen.[253]

The factory buildings were erected on each side of an internal roadway running north/south, with the main entrance to the site, the entrance lodge, office and garage at the south end. On the righthand (east) side of the road is building A, a five-storey block with basement, constructed of reinforced

Fig. 41 British Bemberg Ltd, Doncaster, Yorks: Building A, *c*. 1930

concrete; it was erected on a high-tower gravity feed system with concrete puddled in by its own weight (Fig. 41). Fronting and running northward from A are attached buildings B and C; a two-storey block parallel to the road, for offices and ancillary support departments (B) and, to its rear, a single-storeyed manufacturing block with north-light roofs clad in three-inch pumice and felt (C). The three buildings together cover an overall area of 900 feet by 200 feet.

On the west side of the road are building E, double-storeyed, steel-framed, north-light sheds for storage and engineering services; buildings F and F1, processing tanks for raw materials; and building G, the boiler house and chimney. Space and water heating were provided by the self-serving *Calique* system, mostly piped, but by blown air in the spinning department. The interiors were (and many so remain) spartan, even on the visitor's path to the executive and directorial offices. The absence of decoration (and/or a marked processional way) may have been for the sake of economy, given that the special manufacturing features would have been very expensive; or due to the need for, and ease of, maintaining strict cleanliness; or, and possibly most likely, in view of the exterior appearance, due to the personal preference of the clients.

All the buildings, whether of infilled steel or reinforced-concrete frame, were externally rendered in white cement. The appearance is very German-ic Modern, revealing the continental origins of the design. Lines are clear cut, strongly trabeated and devoid of decoration. Pure rectilinear form is articulated by the size and disposition of windows, different in pattern in each building because the arrangement was dictated by the plan and by internal usage. Nevertheless, there is such consistency of outward treatment as to constitute a style. Although stanchion and beam structure is evident, the windows appear not so much apertures created by the frame, but holes punched into solid walls. This concept is apparent, for instance, in the German Air Ministry building in Berlin, the Roche factory at Welwyn Garden City, Herts, England, and the Behren's design for a foundry at Oberhausen, Germany.

Night-time floodlighting at British Bemberg did not soften the hard lines and corners but, within a reasonable growing time, landscaping with trees, ponds, flowers and lawns eased the alien contours into the rural setting and made them beautiful. In subsequent years, some alterations have been carried out, additional large buildings with no pretence to attractiveness or association have been erected on the site, and the surrounding area has been built up. But good maintenance of the original buildings has preserved their historic aesthetics and ensured their pristine survival.

During the Second World War, the factory was controlled by the Custodian of Enemy Property and was taken over by British Nylon Spinners in 1954. Buildings were then stripped out, obsolete machinery was disposed of, and new machines were installed. But the factory itself was found to be very amenable to usage with new processes. There was a need only to demolish a few walls, which was contracted to the McAlpine company—'and a right job they had there'.[254] The initial contract for construction had been awarded to McAlpines, but was withdrawn early when problems arose and a new contract was negotiated with Doncaster builders Harold Arnold.[255] More recently, and for some years, the property has been owned, operated and excellently maintained by ICI Fibres, a division of Imperial Chemicals plc.

The Michelin and Bemberg factories could be cited as examples of the Modernist maxim that form should follow function. Construction of factories in concrete, steel and glass offered a variety of formal arrangements. There was the exposed frame of the Kahn Daylight system; the 'punched holes' version with overhung flat roof favoured by Bemberg; or, possibly the most popular, the horizontal layering of solid and void; or there was cantilevering, a system based on the mushroom column or the Domino slab, which permitted glass curtain walling at, for example, the van Nelle factory at Rotterdam in The Netherlands. These formal arrangements could be employed singly or in concert, with straight or curved lines but, since in most cases any one of the forms was as suitable as another, it cannot be said that function alone dictated the choice. Indeed, the 'most' Modern of them, glass curtain walling, actually created functional problems, such as excessive heat gain or loss, too bright natural light, danger at floor edges and wasted space between stanchions and cladding.

Aesthetic preference clearly influenced choice. Aesthetic considerations converted the movement into a style and supported the view that Modern form was sufficient unto itself, requiring no decoration. More fundamental to factory design was J. van Nelle's assertion, with which his architects Brinkman and van der Vlugt concurred, that decoration had an adverse effect upon the workers.[256] In that context, decoration may have been considered a commercially unwarrantable distraction, or its absence, arising from Bauhaus and Modern theories, a means of improving the mind and outlook of the worker. But either way was contrary to the views held by Wallis, Gilbert & Partners and, by inference, their clients. Thomas Wallis believed that people wanted and needed decoration and that it enhanced the advertising potential of a factory. Moreover, Modern architecture was intended to be adaptable to any building type and to eradicate individualism, while Wallis, Gilbert's philosophy aspired to the creation of an architecture intrinsic to industry but adaptable to the individual company's image.

Columbia Gramophone Company Limited

It is apparent from the group (c) buildings, designed when Modern styling was more influential in Britain, that Wallis was never entirely at home in the medium. Although he produced some attractive forms in that group, the forms themselves resisted the kind of decoration he applied to them. In 1929, however, when Wallis, Gilbert & Partners designed a factory at Chatou, Paris, France for the Columbia Gramophone Company Limited, although they were coeval with the construction of British Bemberg and despite the continental origin of the commission and its continental location, the buildings were very much in accord with Wallis, Gilbert's British designs of the period. Similarities with the later buildings designed for the Gramophone Company at Hayes, England, may also be explained by the coincidence in time of the two companies' proposals for merger.

Surviving Columbia plans show them to have been first drawn in March 1929 but revised and redrawn in November and on into 1930. Photographs of the executed factory appear in Wallis, Gilbert's *Industrial Architecture* of 1932.[257] No other sources are readily available and it is not known if the buildings are still standing. The main block consists of a flat-roofed, three-storeyed block in hollow square, with a three-bay width gap at the rear, the interior court being infilled with single-storeyed north-light sheds. The multi-storeyed part was constructed of reinforced concrete, the shed areas of steel frame. Overall dimensions, converted to Imperial, are approximately 260 feet on frontage and 200 feet in depth. The building faces south by south-west (called south here for simplification of other orientations), with the front building line angled obliquely to the square. The main entrance is centrally placed on front; works entrances, leading to cloakrooms, lavatories and stairs, are on the east; receiving loading bays on the west side provided access to the raw materials store in the centre, single-storeyed building and the general stores on the west front. The shipping department occupied the righthand, east side of the front block and the rest of the ground floor was devoted to mixing, processing of raw materials, printing and storage of labels, a finishing department and various other storage sections. On the first floor gramophone records were made and the master and mother discs stored; on the second floor, all space to the west of the main stairwell was occupied by offices and all on the east side by stock rooms. Part-glazed, movable partitions sectioned off most departments; where processes attracted fire hazard, there were fireproofed ceilings, tiled floors and solid walls, so that whilst some departments could be internally expanded or contracted, others were restricted by the nature of the processes they housed.

Externally, the building presents itself as a large 'Daylight' block, with windows decreasing in height in ascending order in accordance with ceiling heights. On the front, the double set-backs on the corners are not symmetrical because of the oblique line of the frontage, but they are similarly treated. The middle set-back in each case has glazed corners and rises above the general skyline to give an appearance of corner towers, but with no relevant internal function. At each end of the flat front, twin pairs of projecting colossal piers are joined at the uppermost fascia level and capped with a ribbed band and a rebated 'wishbone' line at the corners (a feature also seen on the Gramophone Company buildings at Hayes). The windows framed by the piers become sets of triple slits by virtue of pairs of narrow, colossal mullions that latch onto the top crossbeam with small hooked motifs. Pendant from mid-storey level on each stanchion are elongated 'tassels' and horizontal ribbed bands running across the centre of each spandrel. The doorway surround is of double-storey height and is decorated with sets of horizontal lines that may be rebated in the concrete or, perhaps, inset with faience. The surviving photographs are not clear enough to be sure.

For all the expanse of glass, the building has a solid stalwart appearance. Its semi-classical lines are similar to those of the early Daylight/Masonry era, without the classicised ornament. The presence of triple windows, glazed corners and certain minor decorative elements align the building with the transitional designs at the Gramophone Company, but without the overall framing effect. In view of the factory designs that were appearing on the European continent at that time and what the architects were producing in Britain, the Columbia building does have a slightly dated air and tends to lack the presence of its Wallis, Gilbert contemporaries.

The free-standing power house is also block-like and stalwart, but is more architecturally interesting, with a suggestion of Constructivism. It is expressive of its function in the arrangement of its parts and, by its nature, exudes power in the massive capping and overhang. It is also expressive of its structure and materials, in that they permit the insertion of long vertical and horizontal window slits and large expanses of glass beneath a mass head load. Applied narrow mullions here articulate the form, intercept strong light and heat gain and, with the minor decorative elements at the heads of the frontal piers and in the overhang, establish an association with the main building. The Columbia power house is a bold and impressive design. A plan dated 19 September 1930 exists for a single-storeyed, flat-roofed hospital centre and a men's shower room for Columbia, but it is not known whether it was executed.

Lamson Paragon (South Africa) Limited

Another overseas commission was for a factory facing west to Telford Street, Johannesburg, South Africa, for Lamson Paragon (South Africa) Limited, in September–November 1930. Photographic illustrations in Wallis, Gilbert's *Industrial Architecture*[258] show the design to have been executed but perhaps not wholly in accordance with the surviving plans.

The factory was rectangular in shape, fitted into undulating ground. Long-fronted to the road, on-plan measurements are approximately 170 feet by 100 feet; construction was of steel frame on a grid of seven bays by four, infilled with brick and glass and covered with (antipodean) south-light trussed roofs. Most of the floor space is single-storeyed, open-plan manufacturing area, with sanitary facilities in the south-east corner and the boiler house and coal store in a single bay abutted to the north end of the east elevation. On front, the end bays gave access to the works for delivery at the left (north) end and despatch at the right (south) end. The five centre bays, to one bay's depth, were walled off for offices and the central entrance hall.

The brick front elevation was built to a high parapet, with shallow central pediment, to obscure the factory roofs and bear the company flag. The solid corners on front were decorated with concrete nail-heads at the lower corners and with tasselled discs in the upper centre, not as on plan. There is no illustration giving a full view of the façade but the drawn plan shows an elaborate main entrance with moulded concrete surround, curved and decorated and surmounted by an up-surging 'botanical' spray form. The elevation plans also show an upper row of windows on front and a two-storeyed south elevation, yet there are no stairs or lifts on the ground-floor plan. Clearly revisions were made, but 1930 is still a little late for nail-heads and tasselled discs. From the narrow view available, however, the building appears pleasant enough.

Murray House

Very little source material indeed has been discovered about Murray House in Cape Town, South Africa—not even the name of the client, unless there is a connection between the name of the building and the Murray tobacco firm in Ireland. The illustration of a nine-storey block on a smallish, square corner site shown in *Industrial Architecture*[259] is of a colour wash impression. It is stated there to be designed by Douglas Wallis and located in Hout Street. An illustration in a newspaper cutting from the *Cape Argos* of — 1929[260] shows an executed building of similar appearance but with a canopy and much more moulded decoration at eighth-storey level. The newspaper describes the building:

> Murray House, in Burg Street, is a splendid work in concrete; it is without a scrap of superfluous decoration; its high vertical lines reach up, tall and severe; its steel windows, suitably spaced, are the only marks of the storeys as they ascend. Murray House is a unity with nothing whatsoever to destroy or impair its vertical design.

On such slender evidence it is difficult to pass judgement but, in comparison with the other buildings shown in the *Cape Argos*, Murray House is fairly plain and the most modern of them. The colour wash design is, however, tidier, better balanced and generally superior to the executed building. Douglas Wallis visited South Africa to oversee the construction of Murray House and may have revised the building's appearance on location, to be in closer accord with the province's local architecture.

This sub-section refers to two rather 'quaint' designs by Wallis, Gilbert, their involvement in two of continental origin, and four of their own for foreign locations. Compared with the modernity of the imports, Wallis, Gilbert's are all but untouched by *avant garde* theories, their overseas designs are distinctly *devant garde*. But all were acceptable to their commissioning clients.

(ii) Miscellany

There are a few commissions about which little has been discovered; they are described in chronological order.

Auto Carriers Limited

Based at Thames Ditton, Surrey, this company made invalid chairs but went on to produce the beautiful AC Cobra sports car. Founded before the First World War, it sought expansion afterwards. The only trace of Wallis, Gilbert involvement is a ground plan in E. G. W. Souster's *The Design of Factory and Industrial Buildings* (1919); neither the local history/planning offices nor the company, which is still in existence, has any record of any building to which the plan refers.

Dent & Hellyer Limited

Dent & Hellyer Limited were plumbers and sanitary engineers with a history dating back to 1706. The main works were at Red Lion Square, London, in a building that ran through to Theobald's Road. A single Wallis, Gilbert plan, dated 10 October 1918, proposes alterations to the premises fronting Theobald's Road, with restructuring of and within the basement, four storeys and a skylight. If the alterations were carried out they have not survived; all of the Dent & Hellyer premises were destroyed by enemy action in 1941 and the site has been redeveloped.[261]

Doyle & Son

For this firm, of Newcomen Street, London, the only information about alterations to the company's premises is in a letter dated 29 November 1923 to the architects enclosing payment of account, expressing satisfaction with the work and mentioning that the members of the architects' staff with whom they had been in contact had been 'particularly courteous, efficient and obliging'.[262]

Pressed Steel Limited and British Paint & Lacquer Company

Both these companies set up their own works at Garsington Road, Cowley, Oxfordshire, to service the Morris Motor Works at that site. The buildings and the first-named company were later absorbed into the conglomerate Rover Group plc. The commission from Pressed Steel was for an office extension in November 1930. The building is still standing and in use. Plans for British Paint & Lacquer, dated October and December 1930, are for a single-storeyed office block, 30 feet by 35 feet, with basement boiler house. The building cannot be identified on site and enquiry elicits the surmise that the company may have been taken over by Pinchin Johnson Paints (now part of the International Paint Group) which, for many years, was supplier of paint to the motor industry, particularly Morris Motors and its successors.[263]

Edward Manwaring Limited

This company, based in Peckham, London, was a pickle manufacturer. Surviving plans, dated early in 1932, are for the rebuilding of the company's premises and show a three-storey 'Daylight' factory. There is no record of the commission being carried out. The business was located at Radnor House, Hill Street, Peckham, but whatever building was there has been demolished. The site is derelict and overgrown; what bits of buildings remain do not resemble those on plan. It appears that the company was taken over by Haywards Pickles Limited, which became part of Brooke Bond Oxo in 1970. The last-named company has expressed its unwillingness to be of assistance.

Horsham Factory

In this case the name of the client is not known. Two plans bearing date May 1932 show a single-storeyed, north-light factory approximately 198 feet by 70 feet, with its narrow end fronting Queen Street, Horsham, Sussex. The road-front bays are two-storeyed, for offices on the first floor and shops at ground level, the design of the shop fronts to be 'to client's requirements'. The long south-east elevation was evidently open to public view; the north-light roofs were to be obscured by pitched gables with an unusual arrangement of windows enhanced by 'projecting concrete mullions' against rendered brickwork.

Other buildings by Wallis, Gilbert & Partners may come to light; the present chapter concludes with a survey of the architects' designs for the most basic form of industrial building.

(iii) Sheds

The buildings in this group were designed and erected over a period of 20 years, 1916 to 1936. They are grouped separately because all were designed for strictly utilitarian purposes, that is, internal, physical operations were the prime determinant of the design. Most of the buildings were additions to existing works; all of them were for housing new industrial developments, processes or inventions. Product innovation often called for innovation in building design, which affected the architectonic form, called for the architects' close collaboration with works managers and engineers, and would have extended Wallis, Gilbert's knowledge of factory design. Three interesting points arise from a survey of this group: the effect of utility on form and style; how closely the projects related to their historical context; and how those two points contributed to the fate of the buildings.

New industries and new products played no small part in the historic changes of the interwar years. Buildings in this group reflect decision making at a fundamental level, for instance, between expansion into total production or the buying in of some goods and services; of entering volume production of inventions or preferring smaller-scale product development; and of producing components or materials for inter-industry trading or assembly elsewhere. Yet, by their contribution to industrial progress, they become vulnerable to the same process.

An accelerating feature of company structure in the interwar years was consolidation, by vertical or horizontal integration or the taking over of competitors. Companies marketing innovative goods or services were always at risk from wealthier competitors, of needing new capital and the wider markets offered by consolidation or, as pioneers, of being overtaken by later advances that rendered their product obsolete. Of the 12 companies in this group, the very few still operating under their own flag do so under the auspices of a giant concern or conglomerate. Almost all of the buildings have been demolished. Some were too purpose-designed and became impossible to re-use. In other cases, only the innovation and/or the vendor company's long-standing name was acquired by a competitor, so that satellite production became defunct. Often the value of an asset-stripped site for redevelopment was greater than by the sale or leasing of a standing building.

British Westinghouse Electric and Manufacturing Company Limited

The first of the shed-type buildings were for the British Westinghouse Electric and Manufacturing Company Limited at Trafford Park, Manchester, in 1916. In 1899 George Westinghouse of the Westinghouse Electric and Manufacturing Company of Pittsburg, Pennsylvania, USA purchased 100 acres of the new industrial estate at Trafford Park, Manchester,[264] with the intention of entering the British and British colonial markets. The British Westinghouse company was formed on 10 July 1899 for the production of steam and gas engines, steam turbines and all forms of electrical engineering apparatus, under licence from the American parent company and from Parsons Engineering, USA.[265]

The main factory, covering some 30 acres, was completed in 1902 and was fronted by the company's headquarters built in Gothic style in red Accrington brick and terracotta.[266] Initially, the works produced only Parson engines. As the company expanded to related products, additional production units were added; the site was extended to 130 acres and the plant thereon grew in a Topsy-like fashion. With the increasing use of electricity, the manufacture of electricity transformers by British Westinghouse began in 1916. Wallis, Gilbert were commissioned to design a building for the production of tanks in which transformers were contained.[267]

British Westinghouse transformer tank shop
As a wartime project and unlike other buildings on site, the British Westinghouse transformer tank shop was of reinforced concrete frame (by Truscon) with glass and brick infill. It was placed to the rear (north) of the existing transformer shop and measures 322 feet by 81 feet on a grid of 13 bays by 6. The building is double-storeyed and has a part-glazed, specially ventilated, steel-trussed, double-pitched roof over gantries that support travelling cranes. Originally each bay was glazed from eaves to ground-level sill, but the lower portions have since been bricked in and the centrally placed doors on the long sides have been repositioned. The twin double doors on the front, gabled end remain, although the doors themselves have been replaced by steel roller shutters. Top ventilation and maximum natural light provided appropriate conditions for processes that produced heat and fumes. This was purely a production unit, designed in accordance with its internal operations and as expressed in its structure and form. The dimensions of the building reflect the large size of the product, as does the gantry support for the station-to-station movement of the product.

The building was not visible to the general public, was one of many production units on site and had no direct relation to or view from the company's main flag building. Yet the architects chose to identify the transformer tank shop by (albeit minor) decoration related not to its operative purpose but to the company, to the basic architectural format of the building and to the designer. Circular company monograms were inserted in the gable ends, the classical lines of the building were emphasised by stepped pediments and a frieze; the nail-heads marking the heads of columns/ stanchions and the broken parapets that suggest corner towers, all elements that became a familiar feature of Wallis, Gilbert buildings. Wallis believed that an industrial building should have dignity and an expression intrinsic to itself and to the importance of its purpose and use. Here the monumentality of the product is expressed in the monumentality of the building; it does not imitate classical architecture, but the lines were already there in the basic structural requirement and had only to be accentuated to produce an assured dignity. The tenets of Modern architecture were not then formulated in Britain, but this building does grow from the nature and form of the machinery—it is clearly for heavy engineering. But it also shows an aware-ness of the human element; the factors conducive to good working conditions are integral to the design and style of the building.

The copper shop and canteen
The purpose and uses of the second building for British Westinghouse were somewhat diverse. The combined copper shop and canteen was sited parallel to the original main building, with its long frontage facing west. Constructed of steel, brick and concrete, with glazed infill, the building had a trussed, double-pitched roof and measured, on plan, 320 feet by 80 feet on a grid of 20 by 16 bays, although a more recent map of the company site shows measurements of 355 feet by 73 feet. The ground floor, with ceilings at 20 feet, housed the copper shop—for drawing, plating, welding and producing copper bars for other units. Above, with a ceiling height of 10 feet, was the works canteen. On plan, corner towers projecting on front contained stairways leading to the canteen; a central projection of three storeys contained stairs for the canteen staff and, at either side, at ground level, male and female lavatories; at mezzanine level, stores, and at canteen level, offices. The kitchen was placed centrally, with counter service on its west side. The fire escapes stood externally at the corners of the rear elevation. Access to the copper shop was by two doors at the rear and two at each end of the building.

The elevation on plan shows the frame structure of the building, large expanses of glazing, and the various floor levels. Nail-heads in the frieze mark the heads of stanchions; the main columns of the projecting parts are decorated with discs, panels and cornices. A photograph of 1960 shows only one stair tower access some bays in from the corner; the central projection is as on plan, but both appear to be different in style. Photographs taken when fire destroyed an adjacent building show only the southern end of the copper shop but, from those, it appears that the building was constructed of steel frame with brick encasement and infill, with concrete beams and floors.[268] As a combined industrial building and personnel facility, it was a realistic solution to make an architectural feature of the access points for the latter, whilst relating the overall appearance of the building to the more utilitarian usage of the former. But such odd bedfellows would scarcely be permitted today.

More recently, as the functions of the copper shop were depleted or redeployed, the building was variously used as a cabinet shop, pattern shop and warehouse. Reductions in staffing levels produced over-capacity in the canteen, which was then resited and the original altered to office space. When the total GEC site was reduced from 130 to 90 acres the building was demolished to make way for an internal car park. Transformer production was tranferred from Manchester to Stafford. For a while the tank shop, with its welding facilities, was used as a light machine shop until maintenance and. local authority rating of so large a building for such an incompatible purpose became too uneconomic. It has always been regarded as a 'good building' but now stands unused, designated 'derelict', outwith the company's boundary.[269]

British Westinghouse was wholly British-owned by 1917; in 1919 it became part of a joint purchase by Vickers Limited and the Metropolitan Carriage, Wagon & Finance Company Limited; on 8 September 1919 its name was changed to Metropolitan Vickers Electric Company Limited, which name it retained, despite amalgamation with AEI Limited (Associated Electrical Industries Ltd) in January 1929, until the merger of AEI Limited and English Electric Limited with the General Electric Company in the late 1960s. Since that time, the company at Trafford Park has been registered as GEC Turbine Generators Limited, part of the massive GEC Holdings.[270]

The two British Westinghouse buildings by Wallis, Gilbert are typical of those that were custom-designed and begotten by industrial progress and then ultimately rendered obsolete by subsequent industrial progress.

Caribonum Limited

Wallis, Gilbert & Partners designed a number of buildings for Caribonum Limited in the early 1920s, one of which was a glassworks at Alperton, North West London. When Caribonum ventured into manufacturing ink, it decided to make its own ink bottles. The new glassworks were sited on the south bank of the Grand Union Canal on unused land at the open end of Northwick Road, and designed as an integrated building containing warehouse facilities, a glass-making plant and glass furnace, with offices, canteen and sanitary facilities at the rear, facing the canal. The whole was constructed of reinforced concrete frame and floors, with brick and glass infill. Extensions were added in 1925.

Although effectively one building, each section was designed in accordance with its internal operations; each section had its own separately pitched roof. The furnace must have presented difficulties and, for Wallis, Gilbert, unusual design problems; there are a number of plans and revisions in the collection. Only the office/canteen elevation shows any pretension to non-industrial appearance. Generally, the building is neat and workmanlike. There was added interest given by the configuration of its silhouette until partly hidden by extensions. But, despite its complete fitness for purpose, there is no suggestion of beauty. Within a few years of operation, Caribonum discovered the project was neither economical nor convenient and thereafter bought in its containers. The plant was disposed of. Its most recent owner, Glacier Limited, has vacated the building, commercial glass manufacture having long since overtaken the methods, quantities and locational advantages at one time available here. The larger site is in course of development; the Caribonum glassworks will be demolished.

Caribonum was founded by the Lamson Paragon Supply Company of Canning Town, London. Another separate development by Lamsons was the founding of Papercraft Limited.

Papercraft Limited

In the latter years of the nineteenth century, paper bag making was a sweated industry carried on in small, slum premises. In 1902 Lamson Paragon gathered a number of these operations into its own works. The project soon outgrew the premises built for that purpose and, in 1922, was re-established as Papercraft at Edgware Road, Hendon, Middlesex, in a factory recently vacated by Thrupp & Mapperley.[271] The Papercraft Company designed its own machinery, developed new methods of printing and colour printing, new forms of retail packaging and wrapping, a mounted 'Visible Planning' card system to show the state and progress of orders, and invented new inks and pastes. All manufacturing took place in a single-storeyed, open-plan structure with essential services placed around the walls. Executive offices were at the front of the building and a warehouse at the rear. Separate from that were the canteen and recreation and sports facilities for the workforce.

As the company expanded and/or introduced new developments, these were fitted into the existing direct line of production by rearward extension in the form of single-storeyed, north-light sheds designed by Wallis, Gilbert & Partners. In a progression of extensions over six years, each additional building was matched to its predecessors. The sheds were steel-framed and had concrete floors and trussed, north-light roofs of patent glazing and Trafford tiles. The sides of the building were covered with corrugated iron attached to wooden slats and intersected by sliding doors. These were sheds indeed, very utilitarian and low cost. The original Thrupp & Mapperley office block, although built in 1915, was reminiscent of Victorian railway station architecture. Papercraft provided exceptional amenities for its employees, but there was no wish to improve upon the appearance of the original production area. All production occurred in one large, undifferentiated shed. That in itself was an aesthetic choice—the ultimate building expressing the integrated nature of internal operations, but by no means a thing of beauty.

The site, when fully developed, covered over 250 000 square feet. Eventually, however, newer materials for and methods of packaging and printing rendered the plant obsolete. It has now been demolished and the new company, Decoflex Limited, operates from a much smaller building, designed by Wallis, Gilbert & Partners in 1962 and built on what were the Papercraft tennis courts.

Hall & Company Limited

The engineering workshops designed by Wallis, Gilbert for Hall & Company Limited at Salfords, Surrey, were also concerned with the integration of operations; they slightly predate the commission for the Hall Company headquarters at Croydon, Surrey. The company's volume of trade increased rapidly during the interwar years. Its 50 depots and supply sections in London, Surrey, Sussex, Essex and Middlesex operated almost autonomously as local businesses, but had a common focal point in the head office and an overall linkage in the company's transport organisation. All deliveries within 10 miles of a supply or marketing depot were made by road. In the 1920s a gradual transition was made from horse-drawn to steam and then almost wholly to petrol-engined vehicles, for which the existing repair and wagon-building shops at Redhill, Surrey, were totally inadequate in size and performance. The directors had to choose whether to contract out or build their own maintenance works; they decided that all operations should be kept within company control.[272] Fourteen acres of open land were purchased at Salfords and, in 1929, Wallis, Gilbert & Partners were commissioned to design the new workshops.

The new building was constructed of steel frame encased in brick, some of which was rendered, and measured 270 by 148 feet. A new road, 40 feet wide, was cut across the north front and a 20-feet wide concrete road was laid around the other sides. A central, north-light section, 100 feet wide, housed inspection pits and a body repair shop. On each side, a flat-roofed, 24-feet wide bay contained, on the west: offices, basement boiler house, stores and a blacksmith's shop, all with their own entrances. On the east were the tyre store, machine shop, electricians' department, woodworking shop and paint stores. The offices were partitioned off in glass and wood, the stores by wire mesh caging and the tyre store by a thin wall. The otherwise clear space thus received natural light from the large areas of side glazing as well as from the roof. Satellite buildings for timber storage, heavy vehicle tyre fitting and vehicle washing were placed externally appropriately to their functional connection with the main building.

At the front, four vehicular entrances were flanked by two larger framed entrances; a separate pedestrian entrance to the offices was placed centrally on the front of the west bay. Pairs of double doors at the rear of the building and the four open bays of the paint shop provided vehicle exit routes to the encircling road. The workshops not only repaired, maintained and over-hauled the company's fleet but also maintained the pit plant and built and painted steel lorry bodies made to the company's own design.[273]

The structure and form of this building are very closely related to the layout plan and show both differentiation of function and the interrelation of the internal functions. For the closeness of its ties with every other part of the Hall organisation, the engineering works could be described as a self-contained unit entitled to its own vocabulary. It was the prestigious possession of a company of which transport was a necessary but not primary function. Hence the enhancement of its structure by rendering and of its principal elevation and impressive doorways—enlarged architraves inter-lined with coloured, chequered tiles and the suggestion of columns with coloured faience capping, rather than stanchions—to present a status-conscious 'Classical' façade.

Within 20 years the Salfords works had doubled in size but piecemeal accretion gradually destroyed the compact integrity of the original building. The whole has now been demolished. 'Clean air' legislation brought coal-burning heating to an end in many parts of the country. As building firms consolidated, so did builders' merchants. Hall & Company still operates under its own name as builders' suppliers, but on a reduced scale and as a member of the RMC Group of Feltham, Middlesex.

H. J. Mulliner & Company Limited

The client for the next building in this group represents another instance of a name being perpetuated as a guarantee of product long after the original connections had been severed. The firm of H. J. Mulliner & Company Limited was registered in December 1915 by the purchaser of the founding firm. Mulliner established a carriage and motor body building works at Bath Road, Bedford Park, London, in 1910 as a private, unlimited company. Five years later he sold the business to John Croall & Sons Limited, motor car hirers and body builders of Edinburgh, Scotland, which was responsible for registering the limited company in the Mulliner name.[274]

The commission to Wallis, Gilbert & Partners in 1930 was for extensions to the existing works, in Bath Road, but which would face directly to the curve of Flanders Road. This rather complex project consisted of a new first floor to part of the original building, a two-storey bridging of the outer angle on the road elbow, and a large shed extending along Flanders Road to the east of the main site. All the buildings were of steel-frame construction. The new first storey was clad in match-boarding and roofed in glass and Trafford tiles to join the existing gables at each end; it contained the plating and polishing shops. An entrance to the lower floor from Flanders Road was already in being; the new upper storey was reached by an external iron staircase that turned from the bridging section to a doorway in the east wall of the new storey, and also provided a fire escape.

The two-storey bridging section stood over a sunken petrol tank and was of steel frame with brick and glass infill and a flat roof. Inside were stairs leading to lavatories on the first floor and a lobby with access to the newly-built first floor on its west side. The triangular courtyard at the rear was part-glazed, part Trafford-tiled at single-storey level and was open to both the new shed on the east and the ground floor of the existing works on the west.

The large shed to the east of the above buildings faced north to Flanders Road and was also infilled with brick and glass; it had a trussed, hipped roof of glass and Trafford tiles over the main area, with 'lean-to' bays at front and rear. The roadside lean-to was the building's main entrance—a collapsible gate and sliding doors at the west end. To its left, and extending into the main shed, was the car wash over a sunken pit; in the east corner were the chimney stack, lavatories and the coke and breeze stores beneath which was the basement boiler house. In the rear, south-side lean-to were the blacksmith's shop with pit and forge, the screen-maker's room and a timber store. On the east side the roof was flat to a depth of six and a half feet, which suggests that the differently-roofed perimeters of the building were owed to standardised dimensions of the cross lattice girders (54 feet inches) and steel hips and/or planning restrictions on ridge height, rather than to aesthetic or operational consideration.

Bedford Park is a residential area, a 'garden village' of nineteenth century Arts and Crafts origins; some of its buildings were designed by Norman Shaw. The position amongst domestic housing of a motor body manufacturing establishment in a very utilitarian building is therefore surprising. There appears to have been no attempt to prettify the works, and the extensions added to the hotch-potch of parts. That the buildings were appropriate to the work's craftsmanship functions perhaps prohibited pretension. The site is, in any case, just on the border line of Bedford Park and the more industrialised region of Acton. The name Mulliner became a famous one in relation to car bodies, particularly those for Rolls-Royce and Bentley cars. The name continued in being even when the firm was taken over by Rolls-Royce in the 1950s and when amalgamated by Rolls-Royce with Park Ward (body builders of Willesden) in 1961. Eventually, both firms were moved to the Rolls-Royce works at Hythe Road, London NW10, but the name Mulliner was perpetuated.[275] The works at Bedford Park were demolished; they were replaced in the late 1970s by a new office building, occupied by I. D. C. Europa Ltd and memorially named 'Mulliner House'.

The Northern Aluminium Company Limited

In the 1930s aluminium became an important material for the mass production of motor vehicles, of domestic holloware and, with a rearmament programme in the later 1930s, for the aircraft industry. It was the product of the company for which Wallis, Gilbert & Partners designed three buildings in 1930–31 and, uniquely in their experience, was used in the construction of the buildings.[276] The main values of aluminium to industry were that the metal is light in weight, malleable, ductile, nontarnishable, durable and suitable for a very large range of uses. Its production was a new industry; vertical integration and horizontal combination were marked features of the firms involved in its development. The British industry was dominated by the conglomerate British Aluminium Company; in America, the monopoly was held by ALCOA (the Aluminum Company of America). The latter was able to import ingots into Britain via its Canadian subsidiary, the Northern Aluminium Company and, in 1926, set up production units in Birmingham and West Bromwich in the Midlands under that name.[277]

The Canadian company separated from its American parent in 1929 and decided to manufacture on its own account in Britain as the Northern Aluminium Company Limited on a site selected in 1930 on the outskirts of Banbury, Oxfordshire. The only local industry, manufacturing farm implements, was in decline so that labour was available; the site was central to several industries that purchased aluminium sheeting; it had adequate water supply from a nearby canal and there was a railway on its boundary for transport purposes.[278] Wallis, Gilbert & Partners were commissioned to design a remelt shop/ingot store and two sheet mills.

The site lies to the east of the main road. The remelt shop, to which ingots were delivered, faced north parallel to the railway, towards the rear of the site. Ingots were remelted and cast into billets for rolling in Mill Number 1, placed at right-angles to the remelt shop and extending north–south. Finished goods left the works on the north side to be transported across the rear of the site to the railway. Mill Number 2 was built shortly afterwards and lies parallel to the first mill. As old farmland, the ground was marshy. For each building concrete platforms were sunk seven feet below ground, from each of which concrete pillars 10 feet high formed stanchion bases. The space between the ground and ground floor was packed with ironstone.

The remelt shop, with ingot store at the south front and furnace at the rear, was constructed of steel frame infilled with tall windows and rendered brick. The lattice-girdered roof was covered in aluminium sheeting and top-lit in the raised central portion along the ridge, which has side louvres for ventilation. Steel louvres at ground level on the north side gave additional ventilation to the furnace room. The building measures 200 feet by 90 feet and rises to 36 feet at the ridge, 27 feet at the eaves.

Mill Number 1 was 600 feet long (and since extended) and 140 feet wide, with a double-storeyed central hall 80 feet wide; on each long side is a single-storeyed 'aisle' 30 feet wide. Each section has a trussed, pitched roof and top lighting and is partly covered with aluminium sheeting. The clerestory lights in the raised ridge section and above the junction of the single-storeyed sheds run the full length of the central section. Infill is of rendered brick, corrugated iron and glass. Sheet metal rolling was carried out in the central hall, where gantries support travelling cranes. The side bays contain offices, stores, machine shop and other ancillary functions. No ground plans are available for Mill Number 2, but it is of similar construction, size and layout to its neighbour, except that the roof is of plain, pitched form and wholly covered with aluminium.

The company made public show of its product in its gateway and the door and hall furnishings of an administration block designed in 1937 by Gilbert J. Gardiner, architect of Oxford. Over the years, the site has been very considerably built up and enlarged. The original buildings are still standing and in use but the most striking features of the original Wallis, Gilbert-designed plant are now much less evident. Viewed from the road, the sheer length of the mills in an open, greenfield site must have been quite astounding and the buildings themselves are not unattractive. Like railway sheds, rope works or hose-making works, the mills express an internal use for which no other form of building was appropriate. In 1933 a reporter on architectural matters praised the plant as clean, light, practical and efficient— a fine example of engineering eminently suited to its purpose. He also found the buildings 'attractive' and of an 'advertising value which is not to be overlooked'.[279]

The reporter's comments that Wallis, Gilbert & Partners always gave their buildings 'something distinctive', each a 'character of its own', probably refers here to Wallis' treatment of the south-facing ends of the mills. True, they imitate a style of architecture of superior social status—a modern church could not but be envious. But their appearance does rise from the form the buildings take in relation to their internal usage; the gable heads relate to the roof plan, the large expanses of glass starkly accenting the structural lines, and the cathedral-like reference is inherent in the internal layout of the 'nave' and 'aisles'. For some years, the south faces of the mills were visible from road and rail. Now partially obscured by later accretions, they still present a breathtakingly proud and overwhelming dignity (Fig. 42).

Because of their height, the huge windows did not present problems of glare or heat loss/gain but had to be camouflaged in wartime. The paint still adheres to some extent and so distracts from their impact from inside. The remelt shop, for all the basic industrial nature of its operations, stood happily in its rural surroundings, like a handsome pavilion midst lawns and open

Fig. 42 Northern Aluminium Co Ltd, Banbury, Oxon: mills 1 and 2, south elevations

skies, until hidden by later buildings. Its format was copied when the company built a canteen and recreational facility at the north-west of the site. The original plant is still in good condition and is well-cared for. As new uses were found for aluminium the company expanded, becoming Alcan Industries in the 1960s. The Banbury works is no longer concerned with aircraft material but is still in operation as part of British Alcan Aluminium plc.

Briggs Motor Bodies Limited and Kelsey-Hayes Wheel Company Limited

During the interwar years companies gradually consolidated into fewer but much larger firms; volume production became more a matter of long assembly lines. The Ford Motor Company of America opened its first manufacturing base in England in 1911 at Trafford Park, Manchester, and later, in 1931, migrated to a large, specially-designed plant at Dagenham, Essex. The Dagenham estate covered 600 acres, of which Ford leased land superfluous to its own requirements to other companies attracted by the many facilities and mains services offered by Fords.[280] The American company invited two compatriot companies, whose products Ford had previously imported to the Manchester works, to establish themselves at

Dagenham. Briggs Motor Bodies Limited and Kelsey-Hayes Wheel Company Limited were registered as new companies with partly-British boards of directors. They chose a site on the Ford Industrial Estate between Chequers Road and Kent Avenue, near the London–Tilbury–Southend road and just north of the London Midland & Scottish railway line and station. Wallis, Gilbert & Partners were commissioned to design the two companies' buildings.

No ground plans survive of either plant; photographs were published in Wallis, Gilbert's *Industrial Architecture*.[281] The buildings have been absorbed into the extended Ford factory; the Kelsey-Hayes Wheel company was acquired by Ford in 1947; Briggs Motor Bodies in 1953. Subsequent additions, alterations, demolitions and replacements make for difficulty in identifying the original buildings.

The Briggs plant consisted of two large manufacturing sheds perpendicular to Chequers Road, and (possibly) an office block facing the road. Kelsey-Hayes appears to have consisted of four identical sheds, of which at least two are standing largely unaltered, although the long, single-storeyed office section along the west ends of the sheds is no longer extant; administrative functions would have been centralised into Fords on the takeover. According to contemporary motor vehicle literature, production in both factories was of an advanced nature, but there was also a measure of technical craftsmanship. Both companies made many of the machine tools required for production purposes. Even in the absence of documented layout, it can be assumed that production was organised on direct flow lines; description of the processes suggests that much of the machinery was electrically operated.

Briggs Motor Bodies Limited made motor car and commercial vehicle bodies for Fords; the bodies were either transported complete to the Ford works down the road or transshipped in parts to Ford plants in Europe. They were also available to any other company to order. Body frames were of ash wood, built up into jigs and the panels were then attached. The panels were pressed in small sections (to save time and expense in die-making when models changed), assembled into jigs, held by pneumatic pressure and then electrically welded, automatically, by an electrically-driven machine. The metal bodies were then buffed and chemically treated, hung on an electrically-driven conveyor to reach the paint-spraying section and drying tunnels. They were then trimmed, upholstered and despatched.[282] These operations appear to have run concurrently through the two buildings—one the 'manufacturing' building and the other the 'heavy press shop' to meet for assembly and finishing at the west end, where there was a railway connection. The buildings were of steel-frame construction, each three bays wide and infilled with brick and glass. The trussed, pitched roofs were top-lit and had a raised central section, with rows of windows that opened and closed electrically in banks. Catwalks were placed in the roof for maintenance and cleaning purposes.

The most modern and unusual feature of the Briggs building is its south wall, a sheer cliff of brick and some glass, supported by internal I-stanchions and angle struts, but now much altered and less agreeable or impressive. The height of the building allowed the intersection of mezzanine floors. As at Firestone, sanitary facilities were raised above the processing floor and were reached by independent metal stairs. More for employees' comfort than processing hygiene, washing fountains of the kind installed at the George Kemp factory were fitted in side bays.

The Kelsey-Hayes Wheel Company, as the name implies, supplied Fords and external companies with wheels for light cars and commercial vehicles, but the firm also manufactured brake drums and general machine parts such as cylinder liners, fly-wheels and differential housing. Electric welding of spokes to wheel rims was automated. As well as precision work, the factory was also equipped with an automatically-operated rust-proofing plant, a paint-spraying and dipping department and a machine tool shop, in which the company's production tools and dies were made.[283]

Although there was direct communication between the four parallel sheds, the various product runs appear to have been located separately, to run east/ west to meet the railway sidings. The buildings were constructed of steel lattice stanchions, with trussed, top-lit roofs and a raised ridge for ventilation. On the long sides the walls were of glass with brick infill, the short ends being clad in corrugated metal.

The lateral office block appears to have been of concrete and glass construction with a flat roof. Aesthetically, the Kelsey-Hayes plant as originally designed suffered from the incompatibility of office and works sections, the one having little architectural relation to the other, but the buildings did say quite clearly: here is one function; here is another. Sited across the ends of the sheds, the offices could be departmentalised in accordance with the operations of the shed with which each was co-extensive. The sheds themselves had a monumental quality in their scale and regularity of outline; despite their obvious utilitarian appearance, they were handsome buildings.

On the other hand, the main view of the Briggs factory was unusually, magnificently modern, engineered as precisely as its internal operations, but aesthetically neutral. For all the individuality of its form, it says nothing about internal usage, nothing about the company and nothing about the people engaged within it. Here, perhaps, Wallis came as near to the anonymity of the Modern 'machine age' as is to be found. As the interwar car market enlarged, Briggs dispersed some of its operations to individual process buildings. Demands during the Second World War found the company in dire need of large, integrated premises. After the war, however, methods of vehicle construction changed; parts were pressed in much larger sections for monocoque construction, with components added on very long assembly lines. Both the Briggs and Kelsey-Hayes factories then became part of Fords.

Greaseproof Paper Mills Limited

The manufacture of paper in Britain has a very long history. The industry expanded rapidly from the late nineteenth century onwards with the increase in literacy and reading matter and, in the twentieth century, new forms of office stationery, wrapping and packaging. The production of greaseproof paper was a new industry in the interwar years and was welcomed as a contributor to improved hygiene in food supply. Until the early 1930s almost all greaseproof paper had been imported but tariffs were imposed and were soon to be increased. Dartford Paper Mills Limited, established in 1861 as Ettrick Forest Mills, occupied a five-acre site on the south bank of the River Thames between Priory Road, Dartford, Kent, and the lower reaches of the tidal River Darent, known as Dartford Creek. The company was acquired in 1931 by paper manufacturers Wiggins, Teape & Company Limited with a view to building a greaseproof paper mill on unoccupied land at the southern end of the site, which had been chosen for its plentiful supply of clean water from deep chalk wells, its river access for bulk transport of goods and materials, and for its proximity to London.

The new venture was in collaboration with Belgian manufacturers of greaseproof paper, Louis de Naeyer. A new company, Greaseproof Paper Mills Limited was founded, whose products were to be unbleached grease-proof paper for ordinary wrapping purposes, a higher quality bleached paper for biscuit and sweet manufacturers, and 'Glassine', a patent, durable, transparent, damp-proof paper for cigarette wrappers, laundry and haber-dashery bags.[284] The Belgian company expected thereby to enter the British market tariff free and the British company thought to acquire an early monopoly of the home market. In anticipation of an expanding market, as new uses for the product stimulated competition, no expense was spared to ensure that the new mills were the 'most up-to-date in the world'.[285] They were to be designed precisely in accordance with their operational purposes. The managing director of the Belgian firm planned the machinery and its layout; Wallis, Gilbert designed the buildings.

A drainage plan and rough sketch map of the site show the new buildings crossed the southern portion of the site, running north-east to south-west. The single-storeyed 'Collergang House' (purpose unknown) faced directly onto the river wharf and was constructed of concrete frame, infilled with brick and glass and corrugated sheeting. Obliquely to its rear was the main manufacturing plant—a large machine shop with a three-storeyed building, 'Hollander House', across its south end. Raw pulp was unloaded from the Creek Wharf, conveyed by electric cranes to the 'thickening' room on the top floor of Hollander House, thence gravitationally through the 'beater' floor to the 'chest' room, to be fed into the paper-making machines running along the building's ground floor in direct production line to the 'finishing' mill on the ground floor of the northern block. After completion, the product was transferred by lorries to the Goldsmith Wharf for shipment.

Erected on marshy land, the buildings' foundations were of mass concrete blocks below stanchions. A basement beneath most of the machine shop had waterproof concrete retaining walls and platform base, with extra pillars and concrete dwarf bearer walls where additional support was needed for the two paper-making machines on the floor above. Floor channels for run-off water were connected to the basement pump room at the north-east end. All the buildings were of reinforced concrete frame, fully glazed and with concrete floors overlaid with granolithic or brick as appropriate.

The machine shop measured 226 feet by 113 feet, of 16 bays by 4, at 21 feet centres, of which the single-storeyed side bays were 18 feet. Two double-storeyed central bays, each 38 feet wide, had asphalt-over-felt-clad pitched roofs, supported by steel lattice girders and trusses over concrete ceiling slabs, and were top-lit at the ridges. Paper-making produces steam and condensation; a system of fans and double glazing of all windows to prevent condensation was combined with a steam outlet in the form of a concrete-clad ventilator with louvred roof rising above the ridge over a span of six bays. It had internal valves and, below, a large metal drip tray. The drawings of this building are quite something to behold.

Hollander House measured approximately 69 feet by 164, three bays by eight. The pitched roof with raised square section above the ridge, was of reinforced concrete clad in asphalt. Above, on reinforced concrete stilts, was a water tank made of reinforced concrete. Running the length of the two upper storeys were six-ton runways in each of the side bays and an overhead crane at the top floor. Loading bays at each floor of the east end of the building were served by an overhead hoist; here too was an external fire escape. Internal stairs were placed at the west end, as were the goods lifts to all floors, the pipe ducts and sanitary facilities. The finishing mill, two storeys high, 69 feet by 154, three bays by seven, had a pitched roof that was top-lit above a raised ridge and was supported by steel trusses and lattice girders. There were loading bays at both ends and centrally on the west elevation, all at ground level. Stairs, lavatories and cloakrooms were situated at the west end; a fire escape at the east end. All machinery was driven by electricity supplied by a specially-designed power house. Three steam boilers drove three turbines which operated GEC electricity generators. Low pressure steam was drawn from the turbines to warm the cylinders of the paper-making machines.[286]

The new mill was ceremonially opened on 20 July 1933. Three months later Wallis, Gilbert & Partners were engaged in designing extensions of the paper store and offices, to be sited at the rear of houses facing Priory Road and turning around the west side of the mill. Copies of the existing plans are largely illegible but show a store shed with trussed, pitched roof, top glazed and clad in corrugated asbestos. The north end was left in a 'temporary' condition for later extension. The south end ran into an elbow section of similar construction that abutted the three-storey office block which, itself, was attached to the finishing mill. The half-hipped roof was clad in corrugated asbestos; the building appears to have been of frame construction with brick infill and domestic-sized windows.

The founders of Greaseproof Paper Mills Limited had decided that, at a cost of £500 000 their mills should be purpose-designed and as technically advanced as was possible at that time. They were in operation for many years but, eventually, markets and production material and techniques changed. Greaseproof paper-making was transferred to Wiggins Teape's mills at Cardiff and the Dartford factory was used for production of an up-dated form of 'Glassine' for chocolate and sweet wrappers, as used by, for instance, Mars and Bounty Bars. The Wiggins Teape company was taken over in 1985 and production was discontinued. In size, layout, internal dimensions and constructional materials, the mill was too closely planned in relation to one product to be altered for economic re-use. The other buildings thereby lost their ancillary use and all were demolished.

Beaton & Son Limited

The company Beaton & Son Limited, of Beatonson House, Victoria Road, Willesden, London, owed its origins to George Beaton who, in 1881, set up as a 'coach joiner' at High Holborn. Shortly before the First World War, as George Beaton & Son, the firm made windscreens, car hoods and other fittings for motor cars. After the war, as a private, limited company, it moved to Notting Hill and, eventually, converted to a public company, was established at Willesden. At that time, the company manufactured all kinds of motor body fittings and car accessories. By 1934 it had recovered sufficiently from the 1931 slump to commission Wallis, Gilbert & Partners to design extensions as replacements for the various small buildings that stood in the yard at the rear of the main premises and opened on to St Leonard's Road.

The extensions were all of steel-framed construction with infill glazing and cement-rendered brickwork. They consisted of a large, square building, six bays by seven that was two storeys high and flat-roofed in an L-shape to St Leonard's Road and the road into the yard. The rest of the building was single-storeyed and flat-roofed, except for a six-bay section in the overall centre that had a top-glazed, trussed, pitched roof. All flat roofs were intended for future upward extension. To the rear of that building, in the crook of the turn of the site, were a single-storeyed garage with twin double doors opening to the yard, and a workshop. A larger workshop was double-storeyed and fitted into a vacant square in the existing works. These buildings all had pitched, trussed, top-glazed roofs clad in asbestos cement. There were no windows in the external perimeter walls. Difficult as this jigsaw of buildings must have been to fit into the yard, there was also a step-down to the level of the existing works as the ground sloped down to the east. The whole of the new-built area appears to have been for production purposes. On the first floor of the two-storey portion were the canteen and kitchen. There are plans extant dated 1937 for a third storey with a hipped, top-lit roof and more sanitary facilities, but it is not known if these were executed.

These buildings were straightforward production units, albeit built directly on to a public road, but in a manufacturing area. And here the 'Daylight' factory had been sacrificed to style—perhaps the shallow depth of the windows made them look longer but, on the road elevations of the two-storey block 'standard longitudinal-pane steel sashes' were used to emphasise horizontality. 'Rustic fletton facings' to the piers for only the depth of the windows would further accentuate the horizontal lines of cement rendering. Verticality was introduced in the tall narrow light of the stair tower; that and the smaller windows in the solid wall brought the stack of long lines to a gentle, asymmetrical halt. The structure was, therefore, expressed to a certain extent, but the overall aesthetic said nothing about the building's purpose or, indeed, any other purpose. Utility was served here only by anonymity. The Beaton works have been demolished, along with some of their neighbours to make way for a modern industrial estate.

Frederick Parker & Son Limited

Frederick Parker & Son Limited, long-established as makers of very fine furniture, moved from London to High Wycombe, Bucks, in 1898. In 1930 the company was in financial difficulties, which were resolved by the purchase of a patent for tension springing, invented by Willi Knoll of Stuttgart and registered under the name of 'Parker-Knoll'. Tension-sprung chairs and settees were more comfortable and durable, smaller in size to suit smaller homes, and sufficiently low priced to attract a wider market because they could be produced mainly by machines operated by unskilled labour. Standardisation and variety of choice were reconciled by the many permutations arising from a number of basic designs and a selection of woods, fabrics and colours, that could be modified to meet the demands of fashion.[287]

At first, production of the furniture at Parkers was fitted into excess capacity in the workshops where hand-built traditional furniture was made, but the simple, modern designs soon reached a popular market. To meet increasing demand, a new factory designed by Wallis, Gilbert & Partners was commissioned in 1935. The company was thereby able to launch the venture as an entirely new product under the Parker-Knoll trade name without reflecting upon its reputation as fine cabinet-makers. The new building and its extensions of 1942–43 were destroyed by fire in 1970. No information about them is available from the present company. Only copies of already damaged plans have survived.

If it was built as planned, the factory would have consisted of a long, two-storeyed north-light shed, with side windows only on the ground floor; a two-storeyed building attached at the north end of the shed; and a three-storeyed building, the ground floor of which was double-storeyed, with a vehicular entrance, attached to an existing four-storeyed building at the south end of the shed. All construction was of steel frame on concrete bases, with concrete floors and trussed, top-lit roofs, with Trafford-tile cladding. Glazing is shown on plan, but other infill is not indicated. Except for their unusual height, these buildings are of traditional, utilitarian appearance and identify themselves as industrial buildings. High Wycombe was the veritable home of traditional furniture craftmanship and, as the Parker company moved into volume production of modern furniture, it may have decided not to advertise the fact too publicly or to equate its Parker-Knoll furniture with the quality reputation of the area.

The company is now known only as Parker-Knoll; modern furniture in the quality range has become its major product. Although designs and materials have, over the years, been changed and modernised, the Wallis, Gilbert buildings remained suitable for their purpose and were still in use at the time of their destruction by fire. A new factory has been built in replacement.

Vandervell Products Limited

Vandervell Products Limited was named after Guy Anthony (Tony) Vander-vell, playboy and ruthless businessman, who is best remembered for his famous 'Vanwall' Formula 1 racing car, his own motor racing career and as the son of C. A. Vandervell, founder of the company that pioneered electrical lighting and starter mechanisms for motor vehicles. When Vandervell Senior retired, the family business was sold to Joseph Lucas & Company, but Tony Vandervell was unable to settle to routine work with Lucas. His father purchased for him the near-moribund company O. & S. Oilless Bearings Limited of Willesden, London. Acquisition of licence to manufacture thin wall bearings invented by the Cleveland Graphite Bronze Company of America, and further parental funding, led to a new factory (designed by Sir Aston Webb) being built in 1935 on the north side of Western Avenue, Perivale, Middlesex.[288] Major orders from large motor manufacturers brought almost instant success, further development of the product and expansion of the works premises. In 1936–37 Wallis, Gilbert & Partners designed a production shed, followed by a storage/office/laboratory building.

No block plan survives to show the position on site of the new buildings; company archives give no indication, and the orientation of existing plans is confusing. The production shed extension lay west of and parallel to the existing works. It measured 180 feet, with steel stanchions at 20 feet intervals, by a single span of 35 feet. The pitched, trussed roof and top lights and the shed walls were clad in asbestos sheeting attached to timber framing. The ground plan shows a proposed further extension of two bays at the south end and a similar shed to lie parallel with the first. The latter, however, appears to have been amended in format shortly afterwards, or another different extension may have been added to a different existing building.

A new two-storey building was of five bays' length, each of 20 feet by 35 feet, with a further three bays half the width of the main building recessed at the south end. The lower floor of the recessed part contained lavatories, with offices on the upper floor. The ground floor of the larger block was wholly for storage and had a loading bay at the south end; the upper floor contained offices, store and a laboratory. The building was steel framed with rendered brick infill, long-paned windows and concrete floors over timber joists. The block was flat-roofed and, designed as a separate unit, cannot accurately be described as a 'shed'. An interesting feature, however, was that, whilst the first shed extension had a simple concrete block foundation beneath each stanchion, the storage/office block had concrete-encased ground beams on the long sides between stanchions, and concrete cross sleepers at 10 feet intervals. The site dipped between the raised embankment of Western Avenue at the front (south) and that of the railway at the rear (north), so there may have been need for infilled levelling and stronger support for the heavier buildings on made ground.

The first shed extension was very utilitarian in appearance, expressing both its structure and use. The second building was designed for only partly utilitarian purposes and was perhaps more publicly visible. Its elevations, however, appear to be more representative of its administrative purposes, but they were similar to the roadside elevations of the production unit for Beaton & Son.

Further expansion of the Vandervell plant was designed by Wallis, Gilbert & Partners and executed in 1942–43 to house production of more advanced developments of the Vandervell racing car, which originated before the Second World War and dominated the Grand Prix circuit for 16 years. In 1967 Tony Vandervell died. In the same year the company was taken over by GKN Limited which, interested in Vandervell bearings, transferred that part of production to Maidenhead, Berks, as GKN Vandervell Limited. The Western Avenue plant was closed in 1970 and demolished in 1975.[289]

Assessment of other designs

Many of the factories discussed in Chapter Three are no longer standing, the owning companies failing to withstand the late twentieth-century economic recessions. The demise of so many of the production units discussed in this section was due, however, not to failure but to success. Built to accommodate innovative developments, they were rendered obsolete by subsequent innovation and/or developments in company structure. In almost all of the above designs, the nature of the product and processes dictated the layout and planning. Even so, the general form was based upon precedent—the accepted notion of an industrial shed, with north-light or pitched, trussed roof, modified to suit individual requirements. In 1929 in an article based upon his visit to America, Douglas Wallis suggested that new kinds of roof structure not only improved the appearance of industrial buildings but could improve internal lighting and ventilation.[290] It was not until after the Second World War that roof architecture for factory units in Britain changed perceptibly, but variations on north-light, east/west, monitors and butterflies often presented more problems than they solved.[291]

In the interwar years there were a number of reasons why traditional forms of shed were perpetuated. As building components became increasingly standardised, the standards arrived at were those of known performance for known types of buildings. That, in itself, tended to constrain innovative design. Further, a building that was 'standard' in materials and form was more economical and speedier to construct. When the object of a commission was to float a new product or venture, capital outlay on buildings would be restricted and extra expense permitted only for specific technical reasons. And, where a company was already in viable operation with an existing flag building, there was no point in constructing an expensive, handsome building for a new development until that development had proved itself.

But styles did change. The British Westinghouse tank shop and the Briggs body shop are recognisably of their own time. By and large, however, styles changed only with popular consent; standard components changed in dimension and form only for a proven market. The introduction of long, shallow windows in the 1930s is a case in point. Some of the sheds reviewed here, no matter how well fitted for their purpose, could never claim to be beautiful. Others were certainly distinctive, in the form produced by technical demands of the process concerned or the manner in which the architects were free to enhance the structure. Others were dignified by their monumentality; the more 'Modern' ones were not recognisably industrial buildings, since the style was used for other types of buildings, but they were fashionable. In no instance, and no matter how closely the design related to production or the housing of machinery, did any of them of their own utilitarian accord, produce a 'machine aesthetic' of the kind extolled by the Modernists.

In these 'bread-and-butter' commissions for basic industrial sheds the very considerable amount of expert industrial, technical and economic knowledge and understanding expended was not readily apparent in their appearance. But appearance was important only when it was important. A complete factory has other roles and functions, which can be differentiated by architectural design and appearance.

Chapter Four

About it and about, and some conclusions

A Successful Philosophy

Between the years 1916 and 1939 Wallis, Gilbert & Partners established a substantial reputation as designers of factories and factory buildings. Throughout that period of social, economic, technological and architectural change, by adapting their skills and creativity, they continued to flourish, serving clients from a wide range of manufacturing industries in a wide variety of locations.

What induced Thomas Wallis to enter that field could well have been Truscon's notion of producing The Model Factory. Not, that is, a standardised model into which any manufacturer could fit his operations, rather a model whereby the method of construction permitted flexibility of planning to suit particular manufacturing requirements. Opportunity to realise that aim could have fed Wallis' ambition—perhaps to make his name as a pioneer? It would challenge his artistic creativity as well as his planning skills, marrying art and engineering.

The Kahn Daylight unit system already offered most of the fundamental requirements—speed of design and construction of a fire-resistant building with large, uncluttered floor spaces, improved natural lighting and ventilation, and better working conditions for the operatives. And the apparent weightiness of the design was, at least, a visible assurance of the building's stability when so much glass was involved.[1] Bays and units gave freedom in disposition of doorways, lift and stairwells, sanitary facilities, solid walls or movable partitions and inbuilt systems for services and power lines. It was adaptable to different shapes and sizes, to extension without too great disruption and to construction part-by-part or floor-by-floor as funds permitted or capacity requirement demanded. There was potential for alteration, addition and different usage which extended the building's lifespan and retained its asset value. Wallis' decorative additions were based upon similar principles—a limited repertoire of formwork with great potential for permutation.

These criteria for effectiveness formed the basis of Wallis, Gilbert & Partners' philosophy of approach to factory design. But dedication to improvement was itself an agent of change; thus, while the philosophy stayed constant it was not static. It was necessary to respond to external change and to assimilate external influences.

Severance of direct collaboration with Truscon occurred within a few years. Although the practice was gaining a reputation for itself, laurels could not be rested upon. Personal association with manufacturers—getting to know what kind of men they were,[2] what were their problems and needs, what was happening in the industrial world—was very productive in bringing in commissions and in extending the architects' knowledge. Meeting socially eased relationships and gave opportunity for introduction to potential clients who, in like manner, were able to get to know the architects before approaching them professionally. Friendship with the Lamson, Caribonum, Papercraft connection and with Shannon was helpful, since those firms were in routine contact with the administrators of many other manufacturing concerns. And when commissions were received, it was works managers and engineers, who knew exactly 'what went on' in their factory, with whom the architects preferred to consult.

By the later 1920s, however, Wallis, Gilbert & Partners were regarded as experts in factory design and manufacturers outside the earlier network of known company principals were becoming increasingly convinced of the benefits of retaining their services. Awareness of the architects' planning talents and discernment of far-sighted economies favoured their selection, but there was also the perception of entrepreneurial flair in the way the practice operated that suggested a greater understanding of manufacturing industry there than elsewhere.

Concepts are difficult to define and the concept of entrepreneurship still exercises the mind of economic historians. The main attributes appear to be, however, the ability to react to market signals, to organise and control, to take on risk and uncertainty, to initiate and, perhaps should be added, the ability to move things forward, creating change—the 'disturber of the peace, the destroyer of existing values'. Over the range of their works, Thomas Wallis and the like-minded persons he recruited to the practice seem to qualify!

Grasping the 'early start' when it was possible to flourish unmolested by competition, the choice of name for the practice—Wallis, Gilbert & Partner(s) had a nice ring to it that inspired confidence, suggesting a substantial and well-established practice rather than a new, one-man firm—the structure, execution and philosophy of the practice closely modelled on business lines, the ability to grow but with the sense not to outgrow, are ready indicators.

Some of this acumen may have been learned from Moritz Kahn and his knowledge of American industry and salesmanship, but it did not flag when Kahn departed. There was always an insistence on high quality of materials, workmanship and performance with strict overall control. Their good name was not to be sullied by contractors, sub-contractors or suppliers who did not perform to expectation; construction materials were precisely specified, costed, tested and checked upon. Time control was exerted by a number of innovatory measures—flow charts of construction schedules, the 'acceleration clause' in contracts, dated photographic records of progress, interim reports, the retaining of proven personnel and commodity suppliers, and the ability, because of the organisation of the practice, to revise, adapt, rethink a design very rapidly. The methods of progress control permitted certain parts of a building to be completed and in use prior to completion of less-urgently required parts.

These were means of 'moving things forward' in construction; moving things forward in factory operation entailed precise planning of production lines, the elimination of waste in time and effort and increased productivity through the proper placing of machines. But the architects were also people-oriented and so persuasive of manufacturers to regard their workforce as a valuable asset; attending to employees' welfare and well-being also improved productivity and eliminated unrest.

Creating change was one thing; responding to change was to be constantly aware of external influences. At the official level, there was an increasing concern about the workplace; investigations into its influence on health, fatigue and its psychological impact resulted in new regulations, particularly in respect of heating, lighting, ventilation, cleanliness and safety. In the wider world, expansion of the electricity supply industry, advances in transport technology and the building of new arterial roads brought a wider choice of industrial location. Many industries, particularly manufacturers of new products, migrated to the more salubrious regions of the southern counties, near to London markets, and where more land was available, often as greenfield sites on the periphery of the metropolis. Constructional steel became more easily available and layout of factories tended to change from the urban, multi-storey, gravitationally-fed flow lines to single-storeyed, lateral-flow production areas fronted by an administration block. Company structure changed, by merger or takeover, to increased volume production, hence the requirement for more office space and the separation of administrative functions from production and internally into departments.

The national economy improved in the later years of the 1920s. Competition became very fierce indeed. Many were the changes to which Wallis, Gilbert & Partners had to respond. The improvements they had introduced into factory design were mainly on the supply-side for the betterment of production. Orientation toward the demand-side for the improvement of sales mostly affected the architectural style of their designs.

Changing the Style

The market then available to most British manufacturers was the home market. So, while it was necessary to impress the wealthy and well-off, there was also an expanding middle range—a vast increase in white-collar workers, management, scientific and technical staffs. The rôle of the middleman was declining and manufacturers were selling direct to retailers and the public, or through their own agents. Although high levels of unemployment reduced spending power in some regions, those in employment were better off. In some respects, industry was providing itself with customers, as volume production offered more work to women and the unskilled of both sexes. The new locations brought factories very much into the public view; the expression of a company image that was attractive to so wide a social range of potential customers had to be popular, comprehensible and of high quality.

People were becoming more knowing, their horizons broadened by the new kinds of communications. Travel, cinemas, radio, a greater selection of reading matter and many more leisure pursuits affected fashions and ways of thinking. Hire purchase enabled new householders to furnish their homes. Advertising, creating images of the 'better life' and always of a higher lifestyle to encourage upward mobility, informed about what there was to be had, cunningly exploiting the interrelation of new money, new horizons, new aspirations and new products.

Stylistically, Wallis, Gilbert & Partners responded to the changing scene with, first, a transitional phase—still multi-storeyed blocks but reflecting social changes by releasing the surface from the heaviness of the structure, making more of its relation with glass and expanses of glass, with aesthetic framing and lighter, more stylised decorative motifs. There was a further development of the Egyptian theme as an identifying feature and the introduction of tiling to delineate the framing.

Then came Wallis' 'Transgressional' challenge to orthodoxy.[3] The Fancy factories coincided with an ethos that was more daring, that was brighter, more colourful and looking for glamour. With the introduction of exotic forms and colours the buildings were made romantic, exciting, fashionable and glamorous. They were commanding advertisements in a competitive world, and they exuded success. More powerful Egyptianising provided the monumentality that had been inherently present in the multi-storey blocks.

Among Wallis' 'improvement' objectives must also have been the thought, why should manufacturing industry hide its light under a bushel? Why be unobtrusive? Why be anonymous? Public buildings always exhibited their prominent rôle, why not also industry when it was so essential to national well-being and prosperity? Industry should stand bold, proud, vital and different. Peer response to the Fancy factories would, however, suggest that Wallis, Gilbert & Partners also exhibited those entrepreneurial characteristics of disturbing the peace and attacking existing values.

Although Wallis had impressed upon his grandson the importance of learning and enjoying the classical modes of architecture, as soon as the practice began to prosper in the design of factories, the interior of the practice offices were Egyptianised. Perhaps the two began to coalesce—perhaps it was the permanence of Egyptian architecture that seemed appropriate to industrial imagery as well as its monumentality? The influence of Egypt has appeared from time to time in European art, architecture and artefacts throughout the centuries. The stylistic features of pylon, cavetto and Egyptian columnation would be recognised and could be conflated with basically-classical forms. There were also persuasive correspondences. There is a relation between Egyptian emphasis on linear pathways and lateral-flow production lines; between Egyptian designing to a grid pattern and the frame construction of factories; between Egyptian staging posts and the differentiation of industrial functions; and between the Egyptian laws of frontality, prominence of doorways and processional routes and the intercourse of commerce in its hierarchical nature, which permits almost narrative means of communication.

Further, Wallis' façades established communication between the manufacturer and his market in a language understandable and attractive to both. Modernist and traditional architects were both guilty of putting distance between them—the former with abstract, anonymous forms that had no empathetic content for ordinary people, inspired no personal confidence, failed to take account of human irrationality and imposed a way of life that was attractive to very few. Traditionalist architecture expressed a way of life then becoming inimical to the kind of freedom people were looking for; its devotees failed to realise that the effects of change had moved so much faster than the venerable institutions that had hitherto directed how people should live.

In the later years of the interwar period, Wallis, Gilbert & Partners' designs conformed to more Modern forms, again reflecting the mood of the times. There were, nevertheless, attempts to individualise the style, but neither the addition of Fancy elements nor new, thrusting, architectonic decorative or formal devices sat comfortably with such plain, resistant forms. All the personnel of the practice were themselves part of the contemporary ethos and subject to the same forces, influences and changes that they were at pains to interpret in professional terms. Like many of their clients, Thomas Wallis and Frank Cox were 'Victorians' and able to recognise continuity in the ethos against which better, perhaps, to appreciate changes. As the practice grew, too, there would be younger recruits whose attitudes, experience and way of life were different from their seniors', so broadening the range of specialised knowledge, informed opinion and modern attitudes.

Wallis, Gilbert & Partners were, nevertheless, regarded as experts; other designers came to the field in a variety of circumstances. There were manufacturers who regarded the employment of an architect as wanton extravagance and preferred the services of an engineer or building contractor who, it could have been argued, was likely to know more about factory building than architects with no tradition of engagement in the field. There were manufacturing companies who employed their own 'in-house' architects, who would be very familiar with the needs of their companies but could, thereby, become insular in their vision. There were manufacturing companies of great wealth and renown who would engage a prominent architect who had no experience of factory design, but who was nevertheless a very good architect and whose name would attach prestige to the project. A number of architects turned to designing factories when other commissions were few, while others regarded factories as a suitable means of exercising their own architectural theories.

A few architects followed Wallis, Gilbert's lead into the colourful Fancy style;[4] others, more sedately, departed only slightly from traditional styles. There were ventures into Modernism—few that compared with the continental version, but there were outstanding and memorable examples.[5] But most, eventually, settled for a variation of the British form of Modern[6] that was applicable to so many building types,[7] Odeon-inspired curves, or Dudokian massing.

Criticism and Appraisal

Contemporary views

The early buildings designed by Wallis, Gilbert & Partners, in the Daylight/ Masonry form attracted approval. Although comment on factory design was infrequent and usually published in discussion about construction, the architects were praised for their designs, referring to the benefits of the 'Kahn Daylight system' and that Wallis, Gilbert & Partners made utilitarian buildings 'architecturally interesting'.[8] Souster had referred to R. J. Williams' factory for Timsons at Kettering, Northants, as a 'pleasing combination of reinforced concrete with masses of brickwork'; to A. J. Howcraft's for Hirst Bros & Co Ltd, Tameside, as 'designed on unit principles suggesting efficiency'; to Louis de Soissons and Wornum's Shredded Wheat factory at Welwyn Garden City, Herts, as 'designed on unit principles in which the lines of construction are plainly expressed'. The Wallis, Gilbert design for Barker & Dobson Limited at Liverpool is 'a reinforced concrete daylight factory that possesses architectural character'.[9]

Eric Bird, in his article of 1926, had said that Wallis played 'a lone hand' in exploring and understanding the uses of new materials, frankly expressing the plan in the elevations and not hiding factories 'behind bastard Romanesque fronts'.[10] Other commentators preferred the revivalist mode for reinforced concrete. In 1924 T. H. F. Burditt was congratulated on his design for the Kosmos photographic factory at Baldock, Herts, for 'dispelling the myth that concrete cannot be beautiful'.[11] That 'all concrete' factory contained, however, crushed red brick from the old, demolished factory for its aggregate and the facing was scored to look like brickwork; none of the (very) decorative motifs was moulded *in situ*. The building was regarded as 'expressive of an art gallery or public library', qualified by the firm's business being 'closely allied to art'.

A concrete building for the Ford Engineering Laboratory at Dearborn, Michigan, USA, designed by Albert Kahn was also much more revivalist than Wallis' designs, but was described in Britain in 1930 as 'one of the most elegant designs we yet have in the ferro-concrete style; beautifully proportioned, with a few exquisite ornaments, which serve to enhance the charming simplicity of the building'.[12]

Clearly there was no consensus of opinion as to how concrete should be handled, how factories should express themselves, or by what criteria they should be judged. The writer who so admired Albert Kahn's Ford building described Wallis' Wrigley factory as of '*plain* ferro-concrete style', owing its attraction *only* to its 'fine proportions, its suitability to purpose and extreme reticence in ornament'.[13] Other commentators regarded the Wrigley building as a 'fine example', that its 'function and construction may be clearly understood from its form', the architects having 'taught us that commercial building can be very beautiful building'.[14] Another remarked that the building was the 'direct antithesis of steel construction, the floors being expressed as the main consideration, instead of relegated to the place of next importance to the vertical stanchions'.[15]

Judgement appears to be on the personal in-the-eye-of-the-beholder level. Although Modern and Traditional were not yet openly named and the protagonists had not yet drawn their lines, the views expressed above do tend one way or the other. And there also seems to have been some difficulty in deciding how factories ought to be judged—on their planning, construction, appearance as industrial buildings in the context of the genre or as architecture in the general context. Dixon-Spain insisted that

> no first-rate architect claims to specialize. The qualities which go to make a fine design are identical, be it factory or church.[16]

He believed that factories should be 'unobtrusive', emphasising a difference in status. Would all architects, fine or otherwise, agree with him? But then, so many architects regarded factories solely as production units. In order to plan competently, the architect was urged to 'soak himself in the processes of the particular manufacture or industry', but was warned that clients were likely to have little intimate practical knowledge of their manufactures, or would have requirements that were uneconomical or lacking in vision;[17] or that clients might be men who had 'never learned to be civilized'.[18] Perhaps Wallis, Gilbert & Partners received so many commissions because they did not look down upon their clients?

Wallis' dubbing of his Fancy factories as 'Transgressional' suggests that he expected criticism. The planning and layout were praised. What attracted the virulence of peers and commentators were the façades. As well as the unforgivable sin of having a noticeable façade at all, the façades themselves were attacked as commercial, advertising, novelty-seeking, following fashion, vulgar, with the spurious appeal of surface decoration. In such lack of decorum, of a kind that 'appealed to popular, uneducated taste', Wallis debased his profession and thereby encouraged the proliferation of mass culture. Gloag believed, however, that, as Western elitism was not conceived in the 'temples of Mammon' it would prevail over the 'superstition, cowardice and stupidity of the mass mind'.[19] Did it succeed?

But the critical attacks upon the Fancy factories brought no decline in commissions. The later designs were reported in the architectural press, some fairly fully and in praiseworthy terms. Others attracted only minimal comment to illustrations. Criticisms were modest and referred, in the main, only to minor details of appearance. In all, there was general approval chiefly, it must be assumed, because these works respected orthodoxy. If anything, Wallis was much better with white concrete in the Modern style than with brick in British Modern except, that is, for those very courageous and spectacular plain walls at Briggs at Dagenham, Platers at Burnley and Pasold at Langley.

American influence

Initially, much of Thomas Wallis' understanding of factory design and the ways of private industry were derived from American sources. The practice was founded to collaborate with Mortiz Kahn and Truscon in designing their American system in their own type of material, which Wallis anglicised to attract a British market. There are parallels between the practices of Wallis, Gilbert & Partners and Albert Kahn Inc.[20] Both practices operated on team-work principles and worked in cooperation with clients, their managers and engineers. Both designed multi-storeyed, reinforced concrete-framed factories and then moved to single-storeyed, lateral flow structures in steel frame. Both firms were keenly concerned that their buildings should be cost-effective, technically efficient and planned in accordance with internal usage. Neither was concerned with the symbolic expression of the machine as practised by European Modernists.

There are, however, major differences. The collaboration with Truscon and that company's influence lasted a very few years. Although Douglas Wallis travelled widely and was very impressed by Albert Kahn's factories, Wallis, Gilbert rarely subscribed to Douglas' views or assimilated his ideas,[21] Coty and William Burnett excepted.

Albert Kahn abandoned the north-light roof as early as 1920 as inferior to his own designs. Kahn's roofs, as well as being functionally superior were aesthetically superb. Wallis, Gilbert continued to use the north-light or top-lit, pitched roof for production areas. Here they were less progressive or pioneering than in other aspects of their work. But the retention of traditional roofs may be owed to the benefits of familiarity—what their clients already understood and were accustomed to; what they themselves knew how to design with little effort; what contractors, building workers and component manufacturers knew best; and which avoided delays in delivery and construction and/or difficulties and expense arising from untested innovations.

Kahn's non-industrial work was much more ornate and nostalgic than anything designed by Wallis in that field, but Kahn had no interest in consciously providing factories with an aesthetic appearance. He was not concerned with roadside views or with projecting a company image. The American market was so far-flung that money spent to impress the immediate vicinity was largely wasted. Kahn's almost sole concern was with production areas, at the designing of which he excelled. But then, during the interwar years, he had worked almost wholly with the motor vehicle industry and become expert in that one field. There was too the advantage of wide acreage of site and magnitude of buildings—impressive in themselves without additional ornament. In America, his clients were of a different ilk; American industry bred men who were far more hard-headed and aggressively profit-oriented than their counterparts in Britain. Kahn devoted himself to their needs, but the concentration on vast, fast, super-efficient production lines took little account of the human element. There were good quality facilities, but operatives were as robotic as the machinery they tended, which led to not-infrequent labour disputes.

In contrast, the work of Wallis, Gilbert & Partners could be considered insular, lacking in inventiveness and insufficiently production-oriented. But their composite approach to factory design arose from a situation to which American styles and methods were of little relevance. Wallis, Gilbert buildings were very much closer to public view, were on smaller sites and often beside major highways. Attention was directed to a home market, which was much smaller and of different outlook. America had done well out of the First World War and its industry was on a substantial footing; Britain was trying to recover from a much longer war and to get industry back on its feet. With the exception of British·Bemberg and Michelin, which produced their own designs, foreign companies setting up in Britain found it politic to look like British firms.

There were some strong American influences on British life—in fashion, speech, music and other entertainments, including some of the razzmatazz enjoyed by Americans. Some of the new products emanated from America, such as chewing gum and gramophone records. Some manufacturers were impressed by American management techniques and imported American technological aids, such as adding- and weighing-machines. But the overall circumstances in which Wallis and Kahn worked and to which they responded were so dissimilar as to negate comparison—like needs to be compared with like.

In factory design in Britain the urge to be Modern received its external influence from Europe; published exemplars of the new architecture were invariably of continental origin. By 1939 young members of the Wallis, Gilbert practice would say 'for better or worse, the Bauhaus and Corbusier were our mentors in those days'.[22] After the severance of the early American connections, having taken what was useful from that source, Wallis, Gilbert & Partners were no longer influenced by American design. They pursued their own way, knowing their own market.

It is only with hindsight that greater American influence has been attributed to Wallis, Gilbert designs. Their Fancy factories pre-date the American version shown in *Façade*.[23] That there are more differences than similarities between them, in character as well as concept, is in itself sufficient to destroy the illusion of influence. It is nevertheless surprising that, whilst this hindsight view is incorrect and unfounded, the transatlantic reference of the early designs and the importation of the Kahn Daylight factory system at a much earlier date than any continental influence, has been ignored or overlooked.

Retrospective appraisal

It is heartening that more attention is now being paid to the architectural history of factory design. Whatever the scale of approach, when dealing with interwar factories, mention of Wallis, Gilbert & Partners is inevitable. The architects are described as 'ubiquitous', but attention invariably focuses on the incorrectly-dubbed 'Art Deco' factories and, generally, only to comment upon the façades of Firestone and Hoover.

> Their [Wallis, Gilbert & Partners] work may today be described by some who in my view should know better as 'art deco', but I doubt whether the term, even if it had then been in general usage, would have been recognized as pertaining to architectural design. In the late '20s and '30s I am sure it would have had no such connotation either inside or outside the practice of Wallis, Gilbert & Partners or methinks of any other architectural practice.[24]

Perhaps we can now put that appellation to rest? Hillier's search for parentage of the Fancy factories includes the garish ostentation of the Michelin building, Fulham Road, London, transatlantic commercial knock-'em-for-six and showy razzmatazz, the cosmetic cubism of the Paris 1925 Exhibition, the Russian Ballet, the ancient Egyptian style, American Indian art and the machine aesthetic. Perhaps all those, except Egyptian, can also be put to rest?[25]

Taken as a group, Fancy is much more appropriate; Wallis wanted to demonstrate the status of industry and the people who worked in it as more important than contemporary received opinion, thus Fancy, as in fanciful, dressed out in glorious colour, catching the eye and the imagination, romantic, lifting the spirit, freeing the mind from toil and grind. Making the goods, attracting the buyers, improving the lot of the nation—and celebrating it.

In John Winter's survey of factory buildings, Wallis, Gilbert are referred to under a sub-heading 'Ad-men', in respect of the trend led by 'English subsidiaries of American companies' as they had the 'promotional conscious-ness of American business men'. Their aim, he states, was to seek prominent sites on the new arterial roads around London on which to build 'great shiny buildings set in lawns, all floodlit at night and fantastically styled to attract the passing motorist'.[26] Inevitably, 'good examples' are Firestone and Hoover. But for only *two* of the Fancy factories were the commissioning clients of American origin—hardly sufficient to be responsible for the trend or its naming. Wallis never denied that the Fancy fronts had an advertising merit.

Edgar Jones' very admirable survey of factories takes a much more realistic position.[27] He forcefully rejects the narrow, single-faceted approach and the tracing of development backwards from some point in the present, as in J. M. Richards' argument for a 'functional tradition'.[28] He maintains that industrial buildings should be placed in the context of their age, so that developments in structure, planning and appearance may be properly and historically assessed. He discusses Wallis, Gilbert & Partners more fully than do other writers, with something of their history and their contribution to factory design, and mentions a number of their buildings. The main emphasis is once again, however, on Firestone and Hoover, and the architects are dealt with under the sub-heading 'Art Deco Industry'.[29] There is no such architectural style as 'Art Deco'. What makes a factory a factory is not some mistaken means of describing its façade! There are other inaccuracies in Jones' work, copied from secondary sources, and it is disappointing in so worthy a survey to read that Firestone's administration building and the four-storey ware-house were of 'reinforced concrete' while the single-storey was steel-framed. In pointing out the contrast between the 'stark simplicity' of the factory and warehouse and the 'glamorous administrative façades which serve as an architectural bill board to passing motorists', it is unfortunate that Jones does not compare like with like. He groups Firestone, Hoover and Tilling-Stevens as being where such a contrast occurred as opposed to Wrigley and the East Sussex Waterworks where it did not. Tyre-making (Firestone) was (and still is) a dirty industry so that, whatever kind of front was designed, it was sensible to separate main office from production work. Making vacuum cleaners is comparatively clean; Hoover No 1 Building was designed to be used as a factory on the ground floor, offices and canteen on the first floor, giving them all a glamorous façade. The Tilling-Stevens factory designed by Wallis, Gilbert & Partners was for production purposes only and was decorated on front. Wallis, Gilbert did not design the more ornate office building; it was already existing when they received their commission. As a 'food' producer, Wrigley was engaged, essentially and necessarily, in a clean industry. Offices could therefore be contained within the factory block; a separate, glamorous administration building would have detracted from the massive totality of the design and expression of its unusual structure. It had, in any case, no public road for which to be glamorous. As to the East Surrey Waterworks, is it pertinent to wonder for what purpose a waterworks would need to attract the passing motorist?

The prominence Jones gives to the appearance of the Fancy factories does, however, follow from his point that 'it has not always been appreciated that the building itself could play an important part in the success of an industrial enterprise'.[30] Which is rather more perceptive than, for instance, Snowden and Platts' subsumption of all(?) the works of Thomas Wallis under the title 'Great West Road Style'.[31]

Wendy Hitchmough's book about the Hoover factory[32] has an excellence of illustration, including the aborted first proposed design for Building Number 1, and contains finer detail of the history of the Hoover company than could be included here. There is a bibliography, but there are no references and no pagination, at least in the 1994 reprint. Biographical information appears to be anecdotal and there are errors, which include the occupation of Wallis' father, the cause of James Wallis' death and his age at that time, and the designing of the Tate Gallery. Albert Kahn has been confused with his brother Moritz in respect of the early reinforced concrete factories in Britain; Illustration Number 15, Caribonum, was not built; Number 17, Columbia, Chatou, shows the power house not the factory, and where are to be found the butterfly roofs said to be 'pioneered' by the practice?

More serious, however, is the ascription of the Fancy factories to 'Hollywood style' (whatever that may be), their being 'dressed up with Hollywood panache to dazzle the passing public', and having the appearance of a 'shop window' or 'film set'. And they are frequently referred to as 'streamlined'. In fact, any suggestion of cinema architecture in these buildings was to reduce, for the workforce, the gulf between work and leisure. Designing factories was, for Thomas Wallis, a serious business. An architect so involved, who expected his buildings to be recognised as of, in monarchical succession, the 'George V' period, and that they would eventually mature into 'old friends', was unlikely to trim them with ephemeral Hollywood tinsel.

Conclusions

Wallis, Gilbert & Partners designed for a capitalist economy, they operated in a commercial and entrepreneurial fashion and the practice was organised on quasi-manufacturing production lines. Their aim was to produce, as closely as was then possible, a model factory for each of their clients to thereby increase his returns, and to enhance the status of industry. They did not challenge the pyramidal structure of personnel, but were concerned to improve the working conditions, welfare and well-being of operatives—sympathetically certainly, but also paternalistically with a view to raising moral and physical standards, and exploitively, in that such improvements were gainful to employers. In their designs they energetically encouraged advertising and consumerism. But their buildings were understood and enjoyed by those to whom they were addressed.

Wallis was described as a 'lone hand', as 'unconventional', whose designs were 'quite his own' and, before his peers in his own words, 'Transgressional'. Yet the resonance of his buildings with what we now see as the ethos and character of those times is unmistakable. Dissonance came from his peers, with charges of rampant, commercialistic 'façade building'. This was against the Fancy factories. Whilst the critics were jostling for the primacy of their own high-minded theoretical preferences, Wallis was bowing to popularism. In creating an image for his clients, Wallis, Gilbert had created an image for themselves—that was good for business, bad for the profession. Yet was it not good architectural practice to design to the reality of a client's needs?

In the debate about an architecture for the twentieth century, opposing opinions were reconciled conceptually, if not stylistically, under a criterion generalised as 'form follows function'. For a model factory, however, efficiently planned production layout was a necessary but not a sufficient definition of function. Only the wider grammar of the word could lead to a form compatible with the architects' understanding of industry and their all-encompassing approach to the design of a factory. Manufacturing industry had to inspire confidence; it could not afford in those competitive times to be modest or abstractly detached. Wallis' potent images had a vitality and boldness, an emotional content that touched the human psyche, particularly of those to whom the manufacturer owed his living—his workforce and his customers.

Objection to such overt expression went even further than caustic criticism of the Fancy factories. Thereafter, in articles and talks about 'how to design a factory', Wallis, Gilbert & Partners' designs were never used as exemplars. The architects had broken the rules; their influence, innovation, knowledge and achievements were expunged; they were remembered only for their 'transgressions'.

No two Wallis, Gilbert factories were alike, although it is interesting to note how a new idea emerging in one design was re-used or reworked in another. And new ideas there were: the introduction of mushroom columns at Wrigley, Gramophone and Michelin; water reservoirs on the roof of the Gramophone Shipping Building as proposed at Cambrian Candle; the use of precast members at GEC, Witton and at James Hunt; the communications tunnel at GEC, Witton, the power, services and maintenance tunnel at Firestone, and the underground services and maintenance ducts (including air conditioning) at Montague Burton. There was the elevating of facilities to leave clear floor space below at Firestone, George Kemp and Montague Burton; a central control point at Montague Burton, electrically-operated roof lights at Spencer Corsets, Briggs Motor Bodies and again at Montague Burton. There are many instances of embedded flues, chimneys and down-pipes in the structure to preserve a good appearance (for instance, Caribo-num, India, Avon, Pyrene) and a range of solutions of geological problems.

Where the lie or shape of a site presented problems, they were resolved by incorporation or used to advantage. The off-square Tilling-Stevens, inversion of the hollow square at Napier, the triangulation of the Gramophone Record Store are instances of working to the site rather than against it. Rising ground was used to advantage: insertion of part lower-ground floors at Pyrene, George Kemp, S. G. Brown and Glaxo, an attractive levelling up at Huntley & Palmer, and adaptation of the frame at Babbage, Friendship & Hicks and Cambrian Candle. Occupation of a hill or land crest was exploited to enhance the impact of Firestone, Pyrene, Coty, Burnley Platers and Montague Burton. The India building was designed to offset the effects of low ground falling away from the road with substantial, integrated corner towers and provision for upward extension.

A high standard of physical quality is evident in all the buildings: in structure, materials and workmanship, throughout the period. Many of the buildings are still standing, are in use and have survived considerable alteration, extension, war damage and adaptation to new uses. Where buildings have been demolished, it has been for economic reasons, not through fault in the building; the only exceptions are Frederick Parker Ltd which was lost by fire, and Tylors as the result of an accident. Perhaps the difficulties encountered in bringing some of these buildings down may today be considered a disadvantage.

Not all the buildings are, however, of an architectural merit equal to their planning and constructional qualities. Three most obviously defective in compositional integrity are Hoover Number 1, Spencer Corsets and Elizabeth Arden. Others are architecturally commendable but suffer in some minor defect—usually and surprisingly, in places where the architects most often excelled. The entrances at Avon, Glaxo, Simmonds Aerocessories, Burnley Platers, Hall's Headquarters, R. Woolf, and Ault & Wiborg, are not of comparable quality with the rest of the buildings. The decoration of Hoover Number 1, the Hoover Canteen, S. G. Brown, Telegraph Condensers and Laing factories 1 and 3, is excessive and lacking in coherence.

On the other hand, there are buildings designed for a singular or utilitarian purpose, where expression of that purpose is combined with imaginative and well-balanced architectural composition. Amongst these are the GEC machine shop extension, British Westinghouse transformer tank shop, Halls at Salfords, Northern Aluminium Mills 1 and 2 and the remelt shop, and the Gramophone power house.

Finally, there are buildings of architectural stature, where efficient and imaginative planning, unity of form and decoration, visual interest and pleasure make them a presence in the landscape. Quibbles there may be about a few of them; three are no longer here to be enjoyed and one was never built. The first and best of all has to be Firestone. Without rehearsing their particular attributes or placing them in order of merit, the rest are Tilling-Stevens, Napier, Cambrian Candle, Gramophone Record Store and the grouping of that building with the shipping and cabinet buildings, Wrigley, India, George Kemp, Freeder, Coty, Klinger and one that appears to have had all the virtues and the innovations, Montague Burton.

These are outstanding, worthy monuments to British factory design, well deserving of a proper place in architectural history, of comparison with recognised contemporary examples, and of particular interest as examples of Wallis, Gilbert & Partners' unusual and all-encompassing approach to factory design.

Appendix A

Works by Wallis, Gilbert & Partners, 1916–39

This list includes non-executed designs but not those for competition entries. The non-industrial works are those for which plans exist in the practice archive or have been published.

(n/b = not built; ext = extension; alt = alterations; adds = additions)

1916	Factory	J. Tylor & Son Ltd, New Southgate, London
	Factory (n/b)	Brolt Ltd, Birmingham, Midlands
	Factory (n/b)	Williams & Williams Ltd, Chester, Cheshire
	Transformer tank shop	British Westinghouse, Manchester, Lancs
	Coppershop/canteen	British Westinghouse, Manchester, Lancs
	Factory (n/b)	Auto Carriers Ltd, Thames Ditton, Surrey
1917	Factory	Tilling-Stevens Ltd, Maidstone, Kent
1918	Factory (n/b)	Singer Motor Company, Coventry, Midlands
	Factory (n/b)	Jones & Shipman, Leicester, Leics
	Factory (n/b)	Rubery Owen Ltd, Darlaston, Midlands
	Factory alts	Dent & Hellyer, Holborn, London
	Factory ext (n/b)	Albion Motor Car Co, Glasgow, Scotland
1918–22	Machine shop ext	General Electric Co, Birmingham, Midlands
	Switchgear works	General Electric Co, Birmingham, Midlands
	Administration block	General Electric Co, Birmingham, Midlands
1919	Garage	Halley Ltd, Kennington, London
	Factory ext	Commercial Car Co, Luton, Bedfordshire
	Glass works	Caribonum Ltd, Alperton, Middlesex
1920	House	Secton, Gomshall, Surrey
	House adds	Hawkins, Reigate, Surrey
	Boiler house	Albion Motor Car Co, Glasgow, Scotland
	Factory (n/b)	Clayton & Co, Huddersfield, Yorks
	Factory (n/b)	Cambrian Candle Co, Holyhead, Wales
	Factory	Hayes Cocoa Ltd, Hayes, Middlesex
	Factory	Houghton-Butcher Ltd, Walthamstow, London
1921	Factory	Caribonum Ltd, Leyton, London
1922	Omnibus garage, etc	East Surrey Traction, Reigate. Surrey
	House	Davies, Newcastle-under-Lyme, Staffs
	House	Clark, Loughton, Essex
1923	Factory	Babbage, Friendship, Plymouth, Devon

	Factory alts	Doyle & Co, The Borough, London
	House alts	Evans, Addison Road, London
1924	Factory ext	James Hunt Ltd, Fulham, London
	Factory exts – 1929	Papercraft Ltd, Hendon, London
	Factory	Telegraph Condensers, Acton, London
	Factory	S. G. Brown Ltd, Acton, London
	Pumping station	Norwich UDC, Sandyford, Norfolk
	Cottage	Caribonum Ltd, Chingford, Essex
1925	Factory	Wm Stannard & Co Ltd, Leek, Staffs
	Factory	Solex Licensees Ltd, St Marylebone, London
	Offices and factory	Leibig Meat Co, Antwerp, Belgium
	Omnibus garage, etc. – 1930	East Surrey Traction, Swanley, Kent
	Pumping station	East Surrey Waterworks, Purley, Surrey
1926	Factory	Barker & Dobson Ltd, Liverpool
	Factory	Wrigley Products Ltd, Wembley, Middlesex
	Motor showrooms	Great Portland Street, London
	Factory	Michelin Tyre Co, Stoke-on-Trent, Staffs
1927–30	Cabinet shop	Gramophone Company, Hayes, Middlesex
	Record store	Gramophone Company, Hayes, Middlesex
	Administration ext	Gramophone Company, Hayes, Middlesex
	Research laboratory	Gramophone Company, Hayes, Middlesex
	Power house	Gramophone Company, Hayes, Middlesex
	Shipping building	Gramophone Company, Hayes, Middlesex
1927	Factory (n/b)	Graham Amplion Ltd, Crofton Park, London
	Factory	The Shannon Ltd, New Malden, Surrey
	Machine shop ext	Albion Motor Car Co, Glasgow, Scotland
1928	Factory	Firestone Tyre & Rubber Co, Brentford, Middlesex
	Office block	Murray House, Cape Town, South Africa
	Alts and adds	Royal Cromer Hotel, Cromer, Norfolk
	Wharf walls – 1930	Wiggins, Sankey Ltd, Fulham and Hammersmith, London
	Alts	Caribonum Ltd, Leeds, Yorks
	Club house	West Fulham Conservative Club, London
	Factory	Young, Osmond & Young, Welwyn Garden City, Herts
1929	Offices, warehouse	India Tyre & Rubber Co, Inchinnan, Scotland
	Factory	George Kemp Ltd, Cricklewood, London
	Workshops	Hall & Co, Salfords, Surrey
	Pumping station	East Surrey Waterworks, Redhill, Surrey
	Factory	British Bemberg Ltd, Doncaster, Yorks
	Factory	Columbia Gramophone Co, Chatou, France
	Omnibus garage, etc. – 1932	East Surrey Traction, Crawley, Surrey
	Factory	Pyrene Ltd, Brentford, Middlesex
	Car showrooms	Packard Ltd, Brentford, Middlesex
1930	Offices	Pressed Steel Ltd, Cowley, Oxfordshire
	Factory	Lamson Paragon (SA) Ltd, Johannesburg, South Africa
	Offices, factory ext	British Paint & Lacquer, Cowley, Oxfordshire
	Factory ext	H. J. Mulliner Ltd, Bedford Park, London
	Car hire garage	Daimler Hire Co, London
	Stadium ext	Clapham Stadium Ltd, Clapham, London

	Grandstand, multi-storey carpark, club room, tote, cottages, kennels	Clapham Stadium Ltd, Clapham, London
	Omnibus garage – 1938	East Surrey Traction, Goldstone, Surrey
1931	Head Office	Hall & Co Ltd, Croydon, Surrey
	Offices, tyre sales	Avon India Rubber Co, Euston Road, Camden Town, London
	Factory	Northern Aluminium Co, Banbury, Oxfordshire
	Factory and offices	Kelsey-Hayes Wheel Co, Dagenham, Essex
	Recording studios	EMI, Abbey Road, London
	Omnibus/coach station	East Surrey Traction, Dorking, Surrey
	Omnibus garage	East Surrey Traction, Dunton Green, Surrey
	Coach station, garage, offices	East Surrey Traction, Windsor, Berks
	Hotel (n/b)	Dorchester, Park Lane, London
	Factory	Coty (England) Ltd, Brentford, Middlesex
	Factory, offices, canteen	Hoover Ltd Western Avenue, Perivale, Middlesex
	Five factory buildings – 1938	Hoover Ltd Western Avenue, Perivale, Middlesex
1932	Coach station	London Coastal Coaches, Buckingham Palace Road, London
	Factory	Pasold Ltd, Langley, Bucks
	House	Baker, Woodmansterne, Surrey
	House alts	Jamieson, West Worthing, Sussex
	Factory	Roberts Capsule Stopper Co, Peckham Rye, London
	Factory	Horsham, Sussex
1933	Factory	Reid & Sigrist, Malden Way, New Malden, Surrey
	Factory	Sir Wm Burnett & Co (Chemicals) Ltd, Isleworth, Middlesex
	Paper mill	Greaseproof Paper Mills Ltd, Dartford, Kent
	Omnibus, garage, offices	East Surrey Traction (LPTB), Epping, Essex
	Petrol station/garage	Brew Brothers, Old Brompton Road, London
	Showrooms, shops, flats	Brew Brothers, Old Brompton Road, London
1934	Factory exts	Beaton & Son Ltd, Acton, London
	Omnibus garage, offices	London Passenger Transport Board, (LPTB), Hemel Hempstead, London
	Omnibus garage ext	LPTB, Luton, Beds
	Omnibus garage, offices	LPTB, Tring, Herts
	Factory	C. W. Martin & Son Ltd, Bermondsey, London
	Factory – 1945	Glaxo Laboratories Ltd, Greenford, Middlesex
1935	Factory exts	Freeder Bros, Brimsdown, Enfield, Essex
	Factory ext	Lamson Paragon Supply Co, Canning Town, London
	Factory exts	Reliance Cord & Cable Co, Walthamstow, London
	Factory exts	Murray, Son & Co, Belfast, Northern Ireland
	Factory exts	Frederick Parker & Co, High Wycombe, Bucks
	Omnibus garage, offices	LPTB, Addlestone, Surrey
	Tram depot reconstruction	LPTB, Hanwell, Middlesex
	Omnibus garage, offices	LPTB, St Albans, Herts
	Omnibus garage, offices	LPTB, Staines, Middlesex
1936	Factory exts	ASEA Electrics Ltd, Walthamstow, London
	Factory	Richard Klinger Ltd, Sidcup, Kent
	Factory	Spencer Corsets Ltd, Banbury, Oxfordshire

	Factory	R. Woolf & Co (Rubber) Ltd, Hayes, Middlesex
	Factory	Ault & Wiborg Ltd, Watford, Herts
	Factory exts	Vandervell Products Ltd, Perivale, Middlesex
	Offices, bus shelter	LPTB, Tunbridge Wells, Kent
	Omnibus garage, offices	LPTB, Northfleet, Middlesex
	Omnibus garage	LPTB, Leatherhead, Surrey
	Tram depot reconstruction	LPTB, Wood Green, Essex
	Trolleybus ext – 1938	LPTB, Wood Green, Essex
	Car showrooms, service station	Henly Ltd, Brentford, Middlesex
1937	Factory	Slough Trading Estate, Bucks
	Entrance gateway	Slough Trading Estate, Bucks
	Factory	Champion Sparking Plugs, Feltham, Middlesex
	Factory – 1942	Simmonds Aerocessories Ltd, Brentford, Middlesex
	Factory	Glaxo Ltd, Driffield, Yorks
	Car showroom exts	Henly Ltd, North Circular Road, London
	Training ground, test road, engine stores, laboratory	LPTB, Chelsham, Warlingham, Surrey
	Shop front	Hoover Ltd, Regent Street, London
1938	Factory Number 1	John Laing & Son Ltd, Elstree, Herts
	Factory Number 3 (n/b)	John Laing & Son Ltd, Elstree, Herts
	Factory	Platers & Stampers Ltd, Burnley, Lancs
	Factory	Montague Burton Ltd, Manchester, Lancs
	Factory office block	Huntley & Palmer Ltd, Reading, Berks
	Newspaper offices	*Nelson Leader*, Nelson, Lancs
	School	C of E Community, Totteridge, London
1939	Factory	Elizabeth Arden, Acton, London
	Service station	Godfrey Davies Ltd, Neasden, London
	Factory exts	Reliance Cord & Cable Co, Walthamstow, London
	Factory (n/b)	Caribonum Ltd, Leyton, London
	Factory (n/b?)	Lamson Paragon Co, Canning Town, London
	Factory (n/b?)	Lamson Paragon Co, Cambridge

Appendix B

(1) Resumé of Negotiations with Joseph Nathan & Co Ltd in Respect of Glaxo Laboratories, Greenford, Middlesex, 1934–35

Most negotiations between Wallis, Gilbert & Partners and their clients were completed rather more quickly than at Glaxo, but the Glaxo discussions do reveal some of the difficulties that could arise. Because of the complexity of their business, the Glaxo personnel (the firm was called Joseph Nathan & Co Ltd until October 1935) appear to have had considerable difficulty in deciding what exactly they did require, and there is a hint that the architects should have been able to tell them. The undertaking was a huge capital investment for the company and the building had to be exactly 'right'.

During the negotiations and discussions to settle the brief, the architects had no guarantee of being awarded the commission or of receiving a fee for their endeavours. None of the many sketch plans has survived, so that the story is abstracted from reports and correspondence. The company's own deliberations prior to approaching Wallis, Gilbert & Partners had taken some 14 months.

A report by Harry Jephcott, Managing Director, to the board of directors entitled 'Development of the Greenford Site' and dated 11 September 1934 contains a preamble giving the earlier history of the project. By 1933, the company was expanding its business beyond the capacity of its premises at Osnaburgh Street, London, and two satellite units at Hayes, Middlesex, and Bravington Road (?). On 23 May 1933 the board decided to look into the possibility of segregating the food and pharmaceutical businesses, but this was later discovered to be impractical. On 22 September 1933 the board decided that new-built accommodation for its 'Glaxo Laboratories' was feasible and agreed to purchase land at Greenford. A small committee, comprising Alex Nathan (Chairman of the company), a Mr Randall (Finance Director) and Harry Jephcott (Managing Director), was instructed to 'make investigations with a view to developing the site'. On 15 March 1934 the board resolved that plans should be drawn up 'with as little delay as possible' for a building on the Greenford site to house all the Glaxo departments' activities.

The first intention was to invite 'two or three experienced firms of architects' to present proposals and then decide upon which best suited their needs. Discovering that this was contrary to the 'rules of the professional institute of which all responsible architects are members', it became necessary to choose one firm but, should that firm's proposals be unacceptable, their services would be terminated without obligation but under an agreed fee.

Wallis, Gilbert & Partners were the 'one firm' the board decided to approach, in July 1934. Frank Cox visited the company at Osnaburgh Street and, in a letter to the company dated 9 July 1934, the architects agreed to prepare sketch plans, elevations and approximate estimates showing how the site could be developed in accordance with the document handed to them. That document, also dated 9 July 1934, set out the past 10 years of the company's development, the processes presently being carried out at different venues, and the approximate area of space required to put some of them into one new building, but with a view to bringing them all under one roof in the future. Cox's letter stated that 'In view of the importance of the scheme you had in mind', the architects agreed to render their services without fee, with the hope of being eventually appointed, but with no financial commitment by the company if they were not. Arrangements were made for Glaxo's Mr Palmer to act as contact and liaison, and for Jephcott to be available if necessary to 'give essential details'.

Glaxo was advised of the structure and membership of the architects' practice, was given a list of buildings designed by them, and a copy of Wallis, Gilbert's *Industrial Architecture* publication of 1932, so that the company could enquire into and examine their previous work.

Later in July, Thomas Wallis, Frank Cox and G. H. Buckle (of the architects' engineering consultants, E. Wingfield-Bowles & Partners) visited the company's three operational sites and were handed a memo of 23 July 1934 which presented a 'complete picture' of the company's present activities and a diagrammatic sequence of them. Wallis, Gilbert & Partners then presented questionnaires to elicit more detailed and precise information, and then elaborated their earlier sketch plans accordingly.

Frank Cox's report to the practice and the clients (No. 243/34) of his visit on 31 July 1934 notes that the rough model the company had made showed that dimensions needed to be amended but that, in regard to the plans, Jephcott pointed out the company's 'inability to see far into the future as to what requirements would be' and therefore demanded 'maximum elasticity' in the layout. Further, that the company wished the building to be planned so that, in the event of 'the slacking off of one trade the other trade could, if necessary, encroach over its space'. To date, the objective had been to keep the two trades, food and pharmaceutical, separate. Cox thought the layout as prepared would suffice providing 'they [the two trades] were brought together and goods delivered to the point of intersection of the departments'. At that date, the company was still considering the size, shape and number of floors required for office space.

Wallis, Gilbert's more detailed plans were presented on 10 August 1934. They were asked to produce final plans and estimates for the board to see on 13 September 1934, with a view to appointing them architects to the project. Cox had continued to meet Palmer prior to 10 August and Cox's letter of that date, accompanying the more detailed plans, refers to further amendments made, the further 'tentative' agreements with regard to the positioning of the office block, and asks the company to consider its office planning requirements. In setting out the 'proposed sequence of operations' in the manufacturing area, he notes that departmental areas 'are as shown on the plans practically in accordance with your memo of requirements'. No decision had yet been taken with regard to power supply or its housing, or the canteen. Cox put forward suggestions.

Palmer's report to his company, dated 15 August 1934, completely rejects the solution in the plans to 'factory control' being in the central block; he admits that he was responsible for requesting that arrangement but 'the more I think on it the more it seems to be somewhat over elaborate'. He mentions that the workers' route from entry to cloakroom–lavatories–workplace is too long—'we are paying for that walking'. He further points out that the scheme he had agreed for working in the milk powder section 'has all the signs of logicality and practicability' but 'reflection will show that' if tins were supplied to packing tables in direct line they would impede mobility in a crosswise direction. 'I do not suggest that the problem is insoluble,' he wrote, 'but we do not want to rush into a particular idea without having thought out its implication as regards the reorganization of our packing methods.' Finally, he says that 'We have got all the relations of the various parts to the whole fairly well and if a satisfactory solution of the question of central control can be found, then we can throw the general scheme open to discussion'.

According to *Gold on the Green*, Glaxo's 'Fifty years at Greenford' publication of 1985, Mr Palmer was a multi-university graduate, whose 'breadth of vision, capacity for management and boundless energy proved ably ready to accept the delegated challenge of site coordination'. Palmer was personal assistant to Colonel E. A. Rose, the Production Director, who was supposed to be in charge of the development, but whose name rarely appears in the negotiations. Costs had not yet been mentioned and there is some element of delaying tactics; for all the company's dire need of space, there seems to have been no great haste to settle the brief for the new building.

There is reference to a memo from Palmer to Cox of 30 August 1934, but it is not in the bundle of archive material available to the writer. In response to that memo, further plans had been submitted. Cox and Buckle visited Palmer on 6 September 1934 (Cox's report No. 247/34 dated 6 September refers) and agreed a further revised procedure. Cox's report reveals that Jephcott was 'undecided regarding the alternative positions of the building on site', so the architects were to peg out the two front corners and centre on site and 'get Higgs and Hill to put up scaffold poles at either end and in the centre of both positions'. Cox would then visit the site, as arranged, with Jephcott and Palmer on the following Monday, when the matter would be decided 'subject, of course, to [the company] being able to get the land scheduled for housing released and also the pylon and overhead cables altered'. There were some minor alterations to be done in respect of the placing of lavatories. In his report, Cox asked the practice for plans to be prepared 'nicely done for presentation to the Board midday on Wednesday next' (12 September 1934), and asked to see 'Mr Elliott on Monday morning' in regard to estimates to submit to the board. He had arranged for Palmer to 'come here' in the afternoon of Monday to go through the figures with Stanley Elliott. 'I would like Mr Elliott to consider this possibility and telephone Mr Palmer.'

On Monday 10 September 1934, Cox and Thomas Wallis met Alex Nathan, Randall and Palmer at the site and all of them inspected the positions of the scaffold poles erected by Higgs & Hill. The Glaxo personnel decided to 'keep the main building line of the offices back from the frontage line a distance of 87 feet, the centre feature to project in front of this' and to keep the north end '50 feet away from the flank wall of the houses'. That required the company to have the 160 feet frontage to Greenford Road decontrolled and one pylon removed. The architects' drawings would be submitted to the board on those lines but, should the company be unable to persuade Ealing Council and the Electricity Board to meet the company's requirements 'in an economical manner', the building position would revert to the architects' original suggestion—one outside the controlled area (Cox's report No. 298/34 of 11 September 1934, copy attached to his letter to clients of the same date).

Jephcott submitted his report 'Development of the Greenford Site' dated 11 September 1934 to the board on 13 September. As well as the history of the development prior to approaching the architects, the report points out that he, Jephcott, had asked the architects for plans and estimates to be ready for the board meeting, but 'Our problem has been before the firm [Wallis, Gilbert & Partners] for two calendar months, during which time, with the exception of 14 days (holidays) in August, they have had the benefit of all information and criticisms they requested' but, even so, 'the plans would not be ready until the day of the Board Meeting', due to holidays in the architects' offices.

With regard to the appointment of the architects, Jephcott reported that he saw limits in their planning competence and suggested that 'definite arrangements should be made for visiting a number of the contracts with which they have been associated in order that we may benefit from the experience of others'. He realised, he said, that, as the company's manufacturing activities were 'so narrowly conditioned by the peculiar circumstances of our own activities', those parts would 'be much what we ourselves make them within the general framework of the structure'. He suggested, too, that should Wallis, Gilbert & Partners be appointed, the company should reserve the right to call in consultants of 'specialized and acknowledged competence' in engineering and layout. Jephcott adds, however, that 'we find ourselves not competent critically to examine' Wallis, Gilbert's suggestions since 'in the absence of plans or proposals from another firm, we have no standard against which to judge the quality of their work'. If it were possible he would 'welcome the opportunity of obtaining an opinion upon their suggestions of an independent architect of at least equal standing'.

He did, nevertheless, acknowledge that

> our experience with Wallis, Gilbert & Partners has left the definite impression that they are persons with whom it is easy and pleasant to work, since an interchange of criticisms of our respective ideas is invariably carried out in a manner which rapidly leads to the adoption of the best suggestions of both parties. We look upon this ready but critical acceptance of suggestions from ourselves and the pleasant but firm manner in which they criticise our views as being assets of great importance.

In regard to Mr Palmer's services, he states that Palmer had, during the past few years 'been utilised throughout the organisation in a considerable number of capacities' and he had thus '. . . acquired a wider and probably more intimate knowledge of our requirements and difficulties than any other individual member of staff', so that it was felt he was 'peculiarly suited to be liaison officer between ourselves and the architects'. Jephcott therefore took that opportunity of expressing appreciation of the 'able, tactful and effective manner in which he has carried out his duties'. The placing of the building on site, he reported, 'had exercised the minds of Wallis, Gilbert' and was only finally decided by consulting with Mr Nathan, Mr Randall, Mr Palmer and himself 'actually on the site on the 10th inst'.

For all the criticism of the architects, this document is far more revealing of Jephcott than of them. Jephcott's inability to make decisions, his delegation of responsibility to one young man, his not knowing whether the plans *did* meet the company's requirements, and his covering of all aspects of possible future criticism of himself, must have tried the patience of the architects. When the board met on 13 September it did not appoint the architects—not apparently because of Jephcott's indecisiveness or misgivings, but because of cost. Elliott's estimate is not with the papers but, while all the negotiations about planning had been going on—at virtually no cost to the company—the amount of money available or the degrees of economy to be exercised had not been mentioned. When the building was finally completed and occupied, *Gold on the Green* recalls that the new company, Glaxo Laboratories Ltd, was

> not ready, nor even able, to spare hard-won profits on new desks, carpets, curtaining and such like. The lessons and legacies of the long depression remained; pencils were still halved before issue to staff; used envelopes were re-used, incoming paper clips collected and re-issued; out of date stationery . . . was used for notes and memos.

Colonel Rose had his office decorated and furnished at his own expense.

On Thursday 20 September, Cox reported (No. 310/34) that, after meeting Jephcott, Randall and Palmer the previous day, 'we are to prepare rough outline sketch plans showing our preliminary proposals to effect reductions in our estimates'. The front office block was to be redesigned and, with the adjoining bacteriological laboratories, moved back to the position originally planned. The back of the building was to be replanned, omitting the receiving inspection department and placing it inside the building, resulting in alterations but at lower cost for the crush hall and pay box department. The canteen was to be omitted as a separate building and fitted into the first floor. The clients were 'going to see if they could reduce the width' of a number of departments without increasing the length. Cox noted that some economies could be made in staircases and main lavatories. He asked the drawing office to produce outline plans for 'discussion with our clients on Friday morning first thing', that is, virtually overnight.

Cox's next extant report comes more than a month later, No. 371/34 of 31 October 1934, in respect of a meeting held that day. What is different in that report is that Jephcott advised the architects that he had 'held many interdepartmental meetings', resulting in a document entitled 'Factory Committee Minute No. 1'. The 'Factory Committee' consisted of works managers and 'such additional members as [they] may from time to time co-opt', and had met every Tuesday and Thursday from 28 September to 25 October. Minute No. 1 of 31 October (and presumably the missing 'attached precis of the evidence which influenced the particular decision to which it relates') is a very businesslike, detailed assessment of requirements, with proposed dimensions, estimates of space and locations of departments—exactly the sort of information for which the architects had been striving for months. This does seem to have been one of those instances of being 'commissioned by directors having little intimate practical knowledge of their manufacture' of which Dixon-Spain had warned in 1932.

Things seem to have gone very much better after the architects were able to deal with works managers—territory more familiar and customary to their designing of layouts. Other detailed material, in respect of some areas requiring 'special investigation and agreement', were provided over the next week. New plans and Elliott's revised estimate were submitted to the Glaxo board on 13 December 1934, at which meeting the architects were finally appointed. Construction work began on 18 March 1935. In the intervening period, the only available documents refer to exhaustive enquiries by Colonel Rose into comparative costs of self-generating or mains-supplied electricity, which included visits to two factories (one of them Hoover), a large block of flats, two hospitals and a borough council. The company decided to invest in its own generating plant, but this decision was later overturned. Heating tenders are dated 4 March 1935. Elliott's costed-up bills of quantities as a guide to tenders are dated 5 March 1935, which assumes that bills of quantities, specifications and invitations to tender had been dealt with in the previous weeks.

Fourteen tenders were received. As against Elliott's total of £142 730, they vary from £138 670 (Costain) to £150 050 (Trollope & Collis). Costain's tender was accepted. The estimated times to completion vary between 37 and 70 weeks. Costains completed the work to occupation and near-finish in eight months.

Harry Jephcott, knighted in 1946 for 'Government Services rendered' when he became Chairman, included in his report to the board dated 9 March 1935 that

> During the past two months the work in connection with the Greenford Scheme has been continuously heavy and exacting. It has frequently involved excessively long hours on the part of all concerned and we cannot allow the presentation of this report to pass without expressing our appreciation of our architects, their staff and their consulting engineers, who have been unsparing in their efforts to press forward with the maximum speed and have been particularly helpful within the

past few days in seeking jointly with us every possible means whereby the cost of this scheme might be reduced.

The factory was described in the company's house magazine of January 1936 as the accomplishment of the 'primary aim of modern industrial architecture', namely 'fitness for purpose within an aesthetically satisfying framework'.

(2) The Gramophone Company Ltd, Hayes, Middlesex—Decisions about the Machine Shop, 1912

Wallis, Gilbert & Partners were not the architects of this building—the practice had not then been founded—but the problems encountered in respect of the machine shop are another example of difficulties between client and architect.

The Gramophone Company developed the Hayes site in a very piecemeal fashion, as occasion demanded. Extra plots of land were purchased, power arrangements were always in need of expansion, there were problems with adequate water supply, and many instances of additions to buildings and plant. As it was so new an industry, it was not possible to forecast demand and the rapidity of technological advances and changing fashions affected the organisation of supply. Until the appointment of Wallis, Gilbert & Partners for the massive expansion of 1926–30, however, the company employed different architects and contractors for almost every project, with subsequent problems over building defects—such as boilers sinking through a 21 inch thick concrete raft from which the reinforcement had been omitted, concrete found not to meet crushing tests, and cracks in the boiler chimney.

The machine shop was designed by Langton Cole, to be constructed in reinforced concrete in the system of the Indented Bar & Concrete Engineering Company, and the contractors were expected to be Holloways. The contractors' tender turned out to be so in excess of the architect's estimates that Langton Cole was replaced by (Sir) Arthur Blomfield and the Indented Bar company by Trussed Concrete Steel, and Blomfield's endeavours to attract lower tenders resulted in the contract being awarded to C. F. Kearley (Company Main Board Minutes of 8 May, 12 June, 14 August, 11 September 1912 refer).

The Main Board Minutes of the company in regard to development and construction from 1906 to 1931 (copies supplied by the Archives Department, EMI Ltd) are too bulky for reproduction here but a copy of a letter dated 8 June 1912 from a Mr W. Dennison to Alfred Clark, Managing Director of the Gramophone Company, is reproduced below. The position or qualifications of Mr Dennison are not known, but it would appear that, when any project was at a stage to begin construction, it was first vetted by him.

8th June 1912

My dear Mr Clark
I am giving you the following information, which may be of use to you in your discussion on the Building proposition at the next Building Committee, and I make the following suggestion, which will enable us to get Tenders for the Building in a much more comprehensive form than the Tender we have received from Holloways.
My first suggestion is that the architect be requested to write the Specification for the Building in segregated form, i.e.
Structure of Building Only: Structure of Building, including all Concrete and Steel Work, and including Motor Houses for all Lift Shafts, as shown on plan. Alternative

prices should be shown for concrete and brick walls for Lift Shafts and Stairways . . . .

[Here follows a long list of items on which Mr Dennison suggests that detailed
specifications and costings should be made, with costings of alternative methods
and materials; they are mainly in respect of areas where sub-contractors would be
employed.]

Each segregation, as above, of the Specification, should clearly describe and
specify the Material, Work, Fixtures approved by the Company or their equivalent,
and method of their installation (this applies particularly to Plumbing, Window
Frames etc.) so that the price under each segregation shall be complete and
descriptive, in order that we can tell exactly what we are paying for under the
different segregations.

I also suggest that the Architect be instructed to obtain Tenders from contractors
specialising on various work of the Building, such as, Plumbing, Glazing, Flooring
etc. and also to obtain Tenders from Contractors for the entire building, with prices
on segregations exactly as Tenders would be from specialists in each of the
segregated items.

My purpose in suggesting the segregated Tender is so that if the Contractor for
the entire Building is too high on any one of the segregated items, we can eliminate
this part of the Contract from the main Contract, and give it to the sub-contractor
through our architect. I can see no good reason why we should pay the principal
Contractor of the Building a profit on sub-contractors' work, such as the Toilet
Rooms Plumbing, Glazing, etc., unless the price submitted by the principal
contractor is very close to that of the specialist.

On Friday afternoon, with Mr Berliner, I called on the Trussed Concrete Steel
Company, whose representative took us to the Wesleyan Methodist Hall, a
building in which their system is used throughout, and which is a magnificent
specimen of Ferro-Concrete work. We also went to Woolwich to see one of Siemens
Bros' Factories, which is one of three which the Trussed Concrete Steel Company
have constructed for them. This Building, which we saw there, is about half
completed, and is also a very good demonstration of this Company's ability to carry
out a contract such as we have to offer. I have every confidence that the Trussed
Concrete Steel Company are qualified to build our Factory in a satisfactory manner.
I have also received cable advice from Ballinger & Perrot (The Victor Co's
Architects), who have constructed Ferro-Concrete Buildings with the Kahn System
(Trussed Concrete Steel Co's) that this system is a satisfactory construction. I have
also made enquiries as to the financial ability of the Trussed Concrete Steel
Company to carry out Contracts such as ours, and all of these enquiries have been
answered satisfactorily.

If you concur in my opinion that the Tender and Specification should be
segregated as above suggested, it will be necessary to have the Specification
completely re-written, but I consider a Specification written in this manner an
excellent safeguard against disputes with the Contractor. The way in which Mr
Cole's Specification is drawn up leaves plenty of opportunity for the Contractor to
dispute the Architect's intention on various items in the Specfication.

In going over with Mr Berliner this morning the drawings for the Building I
noticed two or three things about the Building which are not in accordance with the
instructions to Mr Cole and the drawings will have to be changed in this respect, but
these changes will have no effect upon the cost of the Building, except that they
might tend to slightly reduce the cost. The two principal changes are, the position of

the North-light Roof on the front wing of the Building, which is planned entirely wrongly, and the other is the Window Frames in the balconies of each Floor of each of the Stair-cases, which Balconies should be without windows, and the central column between the windows can be omitted.

I understand Mr Berliner has written you pointing out the actual difference in cost of the skeleton Building, based upon the quotation I received from the Trussed Concrete Steel Company, as compared with the quotation in Holloway's Tender for all of the Concrete work on the Building. This item, in my opinion, is largely responsible for the excessive price Holloways are asking, and as this difference, as Mr Berliner is pointing out, is based on positive quotation, I think we are justified in assuming that there are proportionate differences in all the other items for which Holloways have quoted. I have been making a very careful analysis of the literature received from the Trussed Concrete Steel Company, and I am very confident that the Building can be constructed to give us a safe working load of 150 lbs. per sq.ft. with a factor of safety of four times the working load on the floors and a factor of safety of five times the working load on the columns, with a very much less quantity of Steel and Concrete than specified by Mr Cole, or his quantity Surveyor. My reason for making this statement is that after carefully analysing the Kahn System I find that the same results of strength can be obtained with a considerably less quantity of Steel, by reason of the members which anchor the steel in the concrete being a part of the steel bar which is used for the main strength of the column or girder. This is confirmed by a question which I put to their engineer yesterday.

In my opinion there is no question about our ability to construct the skeleton of the building, which would include all reinforced concrete work of every kind on the building, and as shown on the original plans made by Mr Cole and which I approved, for less than £12,000. and there is a splendid chance that we can make a material reduction on this price by reason of a more economical system of reinforcement. If this is accomplished we shall have to be very extravagant to spend another £12,000 to make the building watertight and equip it with the necessary plumbing and fixtures!

Yours truly,
W. Dennison

References and notes

Chapter One: Thomas Wallis and Wallis, Gilbert & Partners
(pages 5–23)

1. *The Times* (8 March 1892); *Pall Mall Budget* (10 March 1892) [Tate Gallery Archive Department].
2. Tate Libraries were designed by S. R. J. Smith for Norwood, South Lambeth, Brixton, Kennington, Streatham, Balham, Greenwich and Hammersmith; the Streatham Picture Gallery was also designed for Sir Harry Tate. Sidney Robert James Smith was born in 1857, died 28 March 1913; ARIBA 1879; FRIBA 1891. He served articles with Mr Bedborough of Southampton and London. Became Assistant to Coe & Robinson, then partner with Coe on Robinson's decease, and started independent practice in 1879 with a first commission of a £70 000 contract for Lambeth Guardians for Norwood Schools; was appointed architect to Lambeth Board of Guardians and carried out a number of important buildings [*Journal of the Royal Institute of British Architects* (12 April 1913); RIBA Biog. File 1689].
3. 'The new British Art Gallery', *Lloyd's Weekly Newspaper* (17 May 1896) [Tate Gallery Archive Department].
4. Letter to the Editor, *The Builder* (19 March 1892) [Tate Gallery Archive Department].
5. The National Gallery of British Art, *The Magazine of Art* (June 1893), p. 266 [Tate Gallery Archive Department].
6. Letter to the Editor, *The Times* (8 March 1892) [Tate Gallery Archive Department].
7. *The Builder* (15 February 1896) [Tate Gallery Archive Department].
8. *The Daily News* (27 July 1897) [Tate Gallery Archive Department].
9. S. Games, 'A crypt to cache a national treasure', *The Guardian* (19 April 1983).
10. *The Builder* (20 January 1906), p. 68 [Tate Gallery Archive Department].
11. 'Temporary' as opposed to 'established' post in the Civil Service, that is, not 'casual' labour but a post without benefit of tenure, career prospects, pension rights and so on.
12. Public Record Office, Staff: Office of Works 1869–1921, *Work 22/227*, p. 431.
13. Public Record Office, Assistant Architects: Examination Regulations, nominations and results, *Work 22/11/1*.
14. Public Record Office, Establishment to Principal Architect: *Work 22/12/2* (16 March 1912).
15. Public Record Office, Staff, *Work 22/227* (*op. cit.*).
16. Public Record Office, Item 187, *Work 22/23/3*.
17. Sections: Extensions to Stoke-on-Trent Town Hall, *The Architect and Building News* (11 May 1910).

18. Minutes of the Municipal Borough of Stoke-on-Trent: Quarterly Meeting (24 February 1910); Special Meeting (21 March 1910).
19. *The Builder* (14 October 1949), p. 496.
20. Public Record Office, Mount Pleasant Post Office substation, *Work 13/657* (17 February 1915).
21. B. Jones (ed.), *Reinforced Concrete* (London: Waverley Book Co Ltd, 1913; enlarged edition 1920) 11, pp. 222–23.
22. Trussed Concrete Steel Company Limited, *Truscon: The First Fifty Years 1907–1957* (London: Trussed Concrete Steel Co Ltd, 1957).
23. *Ibid.*
24. *Ibid.*
25. *Ibid.* In 1908 an extension to the Kodak Works, designed by the company, suffered collapse of a section because the contractor had poured concrete when the temperature was below freezing point.
26. Trussed Concrete Steel contract for a machine shop for the Gramophone Company at Hayes, Middlesex, architect Sir Arthur Blomfield, appears to be earlier, dated 1912.
27. The American Club, 95 Piccadilly, London, was founded in 1919 as a meeting place for businessmen and women of the large American colony in England, members of the US Diplomatic Service and British Associate Members representing American concerns in the United Kingdom. Other nationalities were, and still are, welcomed and receive all the privileges of the club. *Anglo-American Trade Directory, 1988* [The Reference Centre, United States Information Service, Embassy of the United States of America].
28. Personal communications: Douglas Burford FRIBA, Elliott, Cox & Partners, as related to him by Frank Cox; W. Todd Roxburgh FRICS, member of the professional staff of Wallis, Gilbert & Partners in the interwar years, surveyor with Sidney Elliott.
29. Wallis, Gilbert & Partners, *Industrial Architecture* (Geneva: Biblos Ltd, 1932).
30. Glaxo Laboratories Ltd, Development of the Greenford Site (11 September 1934) [Glaxo Pharmaceuticals Ltd, Archive Department].
31. Personal communication: W. Todd Roxburgh (*op. cit.*).
32. T. Wallis, 'Factories', *Journal of the Royal Institute of British Architects* (25 February 1933), pp. 301–12.
33. W. Todd Roxburgh, *Notes re Mr Wallis' Paper on 'Factories'* (London: Contract Section, Wallis, Gilbert & Partners, 7 January 1933).
34. For instance, Simmonds Aerocessories Limited was persuaded not to mount 'Nuts and Bolts for All Purposes' around the tower of its building.
35. T. Wallis, 'Factories' (1933) (*op. cit.*).
36. D. T. Wallis, 'Single-story [*sic*] factory roofs of America', *The Architects' Journal* (22 August 1928), p. 269.
37. T. Wallis, 'Factories' (1933) (*op. cit.*).
38. D. T. Wallis, 'Modern factory planning', *Architecture* (May/June 1929), pp. 61–66.
39. Personal communications: W. Todd Roxburgh; D. Burford; Mrs S. Penman, widow of D. Penman who was a member of the professional staff at Wallis, Gilbert & Partners and resigned rather than make the choice.
40. Obituary, *Journal of the Royal Institute of British Architects* (September 1953), p. 465.
41. T. Wallis, 'Factories' (1933) (*op. cit.*).

Chapter Two: Interwar Architecture and Factories
(pages 25–34)

1. J. Summerson, 'History of art and design 1890–1939', broadcast talk (Open University Course A305, 1975); see also J. Summerson, 'Bread and butter architecture', *The Architect and Building News* (25 December 1942).
2. J. Gloag, *Men and Buildings* (Country Life Ltd, 1931), p. 10.
3. R. Blomfield, *Modernismus*, quoted in T. Benton and C. Benton with D. Sharp, *Form and Function* (London: Crosby Lockwood Staples, 1975), p. 175.
4. H. L. Curtis, 'The architecture of public buildings', *International Architecture 1924–34*, RIBA Centenary Exhibition Catalogue (Royal Institute of British Architects, 1934), pp. 116–18.
5. C. Williams-Ellis and J. Summerson, *Architecture Here and Now* (London: Thomas Nelson, 1934), p. 6.
6. Editorial, *Building*, Vol. IV, No. 2 (February 1929).
7. C. Williams-Ellis and J. Summerson, *Architecture Here and Now* (1934).
8. J. Gloag, *Men and Buildings* (1931).
9. O. Faber, 'The relationship between structure and design' in *A Book of Design by Senior Students of the Architectural Association School* (London: Ernest Benn, 1924), p. 10.
10. *Ibid.*
11. M. Bowley, *The British Building Industry* (Cambridge: Cambridge University Press, 1966), pp. 20–21.
12. J. Dixon-Spain, 'Factory design—the opportunity of our time', *The Architects' Journal* (13 January 1932), pp. 52–60.
13. *Ibid.*
14. Sir Frank Baines, 'War factories and sheds: their construction and adaptation to future needs', read before the Royal Institute of British Architects, 17 March 1919. Published in *Journal of the Royal Institute of British Architects*, Vol. 26, third series (August 1919), pp. 230–40 and (September 1919), pp. 249–59.
15. For example: G. M. Price, *The Modern Factory* (London: Chapman & Hall, 1914); M. Kahn, *The Design and Construction of Industrial Buildings* (London: Technical Journals, 1917); E. G. W. Souster, *The Design of Factory and Industrial Buildings* (London: Scott, Greenwood & Son, 1928); W. J. Hiscox, *Factory Layout, Planning and Progress* (London: Sir Isaac Pitman & Sons Ltd, 1929); C. G. Holme (ed.), *Industrial Architecture* (London: The Studio Ltd, 1935); E. D. Mills, *The Modern Factory* (London: The Architectural Press, 1951).
16. F. E. Wylie, 'Industrial buildings', read at the British Architects' Conference, Belfast, 1 June 1951. Published in *Journal of the Royal Institute of British Architects* (June 1951), pp. 309–14.
17. F. Duffy and J. Drury, 'Nice video—shame about the song' in 'Building Update, Industrial Part 1', *The Architects' Journal* (14 April 1982), pp. 73–76.
18. *Ibid.*
19. A. T. Edwards, *Good and Bad Manners in Architecture* (London: John Tirani; first published 1924, reprinted 1941), pp. 154–55.
20. J. Dixon-Spain, 'Factory design—the opportunity of our time' (1932) (*op. cit.*).
21. L. H. Bucknell, 'Industrial Architecture', President's Address to the Architectural Association General Meeting, 26 October 1937. Published in *The Architectural Association Journal*, Vol. LIII, 609 (November 1937), pp. 217–33.
22. 'Topic of the month: obsolete building acts', *Building*, Vol. V (July 1930), p. 24.

23. T. Wallis, 'Methods of producing artistic concrete finishes', *The Structural Engineer* (August 1934), 268–77; F. R. S. Yorke, 'Facings for steel and concrete buildings', *The Architectural Review* (November 1932), pp. 250–64; R. V. Boughton, 'Comparative costs no. 20: coloured cement buildings', *Building* (November 1937), pp. 493–94.
24. H. Martindale, 'When designing a factory: i. Health requirements', *The Architects' Journal* (13 May 1931), pp. 683–86.
25. J. Gloag, *Men and Buildings* (1931), p. 228.

Chapter Three: Analysis and Assessment
(pages 35–260)

1. R. Loader and J. Skinner, 'Management, construction and architecture: The development of the model factory', *Journal of the Construction History Society*, Vol. 7 (1991), pp. 83–103.
2. J. Skinner, 'Flexibility in factory planning', *Construction History Society Newsletter No. 24* (February 1991), pp. 3–6.
3. *The Architects' Journal* (26 January 1921).
4. M. Bowley, *Innovations in Building Materials* (London: Duckworth, 1960).
5. F. H. Heaven, 'The effect of reinforced concrete upon architectural design', *Concrete and Constructional Engineering*, Vol. 10 (1915), pp. 438–39; G. T. Bloomfield, 'New integrated motor works in Scotland 1899–1914', *Industrial Archeology Review*, Vol. 2 (Spring 1981), pp. 126–43.
6. F. H. Heaven, 'The effect of reinforced concrete upon architectural design' (1915) (*op. cit.*); G. & J. Weir Ltd, *A Seed is Sown: G. & J. Weir Ltd 1895–1955*, jubilee publication by the company [Mitchell Library, Glasgow, 1955]; M. Kahn, *The Design and Construction of Industrial Buildings* (1917).
7. M. Kahn, *The Design and Construction of Industrial Buildings* (1917); G. T. Bloomfield, 'New integrated motor works in Scotland 1899–1914' (1981) (*op. cit.*).
8. G. T. Bloomfield, 'New integrated motor works in Scotland 1899–1914' (1981) (*op. cit.*).
9. M. Kahn, *The Design and Construction of Industrial Buildings* (1917).
10. Scotstoun was not, in 1913, within the city of Glasgow and not all of the records and archives were transferred when the boundaries of the city were extended to include Scotstoun.
11. Albion Motor Car Company, *Minutes*; quoted in a personal communication from Brian Lambie, Curator, Biggar Museum Trust, Biggar, Scotland, holder of the Albion Archives (14 April 1987).
12. 'Albion Extensions at Scotstoun', *The Commercial Motor* (23 April 1914).
13. In a personal communication from R. W. Blackwood Murray of Capetown, South Africa, grandson of the founder of the Albion Motor Car Company (12 May 1987), the comment is made: 'I know my Grandfather travelled to the USA a number of times before the 1914–18 war. In fact his first trip was in 1900 to purchase steel spoked wheels for the first Albion car, which incidentally were totally unsatisfactory and the later production cars were fitted with wooden spoked wheels.'
14. Albion Motor Car Company, *Minutes* (1987) (*op. cit.*).
15. Albion Motor Car Company, *Minutes*, Eleventh Annual Meeting (12 May 1913).
16. Letter to T. Blackwood Murray from N. O. Fulton, dated 9 May 1913 (Copy supplied by Robert Blackwood Murray, Capetown). S. Stevenson & Company were also contractors for the Arrol-Johnson factory at Dumfries.

17. The buildings for Arrol-Johnson and G. & J. Weir in Scotland predate the Albion building, as does a similar structure for the Gramophone Company at Hayes, Middlesex of 1912 (see Appendix B). It is noted that British reviews of *The Concrete Atlantis* by Reyner Banham state that the type was not taken up in Britain until the 1920s. In *Automobile Archeology* (Cambridge: Patrick Stephens, 1981) David Burgess-Wise states: '. . . but the man who created the first truly modern automobile factory was Albert Kahn [in America]. . . . Probably the oldest European factory incorporating Kahn's principles is the Ford plant at Cork, Ireland. Work on this plant started in 1917'.

18. London Post Office Directories (1808–1916), City of Birmingham Reference Library.

19. Standard Telephones and Cables Limited, *The Story of STC*, published by the company (1958); Standard Telephones and Cables Limited, *A Brief History of the New Southgate Site*, STC Ltd (1982); Personal communication: Keith Newstead, STC Telecommunications Manager; *Garcke's Manual of Electrical Undertakings and Directory of Officials (1900 to 1930)* (London: Electrical Press Ltd, 1896–1960).

20. Personal communication: Alan Byford, retired Site Administration Manager, STC Ltd, New Southgate site (26 May 1987).

21. *Ibid*.

22. H. Nockolds, *Lucas: The First Hundred Years*, Vol. 1, 'The King of the Road' (Newton Abbott: David & Charles, 1976).

23. M. Kahn, *The Design and Construction of Industrial Buildings* (1917).

24. Personal communication: Oldbury Planning Office (2 July 1987).

25. Heywood-Williams Ltd, *The Window Makers: A Brief Survey of the History of a Chester Engineering Firm*, published by the company (1985)[Chester Record Office file— 'Heywood-Williams Ltd 1972–85']; Heywood-Williams Group, *Williams & Williams Limited*, company papers (21 February 1974).

26. K. White, *Chrysler (UK) Company Heritage* (Chrysler Training Department, 1979); *Motor Sport* (September 1979); *Garcke's Manual of Motor Transport Undertakings* (London: Electrical Press Ltd, 1915–16 [Vol. XIX], 1918–19 [Vol. XXII] and 1923–24 [Vol. XXVII]).

27. 'The utility of reinforced concrete', *The Architects' Journal* (26 January 1921), pp. 100–07.

28. *Ibid*.

29. E. G. W. Souster, 'The Tilling-Stevens engineering works', *Concrete and Constructional Engineering*, Vol. 12 (1917), pp. 653–60.

30. *Ibid*.

31. *The Architects' Journal* (26 January 1921).

32. K. White, *Chrysler (UK) Company Heritage* (1979).

33. C. Wilson and W. Reader, *Men and Machines: A History of D Napier & Son Engineers Ltd 1808–1958* (London: Wiedenfeld & Nicholson, 1958).

34. 'Construction 9: a reinforced concrete factory for motor-cars', *The Architects' Journal* (24 March 1920), pp. 377, 380–85.

35. C. Wilson and W. Reader, *Men and Machines: A History of D Napier & Son Engineers Ltd 1808–1958* (1958).

36. 'New motor works, Acton', *The Architects' and Builders' Journal* (16 January 1918), p. 32.

37. H. Miller, *Tools that Built a Business: The Story of A. A. Jones & Shipman Limited* (London: Hutchinson, Benham, 1972).

38. Rubery Owen Limited, *Sixty Years of Engineering 1884–1944: Rubery Owen & Company Limited*, published by the company (1946).

39. Personal communication: Charles Pinson, Engineering Manager, Rubery Owen Ltd (25 February 1988); Personal communication: R. J. Owen, Rubery Owen Services Ltd (29 February 1988).

40. 'Singer & Company Limited, cycle manufacturers, Coventry', *Coventry (Illustrated) Up-to-Date Views and Reviews* (Robinson, Son & Co, 1896); K. White, *Chrysler (UK) Company Heritage* (1979); 'George Singer remembered', *The Singer Owner* (October 1979); Singer & Company Limited (1928), Directors' Report (31 August 1929) [Coventry Record Office JN 628.2]; *Singer History* (9 October 1931) [Coventry Record Office JN 628.2].

41. K. White, *Chrysler (UK) Company Heritage* (1979); S. Chadwick, 'Pioneering at Deadwaters' (9 July 1971); 'A name of fame—but little fortune' (10 July 1971), *The Huddersfield Daily Examiner*.

42. West Yorkshire Archive Service, letter dated 25 November 1988, confirms absence of any plans deposited by Wallis, Gilbert & Partners. Extensions and alterations to the company's premises were submitted by L. Knowles, G. F. Jepson, E. F. Gilman and none of them bears any relation to the Wallis, Gilbert design; Mr Norman Cullen, resident in St Thomas' Road for fifty years, now watchman at the factory site; interview August 1987; Mr Frank Thomas, whose father worked at the Karrier firm from its founding, holds archive material included in an article by Andrew Flynn in 1983. Contact by courtesy of *The Huddersfield Daily Examiner*.

43. K. White, *Chrysler (UK) Company Heritage* (1979); S. Chadwick, 'Pioneering at Deadwaters' (1971) (*op. cit.*).

44. Personal communication: Mrs I. Parry, Holyhead, daughter of the founder (9 March 1987); Personal communication: Miss W. West, Tenby, one-time employee (25 November 1986); The Area Record Office, Gwynedd—no information on record (25 November 1986).

45. GEC Ltd, *A National Asset for a Hundred Years*, centenary publication by the General Electric Company plc (1985).

46. General Electric Company Limited, *Comprehensive Witton 1902–1952*, jubilee issue (General Electric Company Ltd, 1952); *Visit to Birmingham by the Prince of Wales: The General Electric Company Limited Great Witton Enterprise*, Description of Premises (1923) [City of Birmingham Reference Library, LF 65.32 661145].

47. W. A. Heaton, 'Machine shop extension', *The Magnet Magazine* (GEC Ltd, January 1920).

48. L. P. Francis, 'Construction 12: machine shop extension', *The Architects' Journal* (25 August 1920); cf. failure at the Bauhaus, Germany to raise a pre-cast concrete slab roof for the Haus am Horn.

49. GEC Ltd, 'The new switchgear works', *The Magnet Magazine* (GEC Ltd, February 1921).

50. This impression was vindicated by later discovery that both the company's principals were of German origin. Hugo Hirst was born and educated in Munich, the son of Emanuel Hirsch, and assumed the name Hirst on emigrating to Britain in 1883.

51. 'Our illustrations: modern factories', *The Architect* (30 June 1922), p. 479.

52. Wallis, Gilbert & Partners, *Industrial Architecture* (Geneva: Biblos Ltd, 1932).

53. GEC Ltd, *The GEC and its Engineering Activities* (GEC Ltd, 1925) [GEC Archive Department, Hirst Research Centre, Wembley, London].

54. Wallis, Gilbert & Partners, *Industrial Architecture* (1932).

55. C. A. Clark, *Charles Frederick Clark: A Brief Biography of a Great Character* (London: Caribonum Limited, 1945).

56. Deposited plans No. 96980/1 (July 1920); London Borough of Waltham Forest Planning Department, London.

57. E. R. Jarrett, 'Draughtsmen of today: iii. L. Bucknell', *The Architects' Journal* (13 April 1927).

58. Caribonum Limited, *Caribonum 1908–1948* (London: Caribonum Limited, 1948); Caribonum Limited, 'Our new buildings', *The Polywog*, Vol. 2, No. 14 (March 1923); Caribonum Limited, 'Building a factory', *The Polywog*, Vol. 2, No. 16 (April 1923).

59. *Ibid*.

60. Correspondence with Mr C. A. Clark, Poole, Dorset (March 1988).

61. *Ibid*.

62. 'From gearbox to prosperity', *Rootes Review* (October 1965) [Luton Central Library, Reference Collection]; K. White, *Chrysler (UK) Company Heritage* (1979); *Commer Prospectus* (23 July 1920) [Luton Record Office].

63. 'Commer Cars to close down', *Luton News and Bedfordshire Advertiser* (7 January 1920) [Luton Central Library, Reference Collection].

64. *Ibid*.

65. The Nestlé Company, *Spotlight on Nestlé*, published by the company (1977).

66. E. G. W. Souster, 'The Tilling-Stevens engineering works' (1917) (*op. cit.*).

67. National Museum of Photography, Film and Television, Bradford; London Post Office Directories 1882–1930 [City of Birmingham Reference Library].

68. *Amateur Cinematography*, extracts supplied by the National Museum of Photography, Bradford.

69. F. G. Windsor, 'The layout of a factory building', *Kahn-crete Engineering*, Vol. XIX, No. 95 (August/September 1932), p. 28.

70. Personal communication: William Stannard & Co Ltd, Biddulph, Staffordshire (4 November 1987); *The Building News*, No. 126 (4 January 1924).

71. Folio of archive material in respect of Babbage, Friendship & Hicks, supplied by Mr Alan J. McCarthy, Director and General Manager, Underhill (Plymouth) Ltd.

72. 'The Regent Street Building', research notes in respect of Babbage, Friendship & Hicks compiled by N. P. J., Solicitor to Underhill (Plymouth) Ltd.

73. *Building* (October 1926), p. 319; *Architecture* (May/June 1929), p. 62; Wallis, Gilbert & Partners, *Industrial Architecture* (1932).

74. 'The "sweet" century: Barker & Dobson's romance of progress', *The Liverpudlian* (November 1934), pp. 27–28 [City of Liverpool Record Office].

75. 'Family firm that grew and died', *Liverpool Daily Post* (10 August 1982) [The City of Liverpool Record Office]; Personal communication: Mr Dixon, Company Secretary, Barker & Dobson Ltd, Bury (20 October 1986).

76. 'Colouring for concrete work', *The Building News* (19 July 1912).

77. T. Wallis, 'Methods of producing artistic concrete finishes', *The Structural Engineer* (August 1934), pp. 368–77.

78. M. Horsey, 'Speculative housebuilding in London in the 1930s: official control and popular taste', *Construction History Society Conference* (12 September 1985).

79. S. A. Worden, 'Furniture for the living room: an investigation of the interaction between society, industry and design in Britain from 1919 to 1939', PhD thesis, Brighton Polytechnic (1980).

80. E. L. Bird, 'The industrial work of Wallis, Gilbert & Partners', Current Architecture Section, *The Architects' Journal* (14 April 1926), pp. 553–64.

81. Personal communication: The Wrigley Company Ltd., Plymouth (11 February 1987).

82. *The Westminster Gazette* (23 June 1926).

83. *The Architects' Journal* (7 March 1928), p. 354.

84. *Architecture Illustrated* (December 1930).
85. J. Watson, 'Concrete and cement', *Building* (July 1926), p. 163.
86. R. Edge, Main Board Minutes referring to building of Hayes office, cabinet factory and other Blythe Road buildings, 1906–1931 (1987) [EMI Archives Department, Uxbridge Road, Hayes].
87. Francis Barraud painted a picture of his dog 'Nipper' listening to a phonograph. On 31 May 1899, he asked the Gramophone Company London office for a brass horn as a model to use instead of the dull, black one of the phonograph. The Edison company, which manufactured cylindrical recording phonographs, had not been interested in the picture for publicity purposes, saying 'Dogs don't listen to phonographs.' Gramophone bought the picture for £50 plus £50 for the copyright so long as the phonograph was painted out and a gramophone substituted. Barraud called the picture 'His Master's Voice'. It was used in many different ways in the company's advertising (except that the dog was replaced by a cobra in Moslem countries), but did not replace the original logo (a recording angel) until 1908.
88. R. Miller and R. Boar, *The Incredible Music Machine* (London: Quartet/Visual Art Books, 1982).
89. R. Edge, Main Board Minutes (*op. cit.*).
90. *Ibid.*
91. 'A reinforced concrete office building in London: Friars House, Broad Street, EC', *Concrete and Constructional Engineering*, Vol. III (1909), pp. 113–16.
92. E. G. W. Souster, *The Design of Factory and Industrial Buildings* (London: Scott, Greenwood & Son, 1928).
93. Wallis, Gilbert & Partners, *Industrial Architecture* (1932).
94. D. T. Wallis, 'Modern factory planning', *Architecture* (May/June 1929), pp. 61–66.
95. Wallis, Gilbert & Partners, *Industrial Architecture* (1932).
96. *Ibid.*
97. 'Mushroom construction again . . . 1', *The Architect and Building News* (August 1930), pp. 232–37.
98. R. Edge, Main Board Minutes (*op. cit.*).
99. *The Architect and Building News* (22 August 1930).
100. Correspondence at the London Borough of Merton Development Department, No. 6278/0936/175 (448).
101. Personal communication: Twinlock plc (28 June 1984).
102. T. Wallis, 'Methods of producing artistic concrete finishes' (1934) (*op. cit.*).
103. London Post Office Directories [City of Birmingham Reference Library]; *Garcke's Manual of Electrical Undertakings and Directory of Officials (1900 to 1930)* (1896–1960).
104. A. Lief, *The Firestone Story* (New York: McGraw-Hill, 1951).
105. Personal communication: Sharon E. Savage Stull, The Firestone Tire & Rubber Company, Akron, Ohio, USA (1980–82).
106. 'The Firestone tyre factory', *The Architect and Building News* (4 January 1929); 'Firestone Tyre and Rubber Co factory', *The Builder* (5 July 1929); 'Tyre factory at Hounslow, Middlesex', *The Architects' Journal* (29 May 1929); Note: There are identical passages in *A & BN* and *The Builder*.
107. S. Games, 'A façade of protest', *The Guardian* (30 August 1980); *The Golden Mile: The Great West Road and its Industries, A Short History*, Gunnersbury Park Museum, exhibition publication (1982).
108. *The Architect and Building News* (4 January 1929) (*op. cit.*); *The Builder* (5 July 1929) (*op. cit.*).
109. Personal communication: past employees of the Firestone Tyre & Rubber Company, Brentford, and the India Tyre Company, Inchinnan (1980–82).

110. T. Wallis, 'Factories', *Journal of the Royal Institute of British Architects* (25 February 1933), pp. 301–12.
111. *Ibid.*
112. J. G. Davies, *Temples, Churches and Mosques* (Oxford: Basil Blackwell, 1982); M. Lurker, *The Gods and Symbols of Ancient Egypt* (London: Thames & Hudson, 1974).
113. A. Lesieutre, *The Spirit and Splendour of Art Deco* (New York, 1974).
114. T. Wallis, 'Factories' (1933) (*op. cit.*).
115. Personal communication: past employees of Firestone and India companies (1980–82).
116. T. Wallis, 'Factories' (1933) (*op. cit.*).
117. 'Tyre factory at Hounslow, Middlesex', *The Architects' Journal* (29 May 1929); 'The Firestone tyre factory', *The Architect and Building News* (4 January 1929); *Journal of the Royal Institute of British Architects* (9 November 1929), p. 7; 'Firestone Tyre and Rubber Co factory', *The Builder* (5 July 1929); F. E. Towndrow, 'A monthly review of current architecture', *Building* (February 1929), p. 86.
118. F. E. Towndrow, 'A monthly review of current architecture' (1929) (*op. cit.*).
119. 'The Firestone tyre factory', *The Architect and Building News* (4 January 1929).
120. A. T. Edwards, 'The year's architecture', *Building* (December 1929), p. 548.
121. R. A. Duncan, 'Architecture of 1929', *Building* (December 1929), p. 552.
122. T. Wallis, 'Factories' (1933) (*op. cit.*).
123. E. Maxwell Fry, 'Design in the countryside and town', in J. Gloag (ed.), *Design in Modern Life* (London: George Allen & Unwin, first published 1934; second impression 1946), p. 117.
124. J. R. Leathart, 'A review of current factory design', *Building* (April 1936), pp. 136–42.
125. G. Stamp, Introduction to 'Britain in the Thirties', *Architectural Design Profile 24* (1980).
126. M. Binney 'Disaster on the Great West Road', *Evening News* (28 August 1980); 'Art Deco falls to the demolition man', *Sunday Times* (24 August 1980); D. Hencke, 'Furore at loss of factory', *The Guardian* (27 August 1980); S. Games, 'A façade of protest', *The Guardian* (30 August 1980); S. Jenkins, 'Downfall of a workingman's palace', *The Observer* (31 August 1980); G. Darley, 'An obituary: the Firestone building', *Financial Times* (1 September 1980); D. Atwell, 'Art demo', *Building* (5 September 1980).
127. B. Hillier, Introduction to T. Mackertich and P. Mackertich, *Façade, A Decade of British and American Commercial Architecture* (London: Mathews Miller Dunbar, 1976).
128. Dunlop Limited, Archives of the India Tyre Company.
129. *Ibid.*
130. Correspondence and Reports from and to Wallis, Gilbert & Partners; Dunlop Limited, Archives of the India Tyre Company (November 1929–March 1930).
131. H. Robertson, *The Pyrene Company Limited*, published by the company (1930).
132. F. E. Towndrow, 'A monthly review of current architecture' (1929) (*op. cit.*).
133. 'A biscuit factory, London', *The Architect and Building News* (25 December 1931), pp. 370–71.
134. *Ibid.*
135. Wallis, Gilbert & Partners, *Industrial Architecture* (1932).
136. C. G. Dobson, *A Century and a Quarter—Hall & Co Ltd*, published by the company (1959).
137. 'An office for a builders' merchant', *The Architect and Building News* (24 June 1932), pp. 458–59.

138. C. G. Dobson, *A Century and a Quarter—Hall & Co Ltd* (1959).
139. Avon Rubber Company Limited, *The Romance of Rubber*, published by the company, Melksham (1927); Avon Rubber plc, *One Hundred Years*, published by the company (1980).
140. M. Lurker, *The Gods and Symbols of Ancient Egypt* (1974), p. 44.
141. 'Commercial architecture, the London depot of the Avon India Rubber Co Ltd', *The Architect and Building News* (20 June 1931), pp. 450–51; 'New premises, Mabledon Place, WC1', *Architecture Illustrated* (July 1931), pp. 29–30.
142. Personal communication: J. Hovell, retired Communications Manager, Hoover Limited (October 1987).
143. C. B. Colston, Managing Director of Hoover Ltd in Britain, quoted in 'Architecture today', *Financial Times* (17 February 1933).
144. The front of the building and the walls of the towers were constructed of white cement and calcined flint aggregate; T. Wallis, 'Methods of producing artistic concrete finishes' (1934) (*op. cit.*).
145. B. Hillier, *Art Deco of the 20s and 30s* (London: Studio Vista, 1968), p. 40; T. Mackertich and P. Mackertich, *Façade, A Decade of British and American Commercial Architecture* (1976).
146. C. F. Feest, *Native Arts of North America* (London: Thames & Hudson).
147. In 'A factory and offices for Messrs Hoover Ltd, Perivale', *The Architect and Building News* (4 March 1932), the light fittings are described as chromium-plated. Original fittings still in place have more the appearance of finely-finished matt stainless steel.
148. J. Hovell, personal communication (October 1987) (*op. cit.*).
149. 'Architecture today, reconstruct for prosperity', *Financial Times* (17 February 1933), p. 8.
150. Hoover press release (May 1984).
151. *Ibid.*
152. M. Dugdale, poem 'Ornamentia praecox', drawings by William Edmeston, *The Architectural Review* (July 1932), p. 40 [my thanks to Robert Loader for drawing my attention to this cartoon].
153. T. Wallis, 'Factories' (1933) (*op. cit.*).
154. S. Gardiner, 'A design maligned', *The Observer* (26 June 1988).
155. T. Wallis, 'Factories' (1933) (*op. cit.*).
156. T. Mackertich and P. Mackertich, *Façade, A Decade of British and American Commercial Architecture* (1976).
157. T. Wallis, 'Factories' (1933) (*op. cit.*).
158. 'The Coty factory, the Great West Road', *The Architect and Building News* (13 January 1933), pp. 77–78.
159. T. Wallis, 'Factories' (1933) (*op. cit.*); T. Wallis, 'Factory planning and construction', *The Architects' Journal* (22 February 1933).
160. D. T. Wallis, 'Modern factory planning' (1929) (*op. cit.*); D. T. Wallis, 'Single-story [*sic*] factory roofs of America', *The Architects' Journal* (22 August 1928), p. 269.
161. Personal communication: Mrs Armitage, a retired Coty accounts clerk, states her perception of the building in 1949 as '. . . much more belonging to the forward-looking age of industry' and a 'more agreeable workplace than those which had no character'.
162. E. W. Pasold, *Ladybird, Ladybird—A Story of Private Enterprise* (Manchester: Manchester University Press, 1977).
163. Pasold had planned for only one lavatory as he did not intend to employ female office staff, but was overruled by the local authority planning regulations.

164. The Langley site had been intended for housebuilding. In that rural area in 1932, 'industry' was represented by only a brickworks and a bacon factory. Local opposition to further industrialisation was fierce and an action committee was formed in an attempt to prevent the factory from being built.

165. The building and setting up of the factory were financed by money from Czechoslovakia that had to be secretly diverted into British channels to avoid political and social sensitivities about monetary exchange and foreign infiltration of British industry.

166. The lettering of the company flag was of faience tile by Shaws of Darwin, an unusual sub-contractor for the architects, whose choice of faience supplier was almost always Carter & Company (London) Limited.

167. *Architecture Illustrated* (August 1934), p. 51.

168. *Who's Who in British Aviation* (London: Bunhill Publications, 1936).

169. Personal communications: Mr Tony Twycross, pilot, Desford Airfield (3 June 1996); Mr Peter Stoddard, Archivist, ex-Snibston Discovery Park, Leicestershire (3 June 1996).

170. Directories: Rylands Engineering, London Post Office Directory (Surrey, 1936–37).

171. *Architecture Illustrated* (August 1934), p. 68.

172. C. W. Martin & Sons Ltd, *History of Martin's*, published by the company (1956).

173. GOAD Insurance Plans: Sheet 168 London (October 1887); Sheet 163, London VII, Resurveyed and revised (May 1941) [John Harvard Library, Bermondsey, London; Southwark Collection].

174. Survey plans—Charterhouse Estates Ltd [Howard, Cavanna & Associates, London, 1988]; Alaska Penthouse Plans [ORMS Designers & Architects, London, 1993].

175. *Affair*, House Journal of the Martin Company, cover (March 1948).

176. Glaxo Laboratories Limited, Archives (1934–39).

177. *Ibid.*

178. *Ibid.*

179. *Ibid.*

180. An example of Thomas Wallis' assertion that the architect must be involved in every detail of the building 'from the digging of the first sod to the raising of steam', in T. Wallis, 'Factories' (1933) (*op. cit.*).

181. N. Ollis, J. Saxton, E. Coward and P. Baldwin, *Gold on the Green* (Greenford: Glaxo Pharmaceuticals Ltd, 1985).

182. Strangely for a sober-minded company, Glaxo chose to display its flag in neon-lighting. Green would have been the obvious choice, but the Great Western Railway objected to the use of red or green as either could confuse engine drivers. Thus, turquoise was chosen as a compromise.

183. Editorial, *Nutrition*, Journal of Glaxo Laboratories Ltd, Vol. 4, No. 1 (January 1936).

184. Deposited plans at Waltham Forest Planning Department show the first factory extensions at Fingal Works, Staffa Road, to be for W. Davies (Spitalfield) Limited in 1935. The London Post Office Directory shows Reliance Cord and Cables to be at that address from 1933. It is not known whether this represents a change of company name, a takeover or a merger. The Reliance Company became part of BICC plc.

185. The writer became aware of these buildings very late in the research programme, so that investigation so far has been perfunctory.

186. Building Application Number 14381, Belfast City Hall dated 1 August 1935. Local consulting architect, T. W. Henry, FRIBA, Belfast [information and photographic transparency of the building kindly supplied by Dr P. F. Lamour, Department of Architecture and Planning, The Queen's University, Belfast].

187. The company was founded as the Paragon Check Book Company by two Anglo-

Canadians in 1886 with two machines that could cut, perforate and number in duplicate from a continuous roll of paper. Capital backing for expansion in 1889 was provided by the American company Lamson Store Services Co; the name 'Lamson' related to the inventor of the first cash/change carrying device for retail shops and had nothing to do with Paragon. Thereafter, the British company moved into the production of all kinds of business forms, commercial stationery and equipment, making its own production machinery; T. Elias, *A Half Century of Paragon Progress* (London: Lamson Paragon Supply Company Ltd, 1936).

188. *Paragon Way*, golden jubilee edition of the house magazine of Lamson Paragon Supply Company Ltd, London (1936).

189. 'Mr and Mrs Kahn' could well have been Moritz Kahn and his wife on a visit to Britain in December 1936. Whether 'Mrs Thomas Wallis' was the true wife or Doris Rudland, the woman with whom Thomas Wallis was then living, is not known.

190. Richard Klinger Limited, *1886–1986—Staying Ahead 100 Years*, centenary leaflet produced by the company (1986).

191. Internal photography was permitted but without benefit of flash equipment because of possible fire hazard. In only one of the workrooms was there any artifical lighting, and that was in an area shadowed by a blank wall.

192. Because of economic recession, the extension building is to be demolished to make way for a Tesco supermarket and production is being reorganised and concentrated within the original building (1987).

193. *Fishburn Printing Ink Company, Jubilee 1929–1979*. A. R. F. Fishburn learned the ink trade with Ault & Wiborg in America and worked in its London plant in the 1920s but left when separation from the American parent was being planned. He set up his own business, Fishburn Printing Ink Company in Watford in 1929. That company is now part of the International Corporation of America and remains Ault & Wiborg's closest competitor.

194. Personal communication: Mr A. M. Cyman, Chief Engineer, Ault & Wiborg General Printing Inks, Watford (31 March 1987).

195. The location is referred to in the literature as 'Southall'.

196. Personal communication: Brixton Estates Limited, London (27 July 1987).

197. When EMI investigated problems with the roof, they found wooden joists measuring nine inches by two inches (suffering from wet and dry rot) laid over one-inch boarding packed with three layers of felt fabric. Some brick centres had been removed, so that the structure attached across the outer stanchions was supporting 17 tons of concrete slab surfaced with asphalt. This was as a result of subsequent treatment, not part of original construction. The roof has now been reinstated and lower, false ceilings have been installed.

198. 'George Palmer, 1818–97', in I. C. Bradley, *Enlightened Entrepreneurs* (London: Wiedenfeld & Nicholson, 1987).

199. *The Architects' Journal* (2 December 1937); J. R. Leathart, 'Current architecture', *Building* (September 1937).

200. J. R. R. Leathart, 'Current architecture', *Building* (September 1937), p. 379.

201. Personal communication: Douglas Burford FRIBA, Elliott, Cox & Partners, as related to him by Frank Cox (*op. cit.*).

202. Personal communication: Philip Rice, then Managing Director, Spencer (Banbury) Ltd (11 June 1987).

203. Spencer Corsets Limited, *Company Minute Books* (1935–37).

204. Personal communication: Philip Rice (*op. cit.*).

205. *Council Minutes* Nos 1506/7 of 3 March 1937. Copies supplied by the District Central

Library, Burnley, who point out that the report of 5 January 1937 appears only in the 'Manuscript Minute Book' and not in the public printed books. The amended figure of £84 070 was presented on 27 February 1937 as:

Purchase of land 1852.

Foundation and incidental work £8000.

Contract price for building £65 950.

Estimated cost of railway siding £1800.

Allowance for Architect, Quantity Surveyor, Clerk of Works and Local charges £4468.
    Making a total of £84 070.

206. Correspondence with the District Central Library, Burnley.

207. Alderman Broadley, the prime mover in the gamble to bring industry to the area, in an effort to avoid any possible surcharge, publicly announced that his total disposable capital amounted to 7s 6d (37 pence). Reported by Alan Halstead in 'Burnley's first new industry', *The Burnley Express* (14 April 1971).

208. The factory is presently being reorganised into a conveyor-belt system. The mezzanine floor now contains accounts offices and the original lavatories.

209. At the London end of the Great West Road land appreciated from £500 per acre to £5000 per acre between 1925 and 1935; *Report on the Location of Industry in Great Britain* (Political and Economic Planning [PEP], March 1939).

210. *Ibid.*

211. J. R. Leathart, 'Current architecture', *Building* (June 1938).

212. *Ibid.*

213. *Architecture Illustrated* (December 1939), p. 122: [caption] 'Factory at Bath Road attributed to W. H. L. Price, LRIBA, architect to Slough Estate, whereas the building was designed by Thomas Wallis of Messrs Wallis, Gilbert & Partners, Consulting Architects to the Slough Estates Ltd.'

214. There are 66 plans on microfilm relating to the Simmonds building, dated between December 1937 and October 1942, in the Wallis, Gilbert archive collection.

215. John Laing & Son Ltd, 'Great West Road landmark', *Team Spirit* (London: John Laing & Son Ltd, August 1949).

216. Personal communication: Roger L. T. Jones, Manager, Estates Department, Beecham Group plc [now SmithKline-Beecham] (7 June 1988).

217. H. Coad, *Laing: the Biography of Sir John W. Laing CBE (1879–1978)* (London: Hodder & Stoughton, 1979).

218. A. A. Jackson, *Semi-detached London* (London: George Allen & Unwin, 1973), p. 114.

219. Personal communication: Professor Alan A. Jackson (12 November 1987).

220. Personal communication; Alan Thorpe, John Laing plc (30 September 1987).

221. *Ibid.*

222. Personal communication: Carl Zeiss Jena Ltd, Elstree (10 March 1988).

223. Montague Burton Limited, *Ideals in Industry: The Growth and Progress of Montague Burton Ltd*, published by the company (editions 1936 and 1951).

224. *Ibid.*

225. *Ibid.*

226. Personal communication: Harry Briggs, architect retired, erstwhile assistant to T. H. Rowntree (9 June 1987).

227. Personal communication: D. W. Bartley, Estates Manager, The Burton Group plc (25 March 1987, 22 April 1987, 30 April 1987).

228. Personal communication: Harry Briggs (*op. cit.*).

229. Healey & Baker, *Survey Report 1951* (1951). Copy supplied by Estates Department, The Burton Group plc.

230. Montague Burton Limited, *Ideals in Industry: The Growth and Progress of Montague Burton Ltd* (*op. cit.*).
231. Personal communication: Harry Briggs (*op. cit.*).
232. Healey & Baker, *Survey Report 1951* (1951).
233. Personal communication: D. W. Bartley (*op. cit.*).
234. In 1975 rates were charged on factories that were unoccupied but fit for use. Some companies avoided payment (and disfigured the landscape) by the cheaper expedient of partial demolition (see Barker & Dobson, Liverpool) or removal of roofs.
235. Channel 4 Television, *Beauty Queens: Elizabeth Arden* (4 January 1988).
236. *Ibid.* An ambition eventually achieved, not through successful industry but when, as 'Mrs Elizabeth Graham' with an estate in Maine, USA, she became part of the elite horse racing fraternity by breeding and racing her own horses.
237. Plans deposited with the local authority in 1939, No. 20419 at Ealing Borough Council Planning Department, are still extant but requests for copies are discouraged by a charge of £10 per single A4 sheet of photocopy (1988).
238. Wallis, Gilbert & Partners, *Industrial Architecture* (1932). The location is given as 'Place de Nier' in *The Building News* (4 September 1925).
239. Ealing Borough Council Planning Department: deposited plans and correspondence No. A13215.
240. Deposited plans at Ealing Borough Council Planning Department include an elevation drawing under A13215. The front elevation of the Telegraph Condenser office building is of poor quality for reproduction.
241. The Telegraph Condenser plans were first registered with the local authority under the name of S. G. Brown and then corrected; they refer to buildings on Wales Farm Road and match those extant in the Wallis, Gilbert archive.
242. *Garcke's Manual of Electrical Undertakings and Directory of Officials (1900 to 1930)* (1896–1960) (*op. cit.*).
243. E. L. Bird., 'The industrial work of Wallis, Gilbert & Partners' (1926) (*op. cit.*).
244. *Ibid.*
245. T. Wallis, 'Factories' (1933) (*op. cit.*).
246. Personal communication: Paul Niblett, Public Relations Department, Manufacturing Division, Michelin Tyre Co, Stoke-on-Trent (25 April 1988).
247. G. P. Manning, 'New factory for the Michelin Tyre Co. Ltd. Stoke on Trent', *Concrete & Constructional Engineering*, Vol. XXIII (January 1928). Manning states that the British architects drew up the plans, which then had to be approved by the French architects.
248. The factory is attributed to Wallis, Gilbert & Partners in 'Factory design', *The Architect & Building News* (25 September 1931) and in the architects' own publication, *Industrial Architecture* (1932). Only in C. G. Holme (ed.), *Industrial Architecture* (1935) is the German architect named (pp. 124–25).
249. There are 40 drawings on microfilm in the Wallis, Gilbert archive and a large number of full-scale drawings as deposited plans held, with other British Bemberg material, by Doncaster Archive Department. The present owner/occupant of the factory, ICI Fibres, holds some original German drawings.
250. A. Plummer, *New British Industries in the Twentieth Century* (London: Sir Isaac Pitman Ltd, 1937), p. 213.
251. J. G. Bemberg AG operated under a contracted arrangement with a Dutch textile company in Amsterdam and two other German firms at Elberfeld and Frankfurt. Public Record Office: company file British Bemberg Limited, BT31/36947/231742.
252. Local coal seams were mined by Barber, Walker & Co, which paid royalties on

tonnage to Sir William Cooke, the owner of the mining rights [uncatalogued papers, Doncaster Archive Department].

253. Personal interview: Wilfred Stainthorpe, member of the engineering department of British Bemberg Ltd since June 1930, now retired (29 September 1987).
254. *Ibid.*
255. *Ibid.*
256. C. G. Holme (ed.), *Industrial Architecture* (1935), p. 41; J. Winter, *Industrial Architecture, A Survey of Factory Buildings* (London: Studio Vista, 1970), p. 73.
257 Wallis, Gilbert & Partners, *Industrial Architecture* (1932), pp. 57–65.
258. *Ibid.*
259. *Ibid.*
260. D. T. Wallis, *Scrapbook* assembled by Douglas Wallis; Wallis, Gilbert & Partners archive collection.
261. Personal communication; G. H. Patrick, Administration Manager, MDH Ltd, Andover (30 June 1987).
262. Copy letter in D. T. Wallis, *Scrapbook (op. cit.)*.
263. Personal communication: J. A. Simpson, Property and Building Surveyor, The Rover Group plc. Personal communication: R. A. Westcott, General Manager, British Motor Industry Heritage Trust (1 March 1988).
264. For nine centuries the 1183 acres of Trafford Park, Manchester, had been held by the ancestral family of Sir Henry de Trafford. When the Manchester Ship Canal was cut through the estate, the family decided to leave, selling the land in 1896 to a syndicate headed by Ernest Terah Hooley and registered as Trafford Park Estate Ltd. A brisk programme of development led to the estate becoming the largest industrial complex in Britain. Surrounded by canals and substantial railway links and with access for sea-going vessels, the estate also included 600 houses, with schools and other amenities for local labour.
265. *Garcke's Manual of Electrical Undertakings and Directory of Officials (1900 to 1930)* (1896–1960) *(op. cit.)*, Vol. XV.
266. GEC Turbine Generators Ltd, *85 Years at Trafford Park*, published by the company, Manchester (1986).
267. Personal communication: S. Nelson, Publicity Manager, GEC Turbine Generators Ltd, Manchester (17 September 1987).
268. The plans for the tank shop bear the architects' name with 'Partner' in the singular, which dates them at 1916. There is also a sketch of the building in M. Kahn, *The Design and Construction of Industrial Buildings*. The plans for the copper shop and canteen have no signature and, although drawn when government licence precluded any large use of steel for constructional purposes, the actual date of building may have been later, but there are no revised plans extant to that effect.
269. Personal communication: S. Nelson *(op. cit.)*.
270. *Garcke's Manual of Electrical Undertakings and Directory of Officials (1900 to 1930)* (1896–1960) *(op. cit.)*; GEC Turbine Generators Ltd, *85 Years at Trafford Park* (1986).
271. Thrupp & Mapperley were manufacturers of aircraft during the First World War—the site had a light railway from the works to Hendon Aerodrome for transporting the finished aircraft. Production ceased with the termination of government orders after the war.
272. C. G. Dobson, *A Century and a Quarter—Hall & Co Ltd* (1959).
273. *Ibid.*
274. *Garcke's Manual of Motor Transport Undertakings*, Vols XIX (1915–16), XXII (1918–19),

XXVII (1923–24) and XL (1936–37) (*op. cit.*); Personal communication: Lawrence Dalton, retired, designer and member of staff, Rolls Royce Ltd (21 July 1987).

275. Personal communication: Lawrence Dalton (*op. cit.*).
276. 'Architecture today: reconstruct for prosperity', *Financial Times* (17 February 1933), p. 8.
277. D. C. Campbell, *Global Mission: The Story of Alcan*, Vol. 1 (1950) [extract supplied by the Aluminium Federation Library, Birmingham]. Alcan Extrusions Limited, *Fifty Years at Banbury*, published by the company, Banbury (1981).
278. *Ibid.*
279. 'Architecture today, reconstruct for prosperity', *Financial Times* (17 February 1933), p. 8.
280. Provided on the Dagenham site by Ford were shipping facilities—a 2000 feet long jetty beside the River Thames, with berthing for ships of up to 10 000 tons displacement; railway sidings to the main lines and to the jetty; made-up roads, sewers, electricity, gas, water, blast furnaces, coke ovens, wells; the company was also a supplier of coke, pig iron, coal tar, sulphate of ammonia, naphthalene and furnace slag; M. Simpson, 'Dagenham ways', *The Autocar* (8 July 1932) [Ford Corporate History Office, Brentwood].
281. Wallis, Gilbert & Partners, *Industrial Architecture* (1932).
282. M. Sampson, 'Dagenham ways', *The Autocar* (8 July 1932), pp. 23–28 [Ford Corporate History Office, Brentwood].
283. *The Autocar* (12 May 1939), p. 42 [Ford Corporate History Office, Brentwood].
284. Wiggins, Teape & Company Ltd, Report of Annual General Meeting published in *Wide Awake Dartford* (July 1932) [Dartford Central Library].
285. *Kent Times* (19 September 1933) [Dartford Central Library].
286. 'Dartford's newest industry', *The Bulletin* (March 1933) [Dartford Central Library].
287. S. Worden, 'Furniture for the living room', Vol. II, PhD Thesis (1980) (*op. cit.*), pp. 164–76.
288. H. Nockolds, *Lucas: The First Hundred Years*, Vol. 1, 'The King of the Road' (Newton Abbott: David and Charles, 1976); E. Eves, *The Autocar* (19 July 1973); D. Jenkinson and C. Posthumus, *Vanwall, the Story of Tony Vandervell and his Racing Cars* (Cambridge: Stephens, 1975).
289. Personal communication: D. Pink, Manager retired, GKN Vandervell Ltd (24 July 1987).
290. D. T. Wallis 'Single story factory roofs of America' (1928) (*op. cit.*).
291. For instance, of factories visited by the writer at Wallsend, Northumberland; Aston, Birmingham; and Brynmawr, South Wales, that had monitor roof construction the first two had severe leakage problems. Only the last-mentioned, a Wallis, Gilbert & Partners' design, had required no unusual maintenance over 30 years, but the Brynmawr company was overwhelmed with difficulties arising from the unique roof structure of the main factory, designed by ACT in 1947.

Chapter Four: About It and About, and Some Conclusions
(pages 261–275)

1. In 1926 a commentator reported that a 'well-known designer in concrete stated some time ago that he always made his piers thick enough to satisfy the mind, regardless of

the fact that concrete allows of very slender construction'. 'Peregrine', 'Design and the Builder', *Builder* (November 1926), p. 372.

2. Except for Elizabeth Arden (who was not, in any case, interested in factory affairs), all the manufacturers for whom Wallis, Gilbert & Partners designed were men. This was not unusual, although there may occasionally have been a titled lady member of a board of directors. When Thomas Wallis' father-in-law (uncle) James died, his wife Sarah took on the building business, which was thereafter known in her name. This *was* unusual.

3. T. Wallis, 'Factories', *Journal of the Royal Institute of British Architects* (25 February 1933), pp. 301–12, at p. 302.

4. For instance: H. S. Goodhart-Rendel (Hays Wharf, London, 1928–32); M. E. and H. O. Collins (Carreras Ltd, Hampstead Road, London—*Architecture*, May/June 1929); F. E. Simpkins (Institution of Automobile Engineers Laboratory—*Building*, April 1936); (Loud & Weston Ltd, Brixton—*Architecture Illustrated*, March 1936); Fuller, Hall & Foulsham (Cox Motor Accessories, Watford—*Building*, February 1938).

5. For instance: Sir E. Owen Williams (Boots Ltd, Nottingham—*The Architectural Review*, Vol. 72 [September 1932], pp. 86–88; *The Architects' Journal*, Vol. 76 [3 August 1932], pp. 588, 673); Sir G. G. Scott and Sir Alexander Gibb and Partners (The Guinness factory, Park Royal—*The Architect and Building News* [31 January 1936]); Stanley Hall and Eastern and Robertson (Allom Bros Ltd, Morden—C. G. Holme [ed.], *Industrial Architecture* [1935]).

6. For instance: A. W. Kenyon and Louis de Soissons (Murphy Radio Factory,Welwyn Garden City—C. G. Holmes [ed.], *Industrial Architecture* [1935]); Fuller, Hall & Foulsham (Printing Works, Eastleigh—*Building* [April 1936]); W. A. Johnson (CWS Soap factory, Irlam, Lancs—*The Architects' Journal* [2 December 1936]); Venables & Barker (Silk factory, Congleton, Cheshire—*The Architects' Journal* [2 December 1936]).

7. For instance: Collins & Green—Romford Town Hall; E. Barry Webb—King Edward VI School, Southampton; Sir Bannister Fletcher—Gillette Factory, Great West Road.

8. For instance: Tilling-Stevens in 'The utility of reinforced concrete', *The Architects' Journal* (26 January 1921), pp. 100–07; D. Napier & Sons in 'Construction 9: a reinforced concrete factory for motor-cars', *The Architects' Journal* (24 March 1920), pp. 377, 380–85.

9. E. G. W. Souster, *The Design of Factory and Industrial Buildings* (1919), pp. 143–47.

10. E. L. Bird, 'The industrial work of Wallis, Gilbert & Partners', Current Architecture Section, *The Architects' Journal* (14 April 1926), pp. 553–64.

11. The Concrete Utilities Bureau, *Architecture in Factory Buildings*, published by the Bureau (1924) as reprinted from *Concrete and Constructional Engineering* (September 1924).

12. H. Keatley Moore, 'Façades in Britain', *Kahn-crete Engineering*, Vol. XVII (January/February 1930), pp. 5–11.

13. *Ibid.* (my italics).

14. J. Watson, 'Concrete and cement', *Building* (July 1926), pp. 162–63.

15. J. D. Broughton, 'The architecture of George V', *Building* (February 1928), pp. 47–50.

16. J. Dixon-Spain, 'Factory design—the opportunity of our time', *The Architects' Journal* (13 January 1932), pp. 52–60.

17. *Ibid.*

18. L. H. Bucknell, 'Industrial Architecture', President's Address to the Architectural Association General Meeting, 26 October 1937. Published in *The Architectural Association Journal*, Vol. LIII, 609 (November 1937), pp. 217–33. Discussion: Major V. H. Seymer, Member of the Council of the Architectural Association.

19. J. Gloag, 'The Conquest of the Machine', *The Architectural Review* (December 1932), pp. 273–75.
20. The comments in respect of Albert Kahn are drawn from a reading of the following: G. Hildebrand, *Designing for Industry: The Architecture of Albert Kahn* (Cambridge, MA: MIT Press, 1974); G. C. Nimmons, 'Modern Industrial Plants Part II', *Architectural Record*, Vol. XLIV (1918), pp. 533–49; W. Ferry Hawkins (ed.), *The Buildings of Detroit* (Detroit, MI: Wayne State University Press, 1980); A. Andrews, *Architecture in Michigan* (Detroit, MI: Wayne State University Press, 1982); M. Kahn, 'The planning of industrial buildings', *The Architectural Forum*, Vol. LI, No. 3 (September 1929); L. Robinson, 'Albert Kahn', *The Architectural Review*, Vol. 157 (1975); A. Kahn, 'Industrial architecture—an opportunity and a challenge', *The Architects' World* (December 1940).
21. D. T. Wallis, 'Single-story [*sic*] factory roofs of America', *The Architects' Journal* (22 August 1928), p. 269.
22. Personal communication: Lawrence Butterfield, TD, FRIBA, FCIArb, FRSA, ex-member of Wallis, Gilbert & Partners (28 July 1995).
23. T. Mackertich and P. Mackertich, *Façade, A Decade of British and American Commercial Architecture* (1976).
24. Personal communication; Lawrence Butterfield (*op. cit.*).
25. S. Jenkins, 'The anger of Firestone', *Journal of the Thirties Society*, No. 1.
26. J. Winter, *Industrial Architecture, A Survey of Factory Buildings* (London: Studio Vista, 1970), p. 73.
27. E. Jones, *Industrial Architecture in Britain 1750–1939* (London: Batsford,1985).
28. J. M. Richards, *The Functional Tradition in Early Industrial Buildings* (London: The Architectural Press, 1958).
29. E. Jones, *Industrial Architecture in Britain 1750–1939* (1985), 212ff.
30. *Ibid.*
31. J. Snowdon and R. W. Platts, 'The work of Wallis, Gilbert & Partners, Great West Road style', *The Architectural Review*, Vol. CLVI, No. 929 (July 1974).
32. W. Hitchmough, *Hoover Factory, Wallis, Gilbert & Partners* (London: Phaidon, 1992, reprinted 1994).

Bibliography

Architecture and Architectural History

R. Atkinson, H. Robertson, O. Faber, V. O. Rees, W. M. Keesey and L. H. Bucknell, *A Book of Design by Senior Students of the Architectural Association School, with Introductory Essays* (London: Ernest Benn Ltd, 1924).

R. Banham, *The Architecture of the Well-Tempered Environment* (London: The Architectural Press, 1984).

R. Banham, *Theory and Design in the First Machine Age* (London: The Architectural Press, 1976).

T. Benton and C. Benton with D. Sharp, *Form and Function* (London: Crosby, Lockwood Staples, 1975).

R. Blomfield, *Modernismus* (London: Macmillan, 1934).

M. S. Briggs, *Building Today* (Oxford: Geoffrey Cumberledge, Oxford University Press, 1944).

H. A. N. Brockman, *The British Architect in Industry, 1841–1940* (London: George Allen & Unwin, 1974).

A. S. G. Butler, *The Substance of Architecture* (London: Constable & Co Ltd, 1926).

P. Collins, *Concrete* (London: Faber, 1959).

H. J. Cowan, *A Historical Outline of Architectural Science* (Oxford: Elsevier Publishing Co, 1966).

E. and O. E., *Planning, The Architect's Handbook*, published for *The Architect and Building News* (George Wood & Co Ltd, 5th edition, 1947). Number 8, 'Factory building', p. 161.

A. T. Edwards, *Good and Bad Manners in Architecture* (London: John Tirani Ltd, 1929; reprinted 1941).

Sir Bannister Fletcher, *A History of Architecture*, 19th edition (London: Butterworth, 1987).

Gallery Lingard, *Trad, Jazz and Mod*, catalogue of an exhibition of European architectural drawings of the 1920s and 1930s (London: Gallery Lingard, 1986).

S. Giedion, 'Construction and aesthetics', in J. L. Martin, Ben Nicholson, N. Gabo (eds), *Circle, International Survey of Constructive Art* (London: Faber & Faber, 1937), pp. 220–29.

J. Gloag, *Men and Buildings* (London: Country Life Ltd, 1931).

S. B. Hamilton, H. Bagenal and R. B. White, *A Qualitative Study of Some Buildings in the London Area*, National Building Studies, Special Report 33 (London: HMSO, 1964).

G. Hildebrand, *Designing for Industry, The Architecture of Albert Kahn* (Cambridge, MA: MIT Press, 1974).

H. R. Hitchcock, *Architecture—Nineteenth and Twentieth Centuries* (Harmondsworth: Penguin, 1990).

H. R. Hitchcock and P. Johnson, *The International Style* (New York: W. W. Norton, 1966).

C. G. Holme (ed.), *Industrial Architecture* (London: The Studio Ltd, 1936).

A. A. Jackson, *The Politics of Architecture: A History of Modern Architecture in Britain* (London: The Architectural Press, 1970).

C. C. Knowles and P. H. Pitt, *The History of Building Regulations in London 1189–1972* (London: The Architectural Press, 1972).

C. Le Corbusier, *Towards a New Architecture*, trans. Frederick Etchells (London: The Architectural Press, 1927; reprinted 1974).

T. Mackertich and P. Mackertich, *Façade, A Decade of British and American Commercial Architecture* (London: Matthews Miller Dunbar, 1976).

J. L. Martin, 'The state of transition', in J. L. Martin, Ben Nicholson and N. Gabo (eds), *Circle, International Survey of Constructive Art* (London: Faber & Faber, 1937).

Open University, *History of Architecture and Design 1890–1939, Course A305* (Milton Keynes: Open University Press, 1975).

N. Pevsner, *An Outline of European Architecture* (Harmondsworth: Penguin, 1968).

N. Pevsner, *Pioneers of Modern Design from William Morris to Walter Gropius* (Harmondsworth: Penguin, 1975).

Recent English Architecture 1920–1940, selected by The Architectural Club (London: Country Life Ltd, 1946).

C. H. Reilly, *The Theory and Practice of Architecture* (London: Victor Gollancz Ltd, 1932).

J. M. Richards, *An Introduction to Modern Architecture* (London: Penguin Books, 1940; reprinted, revised 1970).

H. Robinson, *Modern Architectural Design* (London: The Architectural Press, 1932).

H. Robinson, *The Principles of Architectural Composition* (London: The Architectural Press, 1924; second edition 1932).

F. Rogers, *Specifications for Practical Architecture* (London: Crosby, Lockwood & Co, 1886).

Royal Institute of British Architects, *Centenary Catalogue: International Architecture 1924–34* (London: RIBA, 1934).

W. S. Smith, *The Art and Architecture of Ancient Egypt* (Harmondsworth: Penguin and New York: Wiley, 1981).

D. Watkin, *The Rise of Architectural History* (London: The Architectural Press, 1980).

C. Williams-Ellis and J. Summerson, *Architecture Here and Now* (London: Thomas Nelson & Sons Ltd, 1934).

Factories and Industry

G. C. Allen, *The Structure of Industry in Britain*, third edition (London: Longman, 1972).

R. Banham, *A Concrete Atlantis, US Industrial Building and European Modern Architecture 1900–1925* (Cambridge, MA: MIT Press, 1986).

S. R. Dennison, *The Location of Industry and the Depressed Areas* (Oxford: Oxford University Press, 1939; London: Quantum Reprints, 1966).

J. Drury, *Factories—Planning, Design and Modernisation* (London: The Architectural Press, 1976).

J. H. Dunning, *American Investment in British Manufacturing Industry* (London: George Allen & Unwin, 1958).

J. H. Dunning and C. J. Thomas, *British Industry: Change and Development in the Twentieth Century* (London: Hutchinson University Library, 1961; revised edition 1963).

W. J. Hiscox, *Factory Layout, Planning and Progress* (London: Sir Isaac Pitman & Sons Ltd, 1929; second edition, revised by J. Stirling, 1941).

C. G. Holme (ed.), *Industrial Architecture* (London: The Studio Ltd, 1936).

D. A. Hounshell, *From the American System to Mass Production 1800–1932* (Baltimore, MD: Johns Hopkins University Press, 1984). Especially Chapter 6 'The Ford Motor Company and the rise of mass production in America', pp. 217–61.

E. Jacques, *The Changing Culture of a Factory* (London: Tavistock Publications Ltd with Routledge & Kegan Paul, 1951).

E. Jones, *Industrial Architecture in Britain 1750–1939* (London: B. T. Batsford, 1985).

M. Kahn, *The Design and Construction of Industrial Buildings* (London: Technical Journals Ltd, 1917).

E. D. Mills, *The Modern Factory* (London: The Architectural Press, 1951).

Modern Factory Lighting (issued jointly by the British Electrical Development Association and the ELMA Lighting Service Bureau, London, 1940).

A. Plummer, *New British Industries in the Twentieth Century* (London: Sir Isaac Pitman Ltd, 1937).

G. M. Price, *The Modern Factory, Safety, Sanitation and Welfare* (London: Chapman & Hall, 1914).

J. M. Richards, *The Functional Tradition in Early Industrial Buildings* (London: The Architectural Press, 1958).

E. G. W. Souster, *The Design of Factory and Industrial Buildings* (London: Scott, Greenwood & Son, 1919).

Wallis, Gilbert & Partners, *Industrial Architecture* (Geneva: Biblos Ltd, 1932).

J. Winter, *Industrial Architecture: A Survey of Factory Building* (London: Studio Vista, 1970).

W. M. Wulckow, *Bauten der Arbeit und des Verkehrs aus Deutscher Gegenwart* (Taunus and Leipzig: Karl Robert Langweische, 1925).

Building and Concrete

E. Allen, *How Buildings Work, The Natural Order of Architecture* (New York: Oxford University Press Inc, 1980).

R. Banham, *A Concrete Atlantis, US Industrial Building and European Modern Architecture 1900–1925* (Cambridge, MA: MIT Press, 1986).

R. Banham, *The Architecture of the Well-Tempered Environment* (London: The Architectural Press, 1984).

T. P. Bennett, *Architectural Design in Concrete* (London: Ernest Benn Ltd, 1927).

M. Bowley, *Innovations in Building Materials* (London: Duckworth, 1960).

M. Bowley, *The British Building Industry* (Cambridge: Cambridge University Press, 1966).

M. S. Briggs, *Building Today* (Oxford: Geoffrey Cumberledge, Oxford University Press, 1944).

W. F. Cassie and J. H. Napper, *Structure in Building* (London: The Architectural Press, 1952).

P. Collins, *Concrete* (London: Faber, 1959).

N. A. Davey, *A History of Building Materials* (London: Phoenix House, 1961).

E. and O. E., *Planning, The Architect's Handbook*, published for *The Architect and Building News* (London: George Wood & Co, 1947).

G. & T. Earle Ltd, *The Making and Testing of Portland Cement and Concrete* (Hull, published by the company, 1925).

O. Faber, *Reinforced Concrete Simply Explained* (London: Oxford University Press, 1922; second edition 1926; fourth impression 1938).

B. F. Fletcher and H. P. Phillips, *Architectural Hygiene or Sanitary Science as Applied to Buildings* (London: Whittaker & Co, 1899; third edition 1907).

S. B. Hamilton, H. Bagenal and R. B. White, *A Qualitative Study of Some Buildings in the London Area*, National Building Studies, Special Report 33 (London: HMSO, 1964).

C. C. Handisyde, *Building Materials: Science and Practice* (London: The Architectural Press, 1950).

O. C. Hering, *Concrete and Stucco Houses* (New York: McBride, Nast & Company, 1912).

B. Jones (ed.), *Reinforced Concrete: A Complete Treatise on the Practice and Theory of Modern Construction in Concrete-Steel. With a Section on House Construction in Concrete Blocks and By Reinforced Pre-cast Methods* (London: The Waverley Book Co Ltd, 1913; new and enlarged editions 1920 and 1926).

C. C. Knowles and P. H. Pitt, *The History of Building Regulations in London 1189–1972* (London: Architectural Press, 1972).

Modern Factory Lighting (issued jointly by the British Electrical Development Association and the ELMA Lighting Service Bureau, London, 1940).

N. Pevsner, *A History of Building Types* (London: Thames & Hudson, 1986).

C. G. Powell, *An Economic History of the British Building Industry 1815–1979* (London and New York: Methuen, 1980).

C. E. Reynolds, *Concrete Construction* (London: Concrete Publications Ltd, 1938; revision 1945; second revision 1950).

C. E. Reynolds, *Reinforced Concrete Designers' Handbook* (London: Concrete Publications Ltd, 1932).

H. Sutherland and W. W. Clifford, *Introduction to Reinforced Concrete Design* (New York: John Wiley & Sons Inc; London: Chapman & Hall, 1926).

Historical and Economic Background

B. W. E. Alford, *Depression and Recovery? British Economic Growth 1918–1939* (London: The Macmillan Press, 1972).

W. Ashworth, *An Economic History of England 1870–1939* (London: Methuen, 1969).

R. Blythe, *The Age of Illusion, England in the Twenties and Thirties, 1919–1940* (London: Hamish Hamilton, 1963).

N. K. Buxton and D. H. Aldcroft, *British Industry Between the Wars; Instability and Industrial Development* (London: Scolar Press, 1979).

G. D. H. Cole and R. Postgate, *The Common People 1746–1946* (London: Methuen, 1938; revised edition 1968).

D. Fraser, *The Evolution of the British Welfare State* (London: Macmillan, 1980).

F. Gloversmith (ed.), *Class, Culture and Social Change, A New View of the Thirties* (Brighton: The Harvester Press, 1980).

R. Graves and A. Hodges, *The Long Weekend: A Social History of Great Britain 1918–1939* (New York: W. W. Norton & Co Inc, 1963).

Hayward Gallery, *Thirties—British Art and Design before the War*, Exhibition Catalogue, Hayward Gallery 1979–80 (Arts Council of Great Britain, 1979).

C. P. Hill, *British Economic and Social History 1700–1975* (London: Edward Arnold, 1977).

W. L. McElwee, *Britain's Locust Years 1918–1940* (London: Faber & Faber, 1962).

C. L. Mowat, *Britain Between the Wars 1918–1940* (London: Methuen, 1960; reprinted 1960).

A. E. Musson, *The Growth of British Industry* (London: B. T. Batsford, 1978).

D. Nelson, *Frederick W. Taylor and the Rise of Scientific Management* (Madison, WI: University of Wisconsin Press, 1980).

S. Pollard, *The Development of the British Economy 1914–1967* (London: Edward Arnold, 1970).

H. Read, *Art and Industry* (London: Faber, 1934).

Report of *The Royal Commission on the Distribution of Industrial Population 1939–1940* (Public Record Office, Cmd 6153).

G. R. Searle, *The Quest for National Efficiency, A Study of British Politics and Political Thought 1899–1914* (Oxford: Basil Blackwell, 1971).

A. J. P. Taylor, *English History 1914–1945* (London: Penguin Books, 1970).

A. J. P. Taylor, *The First World War, An Illustrated History* (London: Penguin, 1963; reprinted 1970).

M. Ward and N. Ward, *Home in the Twenties and Thirties* (London: Ian Allen, 1978).

R. Williams, *Culture and Society 1780–1950* (London: Chatto & Windus, 1967).

Decorative Influences

C. Aldres, *Egyptian Art* (London: Thames & Hudson, 1980).

W. Bray, *The Everyday Life of the Aztecs* (London: B. T. Batsford, 1968).

J. S. Curl, *The Egyptian Revival* (Boston, MA and Sydney: George Allen & Unwin, 1982).

J. G. Davies, *Temples, Churches and Mosques* (Oxford: Basil Blackwell, 1982).

C. F. Feest, *Native Arts of North America* (London: Thames & Hudson, 1980).

O. Jones, *The Grammar of Ornament* (1856).

D. Hamilton, *Manual of Architectural Ceramics* (London: Thames & Hudson, 1978).

Hayward Gallery, *Thirties—British Art and Design before the War*, Exhibition Catalogue, 1979–80 (The Arts Council of Great Britain, 1979).

B. Hillier, *Art Deco of the Twenties and Thirties* (London: Studio Vista, 1968).

A. Lesieutre, *The Spirit and Splendour of Art Deco* (London: Paddington Press, 1974).

M. Lurker, *The Gods and Symbols of Ancient Egypt* (London: Thames & Hudson, 1974).

W. S. Smith, *The Art and Architecture of Ancient Egypt* (Harmondsworth: Penguin and New York: Wiley, 1981).

R. Whitlock, *The Everyday Life of the Maya* (London: B. T. Batsford, 1976).

E. Wilson, *Ancient Egyptian Designs* (London: British Museum Publications, 1986).

Note: Catalogues for the two exhibitions of the artefacts taken from the Tomb of Tutankhamun (1923, 1970) appear to be out of print/no longer available.

Journals

The following journals were consulted:
Architecture
Architecture Illustrated
The Architect
The Architect and Building News
The Architects' and Builders' Journal
The Architects' Journal
The Architects' World

The Architectural Association Journal
The Architectural Forum
The Architectural Record
The Architectural Review
Building
Building News
Concrete and Constructional Engineer
Economic History Review
Industrial Archaeology Review
Journal of Economic History
Journal of the Royal Institute of British Architects
Journal of the Twentieth Century Society
Kahn-crete Engineering
The Structural Engineer
The Thirties Society Journal

Selections from journals

F. Baines, 'War factories', *Journal of the Royal Society of British Architects*, Vol. 26 (Third series, August 1919), pp. 230–40 and (September 1919) pp. 249–59.

P. Behrens, 'The aesthetics of industrial architecture', *Scientific American Supplement* (23 August 1913), pp. 120–21.

O. Bernard, 'On the tiles', *The Architect and Building News* (13 January 1933), pp. 56–58.

L. H. Bucknell, 'Industrial architecture', Address by the President, Architectural Association, 26 October 1937, *The Architectural Association Journal*, Vol. LIII, No. 609 (November 1937), pp. 217–33.

H. C. Constantine, 'Factories', *The Architects' Journal*, Vol. 86 (2 December 1937), pp. 873–935.

R. A. Cordingly, 'Building for industry—the rôle of the architect', *Architectural Review*, Vol. 83 (March 1938), pp. 117–26.

J. E. Dixon-Spain, 'Factory design—the opportunity of our time', *The Architects' Journal* (13 January 1932), pp. 52–60.

'Factories', *Architecture*, Vol. VII, No. 38 (May/June 1929).

H. S. Goodhart-Rendel, 'The use of precedent', *The Architect and Building News* (11 December 1931), pp. 307–14.

F. H. Heaven, 'The effect of reinforced concrete on architectural design', *Concrete and Constructional Engineering*, Vol. 10 (1915), pp. 433–40.

C. Hussey, 'Faience as a medium for modern architecture', *The Architectural Review*, Vol. 70 (October 1931), pp. 101–04.

C. Hussey, 'The aesthetics of faience architecture', *The Architectural Review*, Vol. 70 (November 1931), pp. 136–40.

M. Kahn, 'Planning of industrial buildings', *Architectural Forum*, Vol. 51, No. 3 (September 1929), pp. 265–72.

J. R. Leathart, 'A review of current factory design', *Building* (April 1936), pp. 136–42.

H. Martindale, 'When designing a factory i. Health requirements', *The Architects' Journal* (13 May 1931), pp. 683–86.

A. Marwick, 'Middle opinion in the Thirties', *English Historical Review*, Vol. 79 (1964), pp. 285–98.

B. Pite, 'The architecture of concrete', *Journal of the Royal Institute of British Architects*, Vol. XXXII, No. 11 (4 April 1925), pp. 329–38.

A. Powers (guest ed. Special Edition), 'Industrial buildings', *Journal of the Twentieth Century Society*, No. 1 (1994).

The Royal Society of Arts, 'Proceedings', *Journal of the Royal Society of Arts*, Vol. CXI, No. 5084 (July 1963).

C. H. Reilly, 'The architectural scene 1901–1934', *The Architectural Review*, Vol. 75 (1934), pp. 170–76.

H. W. Richardson, 'New industries between the wars', *Oxford Economic Papers*, Vol. XIII (1961).

R. S. Sayers, 'The springs of technical progress in Britain 1919–1939', *The Economic Journal*, Vol. LX (June 1950), pp. 275–91.

P. M. Shand, 'Snobbishness in architecture', *The Architectural Review*, Vol. 65 (June 1929), pp. 273–77.

A. G. Shaw, 'Terracotta and faience—its origins', *Building* (May 1930), pp. 236–37.

D. Sugden, 'The anatomy of a factory', *Architecture and Design* (November 1968), pp. 513–53.

E. Temple-Orme (ed.), *Kahn-crete Engineering*, Vol. 95, No. XIX (August/September 1932).

Thirties Society, *Journal*, No. 1 (1981).

Tiles and Architectural Ceramics Society, 'Notes on tile and faience work by Carter & Co in Poole and Bournemouth' (1984).

F. R. Wylie, 'Industrial buildings', *Journal of the Royal Institute of British Architects* (June 1951), pp. 309–14.

Index